VENONA

SOVIET ESPIONAGE AND THE AMERICAN RESPONSE
1939-1957

ROBERT LOUIS BENSON
MICHAEL WARNER
EDITORS

NATIONAL SECURITY AGENCY
CENTRAL INTELLIGENCE AGENCY
WASHINGTON, D.C.
1996

This volume was prepared from official sources. Nonetheless, the interpretation contained in the Preface reflects the views of the editors and comments made by reviewers within the CIA History Staff, Center for the Study of Intelligence, and within NSA's Center for Cryptologic History. Suggestions from other readers have also been helpful. The Preface has not been coordinated within CIA and NSA as a whole and does not represent an institutional or official US Government point of view.

This publication is prepared for the use of US Government officials, and the format, coverage, and content are designed to meet their specific requirements. US Government officials may obtain additional copies of this document directly or through liaison channels from the Central Intelligence Agency.

Requesters outside the US Government may obtain subscriptions to publications similar to this one by addressing inquiries to:

Document Expedition (DOCEX) Project
Exchange and Gift Division
Library of Congress
Washington, DC 20540

or: **National Technical Information Service**
5285 Port Royal Road
Springfield, VA 22161

Requesters outside the US Government not interested in subscription service may purchase specific publications either in paper copy or microform from:

Photoduplication Service
Library of Congress
Washington, DC 20540

or: **National Technical Information Service**
5285 Port Royal Road
Springfield, VA 22161
(To expedite service, call the
NTIS Order Desk (703-487-4650)

Comments and queries on this paper may be directed to the DOCEX Project at the above address or by phone (202-707-9527), or the NTIS Office of Customer Services at the above address or by phone (703-487-4660). Publications are not available to the public from the Central Intelligence Agency.

Contents

	Page
Foreword	v
Preface	vii
Acronyms and Abbreviations	xxxv
Chronology	xxxvii
Part I: The American Response to Soviet Espionage	
Archival Citations and a Note on the Documents	1
Part II: Selected Venona Messages	
A Note on the Translations and List of Messages	191

Venona: Soviet Espionage and the American Response, 1939-1957

Foreword

In July 1995, in a ceremony at CIA Headquarters, Director of Central Intelligence John Deutch released the first group of NSA's Venona translations to the public. The DCI announced that a public conference on the Venona story would be held in 1996 as soon as the declassification of the translations had been completed. This conference is now at hand and follows the release of the last set of Venona translations. Some 2,900 Soviet intelligence messages are now on the Internet and in hard copy at major archives around the country.

While the cryptologic side of the Venona story belongs to NSA and its partners, the overall achievement is one of Intelligence Community cooperation. NSA and its US Army predecessor worked with FBI, CIA, the British, and allied services. This conference volume is itself a cooperative effort in keeping with the spirit of the times. It provides the public with information that had been closely held until recently and which is of extraordinary interest and importance.

It may be some time before historians and the general public sort out the full meaning of Venona. Lou Benson, co-editor of this conference volume, has prepared five historical monographs about the program. Considerable research, discussion, and writing by journalists and historians is already in progress, making this volume and the presentations at its accompanying conference potentially all the more timely and valuable to these scholarly efforts.

There can no longer be any doubt about the widespread and successful Soviet espionage operations against the United States and Great Britain during the 1940s, and that, aside from their own professional skill, Soviet intelligence services could count on the aid of the Communist parties of the target countries.

Earlier in my career I had the opportunity to supervise and participate in the last stages of the Venona program. From that experience I learned of the incredible determination and great skill of the analysts who made Venona possible. The result of their work was the body of translated messages, each one produced with the most painstaking and, I might add, honest effort. This is authentic material deserving of the most careful study.

William P. Crowell
Deputy Director
National Security Agency

August 1996

Venona: Soviet Espionage and the American Response, 1939-1957

Preface

The muggy Washington summer of 1948 grew even hotter when news media reported that a "blonde spy queen" three years earlier had given federal investigators convincing evidence of widespread Soviet espionage in America during World War II. In a few days the world learned her name—Elizabeth Bentley—and heard her and another ex-Communist agent, Whittaker Chambers, repeat their charges before Congress. Republican congressmen and candidates cited the stories as further evidence of the Roosevelt and Truman administrations' softness toward Communism and neglect of national security. Outraged officials both in and out of government, as well as Democrats fearing a campaign issue that would sink President Truman's apparently foundering re-election chances, insisted that Bentley and Chambers were peddling hearsay and innuendo.

Almost lost in the furor was one isolated recollection of Bentley's that ultimately would provide a clue to the truth behind the charges and denials. Bentley, according to press reports, had told a federal grand jury that an aide to President Roosevelt had learned during the war that American intelligence was on the verge of breaking "the Russian secret code." The aide, said Bentley, had passed this nugget to his Soviet contact.[1] For almost 30 years this fragmentary anecdote remained virtually all that the public would hear about one of the Cold War's greatest intelligence coups.

Bentley's charges, and the debates they fueled, typified the American experience with intelligence and related "internal security" issues in the era of totalitarianism and total war. For roughly 60 years the Western democracies struggled to preserve civil liberties and due process while ascertaining the extent of clandestine penetrations by the intelligence services of fascist and Communist regimes. At midcentury the Soviet Union's main strength was "human" intelligence—the collection of information through agents with access to foreign secrets. Washington's forte was "signals" intelligence—the procurement and analysis of coded foreign messages. At the beginning of the Cold War strength met strength in a struggle that still reverberates 50 years later. The tale of this struggle is the Venona story.

The term "Venona" served as an arbitrary codeword stamped on a relatively small number of documents in order to limit access to a particular cryptanalytic breakthrough. This achievement enabled Western counterintelligence

---

[1] "Blonde Leader of Spy Ring Credited With Reds' Arrests," *Washington Post*, 22 July 1948.

specialists to read portions of more than 2,900 Soviet diplomatic telegrams sent between 1940 and 1948. The encipherment of these telegrams shared a common flaw that left them vulnerable to cryptanalysis. It was that flaw—rather than any commonality of dates, origins, or subject matter—that made the messages a unique and discrete body of documents. American and allied services spent almost four decades deciphering the original texts and then puzzling over their meanings. By the time this effort was formally closed in 1980, the codeword "Venona" meant, to a handful of witting US Intelligence Community officers, the entire program of cryptanalytic and exploitation activities based on the messages.

Espionage in America

The United States made a tempting espionage target for allies and adversaries alike in the 1940s. Berlin, Tokyo, and Moscow all wanted to discover Washington's strategic plans and the progress being made in American factories and laboratories. Axis spies fared poorly in North America, however, in part because allied civilian and military counterintelligence services rolled up Axis nets and agents early in the war. Soviet intelligence fared much better. Indeed, the tensions and crises in East-West relations in the 1940s and 1950s unfolded along patterns determined in no small part by the success of Soviet intelligence officers, and, belatedly, by the growing ability of Western services to counter Moscow's espionage campaign.

Several advantages helped Soviet intelligence succeed where the Axis services failed. First, Soviet intelligence services, in many respects, were stronger than their Axis counterparts, with better leadership and more resources. Second, operating conditions in America were easier for several reasons, the foremost being the fact that the Soviet Union was an ally and therefore was able to post large numbers of officials on American soil in various liaison capacities. Beyond this, many Americans regarded their Russian allies as comrades-in-arms who should be helped with material as well as rhetorical support. There were some instances of American citizens volunteering actual secrets to Soviets during the war, and Soviet officials in the United States sometimes enjoyed considerable hospitality and access. Finally, Soviet intelligence benefited directly and indirectly from the activities and infrastructure of the Communist Party of the United States (CPUSA).

Moscow collected secrets in the United States through overlapping organizations. The Communist International (better known as the Comintern) monitored the CPUSA and supervised the Party's clandestine apparatus. The CPUSA had reached the peak of its strength and limited influence in

American life in the late 1930s, when the Great Depression and Stalin's opposition to Hitler and Mussolini convinced thousands of native-born Americans that capitalism was doomed and that the socialist experiment in Russia represented the world's only reliable bulwark against fascism.[2] Party leaders and some trusted members gathered political and industrial information, most of which probably made its way to Soviet intelligence services.[3] Although the CPUSA lost perhaps a third of its members after the Hitler-Stalin pact of August 1939 temporarily made the USSR a junior partner in Nazi aggression, a committed core remained in the ranks.[4] In addition, military intelligence (GRU) officers based in Soviet consular posts worked with the Comintern and with Party-controlled agents in US Government agencies and private industry.[5]

Another Soviet organization, the NKVD (later to become the KGB)—Moscow's secret police and quasi-civilian intelligence service—had its own foreign intelligence arm. The service had long busied itself with internal repression and with foreign counterintelligence that helped guide covert action against émigré Russian political factions. In other types of foreign operations it had been overshadowed by the GRU, at least in the United States.[6] This relationship would be reversed during the war.[7]

---

[2] Maurice Isserman estimates CPUSA membership at between 50,000 and 75,000 in the years before the war; *Which Side Were You On?: The American Communist Party During the Second World War* (Champaign: University of Illinois Press, 1993), pp. 18-21.

[3] Harvey Klehr and John Earl Haynes, with Fridrikh Igorevich Firsov, *The Secret World of American Communism* (New Haven, CT: Yale University Press, 1995), pp. 8-11, 71-73, 323-326.

[4] Translated messages disclose examples of the CPUSA's direct and indirect assistance to both the GRU and KGB. See Moscow 142 [circular], 12 September 1943, Translation 18 in this volume; New York 598-99 to Moscow, 2 May 1944, Translation 29; New York 1065 to Moscow, 28 July 1944, Translation 45; New York 12-13 to Moscow, 4 January 1945, Translation 80.

[5] GRU refers to the Chief Directorate for Intelligence of the Red Army's General Staff (the organization was upgraded to a Chief Directorate in 1943). For a GRU view of operating conditions in the United States, see Washington [Naval-GRU] 2505-12 to Moscow, 31 December 1942.

[6] KGB stands for the Committee for State Security. For the sake of clarity and convenience, the main foreign intelligence arm of the Soviet state is here called the KGB, its final name before the 1991 collapse of the Soviet Union. The organization had been reorganized, reauthorized, and renamed several times. It was called the Cheka or VChK (1917-22), the GPU (1922-23), the OGPU (1923-34), the NKVD (1934-41, 1941-43), the NKGB (1941, 1943-46), the MGB (1946-47, 1952-53), the KI (1947-52), the MVD (1953-54), and the KGB (1954-91). The KI was subordinated to the Ministry of Foreign Affairs from 1949 to 1952. See Christopher Andrew and Oleg Gordievsky, *KGB: The Inside Story* (New York: HarperCollins, 1990), p. ix. See also the new "biographical reference" published by Russian Federation's Foreign Intelligence Service, *Veternay vneshney razvedki Rossii* [Veterans of Russian Foreign Intelligence], Moscow, 1995, pp. 3-4.

[7] One measure of the KGB's growing pre-eminence in the United States can be glimpsed in the message counts from the KGB and GRU residencies in New York. In 1940 the GRU New York residency sent three messages for every one sent by its KGB counterpart; in 1941 that ratio was reversed, and the KGB total remained higher from then on. An indication of the state of the US Government's knowledge of Soviet intelligence can be seen in Joseph A. Michela, Military Attaché Moscow Report 1903, "N.K.V.D. of the U.S.S.R.," 14 April 1941, Document 5.

The KGB and GRU ran parallel "legal" and "illegal" intelligence networks in the United States. One set of operations was run by intelligence officers working under legal (usually diplomatic) cover in the "residencies" located clandestinely in Soviet diplomatic missions, trade, and media organizations—for example, the Amtorg Trading Corporation, the Soviet Purchasing Commission, and the Tass news agency.[8] Other KGB and GRU networks, in contrast, had no apparent connections to Soviet establishments and were run by "illegals"—Soviet intelligence officers usually living under false identities. In addition, some GRU and KGB agents were themselves CPUSA officers whose clandestine activities were known, to a greater or lesser extent, to the CPUSA leadership and the Comintern. KGB officer Jacob Golos (covername SOUND), for instance, ran the Soviet-sponsored World Tourists corporation in New York and allegedly also served on the central control commission of the CPUSA. His lover, Elizabeth Bentley (covernames SMART GIRL and MYRNA), had moved from the open Party into underground work in the late 1930s. She helped Golos service various agents and run the World Tourists business.

Stalin wanted his intelligence officers in America to collect information in four main areas. He directed Pavel M. Fitin, the 34-year-old chief of the KGB's First Directorate, to seek American intelligence concerning Hitler's plans for the war in Russia; secret war aims of London and Washington, particularly with regard to planning for a second front in Europe; any indications that the Western allies might cut a separate peace with Hitler; and, finally, American scientific and technological progress, particularly in developing an atomic weapon.[9]

Soviet espionage operatives in the United States during World War II funneled information to Moscow through a handful of professional intelligence officers who sent reports to the Center and relayed orders and questions from the Center to agents in the field. Operations in America were led by experienced hands such as Vassili M. Zarubin (covername MAKSIM), who served as *rezident* in New York and later in Washington, and Iskhak A. Akhmerov (covernames MER and ALBERT), the senior illegal. Some Soviet case officers, however, were raw recruits recently brought into the services in order to fill out ranks depleted during Stalin's purges of the late

---

[8] KGB use of Amtorg is discussed in Herbert Romerstein and Stanislav Levchenko, *The KGB Against the "Main Enemy": How the Soviet Intelligence Service Operates against the United States* (Lexington, MA: D.C. Heath, 1989), pp. 19-21, 176-177.

[9] Stalin's four requirements are either cited or paraphrased (the text and notes do not specify which) and subsequently became a general directive sent to several residencies. Vladimir M. Chikov claims Stalin issued these requirements in the presence of the newly appointed KGB senior *rezident* in the United States, Vassili M. Zarubin; this suggests that Stalin did so in autumn 1941. See "How the Soviet Intelligence Service 'Split' the American Atom," *Novoe Vremia* [*New Times*; English ed.], 23 April 1991, p. 38.

1930s.[10] For many of these officers, America was their first overseas post. Elizabeth Bentley described her initial meeting with "John" (Anatoli A. Yatskov, Venona covername ALEKSEI), who turned out to be

> *a thin, pale, blond, young man of about my height, who was dressed in badly fitting clothes of obviously European make. . . . He had that half-starved look so characteristic of new Soviet arrivals, his English was so meager I had difficulty in understanding him, and he displayed an astounding ignorance of American life.*

"John," despite his unpromising debut, would play a key role in Soviet espionage against the atomic bomb.[11]

During the latter part of the war, the KGB gradually took over assets and networks originally established by the GRU and the Comintern (particularly after Stalin dissolved the latter body in May 1943).[12] A general re-division of labor among the Soviet services appears to have given political tasks to the KGB, while focusing the GRU more on military collection; both collected scientific and technical data. In addition, agents hitherto run in cooperation with the CPUSA were turned over to direct Soviet control. This streamlining effort faced daunting operational security challenges; Bentley and others who had worked with the Soviets had learned far more than they needed to about other agents and operations—and resented the change in direction.

A Slow Response

The US Government had grown concerned about reputed fascist and Communist subversion in the late 1930s. The war in Europe—and the Nazi-Soviet nonaggression pact of 1939—gave J. Edgar Hoover's Federal Bureau of Investigation an opportunity to move against individuals and organizations suspected of working with the Russians. Tipped by a State Department probe that had uncovered American and foreign Communists

---

[10] According to KGB defector Alexander Orlov, more than 3,000 KGB officers were shot in 1937 alone, even before the *Yezhovchina* reached its full fury. See *The Secret History of Stalin's Crimes* (New York: Random House, 1952), p. 216.

[11] Elizabeth Bentley, *Out of Bondage* (New York: Devin-Adair, 1951), pp. 101-102. See also Yatskov's biography in *Veternay vneshney razvedki Rossii*, pp. 169-171.

[12] See Moscow 142 (circular), 12 September 1943, Translation 18, for more on the dissolution of the Comintern and the transfer of its assets to the professional Soviet intelligence services.

traveling on fraudulent American passports, FBI Special Agents in 1939 raided the facilities of several organizations linked to the CPUSA and found sufficient evidence to arrest General Secretary Earl Browder on charges of passport fraud.[13] In 1940, leads developed by British and Canadian investigators in the Woolwich Arsenal spy case pointed the Bureau toward the senior KGB officer in America, New York *rezident* Gaik Ovakimian (covername GENNADI), whom the FBI arrested in May 1941 for violating the Foreign Agents Registration Act.[14] Information on Soviet intelligence contacts and methods obtained by the Bureau in these early investigations would prove valuable during and after the war.

American authorities, nonetheless, did not act as decisively as they might have at the time. At least three defectors from Soviet intelligence were in the United States (Alexander Orlov, Walter Krivitsky, and Whittaker Chambers) and have given the Bureau relatively current information, had they been questioned in depth—and well protected—by federal officials.[15] In addition, the German invasion of the USSR in June 1941 virtually reversed American attitudes toward the Soviets. The State Department quickly reached an understanding with Moscow that allowed Ovakimian to leave the country. Similarly, President Roosevelt commuted Browder's sentence in May 1942 in the interest of inter-allied relations. The FBI remained watchful, but the raids and prosecutions ceased.

Any foreign intelligence service needs secure communications channels between its headquarters and its officers abroad. Although Soviet intelligence services had clandestine radio transmitters in diplomatic missions located in several American cities, these apparently were to be used only

---

[13] US Senate, Committee on the Judiciary [Subcommittee on Internal Security], "Scope of Soviet Activity in the United States," Part 23, 84th Congress, 2d Session, 1956, pp. 1207-1235.

[14] Ovakimian had been in the United States since 1933, operating under cover of the Amtorg Trading Corporation. US House of Representatives, Committee on Un-American Activities, "The Shameful Years: Thirty Years of Soviet Espionage in the United States," 82d Congress, 2d Session, 1951, pp. 15-17. See also US House of Representatives, Committee on Un-American Activities, "Communist Methods of Infiltration (Education—Part 2)," 83d Congress, 1st Session, 1953, pp. 198-199, 215. In 1937 a British Security Service agent penetrated KGB officer Arnold Deutsch's spy ring in the Woolwich Arsenal. Leads from the case pointed back to Canada and eventually led Canadian authorities to arrest one of Ovakimian's contacts; see Andrew and Gordievskiy, *KGB*, pp. 223-224.

[15] Walter Krivitsky gave some information of value to the Department of State; for a sample, see Loy W. Henderson, memorandum of conversation [with General Krivitsky], 15 March 1939, Document 1. See also Charles Runyon [Department of State], Memorandum for the File, "Walter Krivitsky," 10 June 1947, Document 18.

in emergencies.[16] In consequence, KGB and GRU stations cabled their important messages over commercial telegraph lines and sent bulky reports and documents—including most of the information acquired by agents—in diplomatic pouches. As a new European war loomed in 1939, the US Army had begun collecting enciphered Soviet telegrams, and soon thousands of cables were piling up in the offices of the Army's Signals Security Agency (SSA). A June 1942 agreement with the Navy and FBI gave the Army exclusive responsibility for analysis of foreign diplomatic and military ciphers, and the Army consequently had general responsibility for studying diplomatic traffic.

SSA analysts, based at Arlington Hall in Northern Virginia, soon began to explore whether the collected Soviet diplomatic messages might be readable. The Army and Navy had sporadically studied Soviet codes and ciphers over the preceding decade, but with little success.[17] Decrypted 1942 cables between the Japanese Army's general staff and its military attaches in Berlin and Helsinki showed that Finland's excellent cryptanalysts had made progress on some Soviet military ciphers, had determined the characteristics for sorting the still unsolvable diplomatic messages, and were sharing results with the Japanese.[18] This information was probably the immediate inspiration for SSA's examination of the Soviet telegrams. On 1 February 1943, SSA created a small program to examine the encrypted Soviet telegrams on orders from Col. Carter Clarke, Chief of the Special Branch of the Army's Military Intelligence Service (MID). Clarke seemed particularly concerned that Moscow and Berlin might negotiate a separate peace, and wanted to be able to warn his superiors of such a development.

Gene Grabeel, a Virginia schoolteacher who had recently arrived at Arlington Hall as part of its large civilian contingent, began the effort to read the Soviet diplomatic messages (and would continue working on the project for the next 36 years). She and others assigned to the project in 1943 spent months sorting stored and incoming telegrams by communications circuits. They gradually expanded their knowledge of the characteristics that separated the messages into the groups that the Finnish cryptanalysts had investigated. Five separate cryptographic systems became apparent.

---

[16] Wartime transmissions by Soviet clandestine transmitters in the United States—with the exception of those to Latin America—were usually test messages. It should be noted, however, that Comintern agents in the United States operated clandestine radios in the 1930s, and clandestine radio nets apparently were important for Soviet wartime intelligence operations in Latin America. A hint of the Comintern-CPUSA radio link can be seen in Klehr and Haynes, *The Secret World of American Communism*, pp. 205-208. Examples of Comintern messages to officials in the CPUSA are Moscow 117 of 21 March 1936 and Moscow 121 of 23 March 1936, Translation 1.

[17] See, for example, Stanford C. Hooper, Director of Naval Communications, to D. M. Crawford, Chief Signal Officer (US Army), "Communist Code and Cipher Material," 7 January 1932, National Archives and Records Administration, Record Group 457 (National Security Agency), "Historic Cryptographic Collection," box 138.

[18] Japanese Army General Staff message to military attaches in Berlin and Helsinki, Tokyo Circular 906, 6 October 1942, Document 7. SSA translated this message in early 1943.

More than half the telegrams belonged to a system that analysts dubbed "Trade" because it carried the messages of the Amtorg Trading Corporation and the Soviet Purchasing Commission—most of which concerned the transfer of Lend Lease materiel to the USSR. The other four systems were used by the KGB, GRU, Naval GRU, and Foreign Ministry, but these users would not be fully identified until the mid-1940s.

Moscow had already learned from well-placed agents that both enemies and allies were trying to read its diplomatic cables. Finnish troops found scorched codebooks and cryptographic materials in the USSR's Petsamo consulate in June 1941, and before the end of that year a Soviet agent in Berlin reported that the Germans were trying to exploit a Russian codebook acquired from their Finnish allies.[19] These developments in themselves were not alarming to Moscow, because the security of messages enciphered by one-time pads lies in the cipher and not in the codes per se (see inset). In any event, the compromised KGB codebook was not replaced until late 1943.[20] Another important piece of information came from British intelligence officer and Soviet agent H.A.R. "Kim" Philby in 1944, when he told the KGB that British cryptanalysts had turned their attention to Soviet ciphers.[21]

Philby probably reported nothing at that time about American efforts against the Soviet messages. (US analysts did not begin to collaborate with their British counterparts on Soviet communications in general until about August 1945.) Nevertheless, senior KGB officials may have become worried when White House aide Lauchlin Currie apparently told Soviet contacts (possibly in spring 1944) that the Americans were about to break a Soviet code. Currie had access to signals intelligence at the White House and could have heard overoptimistic rumors that Arlington Hall would soon be reading Soviet messages. Currie's tip probably was too vague to have alarmed Soviet cryptographers, but it might have worried higher-ups in Moscow. Indeed, the only change observed in the characteristics of the Soviet messages around that time appeared to be a cosmetic correction implemented to please higher authority. On 1 May 1944, KGB code clerks began using a new message starting-point indicator for telegrams—a change that ironically would make work easier for Arlington Hall cryptanalysts.[22]

---

[19] John Costello and Oleg Tsarev, *Deadly Illusions* (New York: Crown, 1993), p. 399.
[20] San Francisco 441 to Moscow, 31 October 1943, Translation 19, acknowledges the San Francisco consulate's receipt of the new "075-B" codebook and the scheduled destruction of the "Pobjeda" code, which was almost certainly the one found in Petsamo (and recovered by the US Army in Germany in April 1945).
[21] Genrikh Borovik and Phillip Knightley, *The Philby Files: The Secret Life of Master Spy Kim Philby* (Boston: Little, Brown, 1994), p. 235.
[22] The change is ordered in Moscow [no number] circular, 25 April 1944, Translation 26.

What Made Venona Possible?

The messages broken by the Venona program were both coded and enciphered. When a code is enciphered with a one-time pad, the cryptographer who designed the system expects the encipherment to provide absolute security—even if an adversary somehow obtains an underlying codebook or debriefs a defecting code clerk (such as Igor Gouzenko).

A flaw in the encipherment, however, can leave such messages vulnerable to analysis even in the absence of a codebook. Such was the case for the Soviet diplomatic systems from which the Venona translations came. Arlington Hall's Venona breakthrough in 1943-46 was a purely analytic accomplishment, achieved without the benefit of either Soviet codebooks or plain-text copies of original messages. The 1944-46 messages—which yielded the early translations and the bulk of all translations—were recovered over a period of years by Arlington Hall cryptanalysts and decoded from a "codebook" that cryptolinguist Meredith Gardner reconstructed by using classic codebreaking techniques.

A Soviet code clerk preparing a message first reduced its text into numeric code groups drawn from a codebook (a kind of dictionary in which the words and common phrases correspond to four-digit numbers). After encoding the plain text with numeric code groups, the clerk would obscure the code groups by adding them, digit by digit, to a string of random digits. This second series of digits, called "additive" or "key," was known to both the sender and receiver because it was printed on the pages of a "one-time pad." One-time pads were periodically pouched to Soviet consular missions in sealed packets. The pad pages—with 60 five-digit additive groups per page—were used in order, always starting with the group in the upper lefthand corner (the pad-page number to be used was more or less concealed somewhere on the face of the message). Code clerks in different Soviet missions used up these packets at varying rates, depending on the volume of messages to be enciphered or deciphered.

The security of such an encipherment-decipherment system depends on both the randomness (that is, unpredictability) of the "key" on the one-time pad pages and the uniqueness of the one-time pad sets held by the sender and the receiver. Different Soviet organizations used their own codes, changing them every few years (probably more to improve vocabulary and convenience than to enhance security).

The flaw in the Soviet messages resulted from the manufacturers' duplication of one-time pad pages, rather than from a malfunctioning random-number generator or extensive re-use of pages by code clerks. For a few months in early 1942, a time of great strain on the Soviet regime, the KGB's cryptographic center in the Soviet Union for some unknown reason printed duplicate copies of the "key" on more than 35,000 pages of additive and then assembled and bound these in one-time pads. Arlington Hall's Lt. Richard Hallock analyzed Soviet "Trade" messages in autumn 1943, producing evidence of extensive use of duplicate key pages (often with different page numbers) assembled in separate one-time pad books. Thus, two sets of the ostensibly unique one-time pad-page sets were manufactured. Despite the opinion that a single duplication was insufficient for solution, Hallock and his colleagues continued to attack the Trade messages and made considerable progress in understanding the cryptographic basis of the diplomatic systems. From Hallock's original discovery, additional analysis yielded techniques for finding duplicate pages separated in time and among different users. The duplicate pages began showing up in messages in mid-1942 and were still occurring in one circuit as late as June 1948. Nevertheless, most of the duplicate pages were used between 1942 and 1944—years of rapid expansion of Soviet diplomatic communications.

We do not know how and when the Soviets discovered the flaw, but we believe Moscow learned of it through agents William W. Weisband and Kim Philby. By the time the Soviets saw the consequences of the manufacturing flaw in the late 1940s, however, most of the duplicate one-time pad pages had already been used. The set of potentially exploitable messages thus was bound by the production of the duplicate pages and the West's ability to spot duplicate uses. Finding duplicates, however, only made the messages potentially readable; indeed, some messages and passages remained unexploitable even after 37 years of effort.

Cecil James Phillips
National Security Agency

In November 1944 Arlington Hall analysts solved this new starting-point indicator problem and soon expanded their effort against the "Trade" messages to encompass a second, still unidentified Soviet system. This was the breakthrough that eventually made the cables readable. The method revealed hundreds of instances in which individual pages of additive digits from KGB one-time pads were duplicated by key used for Trade messages. Over a period of years, cryptanalysts were able to determine the one-time pad additive values for significant parts of hundreds of enciphered telegrams, leaving the coded texts vulnerable to crypto-linguist codebuilders trying to recover the meanings of the four-digit words and phrases.[23]

American authorities inferred during World War II that the Soviets were engaged in espionage, but as yet there was little coordination among the various counterintelligence organizations. A June 1939 Presidential directive gave the FBI responsibility for domestic counterintelligence with the Office of Naval Intelligence (ONI) and the War Department's Military Intelligence Division (better known as the G-2).[24] The three organizations comprised a body known as the Interdepartmental Intelligence Conference (IIC) and stood together to protect their monopoly on domestic counterintelligence work from other agencies, particularly the new Office of Strategic Services (OSS) and its activist chief, Maj. Gen. William J. Donovan. OSS eventually developed a capable counterintelligence apparatus of its own in Europe—the X-2 Branch—but it had no authority to operate on American soil.

In keeping with the limited extent of interagency cooperation, American counterintelligence organizations made uneven progress in integrating signals intelligence leads during the war. OSS and the FBI separately launched their own cryptologic intelligence operations, but these were short-lived.[25] (Neither OSS nor the FBI, incidentally, was shown the Army's "MAGIC" intercepts of wartime foreign diplomatic messages.) The X-2 Branch of OSS had been created to provide British intelligence services with a point of contact in OSS for sharing certain sensitive "ULTRA" reports derived from decrypted German military and intelligence communications.[26] Unfortunately for OSS, however, X-2 monitored the agents of Axis—not

---

[23] Several cryptanalysts contributed to this breakthrough, including Genevieve Feinstein, Cecil Phillips, Frank Lewis, Frank Wanat, and Lucille Campbell.
[24] The reasoning and terms of Roosevelt's directive can be seen in Attorney General [Frank Murphy] to the President, 17 June 1939, Document 2; and Franklin D. Roosevelt to Secretary of State, et al., 26 June 1939, Document 3.
[25] Bradley F. Smith, *The Ultra-Magic Deals and the Most Secret Special Relationship, 1940-46* (London: Airlife, 1993), pp. 69, 110-111.
[26] Timothy J. Naftali, "ARTIFICE: James Angleton and X-2 Operations in Italy," in George C. Chalou, ed., *The Secrets War: The Office of Strategic Services in World War II* (Washington: National Archives and Records Administration, 1992), pp. 222-223.

allied—services. It had little influence over security clearances for OSS personnel (some of whom indeed spied for the Soviets).[27]

Coordination was little better between the military's cryptologic services, which in any event had left domestic security largely to the FBI. The Army and Navy signals intelligence organizations barely cooperated with one another, jealously guarding their reports and their access to President Roosevelt. Outside of the Oval Office there was no collation and analysis of the totality of the intelligence information—let alone the counterintelligence leads—collected by the US Government.

Hoover's FBI monitored the CPUSA during the war but did not always share its leads with other agencies. In April 1943, FBI agents began to collect solid information on current KGB activities and personnel. New York consular officer Vassili M. Zarubin (a KGB general operating under the alias Zubilin) called on senior CPUSA officer Steve Nelson in Berkeley, California. Unbeknownst to both, the FBI had been watching Nelson for weeks. Zarubin's conversation made it obvious to Bureau eavesdroppers that he was an important KGB officer (although they could not yet know that he was Gaik Ovakimian's replacement as senior KGB *rezident* in America).[28] The FBI watched Zarubin from that day until he left the United States in 1944 (although he occasionally gave his trailers the slip), and Bureau agents catalogued hundreds of contacts and leads developed by this operation.[29]

More leads dropped into the Bureau's mailbox in August 1943, in the form of an anonymous letter drafted on a Russian typewriter and mailed in Washington, DC. This extraordinary note—the author's identity still is uncertain—denounced Zarubin and 10 other KGB officers in North America, along with two of their assets.[30] Special Agents quickly concluded that the letter was genuine and largely accurate, although they gave little

---

[27] X-2 was prohibited from collecting on Soviet intelligence. Evidence of Soviet penetrations in OSS can be seen in New York 887 to Moscow, 9 June 1943, Translation 11; New York 1325-6 to Moscow, 15 September 1944, Translation 56; and New York 1437 to Moscow, 10 October 1944, Translation 62. For more on penetrations of OSS, see Hayden B. Peake, "Soviet Espionage and the Office of Strategic Services," in Warren F. Kimball, ed., *America Unbound: World War II and the Making of a Superpower* (New York: St. Martin's, 1992).

[28] William Branigan, comment on Herbert Romerstein's "Soviet Intelligence in the United States," in Roy Godson, ed., *Intelligence Requirements for the 1980s: Counterintelligence* (Washington: National Strategy Information Center, 1980), p. 201. Branigan was the Special Agent who recorded the Nelson-Zarubin meeting.

[29] An indication of Bureau operations at the time can be seen in Hoover to Birch D. O'Neal, "Alto Case," 26 February 1944, Document 11.

[30] The anonymous letter is included as Document 10. For an analysis, see the CIA memorandum probably drafted by William K. Harvey, "COMRAP," 6 February 1948, Document 20. Information in Pavel Sudoplatov's controversial memoir suggests the author of the Anonymous Letter might have been Zarubin's assistant, a Lt. Col. Mironov, who was discharged from the KGB in 1944 on psychiatric grounds; see Sudoplatov, with Anatoli Sudoplatov, Jerrold L. and Leona P. Schecter, *Special Tasks: Memoirs of an Unwanted Witness—A Soviet Spymaster* (New York: Little, Brown, 1994), pp. 196-197.

credence to its claim that the Soviets were passing secrets to Japan. The FBI subsequently increased surveillance of persons named in the letter and even doubled two agents recruited by one of them, KGB officer Andrei Shevchenko.[31] Nevertheless, the FBI did apparently not pass copies of the anonymous letter to other agencies until after World War II, nor did Special Agents try to recruit Soviet officers named by its author.

The Atomic Era

US Government agencies ran a wartime security system that was porous for Soviet agents and yet opaque for American counterintelligence agencies charged with protecting secrets. FBI Director Hoover allegedly knew nothing of the super-secret Manhattan Project before Steve Nelson inadvertently informed him in the spring of 1943. High-level political and strategic motivations in Washington also hampered US efforts against Soviet espionage. President Roosevelt wanted to strengthen a distrustful Stalin in his fight against Hitler, and his lieutenants had no desire to antagonize Moscow by suppressing the CPUSA or publicly probing rumors that members of the Party had infiltrated government agencies.[32] Hoover, for his part, kept a close eye on the CPUSA but did not, at least before 1945, try to convince the White House that Soviet officials in the United States were actively engaged in espionage. Donovan's OSS also encountered the administration's reluctance to antagonize Moscow when OSS officers bought unidentified Soviet cryptographic documents from emigre Finnish cryptanalysts in late 1944. Secretary of State Edward P. Stettinius insisted that the papers be given back to the Russians, and Donovan promptly obeyed a White House order to return them to the Soviet Embassy.[33]

The intrigues surrounding the development of the atomic bomb both symbolized and helped widen the growing breach between the Soviet Union and

---

[31] Special Agents monitored Shevchenko's penetration of the Bell Aircraft Corporation in the last year of the war, feeding him innocuous information and developing leads uncovered in the operation. US House of Representatives, Committee on Un-American Activities, "Soviet Espionage Activities in Connection With Jet Propulsion and Aircraft," 81st Congress, 1st Session, 1949, pp. 101-128.

[32] Assistant Secretary of State Adolf A. Berle's and the FBI's slow reaction to allegations by former GRU courier Whittaker Chambers is cited as evidence of Roosevelt administration inattention to Communist infiltration; see Allen Weinstein, *Perjury: The Hiss-Chambers Case* (New York: Alfred A. Knopf, 1978), pp. 329-331.

[33] OSS purchased Soviet code and cipher material (or Finnish information on them) from émigré Finnish army officers in late 1944. The Secretary of State's protest, dated 27 December 1944, is included as Document 12. Donovan might have copied the papers before returning them the following January but there is no record of Arlington Hall receiving them, and CIA and NSA archives have no surviving copies. See Bradley F. Smith, *The Shadow Warriors: OSS and the Origins of the CIA* (New York: Basic Books, 1983), pp. 353-54.

its Western allies in 1945. Washington and London jointly built the bomb but said nothing about their work to Moscow. Stalin's clandestine sources, however, obtained detailed political, military, and diplomatic reports on his allies' strategic planning and war aims.[34] He knew of the bomb project long before the new President Truman finally divulged it to him in July 1945. The KGB effort against the Manhattan Project (codenamed ENORMOUS) represented a shift in collection emphasis. Moscow hitherto had regarded the United States primarily as a source of information useful in the war against Germany; now America became in Russian eyes a rival and even a threat to the Soviet Union itself. Soviet agents penetrated the Manhattan Project at several points. At the Los Alamos facility alone, at least four agents reported through couriers such as Lona Cohen to the Soviet consulate in New York, where a KGB sub-residency under a young engineer named Leonid R. Kvasnikov (covername ANTON) coordinated operations and dispatched intelligence to Moscow.[35]

US perceptions of the Soviets began shifting after the war had been won. Two defections in autumn 1945 galvanized US counterintelligence. Igor Gouzenko, a GRU code clerk in the USSR's Ottawa Embassy, revealed to Canadian authorities that the Soviets had indeed penetrated the Manhattan Project and other agencies.[36] A few weeks later, Elizabeth Bentley gave the FBI details about spies in the State and Treasury Department, OSS, the Pentagon, and even the White House. Both Bentley's and Gouzenko's accounts dovetailed with the story that *Time* magazine editor and former GRU agent Whittaker Chambers had told FBI agents in 1942 and again, in detail, in May 1945.[37] By mid-November, the White House knew the

---

[34] KGB sources, for example, reported accurately on many aspects of Anglo-American planning; see New York 887 to Moscow, 9 June 1943, Translation 11; and New York 1271-4 to Moscow, 7 September 1944, Translation 53. Ironically, the quality of KGB and Communist Party sources was not matched by any particularly insightful KGB analysis of the Western political scene. In particular, KGB officers and CPUSA officials composed some rather confused reflections on the presidential race of 1944; see New York 598-599 to Moscow, 2 May 1944, Translation 28.

[35] The four assets apparently were Klaus Fuchs (covernames CHARLES and REST), David Greenglass (covernames BUMBLEBEE and CALIBRE), Theodore Alvin Hall (covername YOUNGSTER [MLAD]), and a source covernamed FOGEL and PERS; see New York 1749-50 to Moscow, 13 December 1944, Translation 76. PERS seems to have been arbitrarily or erroneously converted to "Perseus" (there is no covername Perseus in the Venona messages) in Russian memoirs as the Soviet and Russian intelligence services sought to describe a high-level source in the Manhattan Project. For more on Russian claims for Perseus, see Chikov, "How the Soviet intelligence service 'split' the American atom," (Part 1), p. 38.

[36] Gouzenko's information helped Western cryptanalysts understand Soviet communications procedures but did not directly contribute to the Venona breakthrough. He brought out GRU messages that identified Soviet assets, but no codebooks or one-time pads.

[37] Weinstein, *Perjury*, pp. 340, 347. The FBI's handling of Chambers is recounted in D. M. Ladd to Hoover, "JAY DAVID WHITTAKER CHAMBERS," 29 December 1948, Document 23.

outlines of the defectors' stories and had heard of their accusations against dozens of US Government employees, including high officials such as White House aide Lauchlin Currie, OSS executive assistant Duncan Lee, and Assistant Secretary of the Treasury Harry Dexter White.[38]

A Canadian Government White Paper on the Gouzenko affair in July 1946 confirmed the gist of press speculation about Soviet wartime espionage and gave the Western public its first official account of the extent of the problem. This confirmation of the essential truth behind the rumors diminished public tolerance for Communism at home and abroad. Truman became convinced of the need for a government-wide tightening of security, but he had no intention of condoning witch-hunts for allegedly disloyal Democratic officials or blanket accusations against federal workers and Roosevelt's New Deal. Little could be done, for the time being, against the individuals named by Gouzenko or Bentley—apart from corroborating their reports and limiting the suspects' access to sensitive information—until Western governments could gather evidence that would stand up in court.

Domestic politics, however, prompted the White House to act. Republicans campaigning in the 1946 Congressional elections accused Democrats of ignoring Communist infiltration and disloyalty; the charge helped the GOP regain control of Congress for the first time since 1931. Truman's response was motivated in part by his own political considerations. Hoping to deter free-ranging Congressional probes and harsh Republican-drafted loyalty legislation, he signed Executive Order 9835, which institutionalized the wartime loyalty regime. The executive order mandated loyalty boards in all federal agencies and defined employee disloyalty to include membership in groups judged subversive by the Attorney General.[39]

During this period, Bentley gave the FBI details that opened a hitherto unnoticed window on the networks run by "illegals"—Soviet citizens abroad under false identities who worked for the KGB or GRU in apparent isolation from official Soviet consular missions. Special Agents fanned out across the country to investigate Bentley's leads and to monitor persons whom she had named, and for about a year the FBI entertained hopes of "doubling" her against the KGB.[40]

---

[38] Hoover sent news of the Gouzenko defection to the White House on 12 September and reported the Bentley allegations on 8 November. See Hoover to Matthew Connelly, 12 September 1945, Document 13; and Hoover to Brigadier General Harold Hawkins Vaughan, 8 November 1945, Document 15.

[39] Alonzo L. Hamby, *Man of the People: A Life of Harry S. Truman* (New York: Oxford, 1995), pp. 428-429. Harry S. Truman, *Memoirs*, Volume 2, *Years of Trial and Hope* (Garden City, NY: Doubleday, 1956), p. 280.

[40] Elizabeth Bentley, with Afterword by Hayden Peake, *Out of Bondage: The Story of Elizabeth Bentley* (New York: Ballantine, 1988 [1951]); see Peake's commentary, pp. 266-267. The Gregory case is summarized in Federal Bureau of Investigation, "Underground Soviet Espionage Organization [NKVD] in Agencies of the US Government," 21 October 1946, Document 17.

The "Gregory" case—as the investigations prompted by Bentley were known inside the government—produced many leads but led to no espionage prosecutions. FBI agents could not use evidence gathered by wiretaps in court, and they were unable to catch suspected spies in the act of compromising official secrets.[41] Meanwhile, Soviet agents and intelligence officers almost certainly surmised the existence of a serious leak. They took precautions even before a federal grand jury, meeting in 1947, probed Bentley's allegations and called as witnesses dozens of individuals named in her testimony.

At roughly the same time, the renamed Army Security Agency (ASA—formerly the Signals Security Agency) developed evidence that would soon corroborate Bentley's testimony and the 1943 anonymous letter. After the war, the "Russian Section" at Arlington Hall expanded. Work on diplomatic messages benefited from additional technical personnel and new analysts—among them Samuel Chew, who had focused on Japan, and linguist Meredith Gardner, who had worked on both German and Japanese messages. Chew had considerable success at defining the underlying structure of the coded Russian texts. Gardner and his colleagues began analytically reconstructing the KGB codebooks. Late in 1946, Gardner broke the codebook's "spell table" for encoding English letters. With the solution of this spell table, ASA could read significant portions of messages that included English names and phrases. Gardner soon found himself reading a 1944 message listing prominent atomic scientists, including several with the Manhattan Project.[42]

Gardner henceforth made rapid progress, reading dozens of messages sent between Moscow and New York in 1944 and 1945. By May 1947 he had read one that implied the Soviets ran an asset with access to sensitive information from the War Department General Staff.[43] It became apparent to Gardner that he was reading KGB messages showing massive Soviet espionage in the United States.

Another problem soon arose—that of determining how and to whom to disseminate the extraordinary information Gardner was developing. ASA's reporting procedures did not seem appropriate because the decrypted messages could not even be paraphrased for Arlington Hall's regular intelligence customers without divulging their source. At this point, ASA knew nothing

---

[41] David C. Martin, *Wilderness of Mirrors* (New York: Harper & Row, 1980), pp. 23-32. For the inadmissibility of wiretap evidence, see Robert J. Lamphere, *The FBI-KGB War: A Special Agent's Story* (New York: Random House, 1986), pp. 101-102. Daniel J. Leab has written a detailed account of the difficulty faced by the Justice Department in its 1946 prosecution of a Soviet officer accused of espionage, Lt. Nicolai G. Redin; "The Red Menace and Justice in the Pacific Northwest," *Pacific Northwest Quarterly* 87 (Spring 1996), pp. 83-88.

[42] New York 1699 to Moscow, 2 December 1944, Translation 74.

[43] New York 1751-1753 to Moscow, 13 December 1944, Translation 77. The actual agent (presumably William Ludwig Ullman, covername PILOT) was not indicated on the message.

about the federal grand jury impaneled in Manhattan to probe the espionage and disloyalty charges leveled by Bentley and other defectors from Soviet intelligence, so no one in the US Government was aware that evidence against the Soviets was suddenly developing on two adjacent tracks. Gardner took matters into his own hands in the summer of 1947, drafting "Special Report #1," which went to a handful of senior ASA officials. One item in it about an unidentified Soviet asset would later prove fateful:

> *LIB?? (Lieb?) or possibly LIBERAL: was ANTENKO* [later understood as ANTENNA] *until 29 Sept. 1944. Occurs 6 times, 22 October–20 December 1944. Message of 27 November speaks of his wife ETHEL, 29 years old married (?) 5 years, ". . . . . . . husband's work and the role of METR(O) and NIL."* [Spelling and punctuation in original] [44]

Cooperation Expands

Deputy G-2 Carter Clarke read Special Report #1 and in late August or early September 1948 asked FBI liaison officer S. Wesley Reynolds for a list of KGB and GRU covernames. Clarke's hint that ASA had broken a KGB code piqued the interest of the Bureau, which at that time was questioning former Soviet agents living in the United States concerning the allegations of Bentley and others and information gathered from surveillance of Soviet officials during the war. The Bureau quickly sent ASA a list of some 200 names, and, although few of them appeared in the translated messages, the long cooperation later known as the Venona program had begun.[45] This cooperative spirit between cryptanalysts and investigators endures to the present day.

Full inter-agency cooperation, however, was still several years away. President Truman, unhappy about the mass of unanalyzed reports that the departments daily sent to the White House, had insisted in 1945 on greater coordination of intelligence information. His new Central Intelligence Group was intended to solve this problem, but it started out slowly. American intelligence agencies on the whole did not do a good job of presenting counterintelligence analyses to the President and his aides. FBI Director Hoover, for instance, frequently sent to the Truman White House

---

[44] New York 1657 to Moscow, 27 November 1944, Translation 73. "Special Report #1" is included as Document 19.

[45] It speaks volumes about inter-allied signals intelligence cooperation that Arlington Hall's British liaison officers learned of the breakthrough even before the FBI was notified. Meredith Gardner kept his British counterpart abreast of developments, and from 1948 on there was complete and profitable US-UK cooperation on the problem. The control term "Venona" did not appear on the translated messages until 1961. In the beginning the information was usually called the "Gardner material," and a formal control term—"Bride"—was finally affixed in 1950. From the late 1950s to 1961 the control term was "Drug."

allegations of Communist plotting and Soviet espionage. It is not clear how much of this information actually reached the President, however, or how seriously it was regarded by White House aides.

Despite the Truman administration's sustained but piecemeal restructuring of the Intelligence Community, the division of labor in counterintelligence functions remained much as it had been set early in World War II. The new National Security Council preserved the FBI's and armed services' monopoly of domestic counterintelligence in NSC-17/4 and 17/6 in 1949.[46] The agencies outside this monopoly were expected to provide information but were not invited to join operations involving domestic security. The new Central Intelligence Agency (CIA), the closest institutional successor to OSS and CIG and, consequently, the inheritor of OSS's dismal security reputation, saw little of the information Gardner and his colleagues were developing. CIA counterintelligence officers, however, now had wider access to signals intelligence than had their predecessors in X-2, and they briefly joined the Army and Navy in a Joint Counterintelligence Information Center (JCIC) to exploit current signals intelligence leads, using X-2's wartime employment of ULTRA as its model.[47] The JCIC received Special Report #1 at roughly the same time Colonel Clarke notified the FBI, but the Bureau never joined the JCIC or sought its assistance with the Soviet translations. When the JCIC inquired about additional Special Reports in early 1949, Clarke apparently instructed his subordinates not to provide anything. The early American effort to use the information from the Soviet messages thus remained understaffed and highly compartmented, and exploitation opportunities were almost certainly lost in consequence. For several years the major investigative burden remained with the FBI, which assigned the most important inter-agency liaison work to a single Special Agent, Robert Lamphere.

"I stood in the vestibule of the enemy's house, having entered by stealth," Lamphere recalled in his memoir of the investigations.[48] Lamphere began sharing liaison duty with Wesley Reynolds in the spring of 1948. That October he had a private meeting with Meredith Gardner and began full-time liaison on the project. It was Lamphere's tenacity that taught the FBI how to use the translations against Soviet espionage. Through him the

---

[46] NSC-17/4 is included under Sidney W. Souers, Memorandum for the President, 22 March 1949, Document 26.

[47] The JCIC worked under the cover of "OP32Y1," an office at the Naval Communications Annex on Nebraska Avenue in Washington. Its CIA contingent was detailed from the Office of Special Operations and included ex–FBI agent William K. Harvey. The Central Intelligence Group became the Central Intelligence Agency with the implementation of the National Security Act of 1947 in September of that year.

[48] Lamphere, *The FBI-KGB War*, p. 86.

Bureau received a steady flow of translations and re-translations, as well as Gardner's insights about the "tradecraft" of Soviet spying. Gardner and his colleagues, in return, received collateral evidence, identifications, and additional leads.[49] The process was essentially a slow comparison of evidence for and against various competing hypotheses, with the knowledge gained in many cases being greater than the sum of its parts.

By the time Lamphere began using the translated messages, the public controversy over "loyalty" and "red-baiting" had risen dramatically amid growing concern over US-Soviet tensions. New allegations that prominent American citizens had spied for the Soviets burst upon the public in July 1948, when Bentley spoke before the House Committee on Un-American Activities. Her testimony recounted, among other things, Lauchlin Currie's alleged distress over US efforts to read wartime Soviet telegrams (this seems to have been the first public clue to the existence of ASA's effort). A few days later Whittaker Chambers charged that Roosevelt administration figures Alger Hiss and Harry Dexter White were secret Communists. Heated denials by the accused and their supporters added to the drama and controversy as elections loomed that autumn. Republican Congressmen and activists hailed the testimony as the long-suppressed proof of Democratic inattention toward Communist subversion. Truman bitterly resented such charges and insisted that the Hiss affair in particular was a GOP "red herring."[50]

Truman's repeated denunciations of the charges against Hiss, White, and others—all of whom appear under covernames in decrypted messages translated before he left office in January 1953—suggest that Truman either was never briefed on the Venona program or did not grasp its significance. Although it seems odd that Truman might not have been told, no definitive evidence has emerged to show he was. In any event, Truman always insisted that Republicans had trumped up the loyalty issue and that wartime espionage had been insignificant and well contained by American authorities.[51]

In December 1948 the FBI identified a Soviet agent covernamed SIMA as Judith Coplon, a young Justice Department analyst recruited by the Soviets

---

[49] Two of Lamphere's blind memos to Gardner can be seen as "FLORA DON WOVSCHIN, with alias," 9 May 1949, Document 25; and "Anatoli Borisovich Gromov," 12 July 1949, Document 27.

[50] Hamby, *Man of the People*, p. 453. President Truman repeated his "red herring" remark late that year; see Truman to Attorney General Tom Clark, 16 December 1948, Document 22. Another glimpse of the White House attitude can be seen in George M. Elsey's note to Clark M. Clifford, 16 August 1948, Document 21.

[51] Mr. Truman wrote in his memoirs in 1956: "The country had reason to be proud of and have confidence in our security agencies. They had kept us almost totally free of sabotage and espionage during the war;" see Truman, *Years of Trial and Hope*, p. 291.

in 1944.[52] Coplon would become the first person arrested on the basis of a Venona lead. FBI agents detained her in March 1949 along with a KGB official under UN cover; her purse contained ostensibly sensitive documents (which the Bureau had routed through her office as bait). Director Hoover or (less likely) someone higher in the Truman administration forbade FBI officials testifying at her trial from introducing the translated messages as evidence. This protection of the cryptanalytic breakthrough forced prosecutors and government witnesses into elaborate cirumlocutions; Special Agent Lamphere, for example, testified that suspicion had fallen on Coplon because of information from a reliable "confidential informant" that was not a wiretap.[53] Although both of Coplon's convictions would be overturned on appeal, subsequent prosecutions developed in the same manner, with the too-sensitive codebreaking secrets obscured behind mounds of corroborating evidence.

The Coplon case set the pattern for an intense series of investigations and prosecutions that followed over the next two years. Meredith Gardner and his colleagues (working from May 1949 under the auspices of AFSA, the new Armed Forces Security Agency) supplied covernames and translations to the FBI; Lamphere and other Special Agents tracked down the leads:

- *February 1949.* ASA observed that messages containing "Material G" were quoting British Foreign Office telegrams sent to the British Embassy in Washington during the war. Not until March 1951, however, did American and British cryptanalysts conclude that "G," "GOMMER," and "GOMER" (the Russian transliteration of HOMER) had to be the same agent who had provided the cables to the KGB. By the beginning of May 1951, the list of possible suspects had narrowed to one name: Donald Maclean of the Foreign Office. Maclean, with compatriot Guy Burgess, soon fled to the Soviet Union.

- *September 1949.* The FBI determined that covernames REST and CHARLES, both denoting a scientist in the wartime Manhattan Project, referred to physicist Klaus Fuchs, author of a paper quoted in one message.

---

[52] New York 27 [to Moscow], 8 January 1945, Translation 82, notes Coplon's transfer to the Department of Justice headquarters in Washington. Lamphere claims the date of her transfer from New York to Washington clinched the identification; see *The FBI-KGB War,* pp. 97-98. See also the KGB's request for information on Coplon in Comintern files; Pavel Fitin to Georgi Dimitrov, 19 October 1944, reprinted in Klehr and Haynes, eds., *The Secret World of American Communism,* pp. 294-295.

[53] Lamphere, *The FBI-KGB War,* p. 115. For more on the administration's handling of the Coplon case, see Clark to Truman, "Proposed Deportation of Valentine A. Gubitchev," 16 March 1949, Document 24.

British authorities interrogated Fuchs in late 1949. His information in turn led the FBI to courier Harry Gold, arrested in Philadelphia on 22 May.[54]

- *February 1950.* Lamphere suspected that a Soviet agent covernamed CALIBRE had to be an enlisted man posted at the Manhattan Project facility at Los Alamos during the war. Subsequent AFSA analysis, and additional information from Harry Gold, led to David Greenglass, who confessed to the FBI on 15 June 1950 and also implicated his brother-in-law, Julius Rosenberg.

- *Spring 1950.* Covername NICK had emerged in 1949 as one Amadeo Sabatini, who had fought in Spain together with KGB asset Morris Cohen. Sabatini apparently kept quiet about Cohen but did point the FBI toward a Jones Orin York (almost simultaneously identified as Venona covername NEEDLE). When questioned in April 1950, York alleged that a former case officer of his was an AFSA employee named William Weisband. AFSA suspended Weisband in May.

- *Late June 1950.* The FBI discovered that information in the messages about an agent who collected technological and scientific secrets, codenamed LIBERAL and ANTENNA, matched the known facts about New York engineer Julius Rosenberg. Two messages also implicated his wife, Ethel. Rosenberg had been questioned on the basis of David Greenglass' information on 16 June and tailed ever since, but he was not arrested until a month later.[55]

- *Sometime in 1949-50.* Gardner translated a 1944 message that described the recruitment of Harvard physics student Theodore Alvin Hall. Soon afterward, the Bureau determined that the covername YOUNGSTER [MLAD], found in other messages, matched Hall. Special Agents questioned Hall in 1951, but he was never prosecuted (probably because a case could not have been made without revealing AFSA's program).

Translated messages also corroborated various charges made by Elizabeth Bentley and Whittaker Chambers. By June 1950 the Bureau determined that the covername ALES, mentioned in one KGB message, referred to former State Department aide Alger Hiss, then serving a sentence for perjury.[56] Around the same time, Lamphere told Gardner that the

[54] See [Lamphere to Gardner], "EMIL JULIUS KLAUS FUCHS, aka; Karl Fuchs," 26 September 1949, Document 28; Lamphere, *The FBI-KGB War,* pp. 133-134. See also W. K. Benson to Chairman, Scientific Intelligence Committee [H. Marshall Chadwell], "Failure of the JAEIC To Receive Counter Espionage Information having Positive Intelligence Value," 9 February 1950, Document 29; Hoover to Souers, 24 May 1950, Document 30.
[55] See Lamphere's blind memo, "Study of Code Names in MGB Communications," 27 June 1950, Document 31; Hoover to Rear Admiral Robert L. Dennison, 18 July 1950, Document 32. See also Lamphere, *The FBI-KGB War,* pp. 178-186.
[56] Washington 1822 to Moscow, 30 March 1945, Translation 89.

covername JURIST meant Harry Dexter White, a former Assistant Secretary of the Treasury, who had died suddenly a few days after denying Whittaker Chambers' August 1948 charge before the House Committee on Un-American Activities.[57] The translations also clarified another sensational spy case a few years later when the FBI identified the covername MARQUIS as Joseph Milton Bernstein, a GRU agent linked to the Institute of Pacific Relations and *Amerasia* magazine.[58]

Double Dilemma

The KGB had not been surprised by the wave of charges, arrests, and prosecutions. Intelligence officials in Moscow nonetheless faced much the same dilemma that confronted the FBI and AFSA. Both sides now had sources too important to risk. The Americans and their allies had to be careful in investigating certain suspects. The Soviets had to be equally wary in protecting their agents.

The Soviets apparently had monitored Arlington Hall's "Russian Section" since at least 1945, when William Weisband joined the unit (see inset). Weisband's earliest reports on the work on Soviet diplomatic systems were probably sketchy and might not have provided clear warning to Moscow about the exploitability of the KGB messages. By 1947, Weisband could have reported that KGB messages were being read, although by then virtually all of the exploitable messages had been transmitted and were in Arlington Hall's possession. Where Weisband had sketched the outlines of the cryptanalytic success, British liaison officer Kim Philby received actual translations and analyses on a regular basis after he arrived for duty in Washington in autumn 1949.[59]

Timely warnings from Philby helped the KGB protect some of its agents and operations. Various accounts indicate that in October 1949 Moscow began advising American agents who had dealt with Klaus Fuchs that they

---

[57] It remains unclear which messages led the FBI to the White identification, but some of the more important messages in which he appeared are New York 1119-1121 to Moscow, 4 August 1944, Translation 50; New York 1634 to Moscow, 20 November 1944, Translation 71; and New York 79 to Moscow, 18 January 1945, Translation 84.

[58] Venona sheds some light on the *Amerasia* affair; see New York 927-28 to Moscow, 16 June 1943, Translation 12; and New York 1103 to Moscow, 8 July 1943. See also Harvey Klehr and Ronald Radosh, *The Amerasia Spy Case: Prelude to McCarthyism* (Chapel Hill: University of North Carolina Press, 1996), pp. 64-65.

[59] Philby's Washington posting has been discussed in many books; a concise account is in Borovik and Knightley, *The Philby Files,* p. 273. The late John Costello clarified the timeliness of Philby's warning somewhat in his notes on Guy Burgess' KGB file (Costello cited it as File 83792, Volume 4, pp. 76-183). The Burgess file indicated that Philby had learned by late September that British and American authorities believed CHARLES was Klaus Fuchs. Mr. Costello summarized some of his notes for Robert Louis Benson in 1995.

Who Was William Weisband?

In 1950 one Jones Orin York (covername NEEDLE) told the FBI that he had passed secrets to the KGB since the mid-1930s. A worker in the aircraft industry on the west coast, York said that his KGB handler during 1941-42 had been one Bill Weisband, who had helped him buy a camera for photographing documents.[a]

York's allegation was disturbing news, implying that the KGB had a mole in the sensitive Armed Forces Security Agency (AFSA). Born in Egypt in 1908 of Russian parents, Weisband emigrated to America in the 1920s and became a US citizen in 1938. He joined the US Army Signals Security Agency in 1942 and performed signals intelligence and communications security duties in North Africa and Italy, where he made some important friends before returning to Arlington Hall and joining its "Russian Section." Although not a cryptanalyst, as a "linguist adviser" (he spoke fluent Russian) the gregarious and popular Weisband had access to all areas of Arlington Hall's Soviet work. Meredith Gardner recalled that Weisband had watched him extract the list of Western atomic scientists from the December 1944 KGB message mentioned earlier.

Weisband always denied involvement in espionage, and the US Government never prosecuted him for it. While suspended from AFSA on suspicion of disloyalty, he skipped a federal grand jury hearing on Communist Party activity. As a result, in November 1950 Weisband was convicted of contempt and sentenced to a year in prison. He died suddenly of natural causes in 1967.

The Venona messages do not hold a definite reference to William Weisband. Nevertheless, three messages mention a "ZVENO" (the Russian word for "link"). The earliest and clearest reference suggests procedures for the KGB's London residency to use in contacting ZVENO, who was awaiting a transfer to England. ZVENO, according to one message, had spent the last four weeks in an Italian-language course in Virginia and would leave for Britain by mid-July.[b] NSA records show that Weisband spent that June honing his skills in a language (probably Italian) at Arlington Hall, shipped out on 17 July, and arrived in London by 29 July.

[a] Information that York provided in a later FBI interview can be seen in the Washington Field Office's memorandum "William Wolf Weisband," 27 November 1953, Document 34.

[b] New York 981 to Moscow, 26 June 1943; this was not fully translated until 1979.

---

might have to flee the country through Mexico.[60] Some operatives, such as Morris and Lona Cohen and their case officer "Mark," avoided the net that was closing around other KGB agents. (The Cohens, as "Helen and Peter Kroger," would be convicted of espionage in the United Kingdom in 1961.)

[60] Ronald Radosh and Joyce Milton, *The Rosenberg File: A Search for Truth* (New York: Holt, Rinehart & Winston, 1983), p. 74.

The long spate of prosecutions and loyalty hearings coincided with, and helped heighten, the atmosphere of suspicion and accusations now known as McCarthyism. Republicans in Congress were echoing widespread sentiment when they criticized the Truman administration for its failure to prevent Communism from conquering Eastern Europe and China. "Softness" on Communism abroad was portrayed by Republicans as the corollary of laxness at home. Suspicions that the Roosevelt and Truman administrations had neglected internal security fed charges of a Democratic-led coverup of the wartime *Amerasia* affair, as well as Eisenhower administration Attorney General Herbert Brownell's 1953 accusation that then President Truman had ignored FBI warnings about Harry Dexter White in 1946.[61] Republican Senator Joseph McCarthy and allies exploited this confusion and rancor, blaming Communists in the State Department for "losing" China and accusing federal workers of disloyalty on flimsy pretexts.

The tacit decision to keep the translated messages secret carried a political and social price for the country. Debates over the extent of Soviet espionage in the United States were polarized in the dearth of reliable information then in the public domain. Anti-Communists suspected that some spies—perhaps including a few who were known to the US Government—remained at large. Those who criticized the government's loyalty campaign as an overreaction, on the other hand, wondered if some defendants were being scapegoated; they seemed to sense that the public was not being told the whole truth about the investigations of such suspects as Julius Rosenberg and Judith Coplon. Given the dangerous international situation and what was known by the government at that time, however, continued secrecy was not illogical. With the Korean war raging and the prospect of war with the Soviet Union a real possibility, military and intelligence leaders almost certainly believed that any cryptologic edge that America gained over the Soviets was too valuable to concede—even if it was already known to Moscow.

Intensified political and legal pressure on the CPUSA coincided with shifts in Soviet intelligence tactics. Two pieces of legislation for a time gave the Justice Department broad powers against the Party. Between 1949 and 1957 the government, invoking the Alien Registration Act (better known as the Smith Act), won convictions of a dozen top CPUSA leaders for advocating the violent overthrow of the government.[62] The following year, Congress overrode Truman's veto and passed the Internal Security Act (often called

---

[61] Attorney General Brownell had President Eisenhower's approval for this November 1953 charge; both men almost certainly had seen translated messages about White (and probably about Hiss as well). Indeed, Eisenhower may have been briefed on the program by the G-2 while he was still Army Chief of Staff in 1947. One of the FBI warnings about White is included as Hoover to Vaughan, 1 February 1946, Document 16.

[62] The Supreme Court's decision in *Yates v. US,* handed down in June 1957, all but voided the Smith Act as a tool for prosecuting Party leaders.

the McCarran Act), which required Communist-affiliated organizations to register with the government and allowed emergency detention of potential spies and saboteurs.

These and other governmental actions sent the CPUSA partially underground in 1951. Party leaders took this step in an effort to protect essential cadres, but the move actually hastened the CPUSA's decline. In addition, Soviet leader Nikita Khrushchev's 1956 critique of Stalinism prompted demoralizing internal debates in the CPUSA and precipitated the departure of still more members.[63] Soviet intelligence officers apparently received orders to steer clear of the closely monitored CPUSA, and they urged assets to avoid open contacts with Communist causes. By 1953 the FBI had concluded that the CPUSA was no longer a serious espionage threat, although the Bureau still regarded it as a potential recruiting ground for spies.[64] Nonetheless, intensive surveillance of Soviet diplomats and nationals did not stop KGB and GRU officers, even those working under official cover, from meeting with assets, and from continuing to operate with some effectiveness in the United States.[65]

Venona in Later Years

Allied efforts to translate the wartime cables would continue for years to come (many translations would be first published in the 1960s and 1970s), but identifications of Soviet agents in America fell off in the 1950s. The CIA finally became an active partner in the Venona effort.[66] After senior manager Frank Rowlett transferred to the CIA in 1952, selected analysts in the Agency's Foreign Intelligence and Counterintelligence Staffs used the translations as a reference point to check the memories of KGB and GRU officers who had defected after the death of Stalin. Defectors once again became the US Intelligence Community's primary source of relatively current information on Soviet intelligence. American analysts sifted the

---

[63] Joseph R. Starobin, *American Communism in Crisis, 1943-1957* (Cambridge, MA: Harvard University Press, 1972), pp. 220-230.

[64] One FBI report of the period claimed that there was "no conclusive indication that the Communist Party, USA, is playing a role [in espionage] at this time;" see "Role of the Communist Party, USA, in Soviet Intelligence," February 1953, Dwight D. Eisenhower Library, White House Office Files, Office of the Advisor for National Security Affairs, box 16, p. 48.

[65] Oleg Kalugin has written a memoir of Soviet operations in the United States during this period; see Kalugin and Fen Montaigne, *The First Directorate: My 32 Years in Intelligence and Espionage Against the West* (New York: St. Martin's, 1994), pp. 1-4, 36. Some of the agents in the late 1950s and early 1960s proved devastating to American intelligence, particularly to the National Security Agency. A contemporary "exposé" can be under Hoover to Brigadier General A. J. Goodpaster, 23 May 1960, Document 35.

[66] CIA received its first Venona translations in 1953, after veteran signals intelligence officer Frank Rowlett transferred to the Agency (the aforementioned Special Reports seen by OSO personnel in 1948 were not translations per se). CIA's William Harvey was formally briefed on the program in August 1952. AFSA was reconstituted as the National Security Agency on 4 November 1952.

defectors' accounts and compared them with information supplied by Venona and various liaison services to catalogue Soviet intelligence officers worldwide.[67] Venona thus became a touchstone for American counterintelligence—a kind of super-secret central reference point for FBI and CIA leaders to use in judging the accuracy of subsequent information.

Spy stories again dominated the headlines during 1957. In January the FBI wound up an operation it had run for almost a decade, hauling in Soviet asset Jack Soble and his associates on the basis of reports from double-agent Boris Morros—whom the Bureau had initially spotted in the company of Vassili Zarubin in April 1943.[68] A timely defection in Paris soon led the FBI to an even bigger catch. In the spring of 1957 the KGB recalled from New York an unreliable illegal, Lt. Col. Reino Hayhanen, who feared punishment at home and sought sanctuary in the American Embassy in Paris. Hayhanen gave the FBI enough information to locate the Brooklyn studio of his superior, an artist whom he knew only as "Mark." Special Agents spotted the elusive Mark when he returned to his studio one last time and found stolen documents and espionage gear in the artist's hotel room. Arrested in June 1957, Mark gave his name as "Col. Rudolf Abel," refusing to cooperate further. He was really William Henry Fisher, a senior KGB officer born in England who had entered the United States in 1948. Abel's arrest marked the first time the government had caught a Soviet "illegal" working in America. Indeed, Abel may well have been Iskhak A. Akhmerov's successor as illegal *rezident* in the United States.[69]

The year 1957 ended with the FBI surveilling a pair of GRU illegals, Walter and Margarita Tairov, in New York. Although the Tairovs vanished and apparently fled the country in early 1958, the operation against GRU illegals was another first for American intelligence. The CIA had spotted one of the pair in Europe with help from its penetration of the GRU in East Germany, Lt. Col. Petr S. Popov. Timely liaison work enabled FBI Special Agents to amass scores of leads from surveillance of the duo.[70] Unfortunately, the couple almost certainly spotted the surveillance, and their flight and subsequent report were among the factors that soon led to Popov's arrest.

---

[67] CIA transferred the management of its portion of the Venona program to James Angleton's Counterintelligence Staff in 1965.
[68] Jack Soble was a Lithuanian whose given name was Sobolevicius; he and his brother had penetrated Leon Trotsky's entourage for the KGB in the 1920s; see Andrew and Gordievskiy, *KGB*, pp. 154-155. Hollywood producer Boris Morros was doubled by the FBI in 1947 and reported on the activities of Soble and members of his almost-moribund spy ring, while also passing low-level secrets and misinformation back to Moscow; see Boris Morros, *My Ten Years as a Counter-Spy* (London: Werner Laurie, 1959), pp. 191, 204-206. Morros is covername FROST in New York 18-19 to Moscow, 4 January 1945, Translation 80. Soble is covername ABRAM in New York 625 to Moscow, 5 May 1944, Translation 31.
[69] See Russian Foreign Intelligence Service, *Veternay vneshney razvedki Rossii* [Veterans of Russian Foreign Intelligence], pp. 158-159. Abel was exchanged for downed U-2 pilot Francis Gary Powers in 1962.
[70] Martin, *Wilderness of Mirrors,* pp. 92-93.

Venona had contributed to just one of these cases. Only a handful of American intelligence officials knew the truth behind the big spy cases of 1957: that US counterintelligence efforts against the Soviets, at least in the United States, had relied on volunteers since the Venona program peaked. This was not for want of trying. NSA had pored over the Soviet traffic and had kept its shrinking Venona team looking for additional leads. The FBI had penetrated the CPUSA and searched for illegals—but still did not catch Rudolf Abel for almost a decade. CIA divisions created clever but only marginally effective programs designed to establish coverage of Soviet installations abroad, to induce Soviet intelligence officers to defect (the REDCAP program), and to monitor the mail of Soviet illegals in America (HTLINGUAL). Despite all these efforts, the Intelligence Community's most important counterintelligence leads in the late 1950s came from volunteers—both walk-ins like Hayhanen and KGB Maj. Peter S. Deriabin, as well as agents-in-place like Popov and Polish intelligence officer Michal Goleniewski.[71] American counterintelligence was once again, as it had before Venona, left to rely on voluntary sources.

Venona, according to US policy at the time, could only be shared with a small, witting cadre of senior American intelligence officers. The tiny fraction of Soviet messages that were read convinced the CIA and FBI that Soviet espionage, at least in the 1940s, was aggressive, capable, and far-reaching—and that at least some wartime spies and agents of influence remained unidentified. Nothing that the West learned in subsequent years suggested that Soviet intelligence had grown any less capable or aggressive. Senior American intelligence officers also knew how poorly American intelligence had fared in its efforts to recruit agents to report on Soviet intelligence operations in the United States. Direct approaches to Soviet officers and illegals in the early Cold War usually failed, and by the 1960s American intelligence was relying on voluntary defectors such as Anatoli Golitsyn and Yuri Nosenko, and defectors-in-place such as Aleksi I. Kulak and Dmitri F. Polyakov, for relatively recent information about Soviet intelligence services. The leads they provided were often valuable but sometimes troubling for Western counterintelligence officers. Remembering how many clues to Soviet penetrations had accumulated in the files before Venona finally provided incontrovertible evidence of espionage against the West, molehunters in the CIA and FBI privately resolved to leave no defector's tip uninvestigated.

Only a short step led from this conclusion to a new concern among some, particularly in the CIA, that the Soviets might try to stage such defections to

---

[71] The ineffectiveness of the CIA's and FBI's mail opening operations is attested in US Senate Select Committee to Study Governmental Operations with Respect to Intelligence Activities (better known as the Church Committee), "Supplementary Detailed Staff Reports on Intelligence Activities and the Rights of Americans," Volume III, 94th Congress, 2d Session, 1974, pp. 576-578, 652.

feed misinformation to American and Western intelligence services. While this possibility is now considered to have been remote, it could not be resolved beyond all doubt at the time. It was impossible to prove the negative and rule out the possible existence of Soviet misinformation operations designed to distract Western services from the most damaging penetrations in their midst. Even so, American counterintelligence services would spend much of the 1960s doing all they could to prove that negative, and to minimize the possibility of deception.

The extreme secrecy of the Venona information tended to ensure that any precautions would be viewed skeptically by some of the very intelligence personnel they were designed to protect. Only a handful of American intelligence officers had access to the Venona secret, and those who did not have such access had no way, in many cases, to judge the reliability of the evidence gathered against alleged Soviet agents in the 1940s. As a result, even seasoned intelligence professionals viewed the spy cases and internal security debates of the 1940s and early 1950s as McCarthyite hysteria. This attitude probably influenced some in the Intelligence Community as a whole to underestimate the Soviet espionage threat.

Elizabeth Bentley died in Connecticut in December 1963, long before the end of the Cold War she had helped to start. She never knew about the Venona secret, or about the way in which her testimony (among that of others) assisted the program. Before she died, she had been denounced as a traitor, a liar, and a criminal by everyone from her old comrades to a former President of the United States. The controversy over her testimony was only a skirmish in the national debate over the true extent of Soviet espionage, and over the federal government's attempts to balance competing requirements of civil liberties and internal security. The declassification of Venona augments and clarifies the evidence in the public domain, and consequently should move the debate from the politics and personalities of those who testified in public to the capabilities and actions of political leaders and intelligence officers—both American and Soviet—who worked in many cases behind the scenes.

Acronyms and Abbreviations

AFSA	Armed Forces Security Agency, 1949-52
ASA	Army Security Agency (US Army), from 1945
CIA	Central Intelligence Agency, from 1947
CIG	Central Intelligence Group, 1946-47
CPUSA	Communist Party of the United States
DCI	Director of Central Intelligence, from 1946
FBI	Federal Bureau of Investigation
GRU	Chief Directorate for Intelligence, Red Army General Staff
G-2	Military Intelligence Division (US Army)
HCUA	House Committee on Un-American Activities, US Congress
IIC	Interdepartmental Intelligence Conference
JCS	Joint Chiefs of Staff
KGB	Committee for State Security, from 1954
MGB	Ministry for State Security, 1946-47, 1952-53
MID	Military Intelligence Division (see G-2)
NIA	National Intelligence Authority, 1946-47
NKGB	Peoples Commissariat for State Security, 1943-46
NKVD	Peoples Commissariat for Internal Affairs, 1934-43
NSA	National Security Agency, from 1952
NSC	National Security Council, from 1947

NSCID	National Security Council Intelligence Directive
OGPU	Unified State Political Directorate, 1923-34
ONI	Office of Naval Intelligence
OSS	Office of Strategic Services, 1942-45
SSA	Signals Security Agency, US Army, 1942-45
USCIB	United States Communications Intelligence Board, 1946-58

Chronology

1939

10 January	Soviet intelligence defector Walter Krivitsky has the first of several debriefings at the Department of State.
26 June	President Roosevelt secretly gives the Federal Bureau of Investigation (FBI), the Military Intelligence Division (MID), and the Office of Naval Intelligence (ONI) exclusive responsibility for counterespionage.
23 August	Germany and USSR sign Non-Aggression Pact.
1 September	World War II begins as Germany invades Poland.

1940

21 May	President Roosevelt authorizes the FBI to conduct warrantless electronic surveillance of persons suspected of subversion or espionage; surveillance was to be limited insofar as possible to aliens.
5 June	FBI-MID-ONI "Delimitation Agreement" further specifies the division of labor in domestic intelligence work.
28 June	The Alien Registration Act (the "Smith Act") criminalizes conspiracy to overthrow the government, requires resident aliens to register, report annually, and provide notice of address changes.
20 August	KGB agent Ramon Mercader assassinates Leon Trotsky in Mexico.

1941

10 February	Walter Krivitsky found dead of a gunshot wound in a Washington hotel; the police rule his death a suicide.
5 May	Federal agents arrest Amtorg employee and KGB New York *rezident* Gaik Ovakimian for violating the Foreign Agents Registration Act.
22 June	Germany invades Russia.

29 June	FBI arrests 29 German military intelligence agents, crippling Germany's clandestine operations in the United States.
23 July	US Government allows Ovakimian to leave the country.
25 September	London KGB *rezident* Anatoli Gorski informs Moscow that his agent reports London has decided to build an atomic bomb.
7 December	Japanese aircraft attack Pearl Harbor; America enters the war.
25 December	Senior KGB officer Vassili M. Zarubin arrives in San Francisco on his way to succeed Ovakimian as New York *rezident*.

1942

20 March	MID's Special Branch begins producing daily "Magic Summaries" analyzing foreign diplomatic messages for the White House and senior military commanders.
13 June	The Office of the Coordinator of Information becomes the Office of Strategic Services (OSS), subordinate to the Joint Chiefs of Staff.
30 June	Interagency agreement divides signals intelligence duties: Navy assigned to handle naval codebreaking; the US Army's Signals Intelligence Service to handle diplomatic and military traffic; and the FBI works clandestine radio communications.
8 July	President Roosevelt bars all agencies except the FBI and the armed services from code-breaking activities. The services interpret this directive as authorization to deny signals intelligence to OSS.

1943

1 February	US Army's renamed Signal Security Agency (SSA) formally begins work on Russian diplomatic traffic.
10 April	KGB New York *rezident* Vassili M. Zarubin meets CPUSA official Steve Nelson in Oakland and discusses espionage.
15 May	Communist International (Comintern) resolves to disband.

7 August	FBI receives an anonymous Russian letter naming Soviet intelligence officers in North America.
31 October	San Francisco KGB residency acknowledges the receipt of a new codebook.

1944

1 May	The KGB, apparently on short notice, changes the indicator system for its cables, leaving the one-time pad page numbers *en clair*.
November	SSA's Cecil Phillips discovers the new KGB indicator, which is then used to detect "key" duplicated in Trade messages.
December	OSS purchases Soviet code and cipher material from Finnish sources; the Roosevelt administration orders the material returned to the Soviet Embassy in Washington.
15 December	The War Department transfers operational control of SSA from the Signal Corps to MID.

1945

12 April	President Roosevelt dies; Harry Truman sworn in as his successor.
27 April	A US Army Target Intelligence Committee (TICOM) team finds Russian code and cipher material in a German Foreign Office cryptanalytic center in a castle in Saxony-Anhalt.
8 May	Germany surrenders.
10 May	FBI conducts a lengthy debriefing of former Soviet agent Whittaker Chambers.
June	Earl Browder ousted as leader of the Communist Political Association, which reclaims its old name, the Communist Party of the United States (CPUSA).
16 July	The Manhattan Project detonates the world's first nuclear explosion, Trinity, in New Mexico; Soviet agents had warned Moscow in advance.
14 August	Japan capitulates.
5 September	Soviet GRU code clerk Lt. Igor Gouzenko defects in Ottawa.

6 September	The War Department authorizes merger of SSA with selected Signal Corps units to form the Army Security Agency (ASA), under MID.
12 September	US-UK signals intelligence Continuation Agreement extends wartime cooperation in this field.
20 September	President Truman dissolves OSS.
7 November	Elizabeth Bentley interviewed at length for the first time by FBI agents about her work for the KGB.

1946

22 January	Truman creates the Central Intelligence Group and the position of Director of Central Intelligence (DCI).
13 June	The State-Army-Navy Communications Intelligence Board adds the FBI and renames itself the United States Communications Intelligence Board (USCIB).
8 July	National Intelligence Authority Directive 5 secretly directs the DCI to conduct, as "services of common concern," all foreign intelligence and counterespionage.
10 July	CIG joins the new USCIB and gains access to signals intelligence.
15 July	A Canadian Royal commission releases its report on the Gouzenko affair to the public.
17 July	Attorney General Tom Clark urges Truman to renew and broaden Roosevelt's 1940 authorization to conduct electronic surveillance on "persons suspected of subversive activities"; the President soon approves.
20 December	ASA's Meredith Gardner translates part of a KGB message containing a list of atomic scientists.

1947

22 March	Executive Order 9835 tightens protections against subversive infiltration of the US Government, defining disloyalty as membership on a list of subversive organizations maintained by the Attorney General.

26 July	President Truman signs the National Security Act of 1947, creating the National Security Council (NSC) and transforming CIG into the Central Intelligence Agency (CIA).
Around 1 September	Col. Carter Clarke briefs the FBI's liaison officer on the break into Soviet diplomatic traffic.
12 December	NSCID-5 reiterates but qualifies DCI's counterespionage authority to avoid precluding certain "agreed" FBI and military counterintelligence activities.

1948

1 July	NSCID-9 puts USCIB under the NSC and increases civilian control of signals intelligence.
20 July	General Secretary Eugene Dennis and 11 other CPUSA leaders arrested and indicted under the Smith Act of conspiring to advocate violent overthrow of the US Government.
31 July	Elizabeth Bentley testifies before the House Committee on Un-American Activities (HCUA), publicly accusing Harry Dexter White and Lauchlin Currie of being Soviet agents.
3 August	Whittaker Chambers names Alger Hiss and Harry Dexter White as Communists in testimony before the HCUA.
19 October	Meredith Gardner and Robert Lamphere meet at Arlington Hall and formally inaugurate full-time FBI-ASA liaison on the Soviet messages.
17 November	Chambers produces the "Pumpkin Papers" to substantiate his new charge that Hiss and White spied for Moscow during the 1930s.
16 December	A federal grand jury indicts Alger Hiss for perjury.
December	FBI identifies covername SIMA as Justice Department analyst Judith Coplon.

1949

4 March	FBI arrests Coplon and Soviet UN employee Valentin A. Gubitchev in New York.

23 March	Truman approves NSC 17/4, which reconstitutes the secret Interdepartmental Intelligence Conference to coordinate jurisdiction of FBI and military counterintelligence.
20 May	Defense Secretary Louis Johnson directs a quasi-merger of service signals intelligence in a new Armed Forces Security Agency (AFSA), subordinate to the JCS.
23 September	Truman announces that the Soviets have exploded an atomic bomb.
1 October	The People's Republic of China is proclaimed in Beijing.

1950

21 January	Alger Hiss is convicted of perjury.
24 January	Klaus Fuchs confesses to espionage.
9 February	Senator Joseph R. McCarthy, in a speech in Wheeling, West Virginia, brandishes a list of Communists allegedly working in the State Department.
22 May	FBI arrests Harry Gold for espionage.
25 June	North Korean troops invade South Korea.
17 July	FBI arrests Julius Rosenberg.
24 August	AFSA assigns Soviet intercept material a restricted codeword ("Bride") and special handling procedures.
23 September	Congress passes the Internal Security Act (the "McCarran Act"), which it would soon pass again over President Truman's veto. The Act requires Communist-linked organizations to register and allows emergency detention of potentially dangerous persons.

1951

25 May	British Foreign Office officials Donald Maclean and Guy Burgess flee Great Britain to defect to the Soviet Union.
July	CPUSA announces that the Party will operate as a "cadre organization," with many of its leaders underground.

1952

                    AFSA detects duplicate key pages in GRU messages.

4 November   Truman creates the National Security Agency (NSA) to supersede AFSA and further centralize control of signals intelligence under the Secretary of Defense and a reconstituted USCIB.

1953

                    NSA places the "POBJEDA" codebook—recovered in Germany in April 1945—against KGB messages from 1941 through 1943. More than half of the burned codebook proves useable.

5 March   Stalin dies.

6 April   KGB defector Alexander Orlov's story appears in *Life* magazine; finally alerting the FBI to his residence in the United States.

19 June   Julius and Ethel Rosenberg executed after President Eisenhower again denies executive clemency.

27 July   Armistice signed in Korea.

6 November   Attorney General Herbert Brownell sparks controversy by claiming in a Chicago speech that former President Truman had appointed Harry Dexter White to head the International Monetary Fund despite FBI warnings that White was a Soviet agent.

1954

20 December   CIA's Directorate of Plans creates the Counterintelligence Staff, with James J. Angleton as its chief.

1956

8 March   NSC approves the FBI's proposed "Cointelpro" operation against the CPUSA.

4 June   The Department of State releases Soviet General Secretary Khrushchev's secret speech to the Twentieth Party Congress, in which Khrushchev denounced Stalin's crimes.

October	Soviet troops suppress a popular uprising in Hungary.

1957

25 January	FBI arrests Jack and Myra Soble for espionage on the basis of evidence provided by double agent Boris Morros.
4 May	KGB officer Reino Hayhanen, en route from the United States, defects at the US Embassy in Paris.
17 June	Supreme Court in *Yates v. US* rules the government had enforced the Smith Act too broadly by targeting protected speech instead of actual action to overthrow the political system; this ruling makes the Act almost useless for prosecuting Communists.
21 June	Federal authorities detain Hayhanen's superior, KGB illegal Col. Rudolf Abel, in New York.
15 November	Abel is sentenced to 30 years and conveyed to prison.

PART I

THE AMERICAN RESPONSE TO SOVIET ESPIONAGE

Part I:
The American Response to Soviet Espionage

Archival Citations and a Note on the Documents

The following 35 documents are reproduced in Part I. They represent an attempt to gather some of the more interesting, important, and revealing original documents available to American policymakers and intelligence officers during the period covered by this volume. It is hoped that these documents will provide researchers with ready access to some of the key decisions of the period, as well as give them a flavor of internal US Government discussions and concerns over Soviet espionage in America. Almost all of the documents are published here for the first time anywhere; although most of the documents were already declassified, 13 were declassified by NSA, FBI, and CIA specifically for this volume. In many cases the date of the declassification is marked on the document's first page.

1. Loy W. Henderson, memorandum of conversation [with General Krivitsky], 15 March 1939, National Archives and Records Administration, Record Group 59 (Department of State).

2. Attorney General [Frank Murphy] to the President, 17 June 1939, Franklin D. Roosevelt Library, President's Secretary's Files (Confidential File), "State 1939-40," box 9.

3. Franklin D. Roosevelt, to Secretary of State et al., 26 June 1939, Franklin D. Roosevelt Library, President's Secretary's Files (Confidential File), "State 1939-40," box 9.

4. J. Edgar Hoover to Major General Edwin M. Watson, 25 October 1940, Franklin D. Roosevelt Library, White House Official Files (Subject File), "Justice Department—FBI Reports," box 12.

5. Joseph A. Michela, Military Attache Moscow Report 1903, "N.K.V.D. of the U.S.S.R.," 14 April 1941, Franklin D. Roosevelt Library, Harry Hopkins Papers, "MID Reports—USSR—Volume V," box 190 [Chart not included].

6. Hoover to Watson, 18 February 1942, Franklin D. Roosevelt Library, White House Official Files (Subject File), "Justice Department—FBI Reports," box 15.

7. Tokyo Circular 906 to Berlin and Helsinki, 6 October 1942, National Security Agency, "Jap Dip Dispatches," Venona Collection, Provisional Box 1.

8. US Army Signals Security Agency, "Memorandum on Russian Codes in the Japanese Military Attache System," 9 February 1943, National Security Agency Archives [Excerpt].

9. Hoover to Harry Hopkins, 7 May 1943, Franklin D. Roosevelt Library, White House Official Files (Subject File), "Justice Department—FBI Reports," box 18.

10. Anonymous letter to Hoover, undated [received 7 August 1943], National Security Agency Venona Collection, 54-001, box D046 [Russian original with English translation].

11. Hoover to Birch D. O'Neal, "Alto Case," 26 February 1944, Central Intelligence Agency, Leon Tarasov file.

12. Edward P. Stettinius, Jr., Memorandum for the President, "Soviet Codes," 27 December 1944, Franklin D. Roosevelt Library, President's Secretary's Files (Subject File), "Russia—1944," box 49.

13. Hoover to Matthew Connelly, 12 September 1945, Harry S. Truman Library, President's Secretary's Files (Subject File), "FBI—Atomic bomb," box 167.

14. Hoover to Frederick B. Lyon, 24 September 1945, Central Intelligence Agency, Igor Gouzenko file.

15. Hoover to Brigadier General Harry Hawkins Vaughan, 8 November 1945, Harry S. Truman Library, President's Secretary's Files (Subject File), "FBI—S," box 169.

16. Hoover to Vaughan, 1 February 1946, Harry S. Truman Library, President's Secretary's Files (Subject File), "FBI—W," box 169 [Attachment not included].

17. Federal Bureau of Investigation, "Underground Soviet Espionage Organization (NKVD) in Agencies of the US Government," 21 October 1946, Harry S. Truman Library, White House Central Files (Confidential File), "Justice" (7), box 22 [Excerpt].

18. Charles Runyon [Department of State], Memorandum for the File, "Walter Krivitsky," 10 June 1947, National Archives and Records Administration, Record Group 59 (Department of State).

19. [Meredith Knox Gardner], "Covernames in Diplomatic Traffic," 30 August 1947, National Security Agency, Venona Collection, box D017.

20. No author [probably William K. Harvey, CIA], Memorandum for the File, "COMRAP," 6 February 1948, Central Intelligence Agency, Vassili M. Zarubin file.

21. George M. Elsey, Memorandum for Mr. [Clark M.] Clifford, 16 August 1948, Harry S. Truman Library, Clark M. Clifford Papers, "Loyalty Investigations," box 11.

22. [Harry S. Truman] to the Attorney General, 16 December 1948, Harry S. Truman Library, Tom Clark Papers, "Attorney General—White House/President, 1948," box 83.

23. D. M. Ladd, Memorandum to the Director [J. Edgar Hoover], "JAY DAVID WHITTAKER CHAMBERS," 29 December 1948, Federal Bureau of Investigation, Reading Room, Alger Hiss File.

24. Tom C. Clark, Memorandum for the President, "Proposed Deportation of Valentine A. Gubitchev," 16 March 1949, Harry S. Truman Library, White House Central Files (Confidential File), "Justice" (4), box 21.

25. [Robert J. Lamphere to Gardner], "FLORA DON WOVSCHIN, With Alias," 9 May 1949, National Security Agency Venona Collection at 49-005.

26. Sidney W. Souers, Memorandum for the President, 22 March 1949, Harry S. Truman Library, President's Secretary's Files, National Security Agency File, "Meeting 36," box 205.

27. [Lamphere to Gardner], "Anatoli Borisovich Gromov," 12 July 1949, National Security Agency, Venona Collection at 49-018.

28. [Lamphere to Gardner], "EMIL JULIUS KLAUS FUCHS, aka; Karl Fuchs," 26 September 1949, National Security Agency, Venona Collection at 49-029.

29. W. K. Benson to Chairman, Scientific Intelligence Committee [H. Marshall Chadwell], "Failure of the JAEIC To Receive Counter Espionage Information having Positive Intelligence Value," 9 February 1950, Central Intelligence Agency, Executive Registry Job 80B01731R, box 35.

30. Hoover to Souers, 24 May 1950, Harry S. Truman Library, President's Secretary's Files (Subject File), "FBI—G," box 168.

31. [Lamphere to Gardner], "Study of Code Names in MGB Communications," 27 June 1950, National Security Agency, Venona Collection, 50-025, box D045.

32. Hoover to Rear Admiral Robert L. Dennison, 18 July 1950, Harry S. Truman Library, President's Secretary's Files (Subject File), "FBI—R," box 169.

33. Armed Forces Security Agency, "Russian Cryptology During World War II," undated [ca. 1951], National Archives and Records Administration, Record Group 457 (National Security Agency), Historic Cryptographic Collection, box 526 [Excerpt].

34. No author [Washington Field Office, FBI], "William Wolf Weisband," 27 November 1953, National Security Agency, Office of Security files [Excerpt].

35. Hoover to Brigadier General A. J. Goodpaster, USA, 23 May 1960, Dwight D. Eisenhower Library, White House Staff Secretary Files (Subject Series), "Expose of Soviet Intelligence," box 23 [Table of Contents and Appendixes not included].

1. Loy W. Henderson, memorandum of conversation [with General Krivitsky], 15 March 1939.

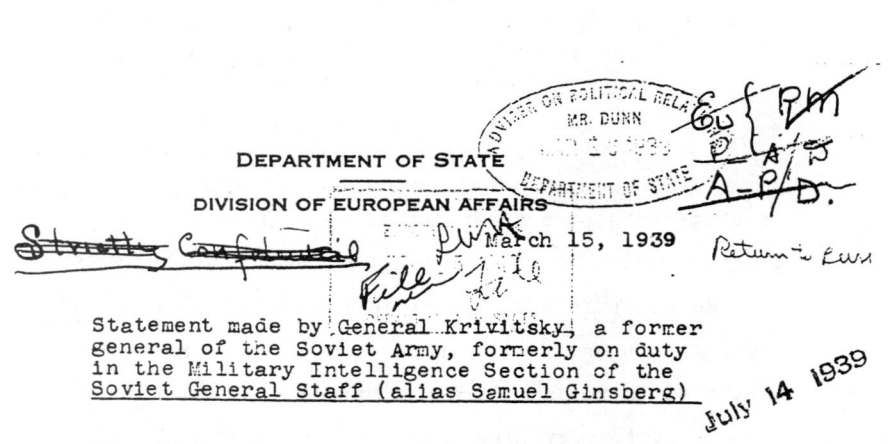

DEPARTMENT OF STATE
DIVISION OF EUROPEAN AFFAIRS

March 15, 1939

Statement made by General Krivitsky, a former general of the Soviet Army, formerly on duty in the Military Intelligence Section of the Soviet General Staff (alias Samuel Ginsberg)

It will be recalled that General Krivitsky, who escaped from the Soviet Union at the time that the eight Red Army generals, including Marshal Tukhachevsky, were seized and executed, and whose civilian name is Samuel Ginsberg, came to this country with his wife on temporary visitors' visas in the latter part of 1938. In January 1939 he called at the Department and discussed at length certain aspects of Soviet developments with which he was particularly familiar. A memorandum prepared by Mr. Page setting forth some of the statements made by General Krivitsky is attached hereto. While the general was in the Department he told me frankly that he feared that agents of the Commissariat for Internal Affairs (the OGPU) might make some attack upon him or members of his family while they were in the United States. He said he was therefore living quietly and endeavoring not to attract attention to his actions.

General Krivitsky came in to see me today and during the course of a rather extended conversation made a number of

1. *(Continued)*

-2-

of statements, the substance of some of which are set forth below.

He has sold a series of four articles to the <u>Saturday Evening Post</u> and is writing a book which he hopes to have published in the not distant future.

On Tuesday evening, March 7, he entered a café near Forty-second and Broadway and took a table with a friend, a Mr. Shoup, one of the editors of the <u>Jewish Daily Forward</u>, whom he had met while in Paris. While they were talking at this table four men entered the restaurant and seated themselves at an adjoining table. One of these men made obvious efforts to attract the General's attention and the General recognized him as <u>Sergei Bassoff</u>, an agent of the OGPU who had been connected with the American work of that organization for many years and whose record had become known to the General while the latter was engaged in intelligence work in Moscow. Bassoff was formerly a Soviet sailor; he joined the Soviet secret police in 1920; he came to the United States as a Soviet secret agent some time during the early twenties; since his arrival in the United States he has been an employee of the Soviet secret service; he has been naturalized as an American citizen; he has been invaluable as a GPU courier traveling between various European countries on an American passport; in June 1937 he was arrested in Holland while transporting funds but was released shortly

thereafter

[Margin note: See Mr. Murphy's memo attached hereto regarding Mr. Bassoff]

1. *(Continued)*

-3-

thereafter, apparently after having called upon the American Consul in Amsterdam for protection; after his release he proceeded to Moscow where he arrived in July 1937 and where he remained for some time.

Mr. Bassoff indicated by gestures that he desired to speak to the General and the General in a somewhat agitated frame of mind suggested to Mr. Shoup that they leave the cafe at once. Before they could get out, however, Mr. Bassoff stopped them and told the General that he desired to have a talk with him. When the General replied that he wished to have nothing whatever to do with Mr. Bassoff, the latter repeated his statement that it was necessary that they should have a talk. Mr. Shoup interrupted to suggest that all three of them go to the New York Times Annex, which was close by, where they could talk in private. The General then asked Mr. Bassoff if he intended to shoot him and Bassoff replied in the negative.

In the office of the New York Times Mr. Sheplin, a member of the editorial staff of that newspaper and a friend of Mr. Shoup, conducted them to a private room. Mr. Shoup withdrew to a distance so the conversation could be carried on without a third person overhearing. The General asked Bassoff who had sent him and Bassoff replied that the meeting had been accidental. The General said

that

1. *(Continued)*

-4-

that he knew that Bassoff must be acting under orders since otherwise he would not dare to talk with a person in such bad standing with the Soviet authorities as himself. Bassoff replied that the General still had friends in Moscow and that many persons continued to have confidence in him. He said, "Of course, we have read all that you have written and we suppose you are writing more." The General then inquired regarding the fate of a number of his friends and was informed that all had been shot. He was also told that the brothers of his wife "had suffered greatly". The intonations and gestures accompanying this statement were apparently made in order to convey the impression that the actions of the General and his wife were responsible for this suffering.

The General asked Mr. Bassoff if the latter was not afraid to approach him in such a manner in the United States. Bassoff said, "I have no fear. I am perfectly safe here." The General then told Bassoff that the latter would not dare take his life. Bassoff made no threat but contented himself with stating that there was nothing particularly to fear; that the penalty for such an act would probably be only a couple of years in jail.

The General told Bassoff to leave at once and not to approach him again. Bassoff thereupon left the building, joined his three friends who had waited outside, and

disappeared.

1. *(Continued)*

disappeared. The General had paid no particular attention to the three men accompanying Mr. Bassoff but Mr. Shoup told him later that they appeared to be of the gangster type.

The General told me that he believed that his life was in danger since the GPU organization in the United States was very strong and since he was certain that Bassoff would not have approached him unless he had been ordered so to do by the highest Soviet authorities and unless it had been decided that come what may the General must not be permitted to continue writing his experiences and memoirs. He said that in 1935 a GPU agent had been killed in New York City by an automobile in suspicious circumstances. There were ways of bringing about his own death in such a manner as to make it appear to be accidental.

I asked the General if he desired police protection and he replied that he did not presume to make such a request; that he hoped eventually to be able to leave New York and live quietly in some more remote place: but that he could not do so until he had finished some of his writings and had obtained an extension of his permit to remain in the United States, which expired on March 31.

Since General Krivitsky has served for many years in the Military Intelligence Service and since the work of that service is closely connected with that of the GPU (The Commissariat for Internal Affairs), I asked him

several

1. *(Continued)*

-6-

several questions regarding the organization of the GPU in the United States. He replied that there were two distinct branches of the GPU operating in this country. One branch was headed by some person in the Soviet Embassy, a person probably who had no diplomatic rank or perhaps a low diplomatic rank and who had little direct contact with the Ambassador or diplomatic members of his staff. Subordinate to this person were GPU centers in Amtorg, Intourist, and the various Soviet consular offices.

The second GPU branch had no connection whatever with the first and like the first, reported direct to Moscow. The head of the second branch lived in New York and undoubtedly many of his agents were American citizens. Although there was some contact between the two branches of the GPU they worked independently.

Eu:Henderson:LF

2. Attorney General [Frank Murphy] to the President, 17 June 1939.

Office of the Attorney General
Washington, D.C.

June 17, 1939

The President,

The White House.

My dear Mr. President:

I desire to direct your attention to the importance of investigations involving espionage, counter-espionage and sabotage. For some time an informal committee composed of representatives of the Department of State, the Department of the Treasury, the Department of War, the Department of Justice, the Post Office Department, and the Department of the Navy, has been acting as a clearing house for data or information concerning such matters. Such data or information was then transmitted to one of the investigative agencies for further action. The great majority of the investigations in this field have been conducted by the Federal Bureau of Investigation of the Department of Justice, the G-2 Section of the War Department, and the office of Naval Intelligence of the Navy Department.

Experience has shown that handling such matters through a committee such as is described above, is neither effective nor desirable. On the other hand, the three investigative agencies last mentioned have not only gathered a tremendous reservoir of information concerning foreign agencies operating in the United States, but have also perfected methods of investigation and have developed channels for the exchange of information, which are both efficient and so mobile and elastic as to permit prompt expansion in the event of an emergency.

As of course you are aware, the Department of Justice has developed in the Federal Bureau of

2. *(Continued)*

2

Investigation a highly skilled investigative force supported by the resources of an exceedingly efficient, well equipped, and adequately manned technical laboratory and identification division. The latter contains identifying data relating to more than ten million persons, including a very large number of individuals of foreign extraction. As a result of an exchange of data between the Departments of Justice, War and Navy, comprehensive indices have been prepared.

With a view to organizing investigative activities in this field on a more efficient and effective basis, I recommend the abandonment of the interdepartmental committee above mentioned, and a concentration of investigation of all espionage, counterespionage, and sabotage matters in the Federal Bureau of Investigation of the Department of Justice, the G-2 Section of the War Department, and the office of Naval Intelligence of the Navy Department.

The directors of these three agencies should in that event function as a committee for the purpose of coordinating the activities of their subordinates.

If the foregoing recommendations meet with your approval, I suggest that confidential instructions be issued by you to the heads of the Departments interested in accordance therewith.

A draft of a memorandum which you may possibly care to use for that purpose, is enclosed herewith for your consideration.

Respectfully,

Attorney General.

Enclosure
No. 2100

3. Franklin D. Roosevelt, to Secretary of State et al., 26 June 1939.

Hyde Park, N. Y.,
June 26, 1939

CONFIDENTIAL

MEMORANDUM FOR — THE SECRETARY OF STATE
THE SECRETARY OF THE TREASURY
THE SECRETARY OF WAR
THE ATTORNEY GENERAL
THE POSTMASTER GENERAL
THE SECRETARY OF THE NAVY
THE SECRETARY OF COMMERCE

It is my desire that the investigation of all espionage, counter-espionage, and sabotage matters be controlled and handled by the Federal Bureau of Investigation of the Department of Justice, the Military Intelligence Division of the War Department, and the office of Naval Intelligence of the Navy Department. The directors of these three agencies are to function as a committee to coordinate their activities.

No investigations should be conducted by any investigative agency of the Government into matters involving actually or potentially any espionage, counter-espionage, or sabotage, except by the three agencies mentioned above.

I shall be glad if you will instruct the heads of all other investigative agencies than the three named, to refer immediately to the nearest office of the Federal Bureau of Investigation any data, information, or material that may come to their notice bearing directly or indirectly on espionage, counter-espionage, or sabotage.

(Signed) Franklin D. Roosevelt

4. J. Edgar Hoover to Major General Edwin M. Watson, 25 October 1940.

JOHN EDGAR HOOVER
DIRECTOR

Federal Bureau of Investigation
United States Department of Justice
Washington, D. C.

October 25, 1940

STRICTLY ~~CONFIDENTIAL~~

Major General Edwin M. Watson
Secretary to the President
The White House
Washington, D. C.

My dear General:

    I am enclosing herewith for the information of the President and you a memorandum which I have just completed upon the present status of the espionage and counter-espionage operations of the Federal Bureau of Investigation to date. I thought the President might wish to have an up-to-date memorandum of exactly what we have done and are doing in this field. As you will note, the contents of this memorandum are highly confidential, in view of the delicacy of some of the operations upon which we are presently working.

    With expressions of my best regards, I am

Sincerely,

J. Edgar Hoover

Enclosure

DECLASSIFIED
E.O. 11652, Sec. 5(E)(2)
Justice Dept. letter, 9-21-72
By DBS, NLR, Date APR 3 1975

4. *(Continued)*

JOHN EDGAR HOOVER
DIRECTOR

Federal Bureau of Investigation
United States Department of Justice
Washington, D. C.

DECLASSIFIED
E.O. 11652, Sec. 5(E)(2)
Justice Dept. letter, 9-21-72
By DBS, NLR, Date APR 3 1975

October 24, 1940

Strictly ~~Confidential~~

PRESENT STATUS OF ESPIONAGE AND COUNTER
ESPIONAGE OPERATIONS OF THE FEDERAL BUREAU
OF INVESTIGATION

    The Federal Bureau of Investigation has been operating for a period of many months on the eastern seaboard a shortwave radio station which is utilized by the German Intelligence Service for transmission of reports of German Agents in the United States to Germany. The directors of the German Secret Service in Germany also communicate with this station furnishing instructions and requests for information to the operators of this station for transmittal to German Agents in the United States. Needless to say, no one knows that this German communication system is actually controlled and operated in the United States by Special Agents of the Federal Bureau of Investigation, who are considered both by German Intelligence Services in Germany and in the United States to be actual members of the German espionage ring. Through this station the Federal Bureau of Investigation has been able to develop voluminous information concerning the identity of German Agents in the United States, their movements, interests and program. All material furnished by German Agents through their complicated channels of communication to this station for transmittal to Europe is cleared by State, War and Navy Department officials prior to the time that it is actually transmitted to Germany. Collaterally, in the operation of this station the undercover Agents of the Federal Bureau of Investigation have been utilized for the transmittal of funds for salaries and expenses of German Agents operating in the United States, which has of course resulted in widening the knowledge of the Federal Bureau of Investigation relative to this espionage group.

    Special Agents of the Federal Bureau of Investigation have under constant observation and surveillance a number of known and suspected Agents of the German, Russian, French and Italian Secret Services. The FBI is able through its counter espionage efforts to maintain a careful check upon the channels of communication, the sources of information, the method of finance and other data relative to these agents. Arrest is considered inadvisable except in extraordinary cases because counter espionage methods of observation and surveillance result in a constantly growing reservoir of information concerning not only known but also new agents of these governments.

4. *(Continued)*

-2-

Of course, when material is observed passing through the monitored channels which should not reach its European destination, such steps as are necessary are taken to prevent the ultimate delivery of this information.

Special Agents of the Federal Bureau of Investigation are assigned in undercover capacities to those plants engaged in the production of materials which are vital to the national defense and to those factories in which the War or Navy Departments have a particular interest. Thus, Bureau Agents work in munitions plants, shipyards, aircraft plants, engine factories and other industrial units whose products and production are vital to the national defense. Agents selected for these posts are men qualified in the skills of the trade in which they are engaged. Their identities as Special Agents of the FBI are of course unknown to their associates in the plants or even to the plant officials. Not only is vital information pertaining to the production of plants in which these men are engaged developed through these Agents, but they are able through their daily contacts to study and observe fellow employees who may be utilized as confidential informants for the FBI in these plants.

Undercover Agents, of course, never contact their fellow employees and disclose their identities but appropriate contacts are established through regional field offices with plant employees known to be dependable in order that arrangements may be perfected whereby these employees will keep the FBI informed of all matters of interest to the national defense. Indicative of the tremendous coverage established by this method, it is interesting to note that in one Ohio city the Federal Bureau of Investigation has 133 confidential informants in a single industrial unit, all of whom furnish to the FBI information deemed of interest to the production of the plant. None of these informants are known to each other and each believes that he is the Bureau's sole source of information within that organization. Extraordinary care is exercised at all times in situations of this kind to avoid the so-called "labor spying", industrial espionage or other matters which would interfere in any manner with employer-employee relationships.

Informants of this character are maintained in more than twelve hundred key industrial facilities. Among the plants in which Special Agents of the Federal Bureau of Investigation are assigned in undercover capacities are the Carl L. Norden Company of New York, manufacturer of bomb sights, the Vought-Sikorsky Aviation Corporation, Stratford, Connecticut, the Newport News Shipbuilding Company of Newport News, Virginia, the New York Shipbuilding Company of Camden, New Jersey, the Federal Shipbuilding Company of Kearney, New Jersey, the Shipbuilding Division of the Bethlehem Steel Company at San Francisco, California, the Bath Iron Works of Bath, Maine, and other plants.

4. *(Continued)*

-3-

Special Agents of the Federal Bureau of Investigation are actually operating in undercover assignments for intelligence purposes in many foreign countries. Included in the posts of assignment where men are stationed as of the date of this memorandum is Shanghai, China, where investigation by Bureau personnel has been under way for several months in connection with the espionage operations of German Agents. Specially qualified and carefully selected Special Agents are assigned in various undercover capacities in Mexico, from whence they operate in Guatemala, Costa Rica, Nicaragua, Honduras, Salvador and British Honduras. Other Agents are operating in Cuba, Colombia, Argentina, Brazil, Peru, Uruguay, Chile and other South American countries. Other Special Agents of the Bureau are on confidential missions in Moscow, Russia, Lisbon, Portugal, Berlin, Spain and Rome, Italy. A large detachment of Agents is stationed in the Hawaiian Islands to devote their entire time to general intelligence matters not only in the Hawaiian group but in other islands of the Pacific.

The office of the FBI at Juneau, Alaska, has been augmented in such a manner as to permit constant control of Bureau Agents in all settlements within the territory of Alaska. Particular care is exercised to constantly maintain appropriate channels of information with its sections of the Territory most adjacent to Siberia. At San Juan, Puerto Rico, the office of the FBI has been further enlarged and serves as the headquarters for a group of specially qualified Agents who from this point cover not only the American insular possessions in the Caribbean Sea but also make frequent visits to the insular possessions of other foreign governments.

Special Agents of the Federal Bureau of Investigation are presently undertaking under appropriate cover a detailed examination of the numerous islands and cays in the Caribbean Sea, with particular emphasis on the minute islands of the Antilles groups. This project contemplates frequent personal contact with inhabitants of all of these islands and periodical physical surveys of the islands to determine whether foreign powers may be concentrating fuel or other supplies in any remote spot.

Bureau Agents are conducting police training schools at the present time in Haiti and another Agent is assisting the Government of Colombia in the improvement of its policing facilities. Another Agent recently completed an assignment in Ecuador, which was designed to improve relations between the United States and Ecuador.

4. *(Continued)*

-3- (a)

Arrangements have been perfected with the following companies to obtain through their facilities in Central and South America information concerning industrial, financial, political and propaganda manipulations and operations of foreign governments:

- Standard Oil Company of New Jersey
- Pan American Airways, New York City
- National City Bank, New York City
- United Fruit Company of Boston, Massachusetts
- W. R. Grace Company, New York City
- Montgomery, Ward & Company, Chicago, Illinois
- Dun and Bradstreet, New York City
- The American Metal Company, Ltd., New York City
- Sterling Products, Inc., New York City (marketers of Bayer aspirin and related products)
- Raybestos-Manhattan, Inc., New York City
- The American-Colombian Corporation, Washington, D. C.
- Stewart, James & Company, Inc., New York City
- American Express Company, New York City
- Smithsonian Institution, New York City
- E. A. Pierce & Company, New York City
- Pan American News Service, Washington, D. C.
- The Hemisphere Corporation, New York City
- Rockefeller Foundation, New York City.

All of these organizations have extensive interests and personnel in Central and South America and are in a position to obtain information of interest and value to the Government of the United States.

The employees of these companies who obtain this information do not know its purpose or the identity of the agency to which it is furnished.

4. *(Continued)*

-4-

A close and constant liaison is maintained by representatives of the Federal Bureau of Investigation with operatives of the British Intelligence Service. These contacts are maintained not only in the continental United States but throughout the Western Hemisphere and a considerable volume of material is received daily from this source. Information so received is of course transmitted to interested governmental agencies.

Close liaison is maintained with the Canadian Intelligence Service, which it is to be noted operates independently of the British Intelligence Service. This agency has established over a period of many years excellent and dependable contacts in the Western Hemisphere. Officials of the FBI and officials of the Canadian Intelligence Service meet at least once a month in Ottawa, New York City or Washington for the purpose of exchanging data of interest to the national defense of Canada and the United States.

The Federal Bureau of Investigation is collaborating with the Pan American Union and the State Department at the present time in perfecting plans for a conference of law enforcement officials and Intelligence Agents of the Western Hemisphere in order to establish a broader medium for the exchange of Intelligence information. Plans are also being perfected for the holding in the training facilities of the Federal Bureau of Investigation at Washington, D. C., in January of a special session of the National Police Academy to be attended only by accredited representatives of the Central and South American countries. A comprehensive and extensive course in police methods, investigative procedure, Laboratory techniques and training methods will be afforded the representatives selected for this school. Invitations will be extended through the State Department to the Central and South American countries to have representatives attend this session of the National Police Academy. Not only will this school enable the FBI to increase its channels of information from Central and South America, but the school will undoubtedly contribute to a greater feeling of good will between the United States and its southern neighbor republics.

For the past year Agents of the Federal Bureau of Investigation have been engaged in the conducting of surveys of plants upon the priority lists of the War and Navy Departments. These surveys are intended to determine the vulnerability of American industrial units to espionage, sabotage and other detrimental efforts of foreign Agents. The Special Agent personnel engaged upon this type of work has received extensive specialized training in all aspects of plant protection and industrial security. To date, complete surveys have been made of more than 350 plants and detailed recommendations made both to the plant management and the War and Navy

4. *(Continued)*

- 5 -

Departments as to the steps which should be taken to minimize the possibilities of espionage and sabotage of these plants.

Actually under survey at the present time are 243 plants, in which the War and Navy Departments are interested, and by November 1st, surveys will have been completed of more than 1,000 plants. Recommendations made to plant management pertain to vulnerable points, hazards, the selection and handling of personnel, the handling of confidential documents, the establishment of identification systems, the initiation or improvement of guard forces, the prevention of fires and other similar subjects pertinent to the protection of such facilities. A staff of more than 250 men is used in making these industrial surveys. Astounding evidence of the lack of comprehension of the potential danger to plant production on the part of plant management is disclosed in many of these surveys.

Collateral to the plant survey program, arrangements have been perfected whereby a special committee representing all of the insurance companies in the United States is cooperating with the Federal Bureau of Investigation in the problem of industrial protection. Hundreds of carefully investigated and specially trained insurance company inspectors make frequent detailed checks of key facilities to insure that all recommended precautions against fire hazard and other interference with continuity of production may be maintained on an absolute minimum.

The Special Agent staff of the Federal Bureau of Investigation is undergoing extensive expansion but great care is exercised to insure that the high standards of personnel selection and qualification are not lowered. The training center on the Marine Reservation at Quantico, Virginia, is filled to maximum capacity and in addition, five Special Agent schools are operated in Washington at all times. Through the combined facilities thus available, eight training schools for newly appointed Special Agents are in operation at all times. In addition, upon completion of the training course in Washington, Special Agents when assigned to field duty are required to continue their training under the supervision of Special Agents in Charge for a considerable period.

The Federal Bureau of Investigation, because of its work in the field of law enforcement, has established and maintained for years friendly contacts with police officials throughout the

4. *(Continued)*

- 6 -

country. To insure a coordination of state, county and municipal law enforcement agencies with the Federal program for the national defense, there have been completed a series of conferences with police executives, these conferences being called by the Special Agents in Charge of each division of the Bureau. A nationwide coordinated plan of procedure under the supervision of the FBI with reference to national defense investigations has been worked out. In every section of the country Special Agents in Charge of the FBI field offices have called together groups of police officers, as a result of which there has been established in each community the machinery whereby thousands of police of local, county and state jurisdiction are available for use in the handling of those types of inquiries and investigations which the FBI believes can be referred to those agencies. This program gives the local officers a high degree of pride in the fact that they are cooperating in the national defense program and it likewise serves to assist the FBI in the handling of routine cases which the police are qualified to handle. The system is presently working in excellent manner and as the emergency becomes greater, the machinery so established will permit an even wider use of the services of local law enforcement agencies.

Closely aligned with the program of enlisting the active assistance of local departments has been the development of the FBI National Police Academy. This Academy, inaugurated in 1935, has trained selected officers from local, county and state police organizations in investigative methods and advanced crime detection. An effort has been made in the three months' course of training afforded officers in this Academy, to qualify them as instructors in their own departments. Thus the 515 graduates of the Academy are in a position to make the FBI methods available in police departments having a total law enforcement personnel of 86,137. Each year a retraining session of the National Police Academy is held. On October 5th there was completed the Fifth Annual Retraining Session of the former graduates of the Academy and considerably more than 300 of the graduates returned to Washington for an intensive course of study and training in the handling of investigations pertinent to the national defense.

In view of the known practices on the part of certain groups of foreign representatives which extend beyond the scope of diplomatic usages, careful and constant observation is made of these groups in Washington and at other strategic and carefully selected places. This operation is productive of considerable

4. *(Continued)*

- 7 -

information of interest to the Federal Government concerning actual and proposed activities contrary to the best interests of the country. This type of work is, of course, done under guarded circumstances and in a most careful manner.

A constant monitoring is maintained of all movements and expenditures of foreign funds, their location, sources and distribution, with special emphasis of course upon those funds in which there is a direct or indirect interest on the part of the German, Italian, Russian, Japanese and French Governments.

Because of the FBI's friendly relationships over a period of many years with various banking establishments, excellent cooperation is received from financial institutions. This monitoring program of course produces much valuable information not only from the standpoint of detecting espionage, sabotage and similar activities for which the funds may be used, but also develops data and information of interest to the Treasury Department in reaching administrative decisions with reference to desirable legislation, etc.

The Bureau has prepared and maintains extensive suspect lists composed of data concerning several thousand individuals located in the United States and its territories whose nationalistic tendencies and activities are considered potentially inimical to the welfare of the United States. These records are maintained according to the nationality of the individuals involved, as well as geographically. In the event of greater emergency or the enactment of additional legislation when it might become necessary to take such individuals into custody or to intern them, the information maintained in these suspect lists, instantaneously available, sets forth the names, addresses, activities and source of information upon each individual in convenient form for necessary action. This list is of course being increased daily as the facts justify. Individual lists are maintained upon German groups and sympathizers, Communist groups and sympathizers, Fascist groups and sympathizers, Japanese and others.

The Federal Bureau of Investigation Technical Laboratory, which is the largest and best equipped of its kind in the world, has trained personnel constantly engaged in the handling of scientific studies and technical crime detection methods in the solution of espionage and sabotage cases by Laboratory procedures.

4. *(Continued)*

- 8 -

The Intelligence operations of the FBI require the constant use of skilled experts in document identification, including the comparison of handwriting and typewriting, chemical, physical and other scientific analyses. This Laboratory has proved itself a most valuable adjunct to the investigation of national defense matters. Constant work is carried on in the solution of cryptograms, in decoding ciphers, and in similar matters. Research is being continued by members of the Laboratory staff to enlarge the possibility of utilization of Laboratory technicians in internal security cases. Members of the technical staff who are authorities upon the subject of explosives have completed a lengthy series of experiments for the purpose of perfecting methods of handling bombs and infernal machines. Detailed instructions upon this subject are being prepared for dissemination throughout the United States. Included in the experiments conducted was a complete study of the efficiency and practicability of a freezing process which would render bombs ineffective and inoperative. Research has been conducted as to the possible use of portable X-ray equipment in the study of bombs at the point of their location. Experimentation has made possible the wider adaptation of spectography in cases involving espionage and sabotage. Extensive research is being conducted in the use of infrared light, ultraviolet light and black light for photographic purposes, particularly in the development of concealed and secret writings.

Radio stations are being operated at strategic points for the purpose of intercepting messages transmitted to European nations by small but powerful portable transmitters in the hands of foreign agents. An experimental radio station is being operated for the purpose of intercepting radio waves carrying impulses transmitted by specially designed teletypewriter machines, which messages are not intelligible to receiving equipment designed to receive either regular code messages or voice messages.

Information concerning sabotage methods utilized throughout the world has been obtained and compiled in comprehensive form in order that Bureau Agents will have first hand knowledge as to the potential means and methods which may be utilized in perpetrating sabotage. The staff of the Identification Division of the Federal Bureau of Investigation has been doubled in the past year and the Identification Division operates on a twenty-four hour a day basis. Daily receipts of fingerprints have doubled in the past year, the daily average number of prints received at the present time approximating 12,000 per day. All of these prints are answered within a 36-hour period. Included in the

4. *(Continued)*

fingerprints being searched at the present time are applicants for appointment to positions in the service of the Federal Government, current enlistments in the War and Navy Departments, and persons being engaged to work upon secret and confidential projects for the War and Navy Departments. Two thousand fingerprints are received each day from the Director of Alien Registration and after appropriate classification these prints are searched and filed as a permanent record of the alien's registration in the files of the Federal Bureau of Investigation. This material, of course, provides a valuable source of information relative to the identity, location and background of aliens. Included in the Federal Bureau of Investigation fingerprint collection at the present time are more than 14,000,000 prints. This constitutes the largest reservoir of information based on fingerprints in the world.

Extensive investigations are being conducted upon the basis of complaints received from officials and citizens relative to violations of espionage and sabotage laws, as well as other statutes designed to maintain the internal security of the nation. Indicative of the volume of this work receiving attention, it may be noted that on a single day 2,985 complaints of this kind were received.

The Bureau has established a special unit to handle cases involving violations of the Selective Service Act of 1940. Based upon a comprehensive study of records available from the World War period, the Bureau estimates that enforcement of the Conscription Act will require the services of 1,085 field Agents. Based upon World War figures, the Bureau estimates that in the course of the registration and conscription of 16,500,000 males between the ages of 21 and 35, there will be violations of the law on the part of approximately 900,000 persons. On the basis of the average number of cases closed per Agent per month, it would require a staff of approximately 5,500 Agents to handle this volume of work. Since, however, the present Selective Service program will be extended over a period of five years, Bureau estimates provide for the use of 1,085 men upon this type of work. A comprehensive program has been outlined which contemplates not only close personal liaison with the 6,500 draft boards throughout the country, but also a systematic check to locate persons failing to register, persons failing to report to draft boards when called, to investigate cases of conscientious objectors and all other possible violations under the statute.

Close relationship is maintained with the State, War, Navy and Treasury Departments, as well as other departments and agencies participating in the national defense program. The heads of the

4. *(Continued)*

- 10 -

various governmental departments are informed promptly of any information obtained which relates to the operations of those departments.

Weekly meetings are held with representatives of Military and Naval Intelligence, the Treasury and State Departments for the purpose of exchanging information of current interest, outlining future programs and otherwise coordinating the work in the Intelligence field.

In a most discreet and careful manner, constant check is being made of those Consular representatives whose conduct is reported to be detrimental to the United States. Their movements, contacts and financial transactions are the subject of constant observation and study.

5. Joseph A. Michela, Military Attache Moscow Report 1903, "N.K.V.D. of the U.S.S.R.," 14 April 1941 [Chart not included].

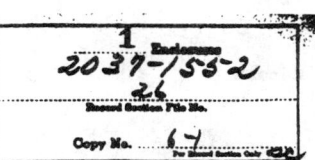

MILITARY INTELLIGENCE DIVISION
WAR DEPARTMENT GENERAL STAFF
MILITARY ATTACHÉ REPORT — Soviet Union

Subject: N. K. V. D. of the U. S. S. R.
I.G. No. 3100
RECEIVED G/2 W.D. MAY 28 1941

Source and Degree of Reliability:
Constitutional Acts 1922-1936; Collection of Laws 1934-1941; Bolshaya Sovietskaya Ensiklopedia, Soviet press and personal contacts.

Summarization of Report:
The history and organization of the N. V. K. D.

INTRODUCTION.

The N. K. V. D. is the abbreviated name most commonly used to designate the NARODNI KOMMISSARIAT VNUTRENIK DEL (the Peoples Commissariat of Internal Affairs). The compounded abbreviation "NARKOMVNUDEL" is also frequently used. The functions and organization of this governmental department are not wholly new, having origin as far back as 1881.

OKRANA.

In 1881 was formed the OKRANOYE OTDELENOYE - loosely translated as the Department of Safety - in the capital city of St. Petersburg (now Leningrad), for the purpose of "preserving public safety and order". It was then a section in the city police department and its duties were to "investigate political crimes and combat the revolutionary movement". Gradually, all the large cities organized similar police divisions. Although these divisions were organic parts of the city police departments, the Tsar's government exercised complete control over all police and used them as an agency to assist in maintaining "state security, order and peace". The Okrana existed up to the February Revolution of 1917.

CHEKA.

During the revolution the Bolsheviks realized that some organization was needed to combat counter-revolutionary movements, and on December 20, 1917 the VSYA-ROSSISKAYA CHREZVICHAINAYA KOMMISSIA PO BORBE S KONTRE REVOLUTSIYEI, SPEKULATSIYEI i SABOTAZHYEI (The All-Russian Extraordinary Commission to Combat Counter-Revolution, Speculation and Sabotage) was created by the Soviet or Peoples Commissars as an All-Union Commissariat.

From M. A. Moscow **Report No.** 1903 **Date** April 14, 1941

5. *(Continued)*

G-2 Report I.G. No. 3100

GPU.

The Cheka lasted until March 1, 1922 when its name was changed to the GPU - GOSUDARSTVENOYE POLITICHISKOYE UPRAVLENIYE (The State Political Administration) with little or no changes in function. Gradually, each republic organized its own GPU and on November 23, 1923 the republic GPU's were united into the OBEDINYONNOYE GOSUDARSTVENNOYE POLITICHISKOYE UPRAVLENIYE (The Unified State Political Administration) (OGPU).

OGPU.

The purpose of the OGPU was to unite all the revolutionary forces of all the republics to "combat the political and economic counter-revolutionary movements, espionage and banditry". The chief of the OGPU was appointed by the Presidium of the then Central Committee of the U.S.S.R. and had a vote in the committee.

The head of the OGPU at that time was also a member of the Supreme Court; and the Chief Prosecutor of the U.S.S.R. was responsible for the legality of all acts of the OGPU. It was simply another CHEKA with broader powers. These powers grew to such proportions that it became for a while the most powerful and feared government agency. It had so much power that its activities were actually curtailed in 1934 when it was incorporated into the N.K.V.D.

N. K. V. D.

At the time of the Civil War all of the republics organized their own republic commissariats of internal affairs. These commissariats controlled the militia, criminal investigations and prisons. But in 1930 these republic N.K.V.D.'s were liquidated and the term was not used again until 1934 when the N.K.V.D. of the U.S.S.R. was formed as an All-Union Commissariat. It was responsible for the following:

(1) Preservation of revolutionary order and state security.
(2) Protection of public property.
(3) Registration of civil acts, and vital statistics.
(4) Protection of the border.

The following administrations were organized and subordinated to it:

(1) State security.
(2) Militia.
(3) Border and internal protection.
(4) Fire protection.
(5) Corrective labor camps and settlements.
(6) Department of civil acts.
(7) Administrative economic administration.

From M. A. Moscow Report No. 1903 Date: April 14, 1941

3855 44

Page 2

5. *(Continued)*

G-2 Report I.G. No. 3100

Although the N.K.V.D. was made an All-Union Commissariat, it again formed the N.K.V.D. in all the republics, except the R.S.F.S.R., which republic became directly under the All-Union N.K.V.D. The same administrations listed above were organized in all the subordinate administrative divisions down to and including the city or district and village.

At the same time, the N.K.V.D. collegium within the Supreme Court was abolished, and certain cases were referred to the court having jurisdiction. Cases of treason and espionage were referred to the Military collegium of the Supreme Court or to the military tribunal having jurisdiction. Cases coming within the functions of the State Security Administration were all referred to the Supreme Court.

To take over all other court functions of the abolished N.K.V.D. collegium, there was formed the Special Advisory Council within the All-Union Commissariat. It consisted of five members and was actually a court in itself. This step gave the N.K.V.D. even more power for it permitted it to try its own cases.

In November, 1935, the N.K.V.D. took over the surveying and cartography administration of the U.S.S.R. with all of the technical agencies to carry out its functions. This latter was taken away in 1938 when it became an All-Union Administration under the Soviet of Peoples Commissars (SOVNARKOM).

In October, 1935, the administration of highways was brought into the N.K.V.D. where it remains today.

When the new Constitution was ratified in December, 1936, the N.K.V.D. became a Union-Republic Commissariat and has remained as such to the present time. In February, 1941, the State Security Administration was removed from the N.K.V.D. and formed into a new commissariat.

Today the N.K.V.D. is organized into six administrations:

    (1) Militia.
    (2) Border and Internal protection.
    (3) Fire protection.
    (4) Corrective labor camps and settlements.
    (5) Registration of civil acts, vital statistics and preservation of state papers.
    (6) Construction and maintainence of highways.

Each republic, autonomous republic, territory, autonomous territory, city or district and village has an agency of some kind for each one of the above named administrations. Theoretically, each one of these subordinate N.K.V.D. Commissariats controls its own six administrations under the next higher N.K.V.D., but there is no doubt that in practice each administration works in close harmony and directly under the administration of the next superior N.K.V.D. administration.

Although it has not been so stated, it may be that since there are seven (7) vice commissars, each administration and the chief inspection is under one of these vice commissars. The chief inspector is responsible to the Commissar only and functions as

From M. A. Moscow   Report No. 1903   Date: April 14, 1941

3855   45

Page 3

5. (Continued)

G-2 Report   I.G. No. 3100

the Chief Inspector of the Commissariat. The attached
chart shows the organization of the N.K.V.D. of the U.S.S.R.
as it is today.

ADMINISTRATIONS.

Since a few of the administrations have little
or no military value they are discussed briefly below.

Fire Protection Administration.

This administration confines its activities to
cities and towns. Each city has its fire department, theoretically subordinated to the city Soviet but with probably
a greater responsibility to the fire administration of the
oblast Soviet above it. Funds for the city departments
come from city budgets and therefore only the fire administration headquarters of the U.S.S.R. and the sixteen (16)
republics are financed by the national budget.

In rural communities all fire administrations are
voluntary, and since the Soviet Union is 67% rural, it means
that 67% of the personnel in the fire administration forces
are unpaid volunteers. In addition, all factories and mills
also have their own volunteer fire brigades. Hence, the
city personnel in the city fire departments is relatively
small. The estimated number of fire administration personnel
is 60,000 for the entire country, exclusive of volunteers.

Civil Acts & Vital Statistics Administration.

This administration is purely civil in character.
It is also charged with the preservation of state papers,
and the personnel for this administration is trained in the
N.K.V.D. Institute mentioned above.* Except for the headquarters of this administration, which are established in
the U.S.S.R., republics, territories, oblasts and cities,
the routine duties of this administration as they apply to
small towns, villages and rural areas, are performed by the
militia. National funds are used to maintain only the headquarters of the administrations of the U.S.S.R. and the Union
Republics. The personnel is estimated at 10,000.

Highway Administration.

This administration is responsible for the construction and maintainence of the All-Union, the Republic,
the regional, and the territorial highways. The responsibility for the district and village roads lies with the
respective Soviets. The personnel in this administration is
made up principally of technicians. The labor for highway
projects comes from the corrective labor camps. When an
important highway must be built it is not infrequent that an
appeal (with rather stiff persuasion) is sent out to the Komsomols, trade unions, Osoaviakhim and the Party, to donate
services to a highway project. This administration is maintained entirely by the national budget. Its personnel is
estimated at 6,000.

From M. A. Moscow   Report No. 1903   Date: April 14, 1941

* See chart.

3855   46

Page 4

5. *(Continued)*

G-2 Report   I.S. No. 2100

See the following reports for other administrations:

Militia	- Report No. 1904	— 2037-2105/1
Border Guards & Internal Troops	" " 1906	— 2037-1552/2
Corrective Labor Camps and Colonies	- " " 1905	— 2037-1552/27

<u>REMARKS</u>.

The personnel strength of the N.K.V.D. of the U.S.S.R. is estimated as follows:

a.	Militia	375,000
	Including:	
	Railway Guards	(25,000)
	Enterprise Guards	(50,000)
b.	Border Guards	150,000
c.	Interior Troops	50,000
d.	Convoy Troops	50,000
e.	Fire Personnel	60,000
f.	Civil Acts Administration	10,000
g.	Highway Administration	5,000
	Total	700,000

Control over this commissariat is actually centralized in the Soviet of Peoples Commissars, where orders are carried out by the Commissar of the N.K.V.D. of the U.S.S.R. In none of the subordinate organs is this control released, but the responsibility of maintainance and financing is forced upon agencies other than the U.S.S.R. Although the Soviets disclaim forced labor in this country, the organization of this commissariat is interesting to note. In it are the means to apprehend (militia), try and sentence (advisory council) and imprison offenders (corrective labor). Any governmental organization that has a crying need for labor simply calls upon the N.K.V.D. to supply it. If the amount of labor is insufficient to supply the need, it is relatively an easy matter to institute a reign of terror on any pretext and fill up labor colonies to meet requirements. There is little doubt that during the purges of the past, one eye was kept on the labor needs of governmental projects.

The N.K.V.D., including the State Security, has protected the present regime but has also prevented the development of the country. Its close supervision over the people, its pogroms, its raids and arrests, has instilled fear to such an extent that initiative in all phases of national economy has disappeared. The individual is too concerned with the problems of simply living that he is

From M. A. Moscow   Report No. 1903   Date: April 14, 1941

3855 47

Page 5

5. *(Continued)*

G-2 Report   I.G. No. 5100

    reluctant to attempt any changes or improvements for fear of a mistake - and a mistake means prison.

    The N.K.V.D. has every individual under observation from birth to death. It registers the birth, assigns quarters, controls internal, as well as external, passports, it prevents or permits travel within the country, its secret agents are everywhere; its actions are swift. An individual simply disappears in the middle of the night and no one ever sees or hears of him again. The N.K.V.D. is used as the check and balance weapon by the government - whenever a group in the government gets too popular, or too powerful, or when Stalin needs scapegoats to cover government mistakes he unleashes his N.K.V.D. The N.K.V.D. and the State Security are the most powerful weapons in the hands of the government. The Soviet Union is in itself a prison and the N.K.V.D. and State Security are its keepers.

                                                  Joseph A. Michela,
                                                  Major, Cavalry,
                                                  Ass't. Military Attache.

1 enclosure:
   Chart.

                                          FORWARDED
                                          Ivan D Yeaton,
                                          Major F A.
                                          Military Attache

From M. A. Moscow   Report No. 1903   Date: April 14, 1941

                                                            3855 48

                                                                  Page 6

6. Hoover to Watson, 18 February 1942.

JOHN EDGAR HOOVER
DIRECTOR

Federal Bureau of Investigation
United States Department of Justice
Washington, D. C.

February 18, 1942

PERSONAL AND
~~CONFIDENTIAL~~

Major General Edwin M. Watson
Secretary to the President
The White House
Washington, D. C.

My dear General Watson:

    As of possible interest to the President and to you, I am transmitting herewith copy of a revised delimitation agreement executed by General Lee, Admiral Wilkinson and myself on February 9, 1942. It will be observed that this agreement outlines the respective responsibilities of Military and Naval Intelligence and the Federal Bureau of Investigation under various conditions.

                        Sincerely,

                        J. Edgar Hoover

DECLASSIFIED
E.O. 11652, Sec. 5(E)(2)
Justice Dept. letter, 9-21-72
By DBS, NLR, Date JUN 25 1975

Attachment

<u>By special messenger</u>

6. *(Continued)*

~~STRICTLY CONFIDENTIAL~~

February 9, 1942

SUBJECT: <u>Delimitation of Investigative Duties of the Federal Bureau Investigation, the Office of Naval Intelligence and the Military Intelligence Division</u>
The Agreement for Coordination of the Federal Bureau of Investigation, Office of Naval Intelligence and the Military Intelligence Division.

I. The undersigned have reviewed the directive contained in the President's Memorandum of June 26, 1939, as augmented by his directive of September 6, 1939, the Delimitation Agreement of June 5, 1940, and the supplemental interpretation and agreements thereunder. It is now agreed that responsibility for investigation of all activities coming under the categories of espionage, counter-espionage, subversion and sabotage, (hereinafter referred to as "these categories") will be delimited as indicated hereafter. The responsibility assumed by one organization in a given field carries with it the obligation to provide a pool of all information received in that field but it does not imply the reporting agency alone is interested in or will work alone in that field. Close cooperation between the three agencies in all fields is a mutually recognized necessity.

II. FBI will be responsible for:

1. All investigation of cases in the categories involving civilians in the United States and its territories with the exception of the Republic of Panama, the Panama Canal Zone, Guam, American Samoas, Palmyra, Johnston, Wake and Midway Islands, the Philippine Islands and the Territory of Alaska other than that specifically described in Paragraph III.

DECLASSIFIED
E.O. 11652, Sec. 5(E)(2)
Justice Dept. letter, 9-21-72
By DBS, NLR, Date JUN 25 1975

6. *(Continued)*

-2-

2. Investigation of all cases directed from foreign countries on those occasions and in those situations in which the State, War or Navy Departments specifically request investigations of designated group or set of circumstances.

3. The coordination of civilian organizations furnishing information regarding subversive movements.

4. Jointly with ONI, the coverage of Japanese activities in these categories. ONI will continue its coverage of Japanese activities as heretofore and FBI will continue to expand its operations in this field.

5. Keep MID and ONI advised of important developments, such as:

   (a) Developments affecting plants engaged on Army or Navy contracts.

   (b) Cases of actual and strongly presumptive espionage and sabotage, including the names of individuals definitely known to be connected with subversive activities.

   (c) Developments affecting vital utilities.

   (d) Developments affecting critical points of transportation and communication systems.
   (for c and d above, no protective coverage is contemplated)

6. Ascertaining the location, leadership, strength and organization of all civilian groups designated to combat Fifth Column Activities (overt acts of all sorts in groups of armed forces of enemies); and transmitting to MID, ONI and State Department information concerning these organizations and any information received concerning their possession of arms.

6. *(Continued)*

- 3 -

7. Keeping ONI and MID informed of any other important developments.

III.

MID will be responsible for:

1. Investigation and disposal of all cases in these categories in the military establishment including civilian employ, military reserve and military control.

2. The investigation of cases in these categories involving civilians in the Canal Zone, the Republic of Panama, the Philippine Islands and the Alaskan Peninsula and islands adjacent including Kodiak Island, the Aleutian and Pribilof Islands and that part of the Alaskan Peninsula which is separated by a line drawn from Iliamna Bay northwest to the town of old Iliamna and thence following the south shore of Lake Iliamna to the Kvichak River to Kvichak Bay.

3. Informing FBI and ONI of any other important developments.

6. *(Continued)*

- 4 -

IV. *ONI will be responsible for:*
 1. *Investigation and disposal of all cases in these categories in the Naval establishment, including civilians under Naval employ or control, and all civilians in Guam, American Samoa, Palmyra, Johnston, Wake, and Midway Islands.*
 2. *Jointly with FBI, the coverage of Japanese activities in the categories enumerated in Paragraph I.*

ONI will continue its coverage of Japanese activities as heretofore, and FBI will continue to expand its operations in this field.

 3. *Informing FBI and MID of any important developments.*

V. *The ultimate test of cooperation and coordination of the Intelligence agencies is the manner in which they function under conditions of national emergency or actual warfare. There should be no doubt as to the identity of the agency or official who is primarily responsible for carrying on intelligence operations under the broad conditions for which the governing principles are listed hereinafter.*

PERIOD OF MARTIAL LAW

VI. *It is further agreed that when a state of martial law has been declared by the President, the Military Commander assumes responsibility for Intelligence coverage. He has authority to coordinate intelligence activities of the participating agencies, within the limits of their available personnel and facilities by the assignment of missions, the designation*

6. *(Continued)*

- 5 -

of objectives, and the exercise of such coordinating control as he deems necessary. He is not authorized to control the administration or discipline of the subscribing agencies to which he does not belong, nor to issue instructions to such agencies beyond those necessary for the purposes stated above.

VII. Personnel of the subscribing agencies will still send reports to and be under the continued supervision of their respective headquarters. The subscribing agencies will render such aid and assistance to the Military Commander and his designated representatives as are possible and practicable. All pertinent information, data, and other material that are or may be necessary or desirable to him shall be furnished by the most expeditious means and methods possible consistent with requisite security. The headquarters of the subscribing agencies will promptly be advised of all information and data appropriately identified as having been furnished to the Military Commander.

VIII. It is assumed that the Military Commander will not hesitate to call upon any governmental agency outside the three subscribing agencies to this agreement for any assistance, cooperation, or activity.

<u>PERIODS OF PREDOMINANT MILITARY INTEREST, NOT INVOLVING MARTIAL LAW.</u>

IX. In time of war certain areas will come into prominence as potential theatres of operation. When a Military Commander of such a potential theatre is designated, he definitely has interest in, though not control of, the civilian life within the area. In order that the Military Commander may prepare himself for the discharge of the possible responsibility which may affix to him, the following procedure is agreed upon:

6. *(Continued)*

-6-

1. Agents of the FBI, of ONI, and of MID will continue to function in accordance with the provisions of paragraphs II, III, and IV.

2. In addition thereto the Military Commander may take steps to analyze the facilities existing and to explore the manner in which complete coverage will be obtained if martial law is declared. Adequate liaison with the other two intelligence services will insure that the Military Commander will have the benefit of the experience, judgment and knowledge of the representatives of the other services.

3. The Military Commander is authorized to request and receive such information from the three agencies as he may desire and they may be able to furnish.

6. *(Continued)*

- 7 -

X. The analysis and exploration referred to above will show the coverage furnished by each of the subscribing agencies and any additional coverage each subscribing agency can undertake. When the Commander feels that more complete coverage is required, it is recognized that his service is authorized to augment the coverage. Prior to any invasion of the spheres normally coming under the cognizance of the other subscribing agency, the Military Commander should obtain the necessary authority from the War Department.

XI. Irrespective of the fact that the preceding recommendations have placed the initiative in the hands of the Military Commander, whenever either of the other two services feel that such a survey to determine adequacy of coverage should be undertaken, it should be so recommended through the director of each service.

XII. The above provisions contemplate that the War Department will be the agency administering martial law. When appropriate, the same principles will govern the Navy Department.

PERIODS OF NORMAL CONDITIONS

XIII. Under these conditions, the Federal Bureau of Investigation, the Office of Naval Intelligence and the Military Intelligence Division will operate in accord with the provisions of paragraphs II, III and IV.

XIV. From time to time it may be desirable in the light of changing conditions to modify or amend this delimitation agreement. Such amendments or modifications when agreed upon by the heads of the

6. *(Continued)*

- 8 -

subscribing agencies shall be issued in the form of a revised delimitation agreement and not as separate instructions.

[signature: Raymond E. Lee]
Assistant Chief of Staff
G-2, War Department

[signature: T. S. Wilkinson]
Director, Office of Naval
Intelligence

[signature: J. Edgar Hoover]
Director, Federal Bureau of
Investigation

7. Tokyo Circular 906 to Berlin and Helsinki, 6 October 1942.

~~SECRET~~

From: Tokyo (WOTNS)
To: Berlin and Helsinki
October 6, 1942
JMA
Circular #906   REVISED TRANSLATION
(Seven parts complete)

To Col. HAYASHI and Major HIROSE.

We have commenced the study of Russian diplomatic and commercial codes, and have obtained the following results. For our information let us know how you are getting along.

1. Extent of interception.

Mostly from Moscow and the Foreign Office in Kuibyshev. Also from the embassies and consulates in Japan and Manchoukuo. Very little material aside from this.

2. Diplomatic.

(1) (Type 8 ?)

Subtracting the first group of the text from the third group, the first and second digits give the additive page; the third digit is the same as the second; the fourth and fifth digits give the vertical and horizontal coordinates; the fifth digit is always even; the code seems to be a 4 figure one.

The additive table is 50 pages each of 50 groups. This type is used in all messages centering in Kuibyshev and about ****** of those around Moscow.

C. I. #896   (Japanese)   Page 1

ARMY   ~~SECRET~~

7. *(Continued)*

S E C R E T

(2) Special form 1 (a).

Subtracting the first group of the text from the second group from the end, the first and second digits give the number of groups in the text of the message; the third, fourth, and fifth digits are all either 4 or 6.

In subtracting the first group of the text from the third group from the end, the first, second, third, and fourth digits are very often all the same. This is believed to be the number of the additive table. The fifth digit is believed to give the consecutively ascending additive page for each message.

The additive table is 10 pages each of 70 groups. This type is used for about half the messages centering in Moscow and between the representatives in Vladivostok and Tokyo.

(3) Special form 1(b).

Only the difference between the second group from the end and the first group of the text mentioned in the previous paragraph.

This type is used between Tokyo, Vladivostok, Seoul, Hakodate, and Dairen. Between Seoul and Vladivostok (they also) subtract the fourth group of the text from the third group from the end, and the seventh group from the end from the fourth group from the end.

(4) Special form 2(a).

The difference between the second and third groups from the end is a series of 2's and 8's. Moreover the sum of the digits in the third

C. I. #896   (Japanese)   Page 2.

ARMY   S E C R E T

7. *(Continued)*

~~SECRET~~

group from the end is a multiple of 10 and, as subtracting the first and second digits from the third and fourth digits gives an ascending sequence in each telegram, it is thought that this indicates the additive page.

The additive table is 40 pages each of 50 groups.

This form is used from Tokyo -- HASHI[a] -- to (LADOGA ?) and from -- HASHI[a] -- to Manchuria.

(5) Special form 2(b).

The second group from the end is a multiple of 10. Aside from this it is the same as the preceding paragraph.

This form is used for messages going in the opposite direction as the previous paragraph.

3. Commercial.

The first and second digits of the first group of the text give the vertical and horizontal coordinates. The third digit gives the length of the message. (Up to 60 groups is 1; and increases 1 for each 60 groups thereafter.) The fourth and fifth digits give the additive page.

The additive table is 50 pages each of 50 groups.

a - Kana spelling.

C I. #896 (Japanese) Inter. 10/6/42 (12)
                       Trans. 1/29/43
                       Retrans. 2/6/43 (B-d)
                                Page 3.

ARMY ~~SECRET~~

8. US Army Signals Security Agency, "Memorandum on Russian Codes in the Japanese Military Attache System," 9 February 1943 [Excerpt].

~~SECRET~~

Feb. 9, 1943.

First Report

MEMORANDUM ON RUSSIAN CODES IN THE JAPANESE MILITARY ATTACHE SYSTEM

footnote 17

The present memorandum records all quickly available information concerning Russian codes which have been transmitted in the Japanese Military Attache (JMA) system of enciphered code.

The transmissions seem all to have taken place from Europe (Berlin, Stockholm, Helsinki, Hungary) to Tokyo-(once to Hsinking). The earliest found is dated July 1, 1941; the most recent, December 22, 1942. All but one (number 8 below), which does not seem to be an ordinary code, were enciphered by the C additive-book, no matter what the date or the cipher-alphabet used (1,2,3).

Cipher text. The text seems to suffer from more than the usual transmission garbles. It is possible that haste and indifference have produced many of the deviations from intelligible Russian and numerals that are found.

Materials used. Circumstances caused the preparation of the memorandum to be hasty. The various message-parts had already been recorded on cards by originating station, station addressed, date, serial number, additive-book page, and the first and last words of the code involved. Unfortunately, the corresponding terminal numbers had not been recorded. Additional information has been sought principally by inspection of the first and last available parts of each message.

It has been impossible in the time spent to correct many garbles and other inaccuracies in the Russian words or to check the work of the compiler of the cards, although some errors of both sorts have been detected and amended in passing.

Types of codes. Each code is classed, when this could be easily done, as one- or two-part and as four- or five-digit.

Treatment of the Russian (Cyrillic) alphabet. The earliest transmissions (1-3) used the code-values for the letters of the Russian alphabet provided in the basic code of the JMA system. These are properly quadriliteral groups introduced by NQ; thus, NQAZ = Russian A. (See 7.) On some occasions, NQ is used only at the beginning and the end of a Russian word, and is to be read before each intervening letter-pair. (See 5.) In the longer code-book messages here treated, NQ never appears, but is to be read before each applicable letter-pair. (See 1,2,3, and compare 8.)

~~SECRET~~

8. *(Continued)*

~~SECRET~~

It seems reasonable to assume that the abandonment of this method was caused by the great time, effort, and expense it entails. In all longer transmissions sent later (beginning with 4), the Russian letters were incorporated as individual-letter (JL) spellings into the message in transliteration, the 26 letters of the Roman alphabet being substituted for the 31 of the Russian (, the hard sign being omitted). This change in method reduces the length of words by half. The table of transliteration is given below. Note that the use of W, V, Q, (for Щ), X, and E (for Э) agrees with the use of the corresponding Morse letters when applied to Russian. The use of the other letters agree both with the Morse and with the usual Slavonic transliteration of the Cyrillic letters (cf. H -- [Serbian X = Croatian H],-- C, Y), except for J (taken away from Й, which becomes I, and assigned to Ч). The special Morse letters for Ш, Ю, and Я have been replaced by Q, U, and A respectively, so that, finally, the following pairs of letters are represented each by the same letter: А Я (a), Е Э (E), И Й (I), У Ю (U), Ш Щ (Q).

Cyrillic	Transl. in messages	Transl. used in BII(b)4a	Cyrillic	Transl. in messages	Transl. used in BII(b)4a
А	A	A	Р	R	R
Б	B	B	С	S	S
В	W	V	Т	T	T
Г	G	G	У	U	U
Д	D	D	Ф	F	F
Е	E	E, YE[a]	Х	H	KH
Ж	V	ZH	Ц	C	TS
З	Z	Z	Ч	J	CH
И	I	I	Ш	Q	SH
Й	I	I	Щ	Q	SHCH
К	K	K	Ъ	***	ʺ
Л	L	L	Ы	Y	Ï[b]
М	M	M	Ь	X	ʹ
Н	N	N	Э	E	E
О	O	O	Ю	U	YU
П	P	P	Я	A	YA

a Transliterated YE when it does not follow a consonant.
b At first the usual Slavonic Y was used for Ы. But since in systems for use in English-speaking countries YU, YA, and on occasion YE are used for Ю, Я, and E, it was thought better, in order to avoid some one's misunderstanding a form like VYUCHIVAT' (for ВЫУЧИВАТЬ), to employ Ï, a symbol widely used by linguists and lexicographers to express the sound of Ы.

~~SECRET~~

9. Hoover to Harry Hopkins, 7 May 1943.

JOHN EDGAR HOOVER
DIRECTOR

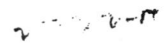

Federal Bureau of Investigation
United States Department of Justice
Washington, D. C.
MAY 7 1943

PERSONAL AND ~~CONFIDENTIAL~~
BY SPECIAL MESSENGER

Honorable Harry Hopkins
The White House
Washington, D. C.

Dear Harry:

    Through a highly confidential and reliable source it has been determined that on April 10, 1943, a Russian who is an agent of the Communist International paid a sum of money to Steve Nelson, National Committeeman of the Communist Party, USA, at the latter's home in Oakland, California.

    The money was reportedly paid to Nelson for the purpose of placing Communist Party members and Comintern agents in industries engaged in secret war production for the United States Government so that information could be obtained for transmittal to the Soviet Union.

    The Russian agent of the Communist International has been identified as Vassili Zubilin, Third Secretary of the Embassy of the USSR. New York City is his headquarters.

    Both Nelson and Zubilin will meet in the near future with other leaders of the Communist International (Comintern) apparatus active in the United States.

    It has likewise been determined through a highly confidential and completely reliable source that the National Headquarters of the Communist Party, USA and, particularly, Earl Browder, General Secretary of the Communist Party, USA are aware of and have approved of the assignment which has been given to Nelson by the Communist International.

    Steve Nelson has used the following aliases: Steve Joseph Nelson, Stephan Mesarosh, Steve J. Mesarosh, Joseph Fleisbinger and "Hugo." It is reported that he was born in Yugoslavia in 1903. His true name is unknown. According to a biographical sketch of Nelson which appeared in the Daily Worker for November 10, 1937 (when the Daily Worker was admittedly the official organ of the Communist Party), Nelson joined the Communist Party, USA in January, 1925. He claims

9. *(Continued)*

- 2 -

to have been naturalized under the name, Stephan Mesarosh, at Detroit, Michigan on November 26, 1928.

According to Nelson's own statements, he performed espionage work for the Soviet Government in 1931 and 1932. In 1935 he was vice president of the Workers Alliance in Pennsylvania and was a subdistrict organizer of the Communist Party in Pennsylvania at the outbreak of the Spanish Civil War. Nelson went to Spain as a political commissar of the International Brigades and rose to the rank of Lieutenant Colonel. He returned from Spain in the latter part of 1937 and became active in the affairs of the Veterans of the Abraham Lincoln Brigade and the American League for Peace and Democracy. Since 1938 he has been a national figure in the Communist Party, USA and is now a member of the National Committee, a high policy-forming body of the Communist Party, USA.

Steps are being taken by the Federal Bureau of Investigation to identify all members of the Communist International (Comintern) apparatus with which Steve Nelson and Vassili Zubilin are connected, as well as the agents of that apparatus in various war industries.

Because of the relationship demonstrated in this investigation between the Communist Party, USA, the Communist International and the Soviet Government, I thought the President and you would be interested in these data.

These matters are being brought to your attention at this time for your confidential information inasmuch as the investigation is continuing.

Sincerely yours,

Edgar

10. Anonymous letter to Hoover, undated [received 7 August 1943] [Russian original with English translations].

~~TOP SECRET~~

Copy No 10
Copy to 7th CIR ?
54-00

Mr. HOOVER,

Exceptional circumstances impel us to inform you of the activities of the so-called director of the Soviet Intelligence in this country. This "Soviet" intelligence officer genuinely occupies a very high post in the GPU (now NKVD), enjoys to a vast extent the confidence of the Soviet Government, but in fact, as we know very accurately, works for Japan himself, while his wife (works) for Germany. Thus, under cover of the name of the USSR, he is a dangerous enemy of the USSR and the U.S.A. The vast organisation of permanent staff [KADROVYE] workers of the NKVD under his command in the U.S.A. does not suspect that, thanks to the treachery of their director, they are also inflicting frightful harm on their own country. In this same false position is also their whole network of agents, among whom are many U.S. citizens, and finally BROWDER himself, who has immediate contact with them. BROWDER passes on to him very important information about the U.S.A., thinking that all this goes to MOSCOW, but, as you see, it all goes to the Japanese and Germans. The "Director of the Soviet Intelligence" here is ZUBILIN, Vasilij, 2nd secretary in the embassy of the USSR, his real name is ZARUBIN, V., deputy head of the Foreign Intelligence Directorate [UPRAVLENIE] of the NKVD. He personally deals with getting agents into and out of the U.S.A. illegally, organises secret radio-stations and manufactures forged documents. His closest assistants are:
1. His wife, directs political intelligence here, has a vast network of agents in almost all ministries including the State Department. She sends false information to the NKVD and everything of value passes on to the Germans through a certain Boris MOROZ (HOLLYWOOD). Put her under observation and you will very quickly uncover the whole of her network.
2. KLARIN, Pavel, vice-consul in NEW YORK. Has a vast network of agents among Russian emigrés, meets them almost openly, brings agents into the U.S.A. illegally. Many of his agents work in very high posts in American organisations, they are all Russian.
3. KhEJFETs - vice-consul in SAN FRANCISCO, deals with political and military intelligence on the West Coast of the U.S.A. has a large network of agents in the ports and war factories, collects very valuable strategic material, which is sent by ZUBILIN to Japan. Has a radio station in the consulate. He himself is a great coward, on arrest will quickly give away all the agents to save himself and remain in this country.
4. KVASNIKOV, works as an engineer in AMTORG, is ZUBILIN's assistant for technical intelligence, through SEMENOV - who also works in AMTORG, is robbing the whole of the war industry of America. SEMENOV has his agents in all the industrial towns of the U.S.A., in all aviation and chemical war factories and in big institutes. He works very brazenly and roughly, it would be very easy to follow him up and catch him red handed. He would just be glad to be arrested as he has long been seeking a reason to remain in the U.S.A., hates the NKVD but is a frightful coward and loves money. He will give all his agents away with pleasure if he is promised an American passport. He is convinced that he is working for the USSR, but all his materials are going via Z. to Japan, if you tell him about this, he will help you find the rest himself.

DECLASSIFIED BY SP2CLCGWM
ON 7-10-96

[Continued overleaf]

~~TOP SECRET~~

10. *(Continued)*

TOP SECRET

- 2 -

5. ShEVChENKO, agent for the Purchasing Commission in BUFFALO. Deals with the same as SEMENOV.
6. LUKYaNOV, agent for the Purchasing Commission in the ports of NEW YORK and PHILADELPHIA. ZUBILIN's assistant for naval intelligence. Has a lot of agents in these ports. His materials are very valuable and dangerous to the U.S.A. as they are all being sent on by ZUBILIN through his wife to the Germans.
7. PAVLOV - The 2nd Secretary of the USSR Legation in Canada, Z.'s assistant for Canada.
8. TARASOV - secretary of the USSR Embassy in Mexico, Z.'s assistant for Mexico.
9. DOLGOV - attaché of the USSR Embassy here, Z.'s assistant for WASHINGTON. [A person who] occupies a most special position, ranks next after ZUBILIN in the NKVD, is a 2nd secretary in the USSR Embassy here - MIRONOV, his real name is MARKOV (ZUBILIN is a general in the NKVD, MIRONOV - a colonel). Both hate each other over their positions. In the NKVD line they directed the occupation of Poland. ZUBILIN interrogated and shot Poles in KOZIELSK, MIRONOV in STAROBIELSK. All the Poles who were saved know these butchers by sight. 10,000 Poles shot near MOLENSK was the work of both of them. If you prove to MIRONOV that Z. is working for the Germans and Japanese, he will immediately shoot him without a trial, as he too holds a very high post in the NKVD. He has some high level agent in the office of the White House.

Postmarked: WASHINGTON, D.C., 2. a.m., 7th August 1943.

TOP SECRET

10. (Continued)

Г-н. ГУВЕР,

Несбычайные обстоятельства побуждают нас сообщить Вам о деятельности, т.наз. руководителя советской разведки в этой стране. Этот "советский" разведчик действительно занимает очень высокий пост в ГПУ (ныне НКВД), пользуется огромным доверием советского правительства, но фактически, как нам совершенно точно известно, сам он работает для Японии, а его жена для Германии. Таким образом он, прикрываясь именем СССР, является опасным врагом СССР и США. Огромный аппарат кадровых работников НКВД, находящийся в США под его начальством не подозревает, что благодаря предательству своего руководителя, они также наносят страшный вред своей стране. В таком-же ложном положении находится и вся их сеть агентов, среди которых много граждан США и наконец сам Браудер, имеющий непосредственный контакт с ним. Браудер передает ему очень важные сведения о США, думая что все это идет в Москву, но, как вы видите все это идет японцам и немцам.

"Руководитель советской" здесь - Зубилин Василий, 2 секретарь посольства СССР, настоящее его имя в Зарубин В. заместитель начальника управления разведки за границей НКВД. Лично занимается нелегальной переправкой агентов в США и из США, организует секретные радиостанции и изготавляет поддельные документы. Его ближайшие помощники:

1. его жена, руководит политической разведкой здесь, имеет огромную сеть агентов почти во всех министерствах в том числе и Стэйт Департаменте. В НКВД посылает дезинформацию, а все ценное передает немцам через некого Бориса Мороз (Голивуд). Установите наблюдение за ней и вы вскроете всю ее сеть очень быстро.

2. Кларин Павел, вицеконсул в Н.Иорке. Имеет огромную сеть агентов среди русских эмигрантов, встречается с ними почти открыто, нелегально переправляет агентов в США. Многие его агенты работают на очень высоких постах в различных американских организациях, все они русские.

3. Хейфец - вицеконсул в С.Франциско, занимается политической и военной разведкой по западному берегу США, имеет большую сеть агентов в портах и на военных заводах, собирает очень ценный стратегический материал, который направляется Зубилиным в Японию. Имеет радиостанцию в консульстве. Сам он очень большой трус, при аресте быстро выдаст всех агентов чтобы спасти себя и остаться в этой стране.

4. Квасников, работает инженером в Амторге, является помощником Зубилина по технической разведке, через Семенова - работающего тоже в Амторге, обворовывает всю военную промышленность Америки. Семенов имеет своих агентов во всех промышленных городах США, на всех военных заводах по авиации, химии и в крупных институтах. Работает очень нахально и грубо, его проследить и захватить на месте преступления очень легко. Аресту он будет просто рад, т.к. давно ищет причину остаться в США, ненавидит НКВД но страшный трус и любит деньги. Всех своих агентов выдаст с удовольствием, если ему пообещать американский паспорт. Он уверен что работает для СССР, но все его материалы идут через З. в Японию, если ему об этом рассказать, то он сам поможет вам найти остальных.

5. Шевченко, уполномоченный Закупочной комиссии в Буффало. Занимается тем-же и Семенов.

6. Лукьянов, уполномоч. закупочной комиссии в портах Н.Иорка и Филадельфия. Помощник Зубилина по военно морской разведке. Имеет много агентов в этих портах. Его материалы очень ценные и опасные для США, т.к. все переправляются Зубилиным через жену немцам.

7 - - 2 секретарь миссии СССР в Канаде, помощник З. по Канаде.

8. Тарасов - секретарь посольства СССР в Мексике, помощник З. по Мексике

9. Долгов - атташе посольства СССР здесь, помощник З. по Вашингтону. Совершенно особое положение занимает, второй после Зубилина по

10. *(Continued)*

НКВД, 2 секретарь посольства СССР здесь - Миронов, его настоящая фамилия Марков (Зубилин - генерал НКВД, Миронов-полковник НКВД) Оба друг друга ненавидят по должностям. По линии НКВД руководили оккупацией Польши. Зубилин допрашивал и расстреливал поляков в Козельске, Миронов в Старобельске. Все спасшиеся поляки знают этих палачей в лицо. 10000 расстрелянных поляков под Моленском дело рук их обоих. Если Миронову доказать, что З. работает на немцев и японцев, то он немедленно расстреляет его без суда, т. к. имеет тоже очень большой пост в НКВД? Имеет какого то крупного агента в оффисе Белого Дома.

postmarked Washington, D.C., 2 a.m., 7th August 1943.

11. Hoover to Birch D. O'Neal, "Alto Case," 26 February 1944.

KLARIN
February 26, 1944

DBC-A1036

Mr. Birch D. O'Neal
The American Embassy
Mexico, D. F.

Re: Alto Case

Dear Sir:

Please refer to your cable of February 23, 1944, advising that Jacob Epstein, who has been identified as one of the writers of the secret writing letters emanating from Mexico in this case, met an unidentified individual at a restaurant and conferred with him on the night of February 21, 1944, for forty minutes. This unidentified individual then went to the Russian Embassy and the next day this same individual appeared at the airport in Mexico City in company with Alexei Prokhorov, Russian diplomatic courier who went to Mexico from the United States by plane on January 28, 1944, and was returning to the United States. The unidentified individual then went to the Geneva Hotel, and it was determined that one Paul Klarine was registered at the hotel from 7 East 62nd Street, New York City (the 62 was obtained from a garble and this could be 61), nationality Russian, registered at the Hotel Geneve since November 23, 1943.

Your office stated that it was believed this individual was identical with Pavel P. Klarin, a Vice Consul of the Russian Consulate-General in New York City, and a suspected Russian agent who had left the United States for Mexico in November 1943, but has not been located. You were advised by Bureau cable dated February 24, 1944 that the Russian Consulate General in New York City is located at 7 East 61st Street, and were requested to effect a discreet surveillance of Klarin and to forward a picture taken of him and Prokhorov at the Mexican airport.

Attached for your use are three photographs of Klarin together with his signature. You should advise the Bureau as soon as possible whether Klarin is identical with the unidentified individual mentioned above.

For your information and the information of the offices receiving copies of this letter, the following is set forth. This should be maintained in a strictly confidential manner. You are aware numerous secret writing letters in this case were intercepted up until November 1943, at which time it appears that the subjects became apprehensive of the security of their method of communication. They indicated that couriers were to be used in the future for their communications, and we know that an attempt was actually made to use Mrs. Anna Collons, New York City, as a courier.

DECLASSIFIED BY
ON 7-30-96

11. *(Continued)*

It now appears from the information furnished by your office relative to Epstein's meetings with the unidentified individual believed to be Klarin, that the subjects are using either Russian diplomatic couriers or the Russian diplomatic pouch or both. This consideration should be borne in mind by all offices investigating this case.

The following is background information regarding Klarin as furnished to the State Department when Klarin became attached to the Russian Consulate General in New York. His full name is Pavel Panteleevich Klarin, born August 15, 1903, Izium, former Kharkov, Gubernia, Russia. He graduated from high school in Izium in 1920, and from the Economic Faculty of the Don State University in 1926. He was employed as a field economist for "Tovhozen" in various parts of the Soviet Union from 1925 to 1931. From 1931 to 1935 he was the economist of the All Ukrainian Union of Cooperatives. From 1935 to 1937 he was economist of the All Ukrainian Chamber of Commerce; from 1937 to April 1939, senior economist of the People's Commissariat of Agriculture of the U.S.S.R. From April to June 1939, he headed the Agriculture Section of the Soviet pavilion at the New York World's Fair, and then served as the administrative assistant to the Commissioner General of the U.S.S.R. at the Fair. On February 17, 1940, he became Vice Consul of the Consulate General, located at 7 East 61st Street, New York City. He listed his American address as 11 East 61st Street, New York City. He stated that he came to the United States on April 6, 1939, aboard the S. S. Queen Mary; that he is the father of two children, Kladvia, 12 years old in January 1941, and Rada, 9 years old in January 1941.

There is a copy of a letter from the Immigration and Naturalization Service to the State Department dated March 5, 1941, indicating that Klarin was admitted to the United States at the port of New York on April 6, 1939, temporarily for business, destined to the Amtorg Trading Corporation, and was to leave the United States within thirty days after the close of the New York World's Fair. He requested an extension of five months to complete work as an employee of the Soviet Commission in the New York World's Fair, but this request was denied on January 30, 1940, since the World's Fair was not to re-open in 1940. A request was then submitted by the Consul General in New York for a change in Klarin's status from a temporary visitor to that of a government official, he having been appointed Vice Consul of the Union of Soviet Socialist Republics in New York and his appointment accepted by the United States Government and certified by exequatur on March 4, 1940.

Surveillances conducted by the New York Field Division have established that Klarin has been in considerable contact with Vassili Mikhailovich Zubilin, Second Secretary of the Soviet Embassy in Washington, D. C., and undoubtedly the head of the Soviet intelligence activities in the United States at the present time. It has been found that Zubilin and Klarin have met a number

11. *(Continued)*

of times in the early hours of the morning, sometimes at 3:00 and 4:00 A.M.

Zubilin was born January 22, 1900, in Moscow, Russia. He claims to have been graduated from the Pleichanoff Institute of Economy and to have subsequently held several positions in the People's Commissariat of Finance of the U.S.S.R., which is known as Narkomfin. In 1941 he was appointed attache of the Soviet Embassy in China. In 1942 he was appointed Third Secretary of the Embassy of the U.S.S.R. in Washington, D. C., and he is at the present time the Second Secretary of the Soviet Embassy.

For your strictly confidential information, it has been determined that Zubilin paid a sum of money to a member of the National Committee of the Communist Party in April 1943, for the purpose of defraying expenses of Communist Party members engaged in espionage activities of the Soviet Union and for Communist Party couriers.

According to information received, Zubilin holds the rank of general in the NKVD and is engaged in the movement of Soviet agents into and out of the United States. He reportedly organizes secret radio stations, prepares counterfeit documents, and obtains industrial and military information for transmittal to the Soviet Union.

For your guidance in the investigation of Soviet agents in Latin America, the following information is furnished to show the type of information Soviet agents in the United States, both those who are members of the Communist Party, USA, and those who are Soviet citizens, are attempting to obtain.

1. Formulas and blueprints for all inventions, discoveries and innovations of a military significance.

2. Formulas and blueprints for all inventions, discoveries, and innovations of an industrial significance.

3. Information regarding the means of communication between individuals in this country and persons in occupied European countries who do not wish to have their nations annexed by the Soviet Union at the close of this war.

4. Information regarding the number of students and the curricula of the schools operated by the United States Army for administrative officers who are to be sent to territories freed from Axis occupation.

Zubilin's closest assistant in the Soviet Consulate General in New York was Pavel P. Klarin, now in Mexico. It is reported that in Mexico Zubilin's assistant was Leon Tarasov, First Secretary of the Russian Embassy at Mexico City. It should be noted that

- 3 -

11. *(Continued)*

Leon Tarasov was accompanying Alexei Prokhorov at the time Prokhorov departed from Mexico City by plane on February 22, 1944.

All of the above information is extremely confidential and must be so maintained by all of the offices receiving copies of this letter. It is furnished to aid in the investigation of this case, which is of increasing importance to the Bureau. It is requested that all offices submit investigative reports of investigations to date within the very near future, and that all offices conduct all necessary investigation promptly and thoroughly.

Very truly yours,

John Edgar Hoover

12. Edward P. Stettinius, Jr., Memorandum for the President, "Soviet Codes," 27 December 1944.

~~SECRET~~

DEPARTMENT OF STATE
WASHINGTON

December 27, 1944

MEMORANDUM FOR THE PRESIDENT

Subject: Soviet Codes

You will recall our conversation on the Soviet codes. I have informed General Donovan that he should send through General Deane in Moscow to General Fetin, the Soviet General with whom Donovan deals on all matters connected with the exchange of information in his field, a message informing the Soviet Government that in dealing with other matters one of our agencies had run across certain material which purported to be related to Russian messages sent in code. He was also asked to explain that we had taken advantage of the opportunity to prevent this material from falling into the hands of the enemy and that we would immediately make it available to the Soviet Government if they so desired.

I feel sure that this will take care of the matter, as the Soviet Government will be informed and will see that we are fully disposed to cooperate with them and not retain any material which they themselves might desire to have.

DECLASSIFIED
State Dept. Letter, 1-11-72
By J. Schauble Date FEB 18 1972

13. Hoover to Matthew Connelly, 12 September 1945.

JOHN EDGAR HOOVER
DIRECTOR

Federal Bureau of Investigation
United States Department of Justice
Washington, D. C.

September 12, 1945

~~TOP SECRET~~

Honorable Matthew Connelly
Secretary to the President
The White House
Washington, D. C.

Dear Mr. Connelly:

    The Royal Canadian Mounted Police have advised that they have obtained positive information through a former employee of the Soviet Military Attache at Ottawa, Canada, that the Soviets have an extensive espionage network in Canada. The Soviets have made the obtaining of complete information regarding the atomic bomb the Number One project of Soviet espionage and these data must be obtained before the end of this year. The Royal Canadian Mounted Police report that there is considerable loose talk in the Office of the Soviet Military Attache in Ottawa regarding the "next war" which the Soviet Union will have with the Anglo-American nations.

    The Royal Canadian Mounted Police received from the same source information that an assistant to an Assistant Secretary of State under Mr. Stettinius, was a paid Soviet spy. This man's name, or nickname, is unknown at the present time but further inquiry is being made by the Royal Canadian Mounted Police in an effort to obtain further identifying data. No information regarding this situation is being furnished to the State Department in the absence of further identifying data.

    With regard to the atomic bomb project, Dr. Allen May, a British scientist assigned to the McGill University Laboratory in Canada, has been identified as a paid Soviet spy of long standing. May spent some time during September, 1944, at the Metallurgical Laboratory of the University of Chicago, working on the separation process for uranium and is well informed as to the methods of setting up uranium piles or lattices.

13. *(Continued)*

May is reported to have furnished the Soviets in Ottawa with a small quantity of U233 which is one of the isotopes of uranium and this specimen was flown directly to Moscow.

The information regarding May has been furnished by the Federal Bureau of Investigation to Major General Leslie Groves, head of the Manhattan Engineering District project.

It has also been definitely determined by the Royal Canadian Mounted Police that Dr. May, in the first part of July, 1945, advised the Office of the Military Attache in Ottawa, that the United States Navy was using radar-controlled projectiles against Japanese suicide planes and that the tubes and batteries within the projectile were finished with a special plastic protective device against the shock of firing, which the American authorities have not furnished to the British.

This latter information has been called to the attention of the Office of Naval Intelligence.

The Canadian situation is being followed closely and any additional information will be brought to the attention of the President and you.

With assurances of my highest esteem and best regards,

Sincerely yours,

J. Edgar Hoover

- 2 -

14. Hoover to Frederick B. Lyon, 24 September 1945.

Federal Bureau of Investigation
United States Department of Justice
Washington, D. C.

TOP SECRET
BY SPECIAL MESSENGER

Date: September 24, 1945

To: Mr. Frederick B. Lyon
Chief
Division of Foreign Activity Correlation
State Department
Washington, D. C.

From: John Edgar Hoover - Director, Federal Bureau of Investigation

Subject: SOVIET ESPIONAGE ACTIVITY

Reference is made to my memorandum of September 18, 1945. Additional information has been obtained by a Bureau representative from Igor Guzenko as follows:

INTERNATIONAL ORGANIZATION

Guzenko stated that all intelligence activities outside the Soviet Union and inside the Soviet Union are coordinated by G. M. Malenkov, a member of the Political Bureau of the All Union Communist Party of Bolsheviks, a member of the Central Committee of the same organization and the man who is mentioned by many Soviet officials as Stalin's successor. Malenkov, according to Guzenko, is actually the head of all intelligence activity, and Military Intelligence, Naval Intelligence, the NKVD and the political apparatus are all ultimately responsible to him.

There are numerous jurisdictional clashes, particularly between the Military and Naval Intelligence organizations and the NKVD. All such matters are referred to Malenkov.

Malenkov is the actual head of the political apparatus in foreign countries and all communications, reports, et cetera, from the Political Secretary in any Embassy are sent directly to Malenkov and not to Molotov or any person in the Peoples Commissariat of Foreign Affairs.

Likewise, no communication from the Military or Naval Attaches in any Embassy would go to Molotov. Such communications go to the Chief of Espionage for the area covering the particular Embassy.

In the same way, the Embassy Secretary who represents the NKVD does not send any correspondence to the Peoples Commissariat of Foreign Affairs. According to Guzenko, the only person in the Embassy who would be corresponding with the Peoples Commissariat of Foreign Affairs would be the Ambassador himself, who in every instance is only a front, and possibly one or two men close to the Ambassador who are called "innocents."

14. *(Continued)*

Guzenko stressed that the Ambassador was advised in general terms of political and economic matters which the Political Secretary, the NKVD representative and the Military or Naval Attaches receive and which they felt would possibly be of interest to the Ambassador. The Ambassador, however, is not consulted or advised with regard to the primary functions of these intelligence organizations.

According to Guzenko, he has heard discussions in the Soviet Embassy at Ottawa indicating that the present system of supervising the activities of the Communist Party of a particular country through the Political Secretary in the Embassy is much more efficient and much more effective than the old cumbersome Comintern setup. Under the present organization, the directives issued by Malenkov through the Embassies to the Parties throughout the world are much more direct and there is less possibility of misinterpretation.

The man in the Embassy in Canada who handles political matters is Gousarov, the Third Secretary, who has his own cryptographer, one Patony, who also acts as a door guard at the Embassy.

The aforementioned system is known to Guzenko to be in operation in the United States, Canada and Mexico and possibly in the other Western Hemisphere countries. It is also in effect in Great Britain, to his personal knowledge. He believes that this system is likewise in effect in all other countries in the world where the Soviets have diplomatic establishments, although there are variations for those countries occupied by the Red Army.

Guzenko states that in the Western Hemisphere and in Great Britain no reports are ever made to Moscow directly by individual espionage agents, whether they refer to Military, Industrial or Political Espionage. All such reports clear through the Embassies and are transmitted by the Embassies.

SOVIET PENETRATION OF DIPLOMATIC ESTABLISHMENTS OF OTHER COUNTRIES

Guzenko stated that from conversations which he had heard in the Embassy and from traffic which he had read, it appeared the Soviets were intending to plant many Soviet espionage agents in the diplomatic establishments already in the United States and Canada, as well as in those diplomatic establishments which are yet to be set up in the United States. These espionage agents are to be sent from Eastern, Central and Balkan European countries. These would number between 50% to 100% of the employees below the rank of Ambassador and would actually be Soviet trained Military Intelligence, NKVD or Comintern men.

Guzenko pointed out that Lieutenant Kulakov had told him that one of his, Kulakov's, best friends is an officer in the NKVD. This NKVD officer is

- 2 -

14. (Continued)

the code clerk for the Lublin-Polish Embassy in Moscow. Kulakov's friend wears his NKVD uniform to work and it is apparently a standing joke in Moscow that the NKVD operates the Polish code room.

According to Guzenko, another NKVD man who is a close friend of Lieutenant Kulakov is Marshal Tito's personal cipher clerk in Yugoslavia. Guzenko states that this cipher clerk is almost worked to death because Tito sends messages to Moscow asking for instructions and advice on the most minor matters.

Guzenko stated that Soviet Intelligence had good coverage at the present time in the Czech Embassies and he knows from reading dispatches that the Military Attache who is being assigned to the Czech Legation in Ottawa is a Soviet espionage agent. This individual had expected to be appointed Adjutant to the Chief of the Czech General Staff, but the Soviets decided that he should go to Canada in the immediate future as Military Attache, considering this to be an equally important post.

Guzenko stated that in Washington, D. C. the Czech Military Attache is a Soviet spy named Hess. It seems that Colonel Zabotin, the Soviet Military Attache in Ottawa, made a trip to Washington shortly after his arrival in Ottawa and sent a cable to Moscow telling them that he had met Hess, who seemed to be sympathetic and that Zabotin felt that he could be developed. Moscow immediately cabled back that Zabotin should stay away from Hess because he was already being operated as a spy by General Saraev, Soviet Military Attache in Washington, D. C.

INTERNATIONAL PLANS OF THE SOVIETS

Guzenko was asked what the attitude in the Soviet Embassy in Ottawa was towards the San Francisco Conference and the other conferences in which the United States, Great Britain and Russia played leading roles.

He stated that in the Embassy the meetings of the All Union Communist Party of Bolsheviks, which is known in the Embassy as the Provisional Union, discussed such matters. They were likewise discussed in the meetings of the Komsomols (Young Communist League), which is known in the Embassy as the "Sports League," and there was also considerable loose talk in the Embassy itself. From these incidents, Guzenko understood that the Soviets considered all such conferences as merely "talk fests" which served only to conceal from the Anglo-American powers and from the rest of the world the actual plans of the Soviets. Anything of a material nature which could be gained by the Soviets through such conferences was, of course, all to the good and would not have to be gained by force of arms.

14. *(Continued)*

He stated that he had been told that the Soviet Union's budget for war, which would include intelligence activities, appropriations for the Red Army and Red Navy and for war production, would be greater during the coming year, which was ostensibly a year of peace, than it had been last year during a year of actual warfare.

He further stated that he had been informed that the Soviet Union was not converting its factories to consumer goods production, such as the United States and Canada had announced those countries were doing, but, on the other hand, the Soviets were increasing their war potential by setting up additional plants devoted solely to war production in Siberia. He stated that he was informed that the Soviets would continue to increase their industrial production for war and would obtain consumer goods from factories in the satellite states of Eastern Europe and through purchases in the Western Hemisphere.

Guzenko stated that the Soviets before the use of the atomic bomb were confident that within ten years their military potential would enable them to conquer the world. Since the atomic bomb has been used by the United States, they have set their calendar ahead and have instructed all espionage agents to make the obtaining of the complete construction plans of the bomb itself the No. 1 espionage project. They have issued instructions that this information should be obtained by the end of this year, 1945. Guzenko stated that the last message received at the Embassy from Moscow before he left on September 5, 1945, was stressing the necessity for obtaining the atomic bomb before the end of this year.

He was asked whether this meant the Soviets had set their calendar up the full ten years. He stated he did not know, but that he was merely telling what he knew.

Guzenko stated that all responsible Soviet officials know that the Soviet Union is aiming toward beating the United States and Great Britain in the next war, which will permit the Sovietization of the entire world.

THE IDENTITY OF SOVIET AGENT IN THE STATE DEPARTMENT

Guzenko was questioned carefully regarding the possible identity of the individual in the Department of State under Stettinius who is a Soviet spy. Guzenko stated he did not know the man's name but that he had been told that an Assistant to Stettinius was a Soviet spy. This information came to him in the following manner:

After the arrival of Kulakov in Ottawa in the Summer of 1945, Kulakov and Guzenko got into a discussion on the agencies of the Canadian organization as compared to the United States organization. Guzenko was bearing in mind the

- 4 -

14. *(Continued)*

adverse opinions held by the Soviet inspectors with regard to the American organization in 1944. Kulakov informed Guzenko that although the Canadian organization was closely knit and well operated and most productive, that there were, of course, more agents in the United States and that he had learned in Moscow that an Assistant of Stettinius, then the United States Secretary of State, was a Soviet spy. Guzenko pointed out that this information would necessarily have come to Kulakov's attention prior to May 17, 1945, because Kulakov left Moscow for the United States and Canada on that date. He stated that he did not ask for the name of this individual because Kulakov would have suspected his motives, since it involved an individual who was not being run by Colonel Zabotin.

Guzenko pointed out that the Soviets were frantic to obtain the secrets of the atomic bomb and that an incident had been reported in the press recently which appeared to him to have been inspired by a Soviet agent. This Soviet agent might not necessarily be the same one to whom Kulakov referred, but on the other hand, it had all the earmarks of the technique used by Soviet political espionage agents. He referred specifically to the announcement made in London by Stettinius that the atomic bomb should be turned over to the Security Council of the United Nations. Guzenko suggested that if the Bureau could determine who suggested to Stettinius that this statement be made, the Bureau might be able to identify a Soviet agent, if not the Assistant to Stettinius referred to by Kulakov.

15. Hoover to Brigadier General Harry Hawkins Vaughan, 8 November 1945.

JOHN EDGAR HOOVER
DIRECTOR

Federal Bureau of Investigation
United States Department of Justice
Washington, D. C.

November 8, 1945

~~TOP SECRET~~

BY SPECIAL MESSENGER

Brigadier General Harry Hawkins Vaughan
Military Aide to the President
The White House
Washington, D. C.

Dear General Vaughan:

    As a result of the Bureau's investigative operations, information has been recently developed from a highly confidential source indicating that a number of persons employed by the Government of the United States have been furnishing data and information to persons outside the Federal Government, who are in turn transmitting this information to espionage agents of the Soviet Government. At the present time it is impossible to determine exactly how many of these people had actual knowledge of the disposition being made of the information they were transmitting. The investigation, however, at this point has indicated that the persons named hereinafter were actually the source from which information passing through the Soviet espionage system was being obtained, and I am continuing vigorous investigation for the purpose of establishing the degree and nature of the complicity of these people in this espionage ring.

    The Bureau's information at this time indicates that the following persons were participants in this operation or were utilized by principals in this ring for the purpose of obtaining data in which the Soviet is interested:

    Dr. Gregory Silvermaster, a long time employee of the Department of Agriculture.

    Harry Dexter White, Assistant to the Secretary of the Treasury.

    George Silverman, formerly employed by the Railroad Retirement Board, and now reportedly in the War Department.

    Laughlin Currie, former Administrative Assistant to the late President Roosevelt.

15. *(Continued)*

-2-

Victor Perlow, formerly with the War Production Board and the Foreign Economic Administration.

Donald Wheeler, formerly with the Office of Strategic Services.

Major Duncan Lee, Office of Strategic Services.

Julius Joseph, Office of Strategic Services.

Helen Tenney, Office of Strategic Services.

Maurice Halperin, Office of Strategic Services.

Charles Kramer, formerly associated with Senator Kilgore.

Captain William Ludwig Ullman, United States Army Air Corps.

Lieutenant Colonel John H. Reynolds of the United States Army, a former contact of Gaik Ovakimian, former head of the Soviet Secret Intelligence (NKVD) in New York, is also apparently involved in the Soviet espionage activities stemming from Washington, D. C.

In addition to the foregoing group in the Government it appears at this time that Mary Price, formerly Secretary to Walter Lippmann, the newspaper columnist and presently publicity manager of the United Office and Professional Workers of America, CIO, is also associated with the foregoing group.

The Government documents were furnished to Gregory Silvermaster, who thereafter photographed them and turned over the undeveloped, but exposed film to a contact of the Soviets

15. *(Continued)*

-3-

in either Washington, D. C. or New York City. In the past, it is reported, the contact man made trips to Washington, D. C. once every two weeks and would pick up on such occasions an average of forty rolls of 35-millimeter film.

Investigation of this matter is being pushed vigorously, but I thought that the President and you would be interested in having the foregoing preliminary data immediately.

With expressions of my highest esteem and best regards,

Sincerely yours,

J. Edgar Hoover

16. Hoover to Vaughan, 1 February 1946 [Attachment not included].

OFFICE OF THE DIRECTOR

Federal Bureau of Investigation
United States Department of Justice
Washington 25, D. C.

February 1, 1946

PERSONAL AND ~~CONFIDENTIAL~~
BY SPECIAL MESSENGER

Brigadier General Harry Hawkins Vaughan
Military Aide to the President
The White House
Washington, D. C.

Dear General Vaughan:

    As of interest to the President and you, I am attaching a detailed memorandum hereto concerning Harry Dexter White, Assistant Secretary of the United States Treasury Department.

    As you are aware, the name of Harry Dexter White has been sent to Congress by the President for confirmation of his appointment as one of the two United States delegates on the International Monetary Fund under the Bretton Woods agreement. In view of this fact, the interest expressed by the President and you in matters of this nature, and the seriousness of the charges against White in the attachment, I have made every effort in preparing this memorandum to cover all possible ramifications. As will be observed, information has come to the attention of this Bureau charging White as being a valuable adjunct to an underground Soviet espionage organization operating in Washington, D. C. Material which came into his possession as a result of his official capacity allegedly was made available through intermediaries to Nathan Gregory Silvermaster, his wife, Helen Witte Silvermaster, and William Ludwig Ullmann. Both Silvermaster and Ullmann are employees of the United States Treasury Department, reportedly directly under the supervision of White.

    The information and documents originating in the Treasury Department were either passed on in substance or photographed by Ullmann in a well-equipped laboratory in the basement of the Silvermaster home. Following this step, the material was taken to New York City by courier and made available to Jacob M. Golos, until the time of his death on November 27, 1943. Golos, a known Soviet agent, delivered this material to an individual tentatively identified as Gaik Ovakimian. Ovakimian you will recall was arrested some years ago as an unregistered agent of the Soviet Government and subsequently, by special arrangements with the Department of State, was permitted to return to the U.S.S.R.

    After the departure of Gaik Ovakimian, Golos delivered his material to an individual who has been tentatively identified as Dr. Abraham Benedict Weinstein. Subsequent to the death of Golos, the courier handling material received from the Silvermasters and Ullmann delivered it through an unidentified

16. *(Continued)*

individual to Anatole Borisovich Gromov, who until December 7, 1945, was assigned as First Secretary of the Soviet Embassy, Washington, D. C., when he returned to the U.S.S.R. Gromov had previously been under suspicion as the successor to Vassili Zubilin, reported head of the NKVD in North America, who returned to Moscow in the late Summer of 1944. This whole network has been under intensive investigation since November, 1945, and it is the results of these efforts that I am now able to make available to you.

    I also feel that it is incumbent upon me at this time to bring to your attention an additional factor which has originated with sources available to this Bureau in Canada. It is reported that the British and Canadian delegates on the International Monetary Fund may possibly nominate and support White for the post of President of the International Bank, or as Executive Director of the International Monetary Fund. The conclusion is expressed that assuming this backing is forthcoming and the United States acquiescence, if not concurrence, resulting, White's nomination to this highly important post would be assured. It is further commented by my Canadian source that if White is placed in either of these positions, he would have the power to influence to a great degree deliberations on all international financial arrangements.

    This source, which is apparently aware of at least some of the charges incorporated in the attached memorandum against White, commented that the loyalty of White must be assured, particularly in view of the fact that the U.S.S.R. has not ratified the Bretton Woods agreement. Fear was expressed that facts might come to light in the future throwing some sinister accusations at White and thereby jeopardize the successful operation of these important international financial institutions.

    I thought you would be particularly interested in the above comments, which originated with sources high-placed in the Canadian Government, on the subject at hand.

    With expressions of my highest esteem,

                      Sincerely yours,

                      J. Edgar Hoover

Attachment

17. Federal Bureau of Investigation, "Underground Soviet Espionage Organization [NKVD] in Agencies of the US Government," 21 October 1946 [Excerpt].

~~SECRET~~

UNDERGROUND SOVIET ESPIONAGE ORGANIZATION (NKVD)
IN AGENCIES OF THE UNITED STATES GOVERNMENT

October 21, 1946

17. *(Continued)*

UNDERGROUND SOVIET ESPIONAGE ORGANIZATION (NKVD)
IN AGENCIES OF THE UNITED STATES GOVERNMENT

PREDICATION

BACKGROUND OF CURRENT PRESENTATION

The purpose of this memorandum is to set forth certain charges against officials and employees of the Federal Government. These charges will be dealt with in detail and information arising from other sources and investigation will be coordinated in an effort to give an over-all view of the situation concerning underground Soviet espionage activities in the United States Government at the present time.

A time element exists in making a factual approach to the material set forth. Although the majority of the basic charges against the individuals mentioned herein concern activities dating back several years, these charges must be viewed from the fact that they only became available in November of 1945. Consequently the reader must consider the difficulty of actually proving these activities by investigation at this late date. The facts are strong in many instances and circumstantial in others primarily because of the disparity in time between the date of the activities and the actual report of these activities to the authorities. A determined effort has been made to produce as much actual and circumstantial evidence as possible, either to prove or disprove the basic charges. At the outset it is considered proper to make a statement concerning the source of the basic charges which will be outlined hereinafter. This source who became available and cooperative in November, 1945, for protective purposes in view of continued assistance being received therefrom, is being given the cover name of Gregory. All material originating with Gregory will be so designated and will be set forth as nearly as possible in the very words used by Gregory in reporting the material submitted.

Background of Gregory

Gregory is an individual of American origin and descent, and was educated in both American and foreign educational institutions. Gregory possesses far above the average of academic learning. As far as political affiliations are concerned Gregory first came in contact indirectly with the Communist Party while attending one of the leading educational institutions of New York City. Gregory's first activity was as a speaker for the American

17. *(Continued)*

League Against War and Fascism in late 1934 or early 1935. The American League Against War and Fascism was succeeded by the American League for Peace and Democracy, both of which have been reported from numerous sources to be and generally accepted as Communist front organizations. From contacts made while appearing as a speaker for the American League Against War and Fascism, Gregory was introduced to and became a member of the Communist Party in 1935 in New York City. Following this affiliation Gregory held numerous temporary positions having no relationship to Communist Party activities but at the same time in an extra-curricular manner participated in many of the activities of the Party and its fringe groups. As an example, Gregory, during the summer of 1936, served as an assistant at the Amtorg Camp in Napanoch, New York, a summer camp for the Children of Soviet Nationals, attended by children ranging in age from 2 to 15. In June of 1938 through an employment bureau of the educational institution attended by Gregory, contact was made with the Italian Library of Information, an adjunct of the Italian Propaganda Ministry situated at 595 Madison Avenue, New York City. Gregory there came in contact with information which was thought of interest to the Communist Party. In a then sincere effort to assist the Communist Party, Gregory approached Ferruccio Marini and offered to make available to him what information was learned as a result of employment with the Italian Library of Information. Marini is a former member of the Communist Party of Italy, a former student of the Lenin School, Moscow, USSR; and an individual who since his arrival in the United States in 1928 has been active in the National Administration of the Communist Party. Gregory remained with the Italian Library of Information until March, 1939. In the meanwhile Marini had introduced Gregory to an individual originally known only as "Tim." "Tim" was later identified by Gregory as Jacob M. Golos of World Tourist, Inc. After the introduction to Golos, Gregory delivered all information which was gathered dealing with the Italian Library of Information to him rather than to Marini. The activities of Golos will be set forth in detail hereinafter.

In September, 1939, at the instigation of Golos, Gregory secured a position as secretary to Richard H. Waldo, the President and owner of McClure's Syndicate which published and distributed the "Whirligig." Golos explained to Gregory that Waldo was suspected of being affiliated in some way with the Germans and the Communist Party was seeking information concerning his activities. Gregory, in fact, was successful in securing considerable information regarding Waldo between September, 1939 and February, 1940, but no facts significant in proving what the Communist Party desired were forthcoming. In April, 1941, the United States Service and Shipping Corporation, 212 - 5th Avenue, New York City, was organized, and Gregory became an official of this organization. This company was established with money belonging to the Communist Party - USA, or to the Soviet Union, made available by Earl Browder, then National Chairman of the Communist Party. According to Gregory, Browder made available $15,000 and John Hazard Reynolds, the original President, who was personally selected by Browder for this position, submitted another $5,000 to augment the capital. While it has been claimed by Communist Party functionaries that the funds supplied by Browder in this connection were funds of the Party, Gregory's superiors in the Soviet Intelligence Service described the funds as "Russian Funds." The United States Service and Shipping Corporation, Gregory states, is a cover firm for Soviet espionage, in the same category with World Tourist, Inc., with which Golos

17. *(Continued)*

was associated up to the time of his death on November 27, 1943. The ostensible business purpose of United States Service and Shipping Corporation is to engage in the shipping of parcels and merchandise to Soviet Russia.

<u>Synopsis of Gregory's Courier Activities</u>

As outlined above, Gregory's first contact with the Soviet Intelligence Service was with an individual known only as "Tim" who, in view of definite identification at a later date will hereinafter be referred to as Jacob M. Golos, Secretary of World Tourist, Inc. World Tourist, Inc., was a New York corporation chartered on June 10, 1927. It is interesting to note that Golos pleaded guilty to an indictment along with World Tourist, Inc., charging failure to register as agents of the Soviet Government in March, 1940. He received a fine of $500 and a jail sentence of four months to one year which was later changed to probation.

After the passage of an initial probationary period, when Gregory was supplying Golos with material secured from the Italian Library of Information, Golos began to use Gregory as a courier for the collection of information from various individuals in Washington, D. C., and New York City. The majority of these persons were employed in the United States Government or had sources therein. During early activities as a courier, Gregory became definitely aware of the connection of Golos with the Soviet Intelligence Service, namely the NKVD as distinguished from the Red Army Intelligence. Regular service as a courier began during the summer of 1941 when Gregory came in contact with a parallel of Soviet espionage headed by Nathan Gregory Silvermaster who has held several positions in the United States Government in past years and is now Chief of the Division of Economic Analysis of the War Assets Administration. Silvermaster and his wife, Helen Witte Silvermaster, according to Gregory, were in turn in contact with many other individuals in the United States Government from whom they secured material and made it available to Gregory for transmittal to Golos. This material was delivered to Gregory in the form of written reports, actual documents, exposed but undeveloped film and verbally requiring its recording in shorthand which Gregory later transcribed. Gregory was eventually placed in contact with another parallel of Soviet espionage, headed by Victor Perlo, who was formerly employed with the War Production Board and later by the Foreign Economic Administration. Gregory met Perlo with others at the apartment of John Abt in New York City who was then and is now General Counsel for the Amalgamated Clothing Workers of America, CIO. Abt is married to Jessica Smith, the President of the S.R.T. Publications, Incorporated, and editor of its magazine "Soviet Russia Today," Communist and pro-Soviet propaganda organ. Gregory acted as a courier for the collection of information of interest to the Soviet Government from this group and delivered it in the same manner to Golos. Gregory's activities as a courier for both the Silvermaster and Perlo groups continued for Golos until his death on November 27, 1943. Collaterally, while serving Golos, Gregory also served others in a small way. Gregory mentioned specifically that while working with Golos,

3

17. *(Continued)*

certain material was delivered to one "John" who has not been further identified to date. "John" was introduced to Gregory by Golos and after having made several contacts he introduced Gregory to an individual known only as "Margaret." Gregory's meeting with Margaret occurred in the latter part of 1941 or the early part of 1942. Subsequent to the introduction Gregory met Margaret five or six times over a period of approximately four months. Margaret did not receive material collected by Gregory but merely arranged for contacts between Golos and "Charlie" who Gregory never saw but is convinced was Golos' superior, to whom the material which Golos received was delivered. Just prior to the death of Golos he instructed Gregory to meet Margaret who would make an introduction to a new person who was to receive the material obtained from the Silvermaster group. This contact was made and Margaret introduced Gregory to an individual known only as "Catherine." Material from the Silvermaster group was only delivered to "Catherine" on one or two occasions when these arrangements were apparently upset by the death of Golos. Taking stock for the moment, the only individual who has been definitely identified in this "John," "Margaret" and "Catherine" series of contacts is "Margaret," who is Olga Borisovna Pravdina, a former employee of Amtorg Trading Corporation, a Soviet purchasing agency. Her husband, Vladimir Sergeevich Pravdin, was the head of TASS News Agency, the official news organ of Russia, in New York City. They both returned to Russia in March, 1946.

Immediately following the death of Golos, "Catherine" introduced Gregory to "Bill" who has not been further identified. "Bill" received all of the material collected by Gregory from November, 1943, until September, 1944. In October, 1944, "Bill" turned the operation of Gregory as a courier over to an individual known only as "Jack." Cooperation with Jack continued until December, 1944, when Gregory was removed from duties as a courier for this espionage group. However, during the period of service with "Jack" he introduced Gregory to an individual known only as "Al." Through ordinary investigative procedures it was learned that "Al" contacted Gregory in November, 1945. As a result of this contact he was identified as Anatoli Borisovich Gromov, then First Secretary of the Soviet Embassy, Washington, D. C. Gromov had been under suspicion for a considerable period as a successor to Vassili Zubilin, reported head of the NKVD in North America until the late summer of 1944 when he returned to Moscow, USSR, following the inspection of espionage facilities of the Soviet Government in North America by representatives of the NKVD and the Red Army Intelligence. Gromov departed from the United States for Moscow, USSR, on December 7, 1945. It is suspected that his position has been assumed by Fedor Alexeevich Garanin, an official of the Soviet Embassy, Washington, D. C.

Gregory is unable to state specifically in any instance to whom Golos, "Bill," "Jack," or "Al" (Gromov) delivered the material which was collected for them. However, Gregory does state that during the period of associations with Golos he selected those items of a political, economic or social intelligence character and made them available to Earl Browder,

4

17. *(Continued)*

then National Chairman of the Communist Party. Browder, in no instance kept this information for delivery to a third person since he did not wish to become compromised in the collection of material of this type. It is significant to note, however, that Gregory is definite in stating that Browder was cognizant of the activities of Golos and his use of Gregory as a courier. It is Gregory's opinion that Golos violated his directives in making information available to Browder. This presumably was done on a personal friendship basis. From information submitted by Gregory, "Charlie" whom Gregory never personally observed has been tentatively identified as Dr. Abraham Benedict Weinstein, a practicing dentist at 20 East 53rd Street, New York City. During the course of instant inquiries, Dr. Weinstein has been in contact with several of the individuals prominent in this case and dealt with in full detail hereinafter in addition to other individuals known to be Soviet agents.

It is significant to observe that while working with Golos and his successors, Gregory had specific instructions to have no associations whatsoever with the Communist Party or any of its fringe groups. Gregory's true name had never figured prominently in any of the activities of the Party or its fringe groups until the advent of the current inquiries. It was through Golos that Gregory became associated with the United States Service and Shipping Corporation, New York City, mentioned hereinbefore, and he assisted Gregory from time to time with grants of money plus all traveling and incidental expenses.

As will be seen hereinafter, through the groups previously mentioned as headed by Silvermaster and Browder, as well as various miscellaneous individuals, it is apparent that the Soviet Intelligence Service was successful in securing material from the Department of State, Office of Strategic Services, the Treasury Department, the War Department, the Department of Justice, the Foreign Economic Administration and numerous other agencies of the Federal Government. In numerous instances the documents themselves were made available from these agencies for copying verbatim or for photographing in the basement of the Silvermaster home where investigation has determined a fully equipped photographic laboratory was located.

As pointed out hereinbefore investigation in this case has only extended over the period November 8, 1945, to the present time. Consequently it has not been possible to show that each and every one of the individuals mentioned by Gregory is interrelated in their activity. The normal practice of espionage would not permit contacts between each and every individual during that period. However, it will be observed numerous contacts between the subjects of instant inquiries have transpired and in some instances under very suspicious circumstances. A studied attempt has been made to establish the basic truth or falsity of Gregory's information and certain observations are apropos in this connection. Gregory has mentioned over 150 names and in no instance has investigation indicated that a non-existent person was mentioned.

5

17. *(Continued)*

Only in those instances where only a first name was given and no identifying data was available has it been impossible to identify the person to whom Gregory was referring. In addition, the methods by which the passage of information was effected are those which by experience have been tried, tested and used by all effective intelligence services, including particularly the Russian. It is also significant that Gregory, by actual observation, has identified Olga Borisovna Pravdina of Amtorg as "Margaret" and Anatoli Borisovich Gromov of the Soviet Embassy as "Al." Gregory has reported with a high degree of accuracy situations of the United States Government policy which were only known within the Government itself as examples of material which was passed through Gregory to Golos and his successors for use of the Soviet Government. Also reported by Gregory was the existence of a photographic laboratory in the basement of the Silvermaster home during the time Gregory was acting as a courier. This laboratory was used for the reproduction of documents brought to the Silvermaster home by various component elements of that particular espionage group. Investigation determined that such a photographic laboratory sufficiently well equipped for the copying of documents was located in the basement of the Silvermaster home. In few instances has Gregory reported information which could not either directly or circumstantially be verified. A high degree of accuracy has prevailed throughout the revelations made by Gregory. In conclusion, it should be carefully borne in mind that in no instance has the information furnished by Gregory proved false, unfounded, or materially inaccurate despite intensive and searching investigation thereof.

Set out hereinafter is a summary of the information submitted by Gregory, gathered from other sources and established by investigation concerning the Russians identified to date in this espionage group, the Soviet system of espionage, the espionage agents comprising the Silvermaster and Perlo groups and the miscellaneous personalities serving the Soviet espionage system independent of association with any organized group as far as is known.

17. *(Continued)*

METHOD OF OPERATION OF SOVIET ESPIONAGE SYSTEM

As a result of the revelations made by Gregory, considerable information concerning the modus operandi of the present Soviet underground espionage organization was obtained. Although these methods are related as pertaining to espionage activities of the USSR, it should be noted they differ little from the method used by any country engaged in effective secret intelligence. As an example, their clandestine activities are cloaked with cover companies such as World Tourist, Inc., and the United States Service and Shipping Corporation in this instance. Pertinent material from numerous sources is collected by the use of couriers and cover addresses. Intermediaries of a primary, secondary and tertiary character are apparent. There is a certain but not necessarily significant absence of advanced technical methods, either in the transmittal of communications or the gathering of information itself. The only technical device apparent in the operations of these espionage parallels was the use of the copying camera.

Soviet espionage has one clear cut advantage over that practiced by any other country within the borders of the United States. This advantage centers in the existence of an open and active Communist Party whose members are available for recruitment for any phase of activity desired. As will be seen hereinafter, in almost every instance Soviet espionage agents, particularly sub-agents, are recruited from among individuals closely associated with the Communist Party, or at least strongly pro-Communist and pro-Soviet, who in the main are native born Americans or individuals not native born but sufficiently familiar with the American way of life to avoid detection. Even the Germans with the large German minority in the United States were not so advantageously placed nor does the fanaticism of the most ardent National Socialist exceed that of the militant members of the Communist Party selected for cooperation directly with the USSR.

Briefly, Soviet intelligence is broken into three branches, namely Military-Naval, Political and General. The first, namely Military-Naval, is handled by Red Army Intelligence. The gathering of political and general information is left in the main to the NKVD, now the MGB, or Ministry of State Security, with which this case deals.

Gregory has described what is referred to as the "pole" method of establishing a ring of individuals for the gathering of information. The term "pole" in reality is the designation of the individual at the apex of the organization which is a self-contained unit. For example, six individuals would be active in the obtaining of information for the Russians. No one of these six individuals would know the identity of the other five. Each individual would have a courier whose identity he did not know and/or a mail drop by which he would dispose of the material which he gathered. None of the six individuals in this self-contained unit would know the identity of their

7

17. *(Continued)*

courier or the identity of the person collecting the material from the mail drop. The next step up the ladder would be an individual responsible for receiving the information from three couriers and/or mail drops. He would correlate this material and in turn would have a courier and/or mail drop to which he delivered the edited information. The other three in the unit would operate similarly. The two individuals each handling three sources of information in turn would not know the identity of their courier or the person collecting their edited material from a mail drop if this was used. In this manner a single individual unknown to anyone else in the group would eventually come in the possession of all the information obtained by the original six sources. This individual or "pole" at the apex of the triangle usually knows all the original sources of information, couriers, mail drops and editors in the unit. According to Gregory, the individual designated the "pole" would normally be a Russian who in turn would pass the information on to the proper authorities for transmittal to Moscow by diplomatic coded cable or diplomatic pouch. As will be seen, this system has as its purpose the security of the espionage organization. Any one member of the group with the exception of the "pole" who becomes compromised will be able to directly compromise the minimum of other individuals in the unit. This in intelligence parlance is generally known as the double cutout system. It is possible to vary it, however, by extensions to a triple or quadruple cutout system with little difficulty.

As will be seen hereinafter, the NKVD was interested in securing all types of information including economic, political, social, industrial, technical and military. Instructions were often given to the courier to relate to the Silvermaster or Perlo group directing them to attempt to secure information on specific matters. Requests for specific material, however, were comparatively limited, resulting in the conclusion that this particular parallel of Soviet espionage was operating more or less as a sponge accepting any type of material that might become available from any source that could be recruited. To gain the full benefit of this type of operation, it is absolutely necessary that effective correlation be made on a higher level. It is not possible to learn whether this actually occurred. It is quite obvious, however, that Gregory's handlers were well schooled in the operation of a secret intelligence service. In this regard some of the cautions expressed to Gregory to avoid detection or compromise are of interest.

Gregory was issued repeated warnings to take every precaution possible to detect a surveillance. This included a tour of New York City in order that a prior knowledge would be available of the location of drug stores with two exits, rest rooms with two exits, movie theaters and other establishments that could be entered and left quickly eluding a surveillance.

8

17. *(Continued)*

Gregory never departed from any premises at the same time with any individual with whom contact was made for Soviet intelligence. Further, with respect to surveillances the instructions were issued to observe automobiles, and their occupants. When on foot, crossing and recrossing the street was recommended and walking the opposite direction on one-way streets when an automobile surveillance was suspected. All contacts were made very cautiously and multiple appointments were the order of the day. For example a rendezvous would be set for 4:00, 6:00 and 8:00 o'clock on a certain date and the contact ultimately consummated at any one of these three times.

Precautionary measures were taken concerning the maintenance of incriminating material on the premises of the courier and other units in the system. Methods were described whereby subsequent detection of the entrance of these premises clandestinely by outsiders could be determined. All incriminating material following its use was to be burned or flushed down the toilet. Couriers traveled with no marks of identification in their persons or on their clothing. Meeting places in general were such public establishments as restaurants and theaters. Hotels, private homes and bars were avoided. When bulky material was transported it was left in a locker in a railroad or bus terminal and the key delivered to the individual who was ultimately to receive it. Repeated cautions were given to all participants in this group to avoid discussing anything pertinent over the telephone.

Another interesting factor is the manner in which finances were handled. Couriers and persons serving in other capacities requiring reimbursement did not receive a regular salary but did receive payment for traveling expenses and other incidentals. At least until the fall of 1943 the whole service was operated on a very frugal basis. At least during the probationary period reimbursement for traveling and incidental expenses had to be supported in detail by receipts or sales slips. It is estimated by Gregory that Golos received between $2,000 and $3,000 every two months for the operation of his particular parallel. When considering that he only paid traveling expenses and incidentals, it is quite obvious that he was operating other parallels than the one with which Gregory is familiar. Money in some instances came to Golos through Gregory who received it from unidentified individuals believed to have been officially connected with the Soviet Consulate in New York City. Denominations of money were never in larger amounts than $20 and Gregory's own expenses did not exceed $100 per month. After the death of Golos, finances seemed to be more readily available and requirements concerning receipts and sales slips were somewhat relaxed. Delays in payments were infrequent and one of Golos' successors commented to Gregory that money was no object as long as it was being used for a worthwhile purpose.

It is interesting to note that one of the duties exercised by Gregory was to buy Christmas presents for the individuals supplying information, as well as for the members of their family each year. These presents, for

9

17. *(Continued)*

which Gregory received reimbursement, bore a direct relationship to the usefulness the particular individual had demonstrated to the Russians, and some were of a substantial value, costing approximately $100. With the exception of one instance, Gregory did not pay for any of the information gathered from Golos' contacts. In this instance payment was made on a regular basis to an individual temporarily in financial straits. While Gregory was dealing with others than Golos, substantial sums of money were received personally as remuneration for services rendered. This may be attributable, at least in some instances, to the fact that Gregory was dealing directly with the Russians rather than with an intermediary such as Golos.

As can be seen from the above methods and instructions and handling of finances, the Soviets are not in any sense of the word novices at conducting secret intelligence. The modus operandi, however, is not novel or different from that of any other country where diplomatic relations exist. It is obvious that all of the information gathered eventually filters into the Soviet Embassy or one of its Consulates where it in turn can be forwarded to Moscow by coded cable or diplomatic bag. It is logical to assume that other parallels of Soviet espionage are in operation whereby material can be forwarded to Moscow outside the above indicated methods of transmittal. The present methods of filtering this material through diplomatic establishment is the most efficient during the existence of diplomatic relations and the other systems, although they may be dormant now, will only be used as an alternate means of communication in the event of the breaking of these relations.

The Soviet organization mentioned by Gregory based upon the "pole" principal was stated to have been the type of organization being put into effect by the Soviets at the time Gregory ceased active handling of the groups discussed in detail in this memorandum. During the period that Gregory was active as a courier and intermediary the personnel of the Silvermaster group, the Perlo group and the miscellaneous group in Washington, D. C., mentioned by Gregory and discussed hereinafter, operated on a fairly informal basis, channelling the material to Gregory through the leaders of the groups and occasionally holding group meetings. The gradual elimination of Gregory from active participation as a courier was indicated to have been a part of the Soviet design to place espionage activities in the departments of the United States Government on a more businesslike basis under direct Soviet control.

10

18. Charles Runyon [Department of State], Memorandum for the File, "Walter Krivitsky," 10 June 1947.

June 10, 1947

MEMORANDUM FOR THE FILE:

Subject: Walter Krivitsky

At about 9:30, Monday morning, February 10, 1941, Thelma Jackson, a Negro chambermaid, found sprawled on the bed of his fifth floor room at the Hotel Bellevue, 15 E Street, N. W., Washington, D. C., the body of Walter G. Krivitsky, his death caused by the contact discharge of a .38 caliber bullet into his right temple, approximately six hours previously.

Walter Krivitsky was born Samuel Ginzberg, June 28, 1899, to middle class peasants in the Russian Ukraine near the Polish border. From 1919 to 1937, Krivitsky served in Military Intelligence of the Soviet Army. In 1923 he was sent to organize the nucleus of a Communist army in Germany in preparation for a revolution in Germany. In May 1933, he was called to Moscow by the Soviet War Industries Institute. In 1935, he was sent abroad as Chief of Soviet Military Intelligence for Western Europe, which job he held until November 1937. In the 1937 purge, many of Krivitsky's fellow generals were liquidated. In December, Krivitsky himself was ordered back to Moscow but refused to return. In the course of his 18 years in the Soviet Military Intelligence, Krivitsky was twice decorated for espionage work.

In March 1938, at Paris, Krivitsky gave an interview to a Russian emigré paper on the death of Maxim Gorky. Krivitsky, in this interview, published by Russian emigré paper Les Dernieres Nouvelles on March 4, 1938, said that Maxim Gorky may have been killed on Stalin's orders if he did not die from natural causes, since Gorky had been refused permission by Stalin to attend the International Convention of Anti-Fascist Authors at Paris recently, and had been under close surveillance. Krivitsky stated he himself had a price on his head and had decided to remain abroad "to rehabilitate tens of thousands of so-called spies". On April 29, 1939, the Saturday Evening Post published one in a series of articles by Krivitsky exposing Soviet espionage activities. In this article, Krivitsky predicted the Soviet-German pact which was concluded in August 1939. Krivitsky's articles, following closely after the Moscow trials, were an important factor in the decision of many to leave the Communist Party camp. During 1939, Ignace Reiss, an associate and friend of Krivitsky's

in the

18. *(Continued)*

- 2 -

in the Soviet Secret Service, was machine-gunned at Lausanne, it is believed, by Hans Bruesse, OGPU political assassin who operated in cooperation with a woman agent, Gertrude Shelbach.

In November 1938, Krivitsky entered the United States on a temporary passport, using his original name, Samuel Ginzberg. On July 1, 1939, he was ordered to report to Ellis Island because his temporary visa had expired. He was given a hearing July 6 and his visa was extended to December 31. At about this time, he escorted his family safely to Canada, using the name of Thomas. At this time, Krivitsky's attorney, Louis Waldman, intimated that the Communists were maneuvering through the Labor Department to have Krivitsky deported in order that they might get their hands on him.

On October 11, Krivitsky testified before the Dies Committee as follows:

1. Soviet Intelligence uses the Communist Party here and the real head of the American Communist Party is Stalin.

2. Soviet Intelligence chiefs in the United States have been: Military: Boris Bycob since 1936; Alfred Tilden, 1929-1933; Felix Wolfe, 1924-1929. OGPU: Boris Shpak, 1936-1937; Valentine Markin, 1933-1934; Alexander Karin, 1928-1933.

3. The Communist Parties outside the Soviet Union are 90% subsidized by the Soviet Union.

4. OGPU supervised Military Intelligence and the Embassies after 1935 and 1936 when Stalin came to distrust the military.

5. Soviet agents are restricted to the jobs of recruiting and directing United States Party members who do the actual work of espionage.

On October 17, 1939, Representative Dickstein of New York charged that Krivitsky was "nothing but a phony" and "was induced" to testify to protect the publishers of his magazine articles from libel suit.

On November 9, 1939, Soviet Ambassador Oumansky, returning to the United States on the *Rex*, was asked if he had read any of Krivitsky's magazine articles naming Oumansky as a former OGPU agent. Oumansky appeared annoyed and replied that he had never heard of General Krivitsky and was never in the OGPU.

On December 30

18. *(Continued)*

- 3 -

On December 30, 1939, Krivitsky's departure, three or four days previously from the United States for a secret destination, was revealed by the immigration authorities. The story subsequently delivered was that he went to Great Britain where he helped uncover extensive fifth column activities and to Paris where he collaborated with Paul Wohl, later of 173 Lexington Avenue, New York City, on various articles.

It appears that by March of 1940, Krivitsky was back in the United States, since it is stated in that month he told a story of meeting three men coming toward him on a New York street. One of these he recognized as the OGPU agent, Sergei Basoff, alias Jim.

It appears that Krivitsky, except for his articles and Dies Committee appearance, lived a retiring life and expressed to his friends a fatalistic belief that he would eventually be assassinated by Stalin. Among these friends were Boris Shev, his translator, Isaac Don Levine, Louis Waldman, New York attorney, and Suzanne LaFollette, described by the newspapers as a New York editor.

At some point during his residence in the United States, Krivitsky negotiated with Albert Goldman of Chicago, Trotsky's attorney, with a view to helping solve Trotsky's murder.

In the period before his death, Krivitsky told friends and associates that his assassination had become urgent because of his knowledge of identity and methods of many Party agents entering the Western Hemisphere. At an unspecified date, Paul Wohl, then in New York, wrote a note to Suzanne LaFollette asking her to warn Krivitsky that Hans Bruesse was in New York. Wohl, with whom Krivitsky had had a dispute about money, was the only one among his friends and associates to assert that Krivitsky had contemplated suicide. He was not, however, on close speaking terms with Krivitsky after their quarrel and stated that Krivitsky avoided him.

On Wednesday, February 5, according to his wife, Tanya Krivitsky, Krivitsky left her and his son, Alexander, seven years old, to whom he was particularly devoted, in New York in order to find a refuge in Virginia for himself and his family and in order to see Martin Dies, to whose committee he had already given much information on Soviet espionage.

Mrs. Krivitsky

18. *(Continued)*

- 4 -

Mrs. Krivitsky stated that he did not take a pistol with him. According to Louis Waldman, one of the purposes of Krivitsky's visit to Washington was to push through his naturalization, which, among other things, would enable him to purchase a pistol in New York, something that, as an alien, he could not do. At this time, his friends stated Krivitsky had sufficient money earned from his writings to carry him for several years. It has also been asserted that he had voluminous notes and stacks of documents although the newspaper stories did not indicate their disposition.

According to Eitel Wolf Dobert, a former German Army officer, who has been described by the newspapers as a former political associate of his and who lived at Charlottesville, Virginia, Krivitsky arrived at Dobert's house in Charlottesville on Thursday, February 6. While there, he bought a pistol from Charles Henshaw, the clerk at the local hardware store, who later identified the gun found beside Krivitsky's body as the same gun which he had sold to Krivitsky. In buying the gun, Krivitsky had used the name of Walter Paref of Barboursville, Virginia. With the gun, he bought fifty mushroom bullets. Henshaw's statement was later taken by Detective Horace E. Caranfa and Lieutenant George E. Darnell of the Washington Police Department. The newspaper's story attributes a statement that Krivitsky sat up until 3 Sunday morning, writing the three suicide notes which were later found in his room at the hotel, to Dobert. The notes found were on stationery having the printed address, Charlottesville, Virginia. It does not, however, appear whether Dobert did or could have identified the notes as actually material written by Krivitsky Saturday night and early Sunday morning. On Sunday, February 9, Mrs. Dobert drove Krivitsky to the Hotel Bellevue in Washington where he registered at 6 p.m. as Walter Paref, a name which, according to Waldman, Krivitsky was taking steps to adopt as his legal name in the United States. Hotel employees did not recall that Krivitsky left his room after 6 p.m., Sunday. The occupants of the other rooms on the fifth floor stated that they had heard no shot. Thelma Jackson, the chambermaid, said that she passed the door several times on Monday morning and knocked each time until she finally used her pass key to get in. The body was found sprawled on the bed--it does not appear with the face up or the face down. Krivitsky's shoes were off and near his bed. His socks were still on his feet and he was otherwise dressed. Near Krivitsky's right hand, but with fingerprints obliterated by

blood

18. *(Continued)*

- 5 -

blood from the wound, was the .38 caliber pistol purchased at Charlottesville, Virginia. There were only two openings to the room, the door, which was latched from the inside, and the window, which was either closed or locked--the story varies--which opened out on the sheer side of the building with no fire escape and no ledge. It is not stated whether the fifth is the top floor of the Bellevue. There was no sign of a struggle in the room which was ten feet square. The pistol was discharged close to Krivitsky's right temple and the contemporary comment was that it was not in his hand "where assassins would most likely have placed it".

The body was identified by J. B. Matthews of the Dies Committee who stated that Krivitsky had once told him: If they ever try to prove I took my own life, don't believe it." The case was handled by Bernard Thompson, Chief of the Detective Force of the Washington Police, and Detective Sergeant D. Guest who originally came to the scene.

Three notes were found in Krivitsky's room, one in English addressed to Waldman requesting that he help his family, adding as a postscript that he went to Virginia because he could get a gun there and asking Waldman to help his friends there who did not, he stated, know why he got the gun. A second in Russian was addressed to his wife and son and pitched in an emotional tone. He stated that "it" was very difficult . . . "but it is impossible . . . you will understand that I have to go . . . I think my sins are big . . . P.S. On the farm of Dobertov I wrote this yesterday but I did not have any strength in New York. I did not have any business in Washington. I went to see Dobertov because that is the only place I could get the firearms." A third in German was addressed to Suzanne LaFollette asking her to help his wife and son. The Washington Police compared the notes with samples of Krivitsky's handwriting and decided that they were authentic. Waldman initally denied their authenticity and the last news of this subject is that Waldman had procured photostatic copies which he and Krivitsky's friends had examined and in which he found discrepancies with Krivitsky's other writings. Waldman stated, however, that it was possible that the discrepancies were simply normal variations and that he proposed to have a professional examination made in New York.

Waldman and Krivitsky's friends called for a Federal investigation but the FBI refused to assume jurisdiction. Although Waldman and Krivitsky's friends sought to hold up

issuance

18. *(Continued)*

- 6 -

issuance of a certificate of suicide, the certificate was finally issued although the coroner agreed that he would impanel a jury in case further evidence "cropped up". Representative Rankin told the newspapers that the gun was in the wrong place for the death to have been a suicide. Mrs. Krivitsky felt sure that the Soviet had forced her husband to write the notes with the threat of assassinating her and his boy. She said that Krivitsky was especially devoted to Alexander. She stated that the note to her did not sound like her husband. Krivitsky's body was taken to New York and cremated February 15. On February 22, Representative Parnall Thomas said the Dies Committee should investigate because certain evidence led him to believe that the body found in the hotel was not Krivitsky's. Previously, over the weekend of Sunday, February 16, the offices of the <u>New Leader</u> in New York were raided. The safe was cracked but nothing was taken. Money left in the office was not removed, but the files were strewn about the office. It was suggested that the OGPU had been searching for Krivitsky's unpublished works.

A-P:CRunyon:ock: 6/11/47

19. [Meredith Knox Gardner], "Covernames in Diplomatic Traffic," 30 August 1947.

~~TOP SECRET CREAM~~

WDGAS-93

30 August 1947

Copy # 5

I. D. SPECIAL ANALYSIS REPORT # 1

COVERNAMES IN DIPLOMATIC TRAFFIC

Prepared by ASA I. D.
30 August 1947

Distribution:

- 2 copies — ID
- 1 copy — Chief, ASA
- 1 copy — Chief, OP-20-2
- 1 copy — LSIC (thru Col. Marr-Johnson)
- 1 copy — WDGAS-93-B

Col. Hayes passed on his own copy. To only recipient (Col. Forney, Col. Sow) or suspended further distribution.

~~TOP SECRET CREAM~~

19. *(Continued)*

~~TOP SECRET CREAM~~

COVERNAMES IN DIPLOMATIC TRAFFIC ▓▓▓▓

1. **Limitations of the report.**

    Any report made at this time on the contents of traffic encrypted by the system ▓▓▓▓ must necessarily be fragmentary and subject to correction in detail. In the messages that are in any degree readable, there are large gaps in solution of the cipher key (additive), and in the code book only about 15 per cent of the equivalences are identified, some only tentatively. Both these deficiencies are constantly being ameliorated, with the result that such reports as this will be outdated very rapidly until a much higher degree of recovery has been reached.

2. **Collateral information.**

    The collateral information given about the covernames is both scanty and tentative, for reasons implied in paragraph 1. The most reliable data related to the names are the date and place of origin of the messages containing them. Since most of the readable traffic originated in New York, it will be necessary to indicate the origin only in the case of Washington, Canberra, and Stockholm messages. All the messages used are directed to Moscow.

3. **Use of covernames.**

    It is known from the Report of the Royal Commission /in Canada/ appointed under Order in Council P. C. 411 of February 5, 1946 (report dated June 27, 1946) that agencies of the Union of Soviet Socialist Republics engaged in conspiratorial activities are accustomed, for reasons of security, to refer to persons that are furthering these activities by covernames, and in particular that this is done in encrypted messages sent between diplomatic installations and Moscow.

4. **Covernames in ▓▓▓▓**

    The traffic encrypted by the system ▓▓▓▓ contains many covernames, which are definitely proved to be such by two circumstances, (1) that many of them are so designated in messages (given as a supplement hereto) that describe themselves as dealing with changes in covernames (KLICHKI) and (2) that many of them are contained in the formula: "A (henceforth B)", in which A is evidently the real name of the old covername and B the (new) covername.

- 1 -

~~TOP SECRET CREAM~~

19. (Continued)

~~TOP SECRET CREAM~~

The classic example for the "henceforth" formula is in a message of 23 August 1944, New York-Moscow, internal address SEMION. There occurs the expression "MAMLUIGA Vitaliy Semionovich (henceforth "EM")." The next sentence starts with "EM's". Now, Vitaliy Semionovich Mamluiga (usual transliteration: Vitalii Semenovich Mamlyga) is the name of a person known to have been with the Soviet Purchasing Commission. After giving his name in full, the originator of the message gave him a covername and immediately proceeded to use it. (EM is not known outside this message, the rest of which is not yet readable; but see section 15.) In this case, where perhaps the need for security was not great, the covername seems to be the name of the initial letter of MAMLUIGA--M. This circumstance must not, however, lead us to employ the term "covername" for initials used for the sake of brevity, the expansion of which is always evident from other passages in the message concerned. (Covernames themselves can be so abbreviated.)

5. <u>Reliability of "readings"</u>.

In the following it must be borne in mind that some of the covernames are expressed by single code groups not yet found in other contexts and others contain groups not yet found in other contexts. When any form has been assumed for the equivalent of such a group, it is here generally followed by a question mark. The forms assumed are based (1) on calculations made possible by the fact that ████████ uses a one-part code and that complete one-part codes of the same length are available (this process of comparison and calculation has yielded many values that were later verified) and (2) on the analogy of verified covernames. As mentioned below, the covernames fall in part into "families".

6. <u>Families of covernames</u>.

It has become evident that many of the covernames can be put into categories on the basis of some similarity between them. In the Report of the Royal Commission we find the alliterating family BACK, BACON, BADEAU, BAGLEY (all members of the Group "Research"; cf. p. 729). We find a Promotheus that seems to belong to a "mythology" family, examples of which in ████████ traffic are Jupiter and Cerës. In New York message 798 appended below, we find Erie immediately followed by Huron (in fact, Erie gave the clue for the identification of Huron). There is a family of ancient Phoenician cities: Carthage, Tire, and Sidon.

The arrangement of the material from this point will be based on such categories. First, covernames apparently for persons will be listed: Addresses, signatures, specifically Russian Christian names, Christian names not specifically Russian, relationships and conditions of age, station and calling, mythological names, names of animals, names of plants, and miscellaneous. Then covernames apparently for places and institutions will be listed: Ancient

- 2 -

~~TOP SECRET CREAM~~

19. *(Continued)*

~~TOP SECRET CREAM~~

places, geographical features, and miscellaneous. Names occurring only in the special covername messages are sometimes not listed except in the text of of those messages themselves (see supplement).

7. Addresses.

✓ The addresses and signatures seem to be covernames. The constant address of Canberra and Stockholm messages and the address of by far the greater part of the New York messages is expressed by a group falling in the book just before the group for VIL and five places after the group for VIZ,a (visa). All probabilities favor the value VIKTOR(as an address, it is to be read in the dative case: VIKTORU, to Victor). The only other occurrence of the group is in the spelling VIKTORII (in which, unfortunately, II can be secured only by assuming a one-digit garble) in the expression "of Victoria and New South Wales."

New York messages show at least three other addresses: 8 OTDELU (to the Eighth Division of Department) and SEMIONU (to Simeon or Simon), both confirmed from other uses, and a group falling two places after PETER, hence perhaps PIOTR (Peter) or PETROV or the like.

The frequency of VIKTORU in the latest index is 24 for Canberra, 4 for Stockholm, and for New York 206. New York four times follows this by 8 OTDELU (with a separating dash or period), Canberra 5 times with a period between and once without--once Canberra has simply VIKTORU 8. New York also has VIKTORU, SEMIONU twice, VIKTORU, BORIS(?)OVU once, and once VIKTORU OT KOMISSARI(?)AT(A?) (to Victor from the Commissari(?)at(??). Canberra has one VIKTORU SEMIONU.

SEMIONU occurs 22 times as an address from New York (twice after VIKTORU), once from Canberra (after VIKTORU). All occurrences are after 19 July 1944.

8 OTDELU occurs 22 times, 11 of these after VIKTORU (with or without separating period or dash). One Canberra message begins "To Victor. In reply to your telegram No. 2383. 8 OTDEL(U)."

"PETROVU", or whatever it is, is an address at least 7 times, all from New York, from May to August 1944. (The group occurs in 4 other passages, twice preceded by TOVARISHCH, "Comrade"; once in a Canberra message. Note that in all indications of frequency, unless otherwise stated, anti-garble repetitions have been eliminated.)

BORIS(?)OV occurs once in the phrase VIKTORU, BORIS(?)OVU" from New York, 17 August 1944.

- 3 -

~~TOP SECRET CREAM~~

19. *(Continued)*

~~TOP SECRET CREAM~~

8. Signatures.

The constant Canberra signature is a group that has been tentatively tagged YEFIM (Joachim). Only one case of a Washington signature (?) is known, a group presumably in the range of VAV to VAK. It could be something like VAVILOV or even VAKH (Bacchus). No Stockholm signatures are known.

The most frequent New York signature is MAY, with an overall frequency of 160, only a handful of which occurrences are not signatures. Occasionally, to distinguish his own remarks from a document he is transmitting, MAY will use the expression "PRIMECHANIYE MAYA" (May's note), thus confirming that MAY is a signature and that the value of the signature group is MAY (for MAYA is a different group and certainly means "of May" in dates).

Another signature, in about the range for ANTON (Anthony), occurs 10 times (New York). Once (12 December 1944) the form is "ANTON (?) and MAK" (MAK is possibly a garble for MAY). All occurrences are from October 1944 to January 1945. The name also occurs in the text 8 times (New York, May-December 1944). In a message of 23 August 1944, ANTON (?) is associated with SERGEY (?) and AKIM, apparently in connection with southwestern factories and plants.

A signature in the right range for BORIS occurs at least twice as a New York signature, on 23 October and 31 December 1944.

SERGEY (?) (Sergius): There are 2 candidates for this value. One occurs 2 September 1944 and 11 January 1945; the other occurs 17 times, 16 May 1944 - 15 January 1945. The second one is associated with ANTON (?) and AKIM (see section 8).

ALEKSEY (Alexis): occurs 5 times, 9 May - 14 December 1944.

- 4 -

~~TOP SECRET CREAM~~

19. *(Continued)*

~~TOP SECRET CREAM~~

9. <u>Specifically Russian Christian names.</u>

Some covernames that are Russian Christian names have already been mentioned in sections 7 and 8. Others are as follows:

ARSENIY (Arsenius): in 5 New York messages, 16 June-22 December 1944.

VITALIY (Vitalis): occurs in 3 messages, 9 August, 23 August 31 December 1944. Also occurs in a real name (see MAMLUIGA in section 4.)

YAKOV? (Jacob): was GNOM before September 1944.

AKIM (Joachim): occurs 8 times in 8 messages (all with a SEMION address), 16 June-28 Dec. 1944. See section 8.

10. <u>Christian names not specifically Russian.</u>

Although many Soviet citizens have Christian names virtually identical with name forms in other languages than Russian, it seems safe to set up a category that would include vaguely international forms together with definitely non-Russian forms. In connection with some of these names, the following quotation from *This is My Story* by Louis Francis Budenz, former managing editor of the Daily Worker, (McGraw-Hill Book Company, Inc., New York and London: 1947) pp. 138-139, is given for whatever reference value it may have.

> The so-called "Dutch" or German, comrade--though his accent was indeterminate to my untrained ear--was the first of a long line of personages with foreign accents and foreign origins who paraded through the governing apparatus of the Communist party of the U.S.A. No one, and least of all any well-educated American, has any complaint about full participation of the foreign born in American life; our own ancestors came from afar to make up this land of the free. But the right of those who are agents of a foreign power to cross our borders under aliases and order American citizens about, is another matter. Yet, to my surprise, this was what I found in the building at Thirty-five East Twelfth Street when I entered it and began to work there.
>
> These men of many names and no names bore aliases like Edwards*--- carelessly chosen plurals of "Christian names" such as Roberts, Richards, Stevens, Michaels, Johns and, occasionally, something more distinctive taken from England or the Middle West. The second one of these gentlemen to impress himself upon me was "Roberts," then acting in a vital secretarial capacity in the Party. That is, he was one of the chief factors in the national setup. Still in the stage of pleasantries upon such matters, I had gaily referred to him as "The Cheshire Cat Commissar" because of his perpetual mechanical smile. It was not unpleasant but unreal. Like the

* Budenz had met Gerhard Eisler under the name of Edwards; see pp 135 and 137 and his testimony in District Court, Washington, on 24 July 1947.

- 5 -

~~TOP SECRET CREAM~~

19. *(Continued)*

~~TOP SECRET CREAM~~

celebrated feline, his names kept vanishing. Shortly after my labor editorship began, he suddenly converted himself into "Comrade Peters" and then into "Comrade Steve" and then, after a long time, back to "Comrade Roberts". It kept one busy trying to keep up with these transformations.

Before the publication of Budenz's book, certain groups had tentatively been identified as equivalent to RICHARD, ROBERT, and the like. That such names occur in the code book has been amply verified, e.g. by the message of 2 December 1944, listing nuclear physicists and mathematicians. To serve as surnames in daily colloquy, some of these names would have to take on an S.

The group that seems to stand for ROBERT (it follows next after RO) occurs 35 times. The group for RICHARD (2 places beyond RIT) occurs 6 times (plus once in RICHARD? PALMER). Both are restricted to New York messages. RICHARD is the new covername given in September 1944 to someone whose previous (cover?) name seems to have begun with LO (see message 70ϕ appended below). A ROBERT occurs from 7 June 1944 on through 17 January 1945 -- of course not necessarily one single individual throughout.

It is significant that ROBERT was always "transmitting" written matter to the originator(s) of the messages: the formula "Robert? has transmitted" occurs five times in the index.

Another individual of particular interest is one whose name would seem to begin with HE (or, by the more usual transliteration, KHE). This may be HENRI (Henry), though there is almost certainly another and more usual spelling of "Henry" in the book, GENRI OR GENRIH. HENRI? figures in arrangements for a rendezvous in front of a Mexico City movie house (N. Y. message of 14 June 1944); in other messages also he is located in DEREVNIA (the Country, covername for MEXICO). In a message of 1ϕ August 1944 there seems to be talk of calling him back to TIR (Tyre, covername for New York). He occurs 21 times, from 26 May-1ϕ August 1944. The other group, GENRI, occurs in message 798 (below) and perhaps in a message of 1 June 1944 involving the securing of a DEREVENSKOY (Mexican) visa.

Other such names are:

AL' or EL' (Al?): occurs 1 October in phrase "Al' or EL'" (both attempts to render English Al?)

DIK (Dick): was EKO (Echo) before October 1944; occurs in five messages, 23 October -26 December 1944.

DONAL'D (Donald): became PILOT? September 1944; this second name appears in section 11 below.

DUN?KAN (Duncan): occurs in message of 26 May 1944.

KARL (Carl): was SKAT before October 1944; occurs once 26 December 1944.

~~TOP SECRET CREAM~~

19. *(Continued)*

~~TOP SECRET CREAM~~

GENRI(H) (Henry):	was TAM before October 1944. See the last paragraph above.
DZHON (John):	was GUDZON before October 1944; occurs once 14 December 1944, with AMUR?
PETER:	was CHORNOY? (Black) before October 1944.
CHARL'Z (Charles):	was something else until October 1944.
ERIK?:	was something else until October 1944.
BEN?:	Canberra, twice 1 September 1945. Seems to have furnished information on the Australian Security Service. Same name twice from New York, 26 July and 16 August 1944.'
KLOD (Claude):	Canberra, April-October 1945. KLOD is Canberra's regular purveyor of information; he occurs 13 time 8 times in the formula "'KLOD' has communicated".
NIK (Nick?):	22 July 1944; message contains names DuPont, Ford, Mellon, Weir, Pew.
(CHARL'Z BRUNO (Charles Bruno):	in N.Y. message 14 June 1944, this is the name HENRI? is to give as a password at the rendezvous.)
DORA:	in two messages, 23 October 1944 and 4 January, 1945.
KORA (Cora):	20 December 1944.
OLA:	a Washington female agent; name changed to something else in October 1944. Occurs in 2 messages, 3 May and 10 August 1944, both dealing with KOMAR (that is, probably KRAVCHENKO). It is planned to make these messages the subject of a separate repor In the former OLA is described as seeking more detailed information on the KOMAR affair. In the latter she has something to do with the supposition that (does not think that?) KOMAR is staying at 209 West 97th Street.
RITA:	mentioned 10 August 1944 in the phrase "the first two parts (of?) the business of RITA". (The message also mentions KOMAR, issue of LA VOZ/Mexico City Communist organ/ for 7 June, HENRI?).

11. <u>Relationships and Conditions of Age, Station and Calling.</u>

OTCHIM (Stepfather): in 3 messages, 17 May - 27 December 1944.

SVAT (Matchmaker: Son- or Daughter-in-law's Father): 23 Aug. and 6 Dec. 1944.

- 7 -

~~TOP SECRET CREAM~~

TOP SECRET CREAM

DEDUSHKA (Granapapa or Granddaddy): occurs 5 times in 6 messages, 9 May - 14 August 1944.

NABOB (Nabob): apparently a high American diplomatic official. Occurs 5 times in 3 messages, 9 May, 7 September, 14 December 1947; in message of 7 September, in connection with postwar treatment of Germany.

ATAMAN (Hetman): occurs 4 times in 3 messages, 17 May, 7 June, 6 October, 1944.

PILOT? (Pilot): was DONAL'D before September 1944.

12. **Mythological Names:**

YUPITER (Jupiter): became ORIOL? (Eagle) in October 1944.

SERES (Ceres): in 4 messages, 4 May - 25 July 1944.

MUZA (Muse): 4 July 1944; communicated concerning Secret Funds Division, Emerson Bigelow, aid of 92,000,000 Portuguese escudos, Northern European division of Secret Intelligence Branch, etc.

EKO (Echo): became DIK in October 1944; occurs 14 times, 2 May 23 October, 1944.'

GNOM (Gnome): became YAKOV? in September 1944. Occurs 3 times, 18 May, 16 June, 25 July.

13. **Names of animals.**

TIULEN' (Seal): 10 August 1944, (a KOMAR or Kravchenko message).

ORIOL? (Eagle): was YUPITER until October 1944. Occurs 5 Dec. 1944

LUN' (Hen Harrier): in 4 messages, 3 May - 17 August 1944.

GUS' (Goose): changed to something else October 1944.

KOMAR (Gnat etc.): probably covername for Viktor Alexseyavich Kravchenko. For a complete development of this idea, a separate report would be necessary. Occurs in 8 messages so far partly read, 6 between 3 and 23 May, 1944, 2 on 10 August, 1944; KOMAR is the object of intense interest, including attempts to locate him (20 May: "is living with? KERENSKOY in the state of Connecticut etc.").

- 8 -

TOP SECRET CREAM

19. *(Continued)*

TOP SECRET CREAM

14. **Names of plants.**

    TIUL'PAN (Tulip): 10 August 1944; (a KOMAR or Kravchenko message) changed to something beginning with KAN Sept. 1944.

15. **Miscellaneous.**

    LIB?? (Lieb?) or possibly LIBERAL: was ANTENKO until Sept. 1944. Occurs 6 times, 22 October - 20 December 1944. Message of 27 November speaks of his wife ETHEL, 29 years old married (?) 5 years, ".......husband's work and the role of METR(O) and NIL".

    AMUR? (Amour?): was ZHA---?--et (Jeannette??) before October 1944; occurs once 14 December 1944 with DZHON.

    METR (like many other equivalences in the code book, this might have an alternative reading, perhaps METRO; as METR it means "meter" and as METRO it is a nickname, applied for example to the Paris subway system): was SKAUT until September 1944. Occurs 27 Nov. 194 (something about LIB?'s wife Ethel? ?knowing about her husband's work and the role of METR(O) and NIL; notice in message 700 below how METR(O) and NIL com together). Seems to occur 5 December 1944 in phras "METR(O) and ?HYU?SON (Hughson?)". Note on page 73 of the Report of the Royal Commission: "Metro..... ...The Embassy of the U.S.S.R."

    GRANT: occurs 26 May 1944 in phrase "of GRANT and EARL"; message mentions FFI (Forces Francais de'l Intérieur?) or possibly a name ending in FFI (FFY). In 1945, GRANT was used in Canada as the covername of Colonel Nikoloy Zabotin, Soviet Military Attache in Ottawa and head of military intelligence work in Canada (see Report of the Royal Commission).

    EM (M): covername of Vitaliy Semionovich Mamluiga in messag of 23 August 1944. He was a member of the Soviet Purchasing Commission, having entered the U.S. in December 1943. He was still here in September 1946 This name may be EMA, and may be the same EMA liste 28 November 1944 (see below).

    KANUK? (Canuck?): Occurs 4 times in 2 messages, 24 July and 1 August 1944.

    SI (C?): occurs 23 October and 6 December 1944.

    PA (Pa?): occurs 14 December 1944.

- 9 -

TOP SECRET CREAM

19. *(Continued)*

~~TOP SECRET CREAM~~

List of 28 November 1944; In a message of that date the following names occur, apparently as operating from New York: KRUG (Circle, or the name Krug), KIN--?--(was R--?--OLOV until October 1944), EMA, --?--, St--?-- (this word may not be a name) --MALIAR (Painter), YAN (Jan), ENK........

16. **Covernames apparently for places and institutions:**

    Ancient places (also rivers, etc.).

    TIR (Tyrs):   covername for New York.

    SIDON (Sidon):   covername for London.

    KARFAGEN (Carthage):   covername for Washington.

    NIL (Nile?):   was something beginning with TU (TUMAN, Mist?) until September 1944; linked with METR, which see.

17. **Geographical features.**

    STRANA (Land, Country): covername for the United States.

    OSTROV (Island):   covername for Great Britain; changed October 1944 to something beginning with EK (or EX).

    OSTROVITIANIN (Islander): Briton.

    DEREVNIA (the Country /i.e., rural districts/): covername for Mexico.

    DEREVENSKOY (Country, Rural): Mexican.

    ZEMLIAK (Fellow Countryman): Coverword for some nationality, possibly U.S.

18. **Miscellaneous.**

    BANK (the Bank):   probably covername for the U.S. State Department; occurs 24 times, (once in the plural from Canberra, probably in the literal sense).

    DOM STARUHI (the Old Woman's House): in 2 messages, 26 May and 10 Aug. 1944.

- 10 -

~~TOP SECRET CREAM~~

19. *(Continued)*

TOP SECRET CREAM

19. Conclusion.

In its present state the ▓▓▓▓▓ traffic tends to arouse curiosity more than it does to satisfy it. This unsatisfactory state of affairs makes it imperative that this report be supplemented at intervals. It is proposed that such supplements not be complete revisions of this report, but rather be of such a nature that they would be filed with it and used in conjunction with it. When enough material has been accumulated, a new report will be made.

This report incorporates the previous brief tentative report of 20 June 1947.

A final reminder of the extremely provisional nature of all assumptions made in this report is desirable. Future supplements will not fail to specify those that have become untenable.

- 11 -

TOP SECRET CREAM

20. No author [probably William K. Harvey, CIA], Memorandum for the File, "COMRAP," 6 February 1948.

Approved for release through the HISTORICAL REVIEW PROGRAM of the Central Intelligence Agency

6 February 1948

MEMORANDUM FOR THE FILE

Subject: COMRAP — VASSILI M. ZUBILIN

1. Set out below for record and cross check purposes is a brief summary of an extensive operational Soviet espionage case within the U.S., known to have been, at least until August 28, 1944 and possibly subsequently, under the control and direction of a Major General of State Security (then NKGB, now MGB). This case has been given the code name COMRAP, inasmuch as it involves personnel who, prior to 1943, had been long active in the illegal conspiratorial and quasi-intelligence operations of the Comintern Apparatus.

2. For purposes of clarity the initial portion of this case summary is given in narrative form, from the standpoint of its investigative development.

3. As of late 1942 and early 1943 intensive investigative coverage was being maintained on the activities and movements of Steve NELSON, then head of the Alameda County, California, section of the CPUSA, which is and has been for some years one of the largest County sections of the Party, probably the most powerful section outside greater New York. NELSON at this time was one of the important and long-time Communist functionaries who, on numerous occasions in the past, had been implicated on the periphery at least of Soviet espionage operations. Steve NELSON was born in Yugoslavia, probably Croatia, shortly before 1900. He first entered the United States about 1920 when he jumped ship in New York City and through the laxity of immigration procedures he was permitted subsequently to legalize his status, later becoming, by naturalization, a U.S. citizen. The exact date of NELSON's initial affiliation with the Communist movement is unknown, but there is at least some reason to believe that he was active in Agitprop work in Yugoslavia prior to his first entry into the U.S. Shortly after his arrival he became affiliated with the predecessor organizations of the CPUSA and his Party career has been one of ever-increasing responsibility. About 1930, the exact date being unknown, Steve NELSON was dispatched through the clandestine channels of World Tourist in New York to Moscow as a student from the CPUSA to the Lenin School. It is interesting to recall, in this connection, that World Tourist was the firm headed by Jacob N. GOLOS (RAZIN) who has since become of paramount interest in view of his participation as a leading figure in the Soviet espionage parallels loosely grouped together in the GREGORY case; it being remembered that GOLOS was responsible to a large degree for the operation of these parallels until his death in New York City in November 1943.

4. After graduating from the Lenin School NELSON served for about eighteen months on an undisclosed Comintern assignment reportedly of an operational intelligence

20. *(Continued)*

-2-

nature somewhere "in Central Europe". Before returning to the U.S. in 1933, NELSON is known to have been, for a brief period, in Shanghai, China, and he has stated that while in Shanghai he was closely associated with Arthur EWERT, alias Harry BERGER, who was active in the Comintern Apparatus for many years and was dispatched to Rio de Janeiro, Brazil in 1937 under supporting cover from Yujamtorg for the purpose of guiding the abortive Communist revolution in Brazil the following year. It will also be recalled that EWERT, who was known in Rio as BERGER went insane while being interrogated by the Brazilian police. Upon his return to the States about 1933, NELSON became increasingly active in Communist revolutionary work in the trade union field and was particularly active in the industrial areas of Detroit, Chicago, Pittsburgh, and Cleveland.

5. Shortly after the outbreak of the Spanish Civil War NELSON went to Spain where he became a political commissar of the International Brigades, specifically attached to the Abraham Lincoln Brigade and eventually attaining the rank of Lt. Colonel. Upon his return from Spain, subsequent to the collapse of the Spanish Republic, NELSON was immediately made a member of the National Committee of the CPUSA by co-optation. It is amusing to note that the procedure adopted in NELSON's case in placing him upon the National Committee was an exact parallel of the procedure used to give Stalin his first post on the Central Committee of the Bolshevik fraction of the Social Democratic Party of Russia. Shortly thereafter, NELSON was transferred to the Alameda County section of the Party. The exact intelligence significance of NELSON's service in Spain has never fully been revealed, although it has been reported that he served as an "NKVD agent" during this period. During the period between his return to the U.S. and late 1942, when he is known to have been re-activated as an intelligence agent, his exact intelligence participation also is not known, although there are indications that during this period he may have carried out certain Comintern assignments.

6. On April 10, 1943, it was ascertained through technical coverage of his residence in Berkeley, California that NELSON was in carefully veiled but detailed conversation with an individual, then unidentified, who spoke English with a heavy European, probably Russian, accent. This conversation which last for several hours, revealed without question that NELSON was an important figure in a Soviet net engaged in operational espionage, in the maintenance of illegal Communist seaman courier routes and at least to some extent in the clandestine forwarding of propaganda through illegal means to the Far East, and that the then unidentified visitor was NELSON's Soviet superior. The conversation opened with the unknown visitor counting ten bills or bundles of currency and its significance was almost immediately tabbld by the following interchange:

NELSON: "Jesus, you count money like a banker."

Unknown man: "Vell, you know I used to do it in Moskva."

Through this conversation it was revealed that NELSON had been recruited shortly before January 1, 1943 by a "man from Moscow" and that this recruitment had been with the knowledge of "the old man", which was an obvious reference to Earl Browder,

20. *(Continued)*

then General Secretary and undisputed head of the CPUSA. Both NELSON and his unknown visitor referred to this network as the Comintern Apparatus and as the "Apparat". It is interesting to note that this conversation took place only a month prior to the formal dissolution of the Communist International and that actually, as will be set out below, the unknown man was identified later as an official of the then GUGB, later the NKGB, and now the MGB. During the conversation references were made to one "Rapp" and to one "George". It was indicated that "Rapp" was responsible for West Coast clandestine courier routes and that "George" was responsible for liaison with BROWDER on all Apparat matters. "Rapp" was subsequently identified as Mordecai RAPPAPORT, an old time Communist waterfront figure, and "George" was subsequently identified as Getzel HOCHBERG, who was then acting as BROWSER's bodyguard and was accompanying him on his various Party trips throughout the U.S. HOCHBERG was an active Communist Party member. NELSON complained bitterly to his visitor about the inefficiency of both RAPPAPORT and HOCHBERG and it is interesting to note that a few days afterward both of them were demoted and disciplined, RAPPAPORT being transferred from San Francisco to Los Angeles where he was given a minor Party post and HOCHBERG being transferred from New York to Detroit merely as a Party member.

7. During the conversation frequent mention was made of an individual referred to as "Al" who was described as located in or near New York and as head of the Apparat although obviously Al also was under the direction and control of NELSON's unidentified visitor. Al was subsequently identified as Ralph BOWMAN, a supposedly minor editorial writer for the now defunct New Masses, a leading weekly organ of the Communist Party for many years. It is interesting to note that while BOWMAN maintained an office at the New Masses, his name did not appear on the magazine's masthead and that he was extremely successful in concealing his movements and contacts and in veiling his true significance.

8. Also discussed as a usable recruit, during this conversation, was a woman, later identified as Louise Rosenberg BRANSTEN, wealthy California woman and former wife of Richard BRANSTEN, alias Bruce MINTON, well known Party propagandist for many years and a frequent contributor to New Masses before his "deviation" as a result of the BROWDER-FOSTER split in the CPUSA. It is noted that BRANSTEN, as Bruce MINTON, was partially responsible for the initial recruitment of two of the agents active in the GREGORY case, having referred these two to BROWDER who, in turn, arranged their recruitment with Jake GOLOS. At the time of this conversation in 1943, Louise Rosenberg BRANSTEN was the mistress of Gregori Markovich KHEIFETS, at that time and until the summer of 1944 Soviet Vice Consul in San Francisco, who was identified through independent investigation as an NKGB official active in the running of operational nets on the West Coast. KHEIFETS was mentioned in inference in the conversation between NELSON and his visitor, and reference was made also to William SCHNEIDERMAN, California State Secretary of the CPUSA, it being indicated by NELSON that SCHNEIDERMAN was reluctant to take the chance involved in making Party members available for "special work" (a stock Party term for Soviet Intelligence assignments). A number of other individuals, cryptically referred to in this conversation,

20. *(Continued)*

have never been definitely identified.

9. Almost immediately thereafter the unidentified man conferring with NELSON was positively identified as Vassili Mikhailovich ZUBILIN, then Third Secretary of the Soviet Embassy in Washington, D.C., and shortly thereafter promoted to the position of Second Secretary. Through other cases and collateral information, it was ascertained that ZUBILIN was a Major General of State Security, that his real name is V. ZARUBIN (apparently no relation to Georgi N. ZARUBIN, Soviet Ambassador to Canada during the time of the extensive operation of Col. Nikolai ZABOTIN, Soviet Military Attache and GRU head in Canada from the summer of 1943 until December 12, 1945).

10. Through investigation it was established that during 1943 and 1944 Ralph BOWMAN ("Al") was in frequent correspondence with Steve NELSON, concerning matters pertaining to this intelligence parallel, through a complicated series of Party and Party affiliated individuals serving as mail drops. During this time also Steve NELSON is known to have been in possession of a complete formula for the preparation of a secret ink adaptable for clandestine secret writing of espionage communications, and he was in possession also of certain ingredients for the preparation of this ink. While no secret writing communications were actually intercepted in this case, it should be noted that it was established that Mordecai RAPPAPORT in 1943 was in possession of a formula for secret ink exactly the same as the one possessed by NELSON.

1. The next major development in this case was the receipt in August, 1943 of an anonymous letter, postmarked at Washington, D.C. on August 7, 1943, mailed from a mail box in the proximity of the Soviet Embassy, and addressed to the Federal Bureau of Investigation. This letter was written on a Russian typewriter in obviously military style, and, as will be noted below, could only have been written by an individual closely acquainted with and undoubtedly deeply implicated in Soviet espionage operations within the U.S. This anonymous letter stated that the Second Secretary of the Soviet Embassy, Vassili M. Zubilin, was actually the head of the Foreign Department (given in Russian as INO) of the NKVD (meaning obviously GUGB/NKVD) for North America, having jurisdiction over not only the U.S. but Canada and Mexico as well. The letter stated that ZUBILIN was running a large network of agents, that his real name was V. ZARUBIN and that he was in Poland at least shortly after the Soviet occupation in 1939 where he was responsible for the massacre of several thousands of Poles. The letter also described him as a Major General of NKVD and listed in detail a number of Soviet officials in North America who, according to the letter, were serving as his assistants in Soviet espionage operations. The other persons named in the letter are listed below, together with a summary of the allegations in the anonymous letter, plus the substantiating information concerning them developed through independent investigation and other sources.

   a. <u>Elizabeta Yurevna Zubilin</u> According to the letter ZUBILIN's wife, Elisabeta, personally was operating a network composed of a large number of agents serving in agencies of the U.S. Government. It has been established independently that

20. *(Continued)*

Elizabeta ZUBILIN was active, at least as early as 1937, as a Soviet agent of importance under the cover name "Helen".

    b. Boris Michael MORROS, a Hollywood film director of Russian extraction. It has been established independently and in fact MORROS has admitted serving as a Soviet agent under ZUBILIN and other individuals with the primary mission of establishing a cover firm or firms for Soviet espionage operations in the U.S. and Latin America. One of the allegations in the anonymous letter, and the only allegation which is considered untrue or inaccurate, was an allegation to the effect that the ZUBILINS were actually betraying the Soviet Union, were passing "disinformation" back to the Soviet Union, but were passing valid intelligence data to the Germans and Japanese through MORROS. Intensive investigation failed to substantiate this allegation in the anonymous letter, although without exception, where possible, all of the other allegations have been independently substantiated. The possible explanation for this rather startling statement is discussed below in connection with the evaluation of this letter and the writer thereof.

    c. Gregori Markovich KHEIFETS, described in the letter as Soviet Vice Consul in San Francisco and an important assistant to ZUBILIN. Through independent sources it is known that KHEIFETS, until his departure for the Soviet Union in the summer of 1944, was active in operational Soviet espionage principally in the San Francisco and Los Angeles areas, it being noted that at least one of his sub-agents was controlled. KHEIFETS, during this period, used among other aliases, the alias of BROWN or "Mr." BROWN. His intelligence contacts were clandestinely made with maximum secrecy precautions and a predilection for the use of public places not readily susceptible to physical or other observation. Access to certain personal papers in KHEIFETS' possession reflected that he maintained a tremendously large number of contacts on the West Coast and that he undoubtedly was responsible for other extensive intelligence operations which were never completely identified. It is interesting to note that when KHEIFETS departed from San Francisco in the summer of 1944 he was replaced as Vice Consul by Gregory KASPAROV, who also was identified as taking over KHEIFETS' intelligence operations and contacts, as well as his overt duties as Soviet Vice Consul. However, KASPAROV did not use exactly the same approach as was frequently used by KHEIFETS, it being noted that KHEIFETS consistently claimed to be assigned to the Consulate in San Francisco as a representative of VOKS and stated on numerous occasions that prior to coming to the U.S. he had been an official of VOKS in Moscow.

    d. Andrei Ivanovich SCHEVCHENKO, described in the letter was a subordinate of ZUBILIN's, active in Technical espionage. For a period of several years until late January 1946 SCHEVCHENKO was an engineer with both the Soviet Government Purchasing Commission and the Amtorg Trading Corporation. Inasmuch as two of SCHEVCHENKO's sub-agents were controlled, it is known that the allegations regarding him in the anonymous letter were without question true. It is interesting to note that SCHEVCHENKO's primary interest, at least as exhibited through his two controlled sub-agents, was in the procurement of technical documents from critical industrial facilities, including the Bell Aircraft Corporation in Buffalo. He is known to have

20. *(Continued)*

expressed a particular interest in jet propulsion, rocket motors, and related matters, and upon at least two occasions he furnished his sub-agents with Leica camera for photographing documents.

e. Leonid A. TARASOV. More commonly known as Lev TARASOV, he was first an important official of the newly opened Soviet Embassy in Mexico City, and was described in the letter as ZUBILIN's chief subordinate in Mexico. TARASOV later became either first or second secretary of the Soviet Legation, later Embassy, in Mexico and was independently identified as deeply involved in operational Soviet espionage. It is interesting to note that TARASOV was at least to a large part responsible for the Mexican end of the Altschuler case, a Soviet espionage case involving numerous secret writing messages which were never completely deciphered between the U.S. and Latin America. This case involved, among other things, efforts to procure the release or disposal of Jacques Mornard VANDENDRESCHD, alias Frank JACSON, the convicted assassin of Lev Davidovich BRONSTEIN (Leon TROTSKY). Shortly after the receipt of the anonymous letter TARASOV departed Mexico for the Soviet Union and his functions, at least in the Altschuler case, were taken over by another Soviet intelligence official, possibly Pavel KLARIN, referred to in greater detail below, and later by Gregori KASPAROV, referred to above.

f. Pavel KLARIN. At the time the anonymous letter was received KLARIN, also known as Paul KLARIN and Pavel M. KLARIN, was Vice Consul assigned to the Consulate General, USSR, in New York City. The letter described him as an assistant to ZUBILIN, responsible for the operation of an extensive espionage net in the New York area. These allegations were substantiated by independent investigation. There appears no question but that KLARIN, during the period he spent in New York before proceeding to Mexico as an official of the Legation there in 1943 or 1944, was responsible for the New York ramifications of the Altschuler case. He has been identified almost without doubt as the writer of the Southbound secret writing letters in this operations.

g. Vassili D. MIRONOV. According to the anonymous letter this individual was a colonel of the NKVD and ZUBILIN's personal assistant and secretary in the Embassy. The letter stated that he also operated an espionage network which included "an important agent in the White House". MIRONOV's Embassy position and his close association with ZUBILIN were verified; however, independent investigation failed to substantiate the allegations concerning his espionage operations.

h. Sergevi G. LUKIANOV. LUKIANOV, an engineer with the Soviet Government Purchasing Commission also was listed in the letter as an assistant to ZUBILIN and as a Soviet Intelligence official actually operating agents. However, LUKIANOV departed from the U.S. for Vancouver, Canada, about the time of the receipt of the anonymous letter, and consequently it was impossible to substantiate the allegations of his espionage activities in the U.S. The Canadian authorities were not able to establish definitely his participation in Soviet espionage in Canada, although they did report that his activities were highly suspect and that he

20. *(Continued)*

assumed to himself on frequent occasions diplomatic prerequisites which were not in accordance with protocol or with his position as interpreted by the Canadian Department of External Affairs.

    i. VITALLI G. PAVLOV. This individual was described in the letter as Second Secretary of the Soviet Embassy in Ottowa, Canada, and, under the direction of ZUBILIN, responsible for NKVD operations in that country. It will be recalled that these allegations were completely substantiated in September 1945 by Igor Sergeievich GUZENKO, Red Army Intelligence code clerk who defected in Canada.

    j. Semen SEMENOV. SEMENOV was named in the letter as a Soviet Intelligence official and engineer representing the Soviet Government in the U.S. It was impossible to substantiate the allegations concerning SEMENOV.

    k. Vassili (?) DALGOV. DALGOV, also a Soviet engineer in the United States, was named by the writer of the anonymous letter as another assistant to ZUBILIN in his espionage operations. In his case, likewise, it was not possible to substantiate this allegation through independent investigation.

12. In connection with the anonymous letter, the pertinent contents of which are set out above, a number of observations appear of importance. Intensive efforts to identify the writer of this communication and/or the Russian language typewriter on which it was written proved completely fruitless, which was and is most unfortunate, since the writer of this letter obviously possessed both authentic and detailed knowledge of Soviet Intelligence operations in the U.S., at least as of 1943. The independent substantiation of so many of the allegations made in the letter, as reflected above, leaves absolutely no doubt as to its basic authenticity. Only one portion of the letter appears open to definite question, i.e., the allegation that Vassili Mikhailovich ZUBILIN and Elizabeta Yurevna ZUBILIN were betraying the Soviet Union, passing "dis-information" to their superiors and transmitting valid intelligence data to German and Japanese authorities through Boris MORROS. As noted above, intensive efforts to substantiate this part of the letter were made without result, and in addition it was not possible to establish the existence of any channel whereby MORROS or the ZUBILINS, through other intermediaries could have passed intelligence information during 1943 to Germany or Japan. Set out below is a possible explanation of the inclusion in this letter of these apparently false allegations, which explanation may have some validity, at least insofar as the motovation for including these statements existed in the mind of the writer of the letter.

13. From the language of the letter and the apparent important intelligence position of the writer thereof, it is believed that the writer was unable to take any personal action against ZUBILIN and his associates, either because of a hostage situation or because the writer felt that he could not safely complain, except anonymously, to U. S. authorities. Remembering that at the time of receipt of the

20. (Continued)

-8-

letter the Soviet Union and the U. S. were in the position of at least quasi-allies, it is believed probable that these allegations were included by the writer of the letter for the purpose of forcing the U. S. authorities to take action on the theory that perhaps no action would be taken against the diplomatic and official representatives of the Soviet Union mentioned in the letter unless some betrayal to the common enemy was alleged.

14. The possible motivation for the rest of the letter is more difficult to speculate upon. It is believed, however, that the letter was written by an officer, either of the Red Army Intelligence or of State Security, sufficiently highly placed to have a detailed knowledge of ZUBILIN's network. It is interesting to note that the letter gave personal characteristics and personal comments concerning each of the individuals mentioned, reflecting with little question that the writer was personally acquainted with the individuals he named. It is, of course, possible that the motivation for this letter stemmed from the writer's past participation in or knowledge of the NKVD purge of Red Army Intelligence in the middle and late 1930's.

15. In the summer of 1944 there began a general exodus of Soviet officials named in the anonymous letter and closely connected with ZUBILIN. The last of the individuals named in the letter to depart from the U. S. was SCHEVCHENKO, who did not finally depart until January 18, 1946. PAVLOV, it will be recalled, departed from Canada for the Soviet Union early in 1946 after the defection of Igor Sergeievich GUZENKO. It will also be recalled that this exodus was a direct result of the inspection conducted in the spring and summer of 1944 of NKGB and GRU facilities in the U. S. by two Soviet Intelligence inspectors, who, according to GUZENKO, represented both Red Army Intelligence and NKGB, and traveled under the guise of diplomatic couriers using the names Mikhail MILSKY and Gregori KOSSAREV. It is recalled further that KOSSAREV, who presumably was an NKGB inspector, has never been identified, but that GUZENKO identified MILSKY as a Colonel MILSHTEIN, Deputy Director of the North American section of Red Army Intelligence in Moscow.

16. ZUBILIN, himself, departed from the port of New York City for the Soviet Union on August 28, 1944, and at about the same time KHEIFETS, KLARIN, and several of the other individuals named also departed.

17. ZUBILIN's successor in the NKGB apparatus in the U. S. is believed to have been Anatoli Borisevich GROMOV, First Secretary of the Soviet Embassy in Washington, D.C., from the summer of 1944 until December 7, 1945, when he departed from the port of New York City ostensibly for the Soviet Union. It will be recalled that GROMOV was identified as the Soviet agent "Al" who was GREGORY's superior in the GREGORY case. Shortly after his departure from the U. S. it was ascertained that GROMOV was assigned as Counselor to the Soviet Embassy in Buenos Aires, Argentina, from where he departed, at least quasi-clandestinely, late in 1946. His present whereabouts are unknown and have been unknown since that time. It is interesting to note that investigation of GROMOV's contacts and activities did not

No, this was FBI Bur [illegible] BENTLEY

112

20. *(Continued)*

reflect his active personal participation in many of the operations ZUBILIN is known to have directed, although it is entirely possible that such implication may have existed inasmuch as GROMOV's full significance was not realized nor his full identity as "Al" ascertained until November 1945, approximately a month before he departed from the U. S.

18. In connection with this case further, it is interesting to note that in addition to his contacts with ZUBILIN, Steve NELSON was also in contact, at least in the spring of 1943, with what appeared to be a separate and distinct Soviet Intelligence operation headed by Peter IVANOV, at that time Secretary of the Soviet Consulate in San Francisco, California. NELSON, during the early months of 1943, made clandestine meets with IVANOV and, in addition, was responsible for putting IVANOV in touch with a number of Communist and pro-Communist professors directly or indirectly connected with the radiation laboratory at the University of California It will be recalled that this laboratory was one of the key installations of the DSM project. It is also known that during the early months of 1943 NELSON made attempts to procure information concerning this project from Party contacts employed therein. While it has never definitely been established, the speculation has been advanced that Peter IVANOV was a GRU official, whereas it will be recalled that ZUBILIN and his assistants were officials of the NKGB. It is interesting to note that the approaches used by IVANOV in his efforts to recruit agents to secure information concerning the DSM project very closely paralleled approaches known to have been made by Arthur Alexandrovich ADAMS, a highly important Soviet espionage agent definitely identified as working for Red Army Intelligence, who was intermittently active in the U. S. from 1919 to 1946. ADAMS was last active in the U. S. from 1938, when he entered this country on a fraudulent Canadian passport, until he disappeared in New York City late in January, 1946. IVANOV departed from the U. S. shortly after his series of contacts with NELSON, and his present whereabouts are not known. The full scope of IVANOV's activities and operations was never definitely ascertained.

19. In 1945 Steve NELSON was made a member of the National Board of the National Committee of the CPUSA, which required, under Party rules, his moving to the vicinity of New York City. In the fall of 1945 NELSON proceeded to New York where he became a full time official at Party Headquarters, 35 East 12th Street, assuming, in addition to his membership on the National Board, the position of Director of Foreign Nationality Group work for the Party. Since that time NELSON has made a number of highly suspicious contacts, but there has been little definite indication of operational espionage on his part. However, he has been in frequent contact with individuals highly suspect as Soviet espionage agents, including a number of visiting Polish and Yugoslav officials whose intelligence significane is open to little question. In addition he has continued his interest in Communist seaman courier routes.

20. By the time of NELSON's move to New York, at least the form in which this Soviet espionage parallel existed in the Spring of 1943 appears to have materially changed and its present form is unknown.

20. *(Continued)*

-10-

21. Through the investigation of the COMRAP case, in addition to the large number of individuals identified as major participants, many others were involved as strongly suspect Soviet agents. Very briefly, there are set out below the identities of a number of these individuals.

Max and Grace GRANICH. These two individuals, husband and wife, who have long been active in Communist and Communist Front Circles in the New York area, were identified as mail drops used in the operation of this parallel by NELSON and BONMAN. Both of them have been active in the past in the Far East and have maintained an intense interest in Far Eastern affairs. In 1947 they moved to a farm in New England, and are known to have expressed to associates a desire to return to China at some time in the future. During 1943 and 1944 the GRANICH's were receiving mail from Madame Sun Yat Sen containing conspiratorial messages and signed by her with the cover name "Suzy". It is noted that one of these letters to the GRANICH's mentioned the return to the U. S. of John S. SERVICE, State Department official implicated in the illegal disclosure of classified documents in connection with the Philip Jacob JAFFE case and strongly suspect, in that connection, of working for Soviet Intelligence. Madame Sun Yat Sen's letter mentioned SERVICE as a "reliable individual" who "thinks as we do".

In the summer of 1945 three Chinese Communist delegates to the United Nations Conference in San Francisco visited Max and Grace GRANICH in New York and were almost immediately escorted by Grace GRANICH to an apartment in lower Manhattan, subsequently identified as occupied by Aube TZERKO, a concert pianist, born in Canada under the name of Abraham KOTZER. TZERKO became of extreme interest in February 1946, when he was contacted by Sam CARR (real name Schmil KOGAN). It will be recalled that CARR was one of the principal recruiting agents in the GRU espionage ring operated in Canada by Colonel Nikolai ZABOTIN from the summer of 1943 until the fall of 1945. At the time he contacted TZERKO in February, CARR was enroute back to Canada from Havana, Cuba, where as a fraternal delegate of the Canadian Communist Party of Canada) he had attended a National Congress of the Cuban Communist Party. Subsequent investigation reflected that TZERKO and CARR have been close associates and there appears little question but that TZERKO was involved in the disappearance in Canada of Sam CARR in April 1946. It was never possible to ascertain the exact significance of the visit to TZERKO's apartment by the three important Chinese Communists attending the UNCIO.

Alexander BITTELMAN (real name Uschur BITTELMACHER). BITTELMAN was drawn into the COMRAP case through his close and frequent contacts with the principal figures therein and it was strongly indicated by the investigation that he was at least indirectly connected with the activities of this net. BITTELMAN, who was born in Russia, and whose deportation was requested very recently by the Department of Justice, has long been an important national functionary of the CPUSA. He has interested himself particularly in Party organization and propaganda among the Jewish minority elements and he is considered by many Party leaders to be the

20. (Continued)

foremost Marxist, Leninist, Stalinist dialectician in the Party. The exact extent of BITTELMAN's intelligence activities has never definitely been ascertained.

Alexander TRACHTENBERG. TRACHTENBERG, a member of the National Committee of the Party, is the director of International Publishers, most important of the Communist Party publishing firms. TRACHTENBERG figured in the COMRAP investigation through his intimate association with many of the other subjects thereof. Collaterally, it was ascertained that he was in close contact with a number of other strongly suspect Soviet agents, not implicated, so far as is known in this case, but definitely implicated in other Soviet espionage operations. Of particular interest in this regard is TRACHTENBERG's association with Joseph Milton BERNSTEIN, alias Joe BERNSTEIN, alias Joe B., alias Joe BURSLEY, alias Joe BURSLER BERNSTEIN, a minor Party figure for many years, has been closely connected with a number of individuals who have figured in the GREGORY case, involving, it will be recalled, the operation of extensive Soviet espionage parallels centered in agencies of the U. S. Government. In addition, BERNSTEIN appears identical with an individual known to have been described by Philip Jacob JAFFE as an important Soviet espionage agent. There is good reason to believe, on the basis of certain correspondence between subjects in the GREGORY case referring to BERNSTEIN, that at least for several years during World War II BERNSTEIN may have been operating a Soviet espionage parallel in Washington, D.C., identical with the so-called Third Parallel referred to by GREGORY about which GREGORY knew practically nothing.

21. George M. Elsey, Memorandum for Mr. [Clark M.] Clifford, 16 August 1948.

THE WHITE HOUSE
WASHINGTON

August 16, 1948

Memorandum for Mr. Clifford:

The following represents the consensus of opinion at our meeting this morning with the Attorney General and Mr. Peyton Ford:

(1) The President should not at this time make a statement regarding "spies" along the lines proposed by Mr. Spingarn.

(2) Attention will be given by Justice to the possibility and desirability of referring the question of Soviet espionage in the Federal Government to a bi-partisan commission, such as the Hoover Commission.

(3) Justice should make every effort to ascertain if Whittaker Chambers is guilty of perjury.

(3A) *Investigation of Chambers confinement in mental institution.*

(4) The Attorney General will furnish the White House with a description of the data Miss Bentley claims to have obtained for Soviet agents during the war, and the White House should endeavor to determine how much of this information was freely available to the Soviet Government through routine official liaison between the U.S. and the U.S.S.R. The purpose of this would be to make it clear that Miss Bentley was not successful in transmitting secret material to the Russians that they did not already have.

(5) The White House should ascertain the facts concerning the retention of Mr. Remington in OWMR, his transfer to the Council of Economic Advisers and his subsequent transfer to the Department of Commerce.

GEORGE M. ELSEY

22. [Harry S. Truman] to the Attorney General, 16 December 1948.

The President

THE WHITE HOUSE
WASHINGTON

December 16, 1948

Memorandum for: Attorney General

From: The President

I wonder if we could not get a statement of facts from the FBI about the meddling of the House Un-American Activities Committee and how they dried up sources of information which would have been accessible in the prosecution of spies and communists.

Their meddling efforts were in fact a "red herring" to detract attention not only from the shortcomings of the 80th Congress but also contributed to the escape of certain communists who should have been indicted.

I'll appreciate it if you will look into this a little bit and we will talk it over at the Cabinet meeting tomorrow.

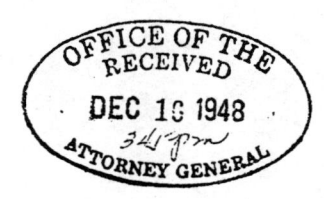

HST

23. D. M. Ladd, Memorandum to the Director [J. Edgar Hoover], "JAY DAVID WHITTAKER CHAMBERS," 29 December 1948.

Office Memorandum • UNITED STATES GOVERNMENT

TO : The Director

FROM : D. M. Ladd

SUBJECT : JAY DAVID WHITTAKER CHAMBERS, with aliases; et al; PERJURY ESPIONAGE - R

DATE: December 29, 1948

Reference is made to my memorandum to you dated December 14, 1948, in which you were advised that the notes of Mr. Adolf Berle concerning his interview with Whittaker Chambers were turned over to the Bureau in June of 1943. You attached a routing slip to my memorandum and inquired, "Do I understand correctly that Chambers talked to Berle in 1939; we interviewed him first in May 1942; and Berle gave us information first in June 1943? How did we come to contact Chambers in 1942 and did we take any investigative action then? What did we do in the year from May 1942 to June 1943 about the data received from Chambers? H."

You subsequently inquired by phone on December 27 as to why we did not interview Chambers sooner than May 13, 1942.

The following sets forth in chronological order the various investigative steps taken by the Bureau.

The Bureau's first reference to Whittaker Chambers appeared in a pamphlet published in 1932 by International Pamphlets, 799 Broadway, New York. (61-7562-Sub 2-161) This pamphlet is a reprint of a short story by Whittaker Chambers entitled "Can You Hear Their Voices? - The Arkansas Farmers' Fight For Food" which was first published in the "New Masses" for March, 1931. This item was referred to by a Miss Hazel Huffman of the Federal Theater Project in New York City in testimony before the Special Committee on Un-American Activities (Dies Committee) on August 19, 1938. (61-7582, Volume 1, page 778)

The New York Office of the Bureau on October 18, 1940, submitted the original report of Confidential Informant Bob M dated September 16, 1940, advising that Ludwig Lore, a former member of the Communist Party and likewise a contact of this Bureau, had told Bob M about an unidentified individual who had been a high officer in the GPU for eight years abroad and seven years in this country. (There was nothing at this time to identify the individual referred to by Lore as Whittaker Chambers.)

By letter dated November 13, 1940, the Bureau instructed the New York Office to make every effort to determine the identity of this unidentified individual for the purpose of securing whatever information he had in his possession (61-7566-1977; 100-25824-1)

23. *(Continued)*

Memorandum to the Director

On February 28, 1941, Mr. Adolf Berle of the Department of State requested someone from the Bureau to contact him regarding Chambers. On March 1, 1941, Mr. Rosen advised Mr. Berle's secretary that it was his understanding that Mr. Carson and Mr. Foxworth of the Bureau had an appointment with Mr. Berle. (100-25824-1X)

At this time there was a nationalistic tendency card filed in the Bureau indices which indicated that Whittaker Chambers was alleged to be a Communist and formerly a member of the IWW, also former staff editor of the "Daily Worker" and contributing editor of "New Masses."

On March 3, 1941, Mr. Foxworth in a memorandum to you made reference to his conversation with you that date concerning Whittaker Chambers. Reference was made to the aforementioned nationalistic tendency card and Foxworth stated, "We are not conducting any investigation and I have accordingly informed Mr. Berle." (100-25824-1X1)

On March 10, 1941, Mr. Berle telephonically advised Mr. Foxworth that he was afraid that the Russian agencies were looking for Whittaker Chambers. This matter was not followed up and the memorandum concerning it was merely filed. (100-25824-1X2) (This is the memorandum which was referred to in the memorandum to you from Assistant Director L. B. Nichols dated September 1, 1948, which prompted the memorandum to all Assistant Directors bringing to the attention of Supervisory personnel the significance of initialing communications.)
(100-25824-52) (ATTACHED)

Information was received on April 29, 1941, from Confidential Informant Victor Riesel, then assistant editor of "New Leader" newspaper, that Whittaker Chambers, a former member of the Communist Party, was then a motion picture reviewer for "Time," "Life" and "Fortune" magazines and was at that time (1941) strongly anti-Communist. (100-5740-5)

On May 9, 1941, the New York Office reported an interview with Mr. Ludwig Lore on May 8, 1941, pursuant to the Bureau instructions of November 13, 1940. Lore declined to furnish the name of the unknown former GPU agent and stated that he had been advised that this man's case had been discussed with the Director of the FBI some six or seven months previous by an intermediary who had suggested that the former GPU agent wanted some sort of immunity guarantee before exposing himself and that the Director had stated that no such agreement could be entered into. Lore also alleged that this former GPU agent had delivered to the President of the United States through a trusted friend who had the necessary

- 2 -

23. *(Continued)*

Memorandum to the Director

contact a list of persons in the Government who were Communists or pro-Soviet and that this list had been on the President's desk for several weeks but nothing had been done about it. (100-25824-2)

The New York Office was advised on May 16, 1941, that you had no recollection of ever having been approached by any intermediary who discussed some type of immunity guarantee which could be given to an agent of the GPU if he were willing to expose himself. The New York Office was instructed to obtain from Ludwig Lore the identity of the former GPU agent. (100-25824-2)

On <u>August 3, 1941</u>, the New York Office advised that <u>Ludwig Lore had identified the individual to whom he had referred as Whittaker Chambers, an associate editor of "Time" magazine.</u> (100-25824-5)

On <u>August 18, 1941</u>, Assistant Director E. J. Connelley in New York was <u>instructed to institute a detailed investigation regarding Chambers</u> to determine his character, background, activities and affiliations in a highly discreet and tactful manner. At the completion of the investigation the feasibility of openly interviewing Chambers would be considered. (100-25824-6)

During the conduct of this investigation Mr. Will Allen of the "Washington Daily News" contacted Assistant Director L. B. Nichols during October 1941 and advised that Ludwig Lore, a former Communist in New York City, knew an individual familiar with OGPU activities whom Allen subsequently contacted. Allen obtained from this person the names of three alleged OGPU agents - Hyman Kalodny, Helen Kalodny and Sophie Menken. Investigation was immediately instituted by the Bureau on the three individuals named. (100-25824-18)

Allen was again interviewed by a representative of the Washington Field Office on November 28, 1941, but stated that he could not under any circumstances divulge the identity of his informant in New York City. Allen was again interviewed by Assistant Director Nichols on January 28, 1942, at which time he stated that his informant's initials were W.C. (obviously Whittaker Chambers) (100-25824-19)

On February 11, 1942, the New York Office advised that Ludwig Lore did not introduce Allen to Chambers, but Lore claimed that Allen had been introduced to Chambers by Isaac Don Levine. (100-25824-20)

- 3 -

23. *(Continued)*

Memorandum to the Director

The logical leads in the investigation into the background of Whittaker Chambers having been completed, the New York Office advised the Bureau on March 4, 1942, that an effort would be made to interview Chambers. In this regard a follow-up letter was sent to New York on April 30, 1942.(100-25824-21)

It will be noted that there was an investigative delay from August 18, 1941 until March 4, 1942, in conducting the necessary investigation into the background and activities of Chambers for the purpose of laying the proper predication for an interview. The Field was followed by the Bureau on this matter in October, November and December, 1941, and in January, 1942, as new information was received or investigative suggestions made. (100-25824-8, 13, 15, 16, 17, 18, 19)

It is possible that this investigative delinquency was a reflection of the general investigative delinquency in the Field during the period immediately prior to and subsequent to Pearl Harbor.

Chambers was interviewed by Special Agents John R. Paul and E. J. Greenwald, Jr. of the New York Office on May 13, 1942, the results being transmitted to the Bureau by letter on May 14, 1942. Chambers advised that he had given all of the information which was in his possession to Mr. A. A. Berle of the State Department in Washington, D. C., in September, 1939, and before discussing any of the matters with the Agents put through a long distance call to Mr. Berle at the latter's home.

Chambers advised Berle in the presence of the Agents that there were present in his office two FBI Agents who wished to secure the information that he, Chambers, had given to Berle and asked if this would be all right. Apparently Berle was in accord for Chambers thanked him and thereafter supplied considerable information which he indicated had been furnished previously to Mr. Berle in September, 1939. (100-25824-22)

During the course of this interview Chambers denied that he was directly connected with the OGPU and stated that he was in the underground movement of the Communist Party, USA as a kind of "morale officer" to guide recruits in the Party's policy. He denied that he had ever been to the USSR. (In this regard the investigation conducted by the Bureau prior to the interview failed to disclose any indications of travel by Chambers to or residence in the USSR as originally alleged by Ludwig Lore, who you will recall died shortly after the conclusion of this investigation, and so was not available to recheck allegations made by him concerning Chambers.) (100-25824-22)

- 4 -

23. *(Continued)*

Memorandum to the Director

As will be seen from the foregoing, the first knowledge the Bureau had that Chambers had been interviewed by Adolf Berle on September 2, 1939, in Washington, D. C., came to us as a result of our interview with Chambers May 13, 1942. You will recall in connection with this matter SAC Carson was brought up from Miami to interview Berle on September 3, 1948, regarding the latter's testimony before the House Un-American Activities Committee in order to clarify the ambiguities in Berle's testimony and to cause a correction in the inference left by Berle's testimony that he had advised the FBI in 1939 of Chambers' allegations. Mr. Berle advised SAC Carson that his recollection being refreshed, he could state that he does not recall or have any record of any prior conversation with the FBI prior to March, 1941, concerning Chambers and that he does not recall having furnished to the FBI in 1941 any information concerning Chambers' interview with him. Mr. Berle advised SAC Carson on September 3, 1948, that in 1939 (and by inference in 1941 as well) he did not feel free to divulge the content of Chambers' conversation to the FBI inasmuch as Chambers had indicated that he did not so desire and had further indicated that he would not back up the story and also did not desire the information furnished to the FBI, particularly if the source was to be revealed. (100-25824-50)

The Bureau may have been delinquent in not contacting Mr. Berle immediately upon the conclusion of the Chambers interview regarding the data which Chambers had furnished the Bureau and to Berle, in order to make sure that it was the same. However, Chambers when interviewed on May 13, 1942, had indicated that what he was furnishing to the Bureau at that time was the substance of what he had given to Mr. Berle in September, 1939.

An analysis of the Bureau's action with regard to individuals mentioned by Chambers in the 1942 interview shows that 21 persons were already subjects of Bureau investigations, as well as two organizations, namely, Amtorg Trading Corporation and Tass News Agency. On five other persons, investigations were instituted on the basis of Chambers' allegations. These persons were: Azimov; Harry Kweit, with aliases; Paul Massing; Hedi Massing; and Helen Ware (Cappel). Two individuals, Ralph Bowman and Margaret Browder, became the subjects of investigation at a later date on the basis of information developed through other sources, data furnished by Chambers in each instance already appearing in the Bureau files. With regard to Bowman, it was noted that he was established to be identical with the person mentioned by Chambers as Rudy Baker but Chambers was never able to identify Bowman's photograph as Baker.

Regarding those individuals mentioned by Chambers, concerning whom no investigative action was undertaken, Mrs. Lila Field and Harold Ware were

- 5 -

23. *(Continued)*

Memorandum to the Director

dead and the Bureau files contained considerable information regarding Ware. Gertrude Schilbach, a German Communist involved in the murder of Ignace Reiss in Switzerland, was not indicated to be in the United States. Isidore Miller was not alleged to be either a Communist or an espionage agent. The circumstances regarding the disappearance of Juliet Poyntz were generally known to the Bureau and Chambers' suspicions contributed nothing to the picture at that time. Chambers mentioned one Post who "was obtained from the underground movement of the Party" and, according to Chambers, became a co-editor of a State Department publication. He has subsequently been identified as Richard Howell Post, a State Department employee and a Loyalty investigation has been conducted concerning him. Chambers mentioned an unnamed individual "connected" with the Communist underground who was in the Trade Agreement Section of the State Department. This person has been identified as Henry Julian Wadleigh, who was formerly employed by the State Department and who was recently interviewed in connection with the most current allegations of Chambers. As to the latter two individuals, Chambers' statements with regard to them were less positive than as to other persons and he did not state in unequivocal language that they were Party members at the time he left the movement in 1938, as he did in the cases of many of the individuals discussed.

It should be noted that subsequent to the Chambers interview on May 13, 1942, Bureau files on numerous individuals were reviewed, certain investigations were opened, and efforts were made to identify persons named by Chambers, the principal one of which was his superior "Peter." In a report dated December 1, 1942, in the Chambers file, the New York Office identified "Peter," the reputed head of the underground movement of the Communist Party, as J. Peters, author of "The Communist Party, A Manual of Organization." (100-25824-25)

Whittaker Chambers meanwhile had been bedridden with angina pectoris from November, 1942 until March 5, 1943, when Agents of this Bureau were able to interview him for a period of five minutes. At this time Chambers identified a photograph of Alexander Stevens, with aliases, as "Peter" his superior in the Communist Party underground. (100-184255-67)

Thereafter, the desirability of determining whether the information furnished to Mr. Berle was identical with that furnished to the Bureau by Chambers became apparent and subsequent to Mr. Berle's recovery from an illness which had afflicted him in May, 1943 (94-4-3869-8) the Liaison Section of the Bureau obtained Mr. Berle's notes of the 1939 interview, which were very

- 6 -

23. *(Continued)*

Memorandum to the Director

sketchy and disjointed <u>in June, 1943</u>. Copies of these notes were placed in the Whittaker Chambers file. (100-25824-27)

The Bureau was probably delinquent in not pressing Mr. Berle in June, 1943, for any independent recollection which he might have had to explain or clarify the ambiguities in his notes, although it is probable that Mr. Berle not having reduced these notes to a memorandum would have been unable to contribute materially to the matters under investigation after a lapse of almost four years since the date of his interview with Chambers.

<u>DELINQUENCIES NOTED</u>

1. The Bureau did not press Mr. Berle for information which he might have had concerning Whittaker Chambers at the time he made his inquiry in March, 1941, concerning the Bureau's possible interest in Chambers. The files do not indicate a definite explanation, but if one exists it might be that the Bureau did not feel that it was desirable to press the Assistant Secretary of State for information which he did not see fit to volunteer concerning a subject which had been raised by him.

2. There was an investigative delinquency in the period required for investigation of the background and activities of Whittaker Chambers from August 18, 1941 to March 4, 1942. An explanation, if such exists, might be the general investigative delinquency in the Field immediately prior to and subsequent to Pearl Harbor.

3. The Bureau was probably delinquent in not contacting Mr. Berle immediately upon the conclusion of our interview with Whittaker Chambers on May 13, 1942, to determine the substance of the information which had been furnished by Chambers to Berle in 1939. The Bureau <u>waited until June, 1943</u> to obtain Berle's notes concerning the interview. The only possible explanation for this delinquency was that Chambers' telephone conversation with Berle and his interview with the Agents indicated that he was furnishing the Bureau in May, 1942, the substance of what he had given to Berle in 1939.

4. The Bureau was probably delinquent in not pressing Mr. Berle in June, 1943, at the time his notes were obtained, for any independent recollection which he might have had of the 1939 conversation in addition to the

- 7 -

23. *(Continued)*

Memorandum to the Director

notes. The Bureau files do not indicate what if anything Mr. Berle said at the time the notes were obtained by the Bureau, but it is doubtful that he would have been able to contribute materially to a clarification of the notes in 1943 after a lapse of almost four years from the date of his original interview with Chambers.

Attachment

Of course hind-sight is better than fore-sight but we should learn from this incident & not have any recurrence in other cases & situations.

H.

- 8 -

24. Tom C. Clark, Memorandum for the President, "Proposed Deportation of Valentine A. Gubitchev," 16 March 1949.

Office of the Attorney General
Washington, D.C.

March 16, 1949.

Filed 3-28-49.

MEMORANDUM FOR THE PRESIDENT

Re: Proposed deportation of Valentine A. Gubitchev

As you know, Valentine A. Gubitchev and Judith Coplon have been jointly indicted in New York City for violation of the espionage laws.

Gubitchev was an ordinary employee of the United Nations, not entitled to diplomatic immunity. Coplon was an employee in the Alien Registration Section of the Criminal Division of the Department of Justice.

This charge is one of conspiracy between the defendants to secure and deliver to a foreign government secret papers of the Department of Justice concerning national defense. The charges carry possible penalties against Coplon of a total of 35 years imprisonment, on all counts; against Gubitchev, 15 years.

The case is due to be tried in the lower court within 30 to 45 days.

On March 16 Coplon was indicted alone in Washington, D. C., on a charge of violating the espionage laws and removal of certain records of the Department of Justice, carrying on the first count a possible penalty of 10 years, and on the second of 3 years. This case should be tried in 90 days.

In view of the recommendation of the State Department, a copy of which is attached hereto, that Gubitchev be deported to Russia rather than stand trial with Miss Coplon, I desire to submit the following reasons why I think that Gubitchev should be retained in the United States at least until after the trial of the New York case, for the following reasons:

1. Successful prosecution depends on his presence, for he is one of the principals of the case and his absence affords vast opportunities to Coplon in her defense.

DECLASSIFIED
E.O. 12356, Sec. 3.4
Authority 89-3
By CB NLT Date 4/2/91

24. (Continued)

- 2 -

2. Coplon has pleaded innocent and in the event we deport Gubitchev she will claim it was done to prevent her from having his testimony in defense.

3. The jury would be adversely affected by the <u>prosecution</u> of this young woman alone. The absence of Gubitchev would, of course, be known to the jury and <u>persecution</u> against Coplon would be charged.

4. The deportation of Gubitchev would undoubtedly cause many to think and say that the Department of Justice never had an espionage case against him and never intended to prosecute the case to its conclusion.

5. The public reaction to immediate deportation before trial would, in my opinion, be extremely unfavorable. If Gubitchev were deported the result would be that an American citizen would remain to face possible conviction and imprisonment with the alien Russian being excused from even the embarrassment of a public trial.

I cannot, of course, substitute my opinion for that of the State Department in matters of foreign relations. I only wish to state my view of the problems presented.

The Secretary of State has asked that I advise him of the decision in this matter by Friday morning. I have furnished him a copy of this memorandum.

Another alternative exists, i.e., to prosecute Gubitchev and then permit his deportation to Russia. In this event I am advised by the Secretary of State that this decision could not be made known until the conclusion of the prosecution. However, it might be possible to inform the Russian Government that Gubitchev will have to remain in this country for the trial but that the consideration of his ultimate deportation after trial would remain open.

It is my considered recommendation that I be authorized to proceed with the trial of Gubitchev without delay, reserving until a later time the question of deportation.

Respectfully,

Tom Clark
Attorney General.

25. [Robert J. Lamphere to Gardner], "FLORA DON WOVSCHIN, With Alias," 9 May 1949.

~~TOP SECRET~~ GLINT

49-005

May 9, 1949

FLORA DON WOVSCHIN, with alias

In connection with the investigation to identify Zora, the person who recruited Judith Coplon and Marion Davis Berdecio in the Fall of 1944 as Soviet espionage agents, an identification has been made which indicates that Zora is identical with Flora Don Wovschin.

Miss Wovschin was born February 20, 1923, at New York City. Her mother, Miss Maria Wicher, and her stepfather, Enos Regnet Wicher, presently reside at 229 East 79th Street, New York City. He is a professor at Columbia University. Mrs. Maria Wicher was born in Russia and became a citizen of the United States in 1922. Flora Don Wovschin's father, Dr. William A. Wovschin (deceased), was born in Russia and became a citizen of the United States in 1914.

Miss Wovschin attended the University of Wisconsin, Columbia University, and received her degree at Barnard College. While at Barnard she was active in the American Students Union and was possibly a member of the American Youth for Democracy. She was acquainted with both Judith Coplon and Marion Davis Berdecio while at Barnard. She was employed by OWI from September 9, 1943, to February 20, 1945, when she transferred to the State Department. She stayed at the State Department until September 20, 1945, when she resigned. Her mother and stepfather reportedly were very active in the Communist movement when they resided in the State of Wisconsin.

We have recently received information to the effect that Flora Don Wovschin went to Russia several years ago, after renouncing her American citizenship, and in Russia she married a Soviet engineer. It is reported that she is unhappy at the present time and would like to return to the United States.

On 9 Sept 1954 Lamphere stated Wovschin was reported to have died serving as a nurse in North Korea.

DECLASSIFIED BY SP2CLLGW
ON 7-30-96

~~TOP SECRET~~ GLINT

26. Sidney W. Souers, Memorandum for the President, 22 March 1949.

NATIONAL SECURITY COUNCIL
WASHINGTON

March 22, 1949

MEMORANDUM FOR THE PRESIDENT:

At its 36th Meeting, the National Security Council, including the Secretary of the Treasury and a representative of the Attorney General for this matter, agreed, subject to a dissent by the Secretary of the Army, to recommend that you approve the enclosed draft directive on coordination of internal security (NSC 17/4).

The reasons for the dissent by the Secretary of the Army are stated in the enclosed memorandum dated March 21, 1949.

SIDNEY W. SOUERS
Executive Secretary

APPROVED:

[Signed] Harry S. Truman
HARRY S. TRUMAN

Date: March 23, 1949

26. *(Continued)*

~~CONFIDENTIAL~~   The President

NSC 17/4   COPY NO. 1

A REPORT

TO THE

PRESIDENT

BY THE

NATIONAL SECURITY COUNCIL

on

INTERNAL SECURITY

DECLASSIFIED
E. O. 11652, Sec. 3(E) and 5(D) or (E)
NSC MEMO 5-4-49
By NLT-WC____, NARS Date 11-5-75

March 22, 1949

WASHINGTON

~~CONFIDENTIAL~~

26. *(Continued)*

NSC 17/4 CONFIDENTIAL

March 22, 1949

NOTE BY THE EXECUTIVE SECRETARY

on

INTERNAL SECURITY

References: A. NSC 17/3
             B. Memos for National Security
                Council from Executive
                Secretary, same subject,
                dated November 26, 1948,
                March 3, and March 21, 1949

At its 36th Meeting, the National Security Council considered the references and agreed, subject to a dissent by the Secretary of the Army, to recommend to the President that he approve the proposed directive enclosed herewith. The reasons for the dissent by the Secretary of the Army are stated in the Reference memo dated March 21, 1949.

Subject to the approval by the President of the above recommendations, the National Security Council also directed the NSC representative on Internal Security to arrange for the prompt study of the points outlined by the Secretary of the Army in the reference memo dated March 21, 1949, and to submit for Council consideration such recommendations with respect thereto as are deemed appropriate.

SIDNEY W. SOUERS
Executive Secretary

Distribution:
 The President
 The Secretary of State
 The Secretary of the Treasury
 The Secretary of Defense
 The Attorney General
 The Secretary of the Army
 The Secretary of the Navy
 The Secretary of the Air Force
 The Chairman, National Security
   Resources Board

CONFIDENTIAL

26. *(Continued)*

March 22, 1949 ~~CONFIDENTIAL~~

D R A F T

NATIONAL SECURITY COUNCIL DIRECTIVE

1. There is hereby established under the National Security Council, pursuant to the provisions of Section 101 of the National Security Act, the following arrangements for the purpose of effecting more adequate and coordinated internal security.

2. The following two permanent committees, together with such secretariat as may be required, shall be responsible for coordinating internal security.

    a. The Interdepartmental Intelligence Conference (IIC) is responsible for the coordination of the investigation of all domestic espionage, counter-espionage, sabotage, subversion and other related intelligence matters affecting internal security. It consists of the Director of the Federal Bureau of Investigation, Department of Justice; Chief of the Office of Naval Intelligence, Department of the Navy; Director of the Intelligence Division, Department of the Army; and the Director of the Office of Special Investigations, Department of the Air Force.

    b. The Interdepartmental Committee on Internal Security (ICIS) is hereby created and shall be

NSC 17/4   1.   ~~CONFIDENTIAL~~

26. *(Continued)*

responsible for coordinating all phases of the internal security field other than the functions outlined in paragraph 2-a above. It shall be composed of representatives from the Departments of State, Treasury, and Justice and the National Military Establishment.

3. Both Committees shall invite non-member agency representatives as ad hoc members thereof when matters involving their responsibilities are under consideration.

4. In accordance with arrangements to be determined in each case, there shall be transferred to the IIC and the ICIS for incorporation as subcommittees or for the absorption of their functions such existing committees as are operating in their respective fields of responsibility. The two committees shall also establish such new subcommittees as will assist them in carrying out their responsibilities.

5. The IIC and the ICIS will, whenever appropriate, hold joint meetings or establish joint subcommittees.

6. The National Security Council shall designate a representative who, under the direction of the Executive Secretary of the NSC, shall:

    a. Assist and advise the NSC in coordinating the activities of the IIC and the ICIS;

    b. Assist and advise the IIC and the ICIS in carrying out their respective responsibilities and in collaborating on problems of common interest;

    c. Submit to the IIC or the ICIS questions which, in his opinion, require their consideration;

26. *(Continued)*

CONFIDENTIAL

<u>d</u>. As representative of the NSC, participate as an observer and advisor in all meetings of the IIC and the ICIS;

<u>e</u>. Submit for consideration by the NSC problems which cannot be resolved by either the IIC or the ICIS or by the two committees acting together, outlining any divergent solutions which have been proposed and his own recommendations;

<u>f</u>. Report to the National Security Council from time to time, at least quarterly, on progress being made for the provision of adequate internal security;

<u>g</u>. Have no powers of instruction, direction or supervision over either the IIC or the ICIS.

7. The IIC and the ICIS shall prepare and submit for consideration and approval by the National Security Council proposed charters for the IIC and the ICIS respectively. The Department of Justice representative shall serve as the Chairman of the ICIS for this purpose. The Executive Secretary of the National Security Council shall assist the IIC and the ICIS in coordinating the preparation of the proposed charters. These charters shall define, in accordance with the foregoing, the respective functions and responsibilities of the committees and shall provide for their chairmanship and staff.

NSC 17/4   3   CONFIDENTIAL

27. [Lamphere to Gardner], "Anatoli Borisovich Gromov," 12 July 1949.

~~TOP SECRET~~ COPSE

49-018

✓

ANATOLI BORISOVICH GROMOV

It appears that Bademus (Vadim) is identical with Anatoli Borisovich Gromov. He arrived in the United States on September 15, 1944. He was designated as First Secretary of the Soviet Embassy in Washington, D. C. The early mention in the material of Bademus on July 25, 1944, is not inconsistent inasmuch as it is indicated therein that Bademus was not in the United States at that time. Identifying data concerning Gromov has previously been made available to you.

~~TOP SECRET~~ COPSE

28. [Lamphere to Gardner], "EMIL JULIUS KLAUS FUCHS, a.k.a. Karl Fuchs," 26 September 1949.

~~TOP SECRET~~ COPSE

September 26, 1949

EMIL JULIUS KLAUS FUCHS, aka;
Karl Fuchs

REST

On June 15, 1944, Rest furnished to a representative of Soviet Intelligence (M.G.B.), Part III of a document now identified as MSN-12. This document dated June 6, 1944 is on file with the Atomic Energy Commission and is entitled "Fluctuations and the Efficiency of a Diffusion Plant", and Part III specifically refers to "The Effect of Fluctuations in the Flow of N_2." The designation MSN stands for documents prepared by British scientists who were in New York City working on Atomic Energy research. The author of this document is K. Fuchs, who is actually Emil Julius Klaus Fuchs, who is usually known as Karl Fuchs. He is a top ranking British Atomic scientist.

Information available concerning Rest indicated that he was a British scientist, inasmuch as he had also furnished to the Soviet Intelligence information concerning British participation in the Atomic Energy development. It was also indicated that he had a sister in the United States. There are indications that Rest was actually the author of the document.

Emil Julius Klaus Fuchs also known as Karl Fuchs, was born December 29, 1911, at Russelsheim, Germany. His father, Emil Fuchs was born May 13, 1874, and was a professor in Germany. Emil Julius Klaus Fuchs entered the United Kingdom in 1933, and from 1941 to 1943, was a medical physicist at the University of Birmingham, England. In November 1943, he was designated by the British Government to come to the United States as a part of the British Atomic Energy Commission. He arrived at New York City on December 3, 1943, and went to Los Alamos or ~~to Oak Ridge~~, Tennessee in August 1944. While in the United States, Fuchs worked with a group of British scientists in the period of March to June 1944, on the development of diffusional operational processes working particularly with the Kellex Corporation, which was working under the Manhattan

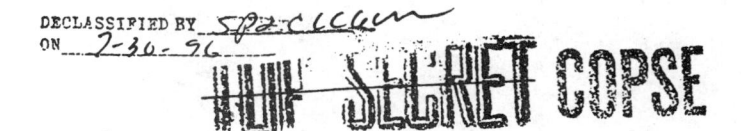

~~TOP SECRET~~ COPSE

28. *(Continued)*

~~TOP SECRET~~ CORSE

Engineering District. Fuchs left for England from Montreal, Canada on June 28, 1946.

In November 1947, Fuchs was back in the United States and visited the Chicago Operations Office of the Atomic Energy Commission. At that time, he attended discussions regarding unclassified and declassified aspects of neutron spectroscopy. He also participated in declassification conferences which were being held between the United States, Great Britain and Canada. Fuchs is presently the senior research worker at the Atomic Energy Commission project at Harell, England.

Fuchs has a sister, Kristel Fuchs Heineman, who prior to January 1941, resided at 55 Carver Road, Watertown, Massachusetts. From approximately 1941, until about 1945, she resided with her husband, Robert Block Heineman at 144 Lakeview Avenue, Cambridge, Massachusetts. They presently reside at 94 Lakeview Avenue, Cambridge, Massachusetts. Robert Block Heineman has been reliably reported as a member of the Communist Party, United States of America in 1947.

The address book of Israel Halperin implicated in the Canadian Espionage network contained the following: "Klaus Fuchs, Asst. to M. Born, 84 Grange Lane, University of Edinburgh, Scotland Camp (possibly comp) N.-Camp L., Internment Operations - Kristel Heineman, 55 Carvel Road, Watertown." The phrase Camp L is encircled.

In addition to the foregoing a captured German document prepared presumably by German Counter Intelligence and which relates to Communist Party members in Germany contains the following:

"Klaus Fuchs, student of philosophy, December 29, 1911, Russelsheim, RSHA-IVA2, Gestapo Field Office Kiel.

"Gerhard Fuchs, October 30, 1909, Russelsheim, student RSHA-IVA2, Gestapo Field Office Kiel."

It is to be noted that Gerhard Fuchs is the brother of Emil Julius Klaus Fuchs.

GUS (GCCSE)

In connection with Rest, who furnished the document MSN-12 and who

~~TOP SECRET~~ CORSE

- 2 -

28. *(Continued)*

TOP SECRET COPSE

is thought to be Emil Julius Klaus Fuchs, it is also known that Rest's sister was a contact of Gus (Goose), who has presumably a scientific background. You will recall, Gus contemplated preparing a work on the production method with respect to the thermal diffusion of gases.

You will also recall, Gus, who has not been identified was also a contact of Abraham Brothman, a Consulting Engineer in New York City, who furnished espionage information to Elizabeth Bentley in 1940.

It is thought that Gus may possibly be identical with Arthur Phineas Weber, who is presently an employee of the Kellex Corporation which is engaged in work under the Atomic Energy Commission. Weber was born March 10, 1920, in Brooklyn, New York and is a chemical engineer. From 1941 to 1942, he worked with Brothman for the Henderick Manufacturing Company. From June 1942 to July 1944, he worked with Brothman in the Chemurgy Design Corporation, and according to some information during a part of this period he was also working for the Kellex Corporation. Weber lists employment with Kellex Corporation as a chemical engineer from July 1944 to March 29, 1946, and again from April 8, 1946, to the present. It should be noted that the Kellex Corporation was closely working in 1944 with the British Scientist group which included Fuchs.

HEILIG

With respect to No. 1390 of October 1, 1944, the Heilig mentioned is believed to be Theodore Heilig, who was born August 6, 1897 in Jersey City, New Jersey and resides at 128 West Walnut Street, Long Beach, New York. He is married and his wife's name is Lee Heilig. In November 1942, Heilig formed the Tedlee Chemical Corporation. This corporation received Government contracts for the filling of methyl bromide ampoules. In July 1943, Heilig formed the Regal Chemical Corporation which received Government contracts for the filling of aerosol containers with insecticide. The prime contractor was the Bridgeport Brass Company.

In October 1943, Abraham Brothman and Arthur P. Weber became associated with the Tedlee Chemical Corporation doing work for Heilig under a contractual agreement to work on an automatic machine to fill aerosol bombs. In an interview Brothman claims that in April 1944, Heilig offered to ask for a draft deferment for Weber if Brothman would sign over to Heilig the automatic filling machine. Brothman refused to do this and broke up with Heilig.

TOP SECRET COPSE

- 3 -

29. W. K. Benson to Chairman, Scientific Intelligence Committee [H. Marshall Chadwell], "Failure of the JAEIC To Receive Counter Espionage Information having Positive Intelligence Value," 9 February 1950.

~~SECRET~~

CENTRAL INTELLIGENCE AGENCY
WASHINGTON 25, D. C.

Executive Registry
O-9082

9 February 1950

MEMORANDUM FOR: The Chairman, Scientific Intelligence Committee

FROM: The Joint Atomic Energy Intelligence Committee

SUBJECT: Failure of JAEIC to Receive Counter Espionage Information having Positive Intelligence Value.

1. It is the opinion of the JAEIC that considerable counter espionage information is and has been available in the files of the FBI and elsewhere which would have been and probably still is of considerable value to the JAEIC in making its estimates of the status of the U.S.S.R. atomic energy program. Some of this information has become available through the investigations conducted by the House Committee on Un-American Activities and the Canadian Royal Commission. However, essentially all information that has become available is of a peripheral nature, incomplete, and of relatively little value because of the length of time which has elapsed since the incidents occurred. The Nuclear Energy Division of OSI made a request for specific information to the Director of the FBI on 21 September 1949, and while some information was furnished in answer to this request, it was only of slight value.

2. More specifically, if the JAEIC had known of the implications of the Fuchs case in June 1949 at the time when the July estimate was being written, the estimate of the time by which the Soviets could have obtained their first bomb would have been appreciably advanced, as no allowance was made in making that estimate for successful espionage on details of bomb design and construction. Of course, the JAEIC does not know how long Fuchs has been under investigation, but the fact still remains that the JAEIC was not informed until after the man's arrest.

3. If the pattern set forth above is followed, it seems obvious that much counter espionage information will not be made available. The only real assurance we have of getting the information at present seems to be as a result of the investigations of a Congressional Committee or the arrest of the offenders in isolated instances. This is very unsatisfactory from the standpoint of time, as the information is so old by the time we get it that it is of little value.

4. The JAEIC desires to point out to the SIC this possibly large area of information which is being denied us. Furthermore, in view of the paucity of information from other sources, the elimination of this deficiency is urgently necessary if the JAEIC is to perform its duties adequately.

~~SECRET~~

29. *(Continued)*

SECRET

Executive Registry
O-9082

5. The JAEIC recommends that this situation be brought to the attention of the IAC as soon as possible in order that remedial action on a high level may be instituted.

F. A. Valente
for
W. K. BENSON
Chairman, Joint Atomic Energy
Intelligence Committee

This document has been approved for release through the HISTORICAL REVIEW PROGRAM of the Central Intelligence Agency.

- 2 -
SECRET

30. Hoover to Souers, 24 May 1950.

Federal Bureau of Investigation
United States Department of Justice
Washington 25, D. C.

May 24, 1950

Rear Admiral Sidney W. Souers   PERSONAL and ~~CONFIDENTIAL~~
Special Consultant to the President   VIA LIAISON
Executive Office Building
Washington, D. C.

My dear Admiral:

    I believe the President and you will no doubt be interested in information concerning Harry Gold who has been identified as the individual who received atomic information from Dr. Emil Julius Klaus Fuchs in the United States for transmittal to the Soviet Union.

    Harry Gold was born December 12, 1910, in Switzerland. In 1914 he came to the United States with his parents, Sam and Celia Golodnitsky, both of whom were born in Russia. At the time of their naturalization as United States citizens their name was changed to Gold. Harry Gold claims citizenship by derivation through his parents. His mother is deceased. Harry Gold resides with his father and his brother, Joseph Gold, at 6823 Kindred Street, Philadelphia, Pennsylvania.

    Shortly after arriving in the United States the Gold family moved to Philadelphia, where, in 1929, Harry Gold became employed by the Pennsylvania Sugar Company in their laboratories. He continued his employment with this company until about February, 1946, at which time he became employed with A. Brothman Associates, Consulting Engineers, New York City. He left this firm in June, 1948. He presently is employed at the Philadelphia General Hospital and is a Civil Service employee of Philadelphia, Pennsylvania. At the hospital he is engaged in the laboratory doing research in connection with serious cardiac cases.

    Gold received his education attending night school at the Drexel Institute, the University of Pennsylvania, and Columbia University. In 1938 he obtained leave of absence from the Pennsylvania Sugar Company to attend Xavier University, Cincinnati, Ohio, where he received a Bachelor of Science Degree summa cum laude in 1940.

    Gold first came to the attention of this Bureau in connection with the activities of Abraham Brothman, concerning whom Elizabeth T. Bentley furnished information. In a signed statement dated November 30, 1945, Bentley advised that in about May, 1940, she was introduced to Brothman, whose photograph she identified, by Jacob Golos, her Soviet espionage superior.

30. *(Continued)*

She stated that Golos told her that Brothman would furnish her with certain blueprints. Following that she met with Brothman about ten times in the summer of 1940 until the fall of that year, and obtained blueprints from him for Golos. She said that in the fall of 1940 Golos claimed to have become disgusted with Brothman and told her he was turning Brothman over to someone else.

As a result of this information an investigation of Brothman was conducted, which resulted in an interview of Brothman on May 29, 1947. At first Brothman denied recognizing the name or photograph of Golos. Upon being shown a photograph of Bentley, which he identified as a person whom he knew as "Helen," he then admitted that he did recognize the photograph of Golos.

Brothman related that some time in 1938 or 1939 Golos had come to his office at 114 East 32nd Street, New York City, and advised Brothman that he had contacts with the Russian Government, by reason of which he was in a position to obtain contracts from that government for Brothman if Brothman would turn over to him blueprints of certain products on which Brothman was working at the time. Brothman advised that the blueprints in question were his own property. He said Golos visited his office on several occasions thereafter until Golos introduced him to "Helen." Golos advised that "Helen" would thereafter obtain the blueprints. "Helen" visited Brothman's office over a dozen times during 1938, 1939, and 1940. Some time in 1940 she stopped coming and another individual named Harry Gold appeared at Brothman's office and said that he represented Golos. Thereafter Gold visited Brothman's office on a number of occasions during 1940 and 1941, and obtained blueprints from Brothman. He said the last time Gold picked up the blueprints, according to the best of his recollection, was late in 1941 or early 1942. He was emphatic in stating that Gold was the last individual to pick up any blueprints or material for Golos. He stated that Harry Gold was, at the time of the interview, namely May 29, 1947, employed by him as a chemist in his laboratory at Elmhurst, Long Island. A signed statement to this effect was obtained from Brothman.

Upon receiving the information about Gold from Brothman, Gold was interviewed the same day at A. Brothman Associates Laboratory, 8503-57th Avenue, Elmhurst, Long Island. Gold related in substance that he had met Jacob Golos in October, 1940, at a meeting of the American Chemical Society at the Franklin Institute, Philadelphia. At this time Golos propositioned Gold, saying that he had connections with individuals in a foreign country, not naming the country, and also had connections with Abraham Brothman in

-2-

30. *(Continued)*

New York who was turning over certain blueprints. Golos told Gold that he required the services of a chemist to go to New York City, obtain the blueprints from Brothman, and then evaluate them on a chemical basis. Gold stated that about two weeks after this, in November, 1940, he contacted Brothman in New York City and introduced himself as a representative of Golos. For the next six months he made visits to New York City on the average of every three weeks to obtain blueprints from Brothman. He said that during this period he received four or five telephone calls from Golos, who always stated that they would have to get together very soon, but that actually this never happened. He said the last telephone call from Golos was in May, 1941, after which time he had no further word from Golos. He denied that he ever had seen Golos except on the occasion when he met him in October, 1940. Gold claimed that after his second or third trip to New York City Brothman became friendly and exhibited an interest in Gold's career as a chemist. He said that ever since that time Brothman had been interested in having Gold join Brothman's organization, but that it was not until February, 1946, that he could see his way clear to accept such employment, which he did at that time. Gold denied any financial agreement with Golos, and claimed he never received a cent from Golos. He insisted that he stood the expenses for the trips to New York City on the first two occasions, after which Brothman became friendly and furnished him a five-dollar bill to cover expenses. A signed statement to this effect was obtained from Gold.

On July 22 and 31, 1947, Abraham Brothman and Harry Gold, respectively, were called before the Federal Grand Jury, Southern District of New York. Both testified in substance before this Grand Jury to that which they had furnished on interview. The investigation of the Grand Jury concerning the charges of Elizabeth T. Bentley culminated in the finding of a "no bill."

After extensive and intensive investigation which developed information indicating that Harry Gold was very probably the United States contact of Emil Julius Klaus Fuchs, he was interviewed at Philadelphia, Pennsylvania, and on May 22, 1950, he furnished a signed statement admitting espionage activity. He admitted that he began the procurement of industrial information for the Soviet Union in the fall of 1936, and continued this activity until 1943, except for the period from 1938 to 1940 while he attended Xavier University in Cincinnati, Ohio.

-3-

30. *(Continued)*

Gold advised that very early in 1944 his then superior made arrangements for him to meet Dr. Klaus Fuchs in New York City. This first meeting occurred on a Saturday afternoon in February or March, 1944, on the East Side of Manhattan, from where they took a cab uptown to a restaurant around Third Avenue in the 50's, possibly Manny Wolf's Restaurant. Following the dinner they walked about and completed arrangements for further meetings. Gold recalled the arrangements for actual recognition to be that he was to carry a pair of gloves in one hand, plus a green-covered book, while Fuchs was to carry a handball. He introduced himself as "Raymond" and Fuchs introduced himself as Klaus Fuchs. He said that Fuchs never used the name "Raymond" because he knew it was fictitious.

At this first meeting no written information was passed, but Fuchs revealed that he was with the British Mission working with the Manhattan Engineer Project. He told Gold that the British Mission was working on the separation of isotopes, and Gold believes there was at least implied the eventual utilization of the energy produced by nuclear fission in the form of a weapon. Following this, Gold had about four meetings with Fuchs in the Bronx, Brooklyn, Manhattan, and Queens. During at least two of these meetings Fuchs furnished written information to Gold, who thereafter delivered it to his superior, "John." He said that he had taken a brief glance at the material on one occasion and found it to consist of a number of folded sheets of paper containing mathematical equations which seemed to concern mathematical derivations.

Gold further advised that he lost contact with Fuchs when Fuchs failed to keep a meeting in August, 1944. He stated that "John" obtained the information whereby he was once more enabled to contact Fuchs. "John" gave Gold the address of Mrs. Heineman in Cambridge, Massachusetts, the sister of Fuchs. As a result of this, he met Fuchs at the Heineman residence shortly after Christmas Day, 1944, or early in 1945. At that time Fuchs told him that he was at Los Alamos, New Mexico, a short distance from Santa Fe. Fuchs also gave him written information at the time and the two made an arrangement to meet in June of that year in Santa Fe. Gold stated that on this occasion he had been given a sum of approximately fifteen hundred dollars to offer Fuchs in a very diplomatic manner so as not to offend him. He said that Fuchs "turned it down cold." Gold returned to New York with the money and information which he delivered to "John."

-4-

30. *(Continued)*

Gold has further advised that he met Fuchs in Santa Fe, New Mexico, in June, 1945, and again in September, 1945. On both of these occasions Fuchs furnished him with written information. He said that during the September, 1945, meeting Fuchs told him that he had been present at the initial large-scale trial of nuclear fission at Alamogordo, New Mexico. He also stated that Fuchs told him at the time that he probably would return to England soon, but that by paying a call to Fuchs' sister he could ascertain just when. Gold said he made one or two attempts to see Fuchs again at the home of his sister, but was not successful. After the possible second attempt, which was either in late January or early February, 1946, Gold missed a scheduled appointment with his superior, "John," and has not seen or heard from him since.

In connection with the current interview of Fuchs in London by representatives of this Bureau, still and movie photographs of Gold were surreptitiously obtained for display to Fuchs. Previously, Fuchs and Robert and Kristel Heineman had failed to recognize a photograph of Gold. On May 20, 1950, Fuchs was shown the new still photographs of Gold and he did not identify them, though he stated he could not reject them.

On May 22, 1950, Fuchs viewed three repeat showings of the moving pictures of Gold, after which he stated that Gold was very likely his contact in the United States. It is most interesting to note that this information was received by cable at 11:08 AM, while Gold had first admitted his espionage activity to the interviewing agents in Philadelphia at approximately 10:45 AM the same day.

On May 23, 1950, a complaint was filed before a United States Commissioner for the Eastern District of New York, Brooklyn, New York, charging Harry Gold and "John" Doe with conspiracy to commit espionage on behalf of the Union of Soviet Socialist Republics in violation of Section 32, Title 50, United States Code. A warrant was issued and Gold was thereupon taken before United States District Judge James P. McGranery at Philadelphia, Pennsylvania, for arraignment. Judge McGranery gave Gold the complaint to read and he admitted that he was the Harry Gold named in the complaint. A preliminary hearing was set for June 12, 1950, and bail was set at one hundred thousand dollars, in default of which Gold was remanded to the custody of the United States Marshal.

-5-

30. *(Continued)*

Further information of interest to the President and you will be furnished as it develops.

With expressions of my highest esteem and best regards,

Sincerely yours,

J. Edgar Hoover

31. [Lamphere to Gardner], "Study of Code Names in MGB Communications," 27 June 1950.

TOP SECRET

June 27, 1950

STUDY OF CODE NAMES IN MGB COMMUNICATIONS

Reference is made to the memorandum dated June 23, 1950, bearing the above caption.

Since the referenced memorandum was prepared it has been determined that one JULIUS ROSENBERG is probably identical with the individual described as ANTENNA and LIBERAL in that memorandum. It is also believed now that DAVID GREENGLASS is identical with the individual described as KALIBR, and that RUTH PRINTZ GREENGLASS is identical with the individual known under the code name OSA.

From the information available to date it is believed that ANATOLI ANTONOVICH YAKOVLEV is identical with the individual described under the code name ALEKSEY in the referenced memorandum.

More complete details concerning these individuals will be furnished to you at a later date.

32. Hoover to Rear Admiral Robert L. Dennison, 18 July 1950.

Federal Bureau of Investigation
United States Department of Justice
Washington 25, D. C.

July 18, 1950

PERSONAL AND ~~CONFIDENTIAL~~
BY SPECIAL MESSENGER

Rear Admiral Robert L. Dennison
Naval Aide to the President
The White House
Washington, D. C.

My dear Admiral:

    I thought the President and you would be interested in the attached memorandum which sets forth information concerning Julius Rosenberg, who was arrested on July 17, 1950, for conspiring to violate the Espionage Statute.

    As further pertinent information regarding this matter is received you will be advised.

    This information has been made available to Rear Admiral Sidney W. Souers, Special Consultant to the President, and Mr. James S. Lay, Jr., Executive Secretary, National Security Council.

    With expressions of my highest esteem and best regards,

Sincerely yours,

J. Edgar Hoover

Enclosure

32. *(Continued)*

July 18, 1950

JULIUS ROSENBERG

ARREST

Julius Rosenberg was arrested by Special Agents of the Federal Bureau of Investigation on the evening of July 17, 1950, in New York City. On arraignment before Federal Judge John F. X. McGohey, he was charged with espionage conspiracy in violation of Section 34, Title 50, United States Code.

BACKGROUND

Julius Rosenberg was born May 12, 1918, in New York City, the son of Harry and Sophie Rosenberg, both born in Poland. He graduated from the College of the City of New York in February, 1939, receiving a B.S. Degree in Electrical Engineering. He also claims to have attended courses at the Brooklyn Polytechnic Institute and at the Guggenheim Aeronautical School, New York University. He married Ethel Guggenheim on June 18, 1939, and has two sons, Michael Allen, age 7, and Robert Harry, age 3. His wife, Ethel, is the sister of David Greenglass who was arrested on June 16, 1950, for conspiring with Harry Gold and Anatoli A. Yakovlev in violation of Section 34, Title 50, United States Code.

Julius Rosenberg was employed by the War Department, Signal Supply Office, New York General Depot, Brooklyn, New York, beginning on September 3, 1940, as a Junior Engineer, Radio. On October 14, 1941, he was transferred to the Signal Corps, Philadelphia, Pennsylvania. He was promoted to Assistant Engineer, Inspection, on January 1, 1942, and on January 13, 1942, was transferred to the Newark Signal Corps Inspection District of the Philadelphia Signal Corps Procurement District, Newark, New Jersey. He was again transferred on October 4, 1942, to the Newark Signal Corps Inspection Zone, Newark, New Jersey, and on February 16, 1943, was promoted to Associate Engineer, Inspection. As of February 9, 1945, he was suspended indefinitely pending a decision by the Secretary of War on the recommendation of his commanding officer for removal by the demands of national security on the basis of information indicating Communist Party membership. His employment by the Signal Corps was terminated as of March 26, 1945. Prior to the

32. *(Continued)*

above employment, Rosenberg worked for various firms in the New York City area and for his father-in-law, Barnett Greenglass. He has reported that he worked for Barnett Greenglass from 1936 to 1938 as a part-time draftsman, machinist and junior engineer. Subsequent to his release from the Signal Corps Rosenberg has principally engaged in his own businesses under the trade names of the G and R Engineering Company and the Pitt Machine Products, Inc., 370 East Houston Street, New York City. He was also employed for some months in 1945 by the Emerson Radio and Phonograph Company, New York City. At the time of his arrest Rosenberg was residing at 10 Monroe Street, New York City.

ESPIONAGE

David Greenglass has stated that in 1944 his wife, Ethel, at the request of Julius Rosenberg, traveled to Albuquerque, New Mexico, where he, David, was then residing in connection with his employment at Los Alamos. Further, and also at Rosenberg's request, she asked David Greenglass to provide information concerning the atomic bomb. This, David Greenglass said, he agreed to do. Subsequently, in January, 1945, Greenglass, while on furlough in New York City, contacted Julius Rosenberg. On that occasion Rosenberg described to Greenglass the "naval type" bomb which was, Greenglass later learned, used at Hiroshima. Greenglass stated that he provided Rosenberg, during this meeting, with the names of personnel at Los Alamos whom he, David, believed were ideologically suited for recruitment to furnish information to the Russians.

In June, 1945, David Greenglass was contacted by Harry Gold in Albuquerque, New Mexico. Gold identified himself by his possession of a half of a Jello box top, the connecting piece of which was in Greenglass' possession. David Greenglass has stated that the box top originally came from Julius Rosenberg, and the latter cut it in half, gave one half to either him, David, or his wife Ruth, and retained the other half. Rosenberg told him that the person who would contact him for information would present the other half of the cover, which Gold did. Greenglass said he provided Gold with information concerning the Los Alamos project, the names of individuals working there, and a sketch of a high explosive lens mold, or something of that type.

-2-

32. *(Continued)*

In the Fall of 1945 Greenglass was in New York City on furlough, at which time he saw Julius Rosenberg. On this occasion he provided Rosenberg with considerable technical data concerning the construction of an atom bomb. He also believes that he gave Rosenberg some sketches having to do with a part of the bomb. Greenglass does not recall if Rosenberg looked at this information, nor does he know what disposition Rosenberg made of it. During this meeting Rosenberg requested Greenglass to remain at Los Alamos following his discharge from the Army, but Greenglass stated he refused.

David Greenglass was discharged from the Army on February 28, 1946, and from that time until September, 1949, was associated with Rosenberg in the G and R Engineering Company, and the Pitt Machine Products, Inc. Greenglass said that when Klaus Fuchs was arrested in England, Rosenberg told him, Greenglass, to leave the country but he refused. On the arrest of Harry Gold, Rosenberg pointed out to Greenglass that Gold was the person who contacted him in Albuquerque. Rosenberg told Greenglass that he must get out of the country. To this end he gave Greenglass five hundred dollars, which sum Greenglass said was not enough. Later, on May 28, 1950, Rosenberg gave Greenglass four thousand dollars in twenty-dollar bills. He told Greenglass to leave the country, taking his wife and children with him. He also provided Greenglass with certain instructions as to how he should travel. Rosenberg indicated to Greenglass that more important people than he, Greenglass, had already left the United States, and he, Rosenberg, intended leaving. Greenglass said that he indicated to Rosenberg that he would leave, but actually he and his wife planned to go to the mountains in New York State until Rosenberg left, and then return to New York City. Greenglass assumed that Rosenberg had been unable to effect his departure from the United States due to his being under surveillance by the FBI.

Ruth Greenglass has stated that Julius Rosenberg, prior to requesting her to approach her husband, David, for information, pointed out to her that he, Julius, and his wife Ethel, had discontinued their open affiliations with the Communist Party. Julius also told her that he always wanted to do more than merely be a Communist Party member, and that he had searched for two years to contact the "Russian underground" in order to do the work for which he felt he was "slated."

-3-

33. Armed Forces Security Agency, "Russian Cryptology During World War II," undated [ca. 1951] [Excerpt].

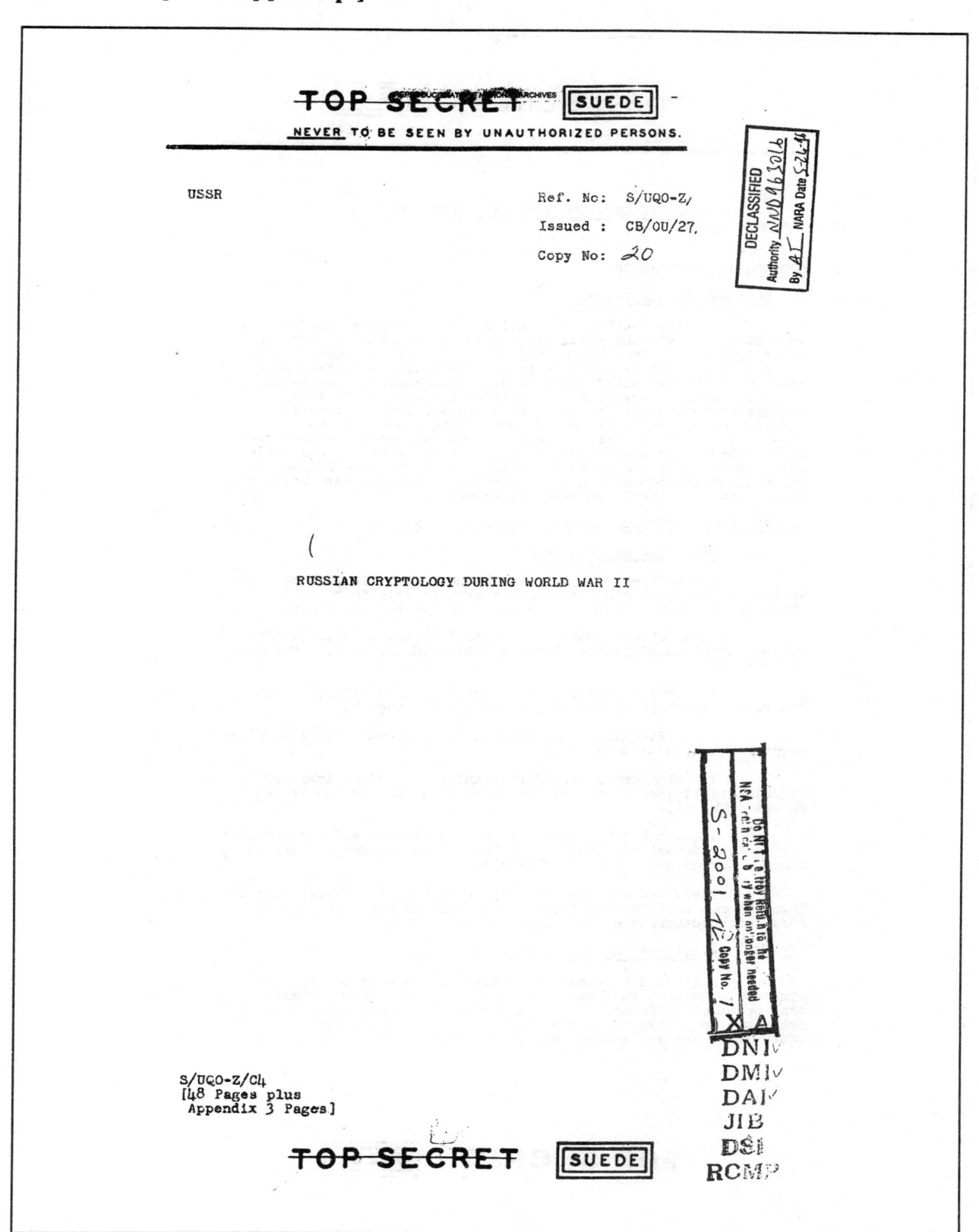

~~TOP SECRET~~ [SUEDE]

NEVER TO BE SEEN BY UNAUTHORIZED PERSONS.

USSR

Ref. No: S/UQO-Z/
Issued : CB/OU/27.
Copy No: 20

DECLASSIFIED
Authority NND 9*****
By AI NARA Date 5-24-**

RUSSIAN CRYPTOLOGY DURING WORLD WAR II

S/UQO-Z/C4
[48 Pages plus
Appendix 3 Pages]

~~TOP SECRET~~ [SUEDE]

DNI
DMI
DAI
JIB
DSI
RCMP

33. *(Continued)*

~~TOP SECRET~~ [SUEDE]

NEVER TO BE SEEN BY UNAUTHORIZED PERSONS.

RUSSIAN CRYPTOLOGY DURING WORLD WAR II

I. SOURCES OF INFORMATION

   A. <u>Captured German Documents</u>

   The information presented in this paper is based solely on a study of relevant documents issued by the Armed Forces Security Agency (AFSA-14) in their TICOM Document Folder (DF) Series. The great majority of these documents are translations from the German of material pertaining to signals communications which the Target Intelligence Committee (TICOM) was able to salvage as cryptologic targets in German and German occupied territories on the continent of Europe were overrun by the advancing Western Armies in 1945. In addition to the discoveries of important Axis cryptologic caches, the interrogations of Axis cryptologic experts and the treatises written by some of them in the postwar era concerning their wartime activities have added to the amount of valuable documentary material.

   B. <u>Home-Work of Former German Cryptologic Experts</u>

   1. <u>Importance of These Men</u>

   Of the treatises written in the postwar era, those written by the following cryptologic experts were found to be the most useful sources of information on Russian Cryptology:

   Alex Dettmann, the former chief of the Russian Section of the Signal Intelligence Agency of the German Army High Command (OKH/Gd NA).

   Kurt Friederichsohn, a linguist and cryptanalyst with the German Army Signal Intelligence Regiment (KONA 6).

   Adolf Paschke, the last head of the German Foreign Office Cryptanalytic Section (Pers ZS).

   Wilhelm Fenner, the former chief of cryptanalysis of the Signal Intelligence Agency of the Supreme Command German Armed Forces (OKW/Chi).

   Wilhelm Flicke, formerly chief evaluator and the officially designated historian of the Signal Intelligence Agency of the Supreme Command German Armed Forces (OKW/Chi).

   These men were key figures in the various German Signal Intelligence Agencies and there is no question but that they can speak with authority on the subject.

   2. <u>Reliability of Their Evidence</u>

   A general agreement regarding the details of many Russian systems is evident in these treatises. Only in a few instances may discrepancies be found. The information on the whole seems to be authentic and there is little reason to question the sincerity of these men. While these sources of information are often not as

- 4 -

~~TOP SECRET~~ [SUEDE]

33. *(Continued)*

~~TOP SECRET~~ [SUEDE]

NEVER TO BE SEEN BY UNAUTHORIZED PERSONS.

III. ORGANIZATION OF CRYPTOLOGY IN THE PEOPLES COMMISSARIAT FOR INTERNAL AFFAIRS

A. The Vastness of the Apparatus and the Consequent Need for a Communications System

Before presenting the few details that are known concerning the organization of Cryptology in the NKVD (Peoples Commissariat for Internal Affairs) it might be well to stress the importance of this organization in the political, military, and economic life of the Soviet Union.

The basic task of the NKVD was to assure the continuance of the political structure of the USSR. To carry out the necessary measures the NKVD had at its disposal various types of troops of its own - NKVD troops - which were assigned and employed according to need by the Central Office in Moscow (GUP NKVD, Central Administration of NKVD Troops).

From an evaluation of the results of traffic analysis and cryptanalysis on Russian traffic the Germans were able to establish the following catagories of NKVD troops:

Troops of the Interior - The "Political Section NKVD" has an extensive network of agents to note any trend hostile to the Soviets. The actual combatting of any such movements is by contingents of these "Troops of the Interior." When there was an occupation of foreign territory during the war, the number of political sections increased materially with consequently a very great increase in the number of contingents of "Troops of the Interior" NKVD.

Escort Troops - The sending away of politically unreliable elements, surveillance, and control of concentration camps as well as the setting up of penal camps and penal battalions fall in the province of the "Escort Troops" NKVD.

Frontier Troops - Because of the special political structure of the USSR, it was necessary to provide for sealing the country hermetically from the outside world. This is the function of the "Frontier Troops" NKVD. Corresponding to their task, these troops have aircraft available and along the water boundaries, appropriate watercraft. Before the war these troops were deployed along the actual frontiers but with the outbreak of hostilities regiments of "Frontier Troops" NKVD were employed some 30 to 60 kilometers behind the combat units of RKKA (Red Worker and Peasant Army) to form an unbroken, very mobile, and deeply deployed security zone. NKVD forward staffs controlled the employment of these regiments; these staffs were located in the immediate vicinity of the forward staffs of the Army but received their orders from NKVD headquarters in Moscow. The task of this security zone was to prevent desertion and infiltration of enemy agents by sealing the sector of the front from the rear area; by mopping up pockets, and clearing areas near the front of cut-off enemy troops and bands; by removal or resettlement of the populace for political reasons; by return of population for repair or new construction of roads, defense installations, air fields, and plants of value to the military economy; by guarding supply; and by collecting and transporting prisoners to the rear.

Railway Troops - The entire economy of the Soviet Union, in particular the military economy and transportation system are under very sharp control and thus under the influence of the NKVD. Whereas before the war this control could be exercised through the local organs of the NKVD, after the outbreak of hostilities it became necessary to take over also the protection

- 17 -

~~TOP SECRET~~ [SUEDE]

33. *(Continued)*

TOP SECRET [SUEDE]

NEVER TO BE SEEN BY UNAUTHORIZED PERSONS.

of the railroads along with their control and for this purpose especially trained troop contingents, "Railway Troops" NKVD were formed. They guarded transports, depots, bridges, junction points, and important as well as threatened stretches of railway track.

<u>Operative Troops</u> - In various phases of the war the need appeared for very daring and reliable units at danger points in the line or at points of concentration. Such elite troops were formed by the NKVD and assigned to divisions of the RKKA armies as "Operative Troops" NKVD.

In addition to the major tasks already outlined the NKVD was charged with the carrying out of the following supplemental tasks: (1) The political training of the RKKA by means of political units, political commissars, etc. (2) The training of a number of military specialists, such as sharpshooter units; selection and training of all replacements for medium and high-grade officers in the RKKA, and all technical signal personnel including those engaged in cryptographic work. (3) The conduct of training schools for dogs and carrier pigeons. (4) The combatting of espionage, sabotage and the activity of enemy agents. This work was done by the SMERSH (Death to Spies), an agency under the control of the NKGB (Peoples Commissariat for the Security of the State). (5) Direction of the activities of partisans and the training of agents for work behind the German front. (6) Mobilization and drafting of recruits for the RKKA. (7) Recruiting workers from among the people of occupied areas into labor battalions. (8) Integration of armies and units of foreign nationality into the framework of the RKKA.

With such a powerful organization having tentacles which reach into the furthermost crevices of the political, military and economic life of the Soviet Union, it is obvious that the NKVD must also have possessed a far-flung communications complex and cryptographic systems of its own.

B. <u>The Centralization of the Productions of Cryptographic Systems</u>

It is said that the Central Office for the cryptographic service of the NKVD organs was located with the GUP NKVD (Central Administration of NKVD troops) in Moscow. Organization and functions of this section in the field of cryptology are not known. In contrast to the cryptographic systems of the Army and Air Force, no cryptographic systems of the NKVD were ever captured by the Germans while they were still in use. At various points on the front 4-figure NKVD codes did fall into the hands of German troops, but either they were then no longer in use or they represented reserve systems which, due to their capture, were not put into use. Consequently there was never the urgent need which brought about the decentralization already noted in the case of RKKA cryptography but instead the NKVD Cryptographic Central Office in Moscow was able to retain the method of centralization for the production, issue and recall of cryptographic material throughout the entire war. For this reason the Section of GUP NKVD corresponding to the 8th Section of the General Staff of the RKKA in Moscow was not obliged to make any radical change in the further development of cryptographic systems but allowed them to remain substantially unchanged from the time the Germans began systematic observation down to the day of capitulation. Therefore in spite of the great number of different NKVD organs there was only a very limited number of NKVD cryptographic systems in use and it was also true that these were valid for a relatively long time, often more than two years. Consequently there was the chance

- 18 -

TOP SECRET [SUEDE]

33. *(Continued)*

TOP SECRET [SUEDE]

NEVER TO BE SEEN BY UNAUTHORIZED PERSONS.

for the German cryptanalysts to do extensive work on great amounts of homogeneous material and to accomplish more with far less personnel against NKVD cryptographic systems than was the case with RKKA systems.

All internal radio circuits of the USSR were not only monitored and controlled by the NKVD but in many cases were directed by it and in all probability the GUP NKVD was also responsible in large measure for the issue of any cryptographic material which might be used for encipherment of such internal radio traffic. The Germans of necessity gave some attention to the interception and decryptment of this traffic. Among other things, special units were devoted to the reception of the Baudot traffic passed on many of these circuits by high-speed transmitters. It is reported that of the entire traffic monitored at great expense by the Germans, at best only 10% was useful for economic leaders while military-political matters constituted hardly 1%. From this traffic German evaluation results lay almost exclusively in the economic field.

C. <u>The Decentralization of Production of Cryptographic Systems for use of Agents</u>

The NKVD also had an important share in the preparation and issue of cryptographic materials for partisan organizations and for the agents and espionage service. In view of the initial multiplicity of partisan groups which operated independently and of the often very extensive employment of agents and spies in the enemy's rear, it was necessary to provide for current replacement of cryptographic systems, in which connection it was of primary importance that these should be convenient, simple to use, and yet secure. This responsibility could not be met by a single central unit, however large; therefore the individual partisan staffs, which for the most part were located in the immediate vicinity of army front staffs, were assigned the task of producing and distributing such cryptographic systems, although all of them were subject to the guidance and control of the NKVD. Although the systems used in partisan, scout, and agent traffic, from the simplest to the most difficult, included some which were neither theoretically or practically capable of solution, it can be stated with good reason that in many respects much latitude was afforded the individual imagination and discretion. A norm, similar to that in the SUV systems of the RKKA, did not exist. The structure and use of cryptographic means had to be adapted here to the momentary needs of agents who often worked alone.

D. <u>The High Sense of Responsibility of Personnel Handling Cryptographic Material</u>

Considering the vastness of the NKVD apparatus and its consequent use of a complex communications system, one unique characteristic was noted by the Germans during the war. This is the high degree of training and the sense of responsibility of NKVD personnel which prevented any cryptographic systems of the NKVD which were still in use from falling into the hands of the Germans during the entire period of the war. This is indeed amazing since the Germans proved conclusively time and again throughout the course of the war that the complete destruction of all secret documents of a nation is a practical impossibility. According to the German account of their experiences in the Balkan Campaign, the Greek and Yugoslav Governments had obviously issued orders for the destruction of all secret documents, yet the amount of captured material was so enormous that it had to be shipped in barges up the Danube to Vienna and from there to Berlin in freight

- 19 -

TOP SECRET [SUEDE]

33. *(Continued)*

cars and nearly two years elapsed before a systematic evaluation of these documents was finally concluded by the Central Evaluation Section in Berlin. But during the German advance into Russia, up to the seige of Stalingrad in 1942, the operational area of the Frontaufklarung (military intelligence in the operational area) comprised upwards of 3 million sq. kilometers of Russian soil and although many, many documents had been abandoned by the Russians in the battle and contrary to orders, over 3,000 comprising only the most important ones having then been registered at Walli III (the German center for tactical counterintelligence on the Eastern Front), still no live cryptographic material of the NKVD was found at this time or even during the entire period of the war. In this connection it might be mentioned that our own TICOM effort against the Germans which saw the first exploitation team dispatched in April 1945 was able to salvage approximately 4000 separate German documents with a weight of about 5 tons and this does not include materials captured in the heat of battle and passed to military intelligence for immediate processing.

E. <u>Lack of German Knowledge Regarding a Russian Organization for Cryptanalysis</u>

Not a thing is known about the possible activities of an agency of the NKVD in the field of cryptanalysis. The subject has already been touched on above in the discussion of a similar function being exercised by the 8th Section of the General Staff of the RKKA. The conclusion is that the NKVD is active, whether in absolute control or merely maintaining its customary surveillance in a more subtle way, it matters little.

33. *(Continued)*

IV. ORGANIZATION OF CRYPTOLOGY IN OTHER AGENCIES:

A. The External Communications

In the organization of cryptology in the Soviet agencies so far mentioned we have been concerned for the most part with strictly internal communications. When we come to an examination of the external communications of the USSR, at least three agencies are mentioned by the Germans as using cryptographic materials during this period. In the diplomatic field we have the Peoples Commissariat for Foreign Affairs, in the commercial field the Peoples Commissariat for Foreign Trade, and in the communist-international field the Comintern as it was called at that time.

B. The Peoples Commissariat for Foreign Affairs

No mention is found in these sources regarding the authority for the compilation, issue and recall of the cryptographic materials used by the Peoples Commissariat for Foreign Affairs. But in view of what has already been elucidated with respect to the activities of the NKVD it seems probable that here too they exercise some sort of control. The use by this Commissariat of the one-time additive pad for re-encipherment of its code is exactly the means employed by the RKKA for the re-encipherment of its operational 5-figure Chiffrecode.

C. The Peoples Commissariat for Foreign Trade

The Peoples Commissariat for Foreign Trade also uses an additive pad system for re-encipherment of its communications. In fact each Commissariat has its own code book and the pad system is generally used for the re-encipherment of the external communications passing to or from the head offices in Moscow.

D. The Communist-International

Only in the cryptographic systems of the Comintern for its signal communications with the Communist parties in foreign countries is there an exception in the use of the additive pad, as such, -- here the most essential parts, the keys for the encipherment, are not outwardly to be recognized as cryptographic material, the necessary digit sequences being derived from a book text by means of a mnemonic key. This development corresponds to the introduction by the NKVD of similar systems in their agent organizations and in point of fact one of the functions of the Comintern is espionage, political, economic or military according to opportunity. While little is known regarding the chain-of-command for issue and usage of cryptographic materials in the foreign services of the USSR, the logical surmise is that the NKVD through some of its many organs exercised its usual surveillance.

34. No author [Washington Field Office, FBI], "William Wolf Weisband," 27 November 1953 [Excerpt].

WFO 121-13210

ESPIONAGE ACTIVITIES

On October 6, 1953, JONES ORIN YORK was interviewed by SA WILLIAM L. BYRNE, JR. and SA FRANCIS D. COOLEY, at which time he submitted the following signed statement:

"Burbank California
October 6, 1953

"I, JONES ORIN YORK, make the following voluntary statement to WILLIAM L. BYRNE, JR. and FRANCIS D. COOLEY, who are known to me to be Special Agents of the Federal Bureau of Investigation. I know I do not have to make any statement, have the right to consult an attorney before making a statement, and that my statement may be used against me in a court of law.

"I was born August 5, 1893, at Bushnell, Illinois, and attended school at Western Illinois Normal School until 1910. After spending approximately one year in Ragan, Nebraska, with my parents I came to Berkeley, California, arriving on December 11, 1911. I worked as a clerk, telephone switchboard installer, and for two automobile agencies. Since 1910 I have been interested in the aviation field; I learned to fly an airplane in 1919 and since that time I have been employed in occupations relating to the aircraft industry. I am presently self-employed as an aircraft engineer, consultant and fabricator of special aircraft apparatus at 2630 North Naomi Street, Burbank, California.

"In 1935 I was employed as an aeronautical engineer at Douglas Aircraft Corporation, El Segundo Division; at that time I met a group of Russians who were touring aircraft plants in the Los Angeles area as representatives of the Soviet Government Purchasing Commission. One of these Russians was STANISLAU SHUMOVSKY. He was identified to me as a technical representative from the Central Hydro-Aerodynamics Institute of Moscow, USSR.

"STANISLAU SHUMOVSKY indicated interest in an airplane engine I was designing and gave me $200.00 as evidence of his interest in my work, with the idea that eventually I might develop something that the Russians would actually purchase. Later, in 1935 or 1936, SHUMOVSKY asked me to furnish him information from Douglas Aircraft Corporation, El Segundo Division, which I did and he furnished me various sums of money.

"About the first part of 1936 SHUMOVSKY introduced me to a man using the name of 'BROOKS' and I continued furnishing information and receiving money from 'BROOKS' until January, 1938, when 'BROOKS' arranged to put me in contact with a man named 'WERNER.' I continued to furnish material to 'WERNER' and receive money from him until about January, 1939. At that time I lost contact with 'WERNER' but in about February, 1940, he recontacted me and I agreed to continue to furnish information to the Soviets. 'WERNER' told me that a new contact had been arranged for me, and it was agreed that my new contact to identify himself would inquire regarding a violin which I owned. Also, 'WERNER' took a picture of SHIRLEY TEMPLE, tore it in half, and said my new contact, upon contacting me, would present the half which 'WERNER' was retaining in order to identify himself.

34. *(Continued)*

WFO 121-13210

"The next individual who contacted me and to whom I furnished information was known to me as 'BILL' and I understood his last name was VILLESBEND. I cannot recall when 'BILL' first contacted me, but I believe it was about two months after I moved into 1301½ North Harper Avenue, Los Angeles, California. I don't know when I moved into that address, but do recall that I obtained a telephone very shortly after I rented the premises. 'BILL' came to my Harper Avenue address and produced the half of the picture of SHIRLEY TEMPLE that had been previously retained by WERNER. 'BILL' also told me he was supposed to tell me the birthdate of my mother, but I said this was unnecessary as I was satisfied he was my new contact.

"At this first meeting 'BILL' asked if I could obtain information, and I said that I could, but advised him that I needed a camera. 'BILL' said that he would furnish me money for this purpose. 'BILL' gave me about $250.00 to purchase a camera, I believe at our second meeting, which occurred about a month after he first contacted me. I purchased a Contax No. 3 camera with an F1.5 Sonnar lens at 'The Dark Room,' a camera shop, located on Wilshire Boulevard, about two blocks west of La Brea Avenue, in Los Angeles for about $250.00, paying a substantial down payment and the balance in monthly installments. I used this camera to photograph information on airplanes being produced at Northrop Aircraft Company, Hawthorne, California. In particular I remember photographing specifications of the P-61 airplane, also known as the 'Black Widow,' and delivering the film I had taken to 'BILL.'

"I also recall that 'BILL' gave me a list of material in which the Russians were interested. When he gave me this list, 'BILL' said that there was some hesitancy about furnishing me this list as it might reflect that the Russians lacked information on those subjects. I don't recall the items on the list, but it was very broad and included many matters on which I had no information and was unable to obtain information.

"I met with 'BILL' about ten times over a period of about one year and I believe that during this time he paid me approximately $1,500.00; during these contacts, I turned over to 'BILL' airplane specifications, the details of which I cannot now recall. I am not certain that these documents were all classified as confidential data but am sure some of them were so classified. I never gave 'BILL' any actual documents but when I gave him the film I would prepare a summary of the information the film contained and any suggestions I had concerning the information. During the course of our meetings, 'BILL' came to my home three or four times, and I recall on one occasion, I showed 'BILL' a copy of a poem I had written entitled, 'The Vandal's Doom," which dealt with the German attack on Russia. 'BILL' stated he liked this poem very much and asked if he could make a copy of it. I agreed and the next time he came to my home he typed out a copy on my typewriter and indicated that his superior would like the theme of this poem, and that he would forward it to him.

"I recall meeting 'BILL' on one occasion at the Florentine Gardens in Hollywood, and on another occasion at a bar near the corner of Wilshire Boulevard and Fairfax Avenue in Los Angeles. At one of my meetings with 'BILL' I recall

34. *(Continued)*

WFO 121-13210:

"that he drank two scotch and sodas and I noticed that he was making some marks on the edge of a newspaper. 'BILL' explained that these marks were in Arabic and indicated the time of our next meeting. He said that anyone could take this newspaper and they would not know what these marks signified. 'BILL' also told me how to say some simple greeting phrases in Arabian such as 'Salaam Alechiem,' meaning 'Peace Unto You,' and the reply, 'Alechiem Salaam.'

"In the early part of our contacts I received a telephone call from 'BILL.' The operator said the call was from Pendleton, and I presume she meant Pendleton, Oregon. 'BILL' said he would not be able to keep a scheduled meeting, and would contact me when he returned to Los Angeles.

"In the latter part of 1942 I met 'BILL' near the Garden of Allah on Sunset Boulevard in Los Angeles, and he told me he would no longer contact me, that my next contact might possibly be a woman, and that the new contact would inquire about my violin. It was arranged that I would meet my new contact at a statue in Westlake Park in Los Angeles on a date I cannot now recall.

"During my meetings with 'BILL' no one else was ever present, and I never met any person with whom he was associated. I did ask 'BILL' about SHUMOVSKY and from what 'BILL' told me I gained the impression he was personally acquainted with SHUMOVSKY. I remember that 'BILL' told me SHUMOVSKY 'was fine,' and that he was 'not in this country.' I remember that 'BILL' was very much concerned over the suffering of the Russian people because of the war and mentioned the sacrifices being made by the Russians.

"I subsequently met my new contact whose name I cannot recall in accordance with instructions I had received from 'BILL' and continued furnishing information to this new contact until the latter part of 1943, when he told me the information he had been receiving from me was unsatisfactory and then did not appear for a scheduled meeting. I have had no further contact with Soviet representatives since that time.

"After the last contact with 'BILL' in the latter part of 1942, I did not see him again until August, 1950. At that time I was at the Federal Building, Los Angeles, having just testified before a Federal Grand Jury. I was standing on the front steps of the Federal Building and I observed 'BILL' walking along the sidewalk about 75 yards away. With me at this time were Special Agents THOMAS E. BRYANT and FRANCIS D. COOLEY and I pointed 'BILL' out to them.

"I have read the foregoing statement consisting six and one-quarter pages and it is the truth.

"/s/ JONES ORIN YORK

"Witnessed:
s/ FRANCIS D. COOLEY Special Agent, FBI Los Angeles 10/6/53

s/ WILLIAM L. BYRNE, Special Agent, FBI, Los Angeles, Calif. 10-6-53."

-8-

34. *(Continued)*

WFO 121-13210

On August 16, 1950, SAS FRANCIS D. COOLEY and THOMAS E. BRYANT of the Los Angeles Office were standing on the steps of the Federal Building in Los Angeles, California, with JONES ORIN YORK. At that time, YORK pointed out the subject, who was then about seventy-five yards away as the individual he knew as BILL VILLESBENI and to whom he furnished information for transmission to the Soviets.

It is noted that YORK placed the date he first met the subject as approximately one month prior to the time he purchased a Contax Camera at "The Dark Room," a camera shop located on Wilshire Boulevard about two blocks west of La Brea Avenue in Los Angeles.

BENJAMIN HUBSCHMANN, owner of "The Dark Room," 5370 Wilshire Boulevard, advised that his records reflected that J. O. YORK, 1301½ North Harper Avenue, Los Angeles, telephone number, Gladstone 8346, purchased a Contax Camera, number 86, a Sonnar F1.5 lens on October 15, 1941, for $257.70. The down payment of $157.70 made at the time of purchase, and payments of $50.00 each were made on January 9, 1942, and March 9, 1942. The lens number on this camera was 1826645 and the book number was B-50419. The records further reflect that on January 25, 1943, YORK purchased lens, Zeiss lens number 1065110, for $133.90.

With regard to the estimate by YORK that he believes subject first contacted him about two months after he moved into 1301½ North Harper Avenue in Los Angeles, California, it is observed that the application records for the Pacific Telephone and Telegraph Company for the years 1941 and 1942 have been destroyed; however, telephone directories for those years reflected that J. O. YORK was listed as residing at 1300½ North Harper Avenue, telephone - Gladstone 8346, in directory dated from September, 1941, until June, 1942.

WEISBAND was interviewed by Washington Field Office agents on May 9, 1950 and May 13, 1950, and by Los Angeles agents on August 16, 1950. When interviewed, WEISBAND denied being implicated in Soviet espionage. He said that to the best of his knowledge, he had never been acquainted with anyone in the Communist Party nor did he know anyone who had been engaged in espionage. He denied ever having removed any documents or material from AFSA nor had he ever advised any unauthorized person any operations being carried on at AFSA. Subject declined to furnish a signed statement denying that he had been involved in espionage activities.

On July 1, 1953, a photograph of JONES ORIN YORK was exhibited to WEISBAND and he stated he recognized the photograph as being that of "YORK," an individual with whom he was acquainted, but he declined to answer any further questions concerning JONES ORIN YORK.

On July 1, 1953, WEISBAND also said he would not admit nor deny he had ever been involved in Soviet espionage activities.

Mrs. PATRICIA BAUMANN, formerly 1952 Marengo Avenue, South Pasadena, California, was interviewed by Los Angeles agents on May 12 and 13, 1950. Mrs. BAUMANN has recently been remarried and is now known as Mrs. ROBERT F. CALLICOTT,

35. Hoover to Brigadier General A. J. Goodpaster, USA, 23 May 1960 [Table of Contents and Appendixes not included].

JOHN EDGAR HOOVER
DIRECTOR

Federal Bureau of Investigation
United States Department of Justice
Washington, D. C.

May 23, 1960

PERSONAL ATTENTION
VIA LIAISON

Brigadier General A. J. Goodpaster, USA
White House Staff Secretary
The White House
Washington, D. C.

Dear General:

I am enclosing herewith a copy of a document entitled, "Expose of Soviet Espionage, May 1960," which we prepared in the FBI and copies of which have been furnished to the Vice President, the Attorney General, Under Secretary of State Dillon, and Mr. Allen Dulles, Director of the Central Intelligence Agency.

The material contained in this document is unclassified and was prepared for use by the State Department in case it desired to use any portion of it before the United Nations or for public release.

I thought that you might desire to have a copy of this in the event there is any portion which you consider should be called to the President's attention.

With best regards, I am

Sincerely,

J. Edgar Hoover

Enclosure

35. *(Continued)*

Exposé of SOVIET ESPIONAGE
May 1960

FEDERAL BUREAU OF INVESTIGATION
UNITED STATES DEPARTMENT OF JUSTICE
John Edgar Hoover, Director

35. *(Continued)*

SOVIET-BLOC INTELLIGENCE ACTIVITIES

1. INTRODUCTION:

Recent Soviet propaganda has denounced the United States for aerial reconnaissance of the Soviet Union in terms designed to convince the world that the USSR would not stoop to espionage. In discussing this subject and the reception which President Eisenhower might expect on his visit to Russia, Premier Khrushchev was quoted in the newspapers on May 11, 1960, as wondering what would have been the reaction of the American people if the Russians had sent a plane over the United States on the eve of his visit to this country.

The facts are that at the very time Premier Khrushchev was advancing to the podium to speak before the United Nations General Assembly on September 18, 1959, two Soviet espionage agents were cautiously surveying a street corner in Springfield, Massachusetts, in preparation for a clandestine meeting with an American whom they were attempting to subvert. At the very time that Khrushchev was declaring that a means must be found to stop mankind from backsliding into an abyss of war, Vadim A. Kirilyuk, Soviet employee of the United Nations, was attempting to induce this American to furnish information regarding United States cryptographic machines and to secure employment in a vital United States Government agency where he could obtain classified information for the Russians. While this meeting was taking place Kirilyuk and the American were under observation by Leonid A. Kovalev, another Soviet employee of the United Nations who was conducting a countersurveillance. Unknown to the Russians, however, this meeting was also being observed by Special Agents of the FBI who obtained photographs of the Russians.

Not only did these Russians stoop to spying, but they callously abused their status as guests of this country to spy in the most reprehensible manner -- the subversion of an American on American soil.

Although FBI Agents observed this meeting and photographed the Russians, no publicity was given to this incident in view of the negotiations which were then in progress. This incident, as contrasted with the recent handling of the plane incident by the Russians, gives ample testimony as to which country is acting in good faith in trying to maintain world peace.

And this is not an isolated incident - nor has the target always been so limited. The facts are that Soviet agents for three decades have engaged in extensive espionage against this country, and through the years have procured a volume of information which would stagger the imagination. This information includes literally dozens of aerial photographs of major

-1-

35. *(Continued)*

U.S. cities and vital areas which have given the Russians the product of aerial reconnaissance just as surely as if Soviet planes had been sent over this country.

<u>2. ACQUISITION OF AERIAL PHOTOGRAPHS</u>:

In a free country such things as aerial photographs are available to the public and can be purchased commercially. The Soviets have been fully aware of this and throughout the years have taken full advantage of this free information, collecting aerial photographs of many areas of the United States.

For example, during October, 1953, two Soviet officials visited Minneapolis where they purchased fifteen aerial photographs of Minneapolis and St. Paul. In October and November, 1953, two Soviets traveled in Missouri and Texas and obtained aerial maps of Dallas, Tulsa, Fort Worth and the surrounding areas covering a Naval air station, an Army airfield, and an Air Force base. In April, 1954, a Soviet official purchased aerial photographs of five Long Island communities. Also, in April, 1954, a Soviet official purchased three aerial photographs of Boston, Massachusetts, and Newport, Rhode Island, areas. In May, 1954, three Soviets traveled to California where they ordered from a Los Angeles photography shop $80 worth of aerial photographs covering the Los Angeles area.

However, they have not been content with acquisition of publicly available data. For example, on May 3, 1954, Leonid E. Pivnev, an assistant Soviet air attache stationed in Washington, who had previously traveled extensively throughout the United States and had obtained commercially available aerial photographs of various areas of this country, requested a Washington, D. C., photographer to rent an airplane to take photographs of New York City which were not commercially available. He specified the scale to be used and the altitude from which the photographs were to be taken. He offered $700 for this activity. Obviously the photographs which he requested would depict vital port areas, industrial facilities, and military installations in the New York area.

For this brazen abuse of his diplomatic privileges Pivnev was declared persona non grata on May 29, 1954, and departed from this country on June 6, 1954.

But this did not stop the Soviets. They continued their systematic program of collecting aerial photographs of major cities and vital areas of the United States. On January 19, 1955, the State Department sent a note to the Soviet Ambassador placing restrictions on the acquisition of certain types of data

- 2 -

35. *(Continued)*

by Soviet citizens in the United States. These restrictions were comparable to restrictions on American citizens in Russia and in part prohibited Soviet citizens from obtaining aerial photographs except where they "appear in or are appendices to newspapers, periodicals, technical journals, atlases and books commercially available to the general public."

Soviet reaction to the restrictions was typical of their philosophy. They began circumventing the restrictions by subverting Americans to purchase aerial photographs for them. One month after the restrictions became effective, Nikolai I. Trofimov, a Soviet official in Mexico, began negotiations for a resident of the west coast of the United States. to obtain aerial photographs of 45 major United States cities. Nineteen of these cities are located near Strategic Air Command bases. The remaining 26 are all strategic cities in or near which are located air bases, naval bases, research or training stations, atomic energy installations or important industrial facilities.

During April, 1958, Vladimir D. Loginov, a Soviet employee of the United Nations used the same technique to obtain an aerial map of New York City. At 10 p.m. on April 26, 1958, Loginov secretly met an individual in a darkened parking lot at the railroad station in Scarsdale, New York, where this map was delivered to Loginov. Months later on November 15, 1958, this same parking lot was again utilized by the Soviets to obtain aerial photographs of Chicago, Illinois. On this occasion, the photographs were turned over to Kirill S. Doronkin, another Soviet employee of the United Nations. In this same operation, the Soviets attempted to obtain aerial photographs of Portland, Oregon; Seattle, Washington; and San Diego and San Francisco, California.

Circumvention of the restrictions also took the form of trickery and deceit. For example, on July 17, 1959, Viktor V. Fomin, assistant Soviet military attache and Anatoli G. Vasilev, an employee of the Soviet Military Attache in Washington, D. C., obtained an aerial photograph of the Glasgow Air Force Base in Montana from the local Chamber of Commerce by posing as tourists without identifying themselves as Soviet officials. On July 24, 1959, they obtained an aerial photograph of Thermopolis, Wyoming, by bullying the clerk at the Chamber of Commerce in an arrogant and insistent manner, again posing as tourists. They were given the photograph in spite of the fact that such a photograph is not normally given to tourists.

Soviet activities did not stop there. At the present time, a Washington, D. C., photographer is under the instructions

- 3 -

35. *(Continued)*

of Petr Y. Ezhov, third secretary of the Soviet Embassy, to take flying lessons at Soviet expense. Ezhov has indicated that the Soviets will purchase a plane for the photographer's use after he obtains his pilot's license. That aerial reconnaissance is the Soviet objective, is amply proven by the fact that this photographer has been requested to obtain aerial photographs of the East Coast from Boston, Massachusetts, to Jacksonville, Florida. He has already been sent on reconnaissance trips throughout the southern states under Soviet instructions to photograph military installations with telephoto lenses. The information obtained on one of these reconnaissance trips including photographs of United States military bases was to be delivered on September 17, 1959, to Vladimir Glinsky, an assistant Soviet naval attache who originally recruited the photographer. At 7 a.m. on that date, however, Glinsky contacted the photographer by telephone and cancelled the appointment, explaining, "my boss is here." Premier Khrushchev on that morning was winding up his first visit to Washington on his tour of the United States. These photographs were subsequently delivered on October 2, 1959.

It is apparent from the examples cited that the Soviet Union reaps the benefits of aerial reconnaissance of the United States just as surely as if planes were sent over this country.

3. RECRUITMENT OF AMERICANS:

The acquisition of aerial photographs is only one phase of Soviet-bloc intelligence activity in the United States, but the manner in which it has been done illustrates two basic Soviet intelligence concepts; namely, to exploit the weaknesses of Americans whenever possible and to take full advantage of all the freedoms of our democratic society.

Following these concepts, the Soviets through the use of such devices as entrapment, blackmail, threats, and promises have exploited human frailty. The record is replete with examples of such exploitation of Americans throughout the years following the Russian Revolution in 1917. For example, Nicholas Dozenberg, a naturalized American, first became associated with the communist movement about 1920. In 1928 he was recruited into Soviet espionage activities with the approval of the Communist Party. He was recruited by one Alfred Tilton, who was an illegal agent of Soviet Military Intelligence, posing as a Canadian citizen and in possession of a Canadian passport. One of the early assignments given to Dozenberg was the sounding out of other Americans for later recruitment by Tilton. Dozenberg, after pleading guilty to violations of the passport laws, served a term in prison in 1940 and thereafter prior to his death cooperated with United States Government agencies.

- 4 -

35. *(Continued)*

Simon Rosenberg, another naturalized American of Polish background, during 1931 was sent to Russia by his employer. While there, he met representatives of a Soviet intelligence agency and under threats of reprisals to be taken against his sister who was then living in Russia, he agreed to work in behalf of the Russians upon his return to the United States. His principal assignment in this country was to obtain technical and industrial information. Rosenberg, who is now deceased, also cooperated with agencies of the Government, prior to his death, as have many other Americans who have been involved in Soviet intelligence activity.

Another example is the case of Hafis Salich, a naturalized American employed by the Office of Naval Intelligence in California who met Mikhail N. Gorin through a mutual acquaintance in 1937. Gorin was then the Pacific Coast manager of Intourist. By advancing Salich money, Gorin ultimately persuaded him to furnish Office of Naval Intelligence reports for which Gorin paid $1700. Gorin and Salich were found guilty of espionage in 1939 and Salich was sentenced to four years imprisonment, which he served. Gorin appealed his conviction and sentence of six years to the Supreme Court of the United States which unanimously upheld the conviction in 1941; however, the trial judge suspended execution of the sentence and placed him on probation provided he would pay a $10,000 fine and leave the United States, never to return.

The decade of 1950 - 1960 has been no exception. It began with the trial and conviction of Valentin Gubitchev, a Soviet employee of the United Nations who had obtained information from Judith Coplon, an employee of the Department of Justice. This conviction was soon followed by convictions of several Soviet agents in the Julius and Ethel Rosenberg network in 1951; by the sentencing of Otto Verber and Kurt Ponger in 1953 after they pleaded guilty to espionage; by the guilty pleas of espionage by Jack and Myra Soble and Jacob Albam in 1957 and later in the same year the conviction of Colonel Rudolf Abel, a Soviet illegal agent in this country.

These prosecutions, although they clearly establish the nature of Soviet espionage activities against this country, involve only a part of the Soviet-bloc espionage attack which has included numerous Soviet attempts to penetrate United States Government agencies. For example, the prosecution of Judith Coplon, an employee of the Department of Justice in early 1950 was followed in October, 1950, by a Soviet assignment to Boris Morros, an American motion picture producer who was cooperating with the FBI, to revive his acquaintance with a member of the United States Atomic Energy Commission; to obtain compromising

- 5 -

35. *(Continued)*

information concerning this individual; and to carefully explore the possibility of placing a secretary in his office who could furnish information to the Russians. Morros previously in 1948 had been given the assignment to attempt to obtain information which could be used by the Russians in an effort to compromise United States General Clay in Germany.

Another example occurred during 1954 when Soviet intelligence officers in Germany approached an American Army officer stationed in Germany who was soon to be retired. They propositioned him to work for the Soviets after his return to the United States and set up a schedule for meetings in New York City. Pursuant to the arrangements, Maksim G. Martynov, counselor of the Soviet Representation to the United Nations Military Staff Committee, carried out a series of clandestine meetings in New York with a person whom he believed to be the Army officer. As a result of his indiscreet abuse of his status, Martynov was declared persona non grata on February 21, 1955.

Another example is that of Evgeniy A. Zaostrovtsev, second secretary of the Soviet Embassy who was declared persona non grata on May 13, 1959, for attempting to subvert a State Department employee to obtain information from State Department files.

A more recent example has been previously cited involving the attempt by Vadim Kirilyuk, an employee of the United Nations, to penetrate a vital Government agency by instructing an American to obtain employment in that agency.

Soviet attempts to recruit Americans during this period have not been confined to attempts to infiltrate Government agencies. For example, in February, 1954, Igor A. Amosov, assistant Soviet naval attache, was declared persona non grata for attempting to obtain information concerning radar and United States naval vessels from a businessman who had commercial dealings with the Russians and who was in a position to obtain such data.

In June, 1956, Ivan A. Bubchikov, an assistant Soviet military attache was declared persona non grata for attempting to obtain data regarding radar, guided missiles, jet fuels and atomic submarines from an American businessman who during World War II had extensive contacts with the Russians on both private and United States Government business. The Soviets attempted to exploit his World War II friendliness.

In August, 1956, Viktor I. Petrov, a Soviet translator at the United Nations, was released from his employment for recruiting an employee of an American aviation company to obtain classified data regarding United States aircraft.

- 6 -

35. *(Continued)*

This activity has continued throughout the decade into 1960, as illustrated by the case previously cited where a Washington, D. C., photographer has been utilized for the purpose of photographing military installations.

4. <u>THE INTELLIGENCE ROLE OF THE SOVIET-BLOC OFFICIALS</u>

Only a few of the many examples of abuse of their diplomatic privileges by Soviet-bloc officials in the United States have been mentioned. In the more flagrant cases, the United States Government has asked the offending officials to leave this country. During the decade, 1950 - 1960, 19 Soviet officials have been asked to leave. Many more have been engaged in intelligence activities throughout the years.

The Soviet Union has maintained a large staff of officials in this country since its first recognition in 1933. These officials have been assigned to Soviet embassies, consulates, trade delegations, news media, the United Nations, and the Amtorg Trading Corporation. It is from these installations that the primary intelligence activities are directed against the United States. A former Soviet intelligence officer who defected from the Soviets has estimated that from 70% to 80% of the Soviet officials in the United States have some type of intelligence assignment. Other defectors have confirmed that a high per cent of the officials are intelligence agents. As of May 1, 1960, there were 328 Soviet officials stationed in this country. They were accompanied by 455 dependents, many of whom are also potential intelligence agents.

Nor is this the full strength of Soviet-bloc intelligence. As of May 1, 1960, there were 272 satellite officials stationed in the United States accompanied by 435 dependents. This almost doubles the potential of Soviet intelligence services. The satellite intelligence services have been developed according to the Soviet pattern, their personnel selected or approved by the Soviets and they are trained and guided by Soviet policies and procedures. Recent defectors from satellite intelligence services have advised that the Soviets have access to all data obtained by the satellites and, in fact, maintain an advisor system at headquarters level to make certain that the satellites operate consistent with Soviet interests.

This coordination is not limited to headquarters' levels. Beginning in November, 1958, the Soviet and satellite military, naval and air attaches stationed in the United States began a series of monthly meetings under the guidance of the Soviet military attache. During this

35. *(Continued)*

initial meeting the satellite representatives were given specific target assignments for the collection of information desired by the Soviets and arrangements were made for the over-all correlation of their activities.

5. <u>INDUSTRIAL SPYING AND CIRCUMVENTION OF REGULATIONS</u>:

This large group of Soviet-bloc officials stationed in the United States has systematically over the years developed a most important part of the modern intelligence machine which was referred to by one Soviet official as the best industrial spying system in the world. Volumes could be written as to the techniques used and the ways and means developed by the Soviet bloc to obtain information regarding the industrial potential of the United States often with the use of subterfuge and deceit as well as deliberate circumvention of Customs regulations.

The following examples illustrate this activity:

In 1924 the Amtorg Trading Corporation was organized in New York for the purpose of acting as an importer and exporter on the North American continent for official trusts of the Soviet Union. Amtorg continued to operate during World War II, although in 1942 the Soviet Government created the Soviet Government Purchasing Commission in Washington, D. C., to purchase war material. This Purchasing Commission was dissolved after the end of World War II, and its activities absorbed by Amtorg. Since its organization, Amtorg Trading Corporation has been staffed primarily by representatives of the Soviet Government who have official status. Former employees of Amtorg have advised that it was standard practice for Soviets attached to Amtorg to request permission for Soviet officials to visit industrial facilities throughout the country on the promise of orders to be forthcoming if the products were found satisfactory. In many instances the officials of the companies would later be advised by Amtorg that Moscow would have to approve the order. In instances where a contract was given to a particular company, Amtorg consistently demanded blueprints of the particular product and other data to which it was not

- 8 -

35. *(Continued)*

entitled by normal business practices. Amtorg officials also consistently insisted on a clause in the contract which would give Soviet inspectors the privilege of inspecting all of the merchandise before it was shipped to Russia.

Another device utilized by Amtorg officials was to gain the confidence of some employee in a plant which had a contract with the Russian Government and, through this employee, obtain blueprints which were copied in the Amtorg office and the copies forwarded to Russia. Amtorg officials would also advertise for employees who, when they appeared for an interview at the Amtorg office, would be instructed to bring proof of their ability in the form of blueprints of former projects. When the applicants for employment later showed up with the blueprints, the blueprints would be photographed and the photographs forwarded to Russia.

Amtorg has also followed a practice of preparing detailed catalogues concerning American industry. Congressman Mundt on January 29, 1947, described one of these catalogues as "a manual for bombing America." It was pointed out that the book contained detailed information including many photographs and maps of vital areas of the United States. In this connection Amtorg Trading Corporation during the 1940's prepared a monthly magazine called "American Engineering and Industry" and an annual guide called "Catalogue of American Engineering and Industry." This latter publication in 1946 was described as a three-volume, 5,000-page document.

In August, 1956, Milos Prochazka, a Czechoslovakian official assigned to the Commercial Office at the Czech Embassy, furnished to an American the specifications for the components of 2 steel mills to be purchased in the United States for the Czechs. He outlined a plan whereby the American would act as an exclusive agent to purchase these mills ostensibly for a private concern in a Western country. He would obtain estimates and if the estimates were approved, the Czechs would furnish the name of the purchasing company, a power of attorney and the necessary bank credit. Thereafter, the mills would be shipped to the Czech agent in the Western country and then transshipped to Czechoslovakia.

- 9 -

35. *(Continued)*

6. *EXPLOITATION OF PUBLIC INFORMATION:*

It is no secret that one of the results of the freedom of our democratic society is the availability of voluminous information to members of the public merely for the asking. Some of the cases previously cited clearly indicate that the Soviet-bloc intelligence services are aware of this fact and have taken full advantage of this democratic freedom; however, it remains for former Soviet-bloc intelligence officers to testify as to its real significance and importance to the Soviet-bloc intelligence services. One defector has stated that the ease with which information is obtained in this country has resulted in a reduction of the hazardous and time-consuming clandestine operations which would otherwise be necessary. Another has estimated that the Soviet Military Attache's office in the United States is able to legally obtain 95% of the material useful for its intelligence objectives. He stated that, in fact, 90% of an intelligence agent's time in any other country in the world would normally be consumed clandestinely obtaining information which is readily available in the United States through Government agencies or commercial publishing houses. He pointed out that Polish military intelligence obtains more technical data in the United States than from all the other countries in the world combined.

Although such information is collected in a number of ways, the following techniques in addition to those previously mentioned have been most productive.

One of the most useful techniques is attendance at conventions of American organizations by Soviet-bloc officials. During the year preceding Khrushchev's visit to this country, Soviet officials alone attended approximately 30 conventions covering various fields of endeavor including aeronautics, electronics, plastics development, education and others. Typical were the activities of 2 Soviets who attended the Western Electric convention held in Los Angeles during August, 1959. As usual, at the inception, they began to collect voluminous literature. When the volume became unwieldy one Soviet left the material at a check stand and resumed his collection activities. It was estimated that the literature picked up by these Soviets at this one convention weighed approximately 250 pounds.

- 10 -

35. *(Continued)*

      Another technique utilized is correspondence with chambers of commerce and industrial facilities throughout the United States through which voluminous information regarding transportation systems, major industries, etc., is obtained. In many instances useful maps of the areas are also secured.

      Still another technique is the subscription to American publications and collection and review of United States Government documents. For example, during June, 1959, it was ascertained that the personnel of the Soviet Military, Naval and Air Attache Offices subscribed to 44 newspapers and 58 magazines of a technical, scientific, military and general news nature. It is apparent that the Soviets have a definite program of subscribing to newspapers published at or in the vicinity of vital United States military bases.

      Purchases from the United States Government have long been a productive source for Soviet-bloc intelligence. For example, on December 28, 1944, the Soviet Government Purchasing Commission in Washington, D. C., ordered copies of 5,810 patents. On the same date the New York office of this Commission purchased two copies of 18,000 patents. On January 1, 1945, the Soviet Government Purchasing Commission in Washington again ordered copies of 5,342 different patents. On January 12, 1945, copies of 41,812 patents were ordered. The next order was for 41,810. The acquisition of copies of patents has been continued throughout the years as illustrated by the fact that in early 1959 Anatoli G. Vasilev, an employee of the Office of the Soviet Military Attache, requested an American to instruct him in the use of the "Search Room" of the United States Patent Office so that he could locate patents in which he was interested.

      The Soviets have, of course, not restricted themselves to the acquisition of patents. For example, on March 10, 1954, an Assistant Soviet Air Attache purchased "The Pilot's Handbook" for the East and West Coasts of the United States from the United States Coast and Geodetic Survey of the Department of Commerce. On March 12, 1954, a chauffeur of the Soviet Air Attache purchased "The Pilot's Handbook" for Canada and Alaska. Six days later an Assistant Soviet Attache ordered "The Pilot's Handbook" for the Far East and Europe. These handbooks contained

- 11 -

35. *(Continued)*

diagrams of all of the principal airfields and the approaches used in landing planes.

In April, 1954, Soviet officials stationed in Washington obtained from the Map Information Office of the U. S. Geological Survey, Department of the Interior, topographic maps covering North Carolina, Michigan, Illinois, Kentucky, and an area within a 50-mile radius of Washington, D. C.

This collection activity has continued unabated up to the present time. Literally thousands of similar documents are obtained in this country every year by Soviet-bloc officials assigned in this country and through registered agents such as the Four Continent Book Corporation and the Tass News Agency.

A statement of a satellite defector illustrates the value to the Soviet-bloc of United States Government publications. He stated that on one occasion, Polish military intelligence obtained an 18-volume edition prepared by the United States Army Engineers regarding United States port facilities. It was purchased from the Government Printing Office at nominal cost, but its estimated value to the Polish military intelligence was placed at $50,000.

Not content with the large volume of publicly available material, Soviet-bloc officials have resorted to deceit. For example, on November 5, 1958, Ion Dubesteanu, an assistant military attache of the Rumanian Legation in Washington, D. C., was declared persona non grata for activity beyond the scope of his official duties. Using a false name and identity, Dubesteanu had corresponded with U. S. military installations soliciting material and had rented post office boxes at North Beach, Maryland, under assumed names to which such material was to be sent.

Reconnaissance trips by Soviet-bloc officials have been a most productive source of intelligence. The officials have been observed to carefully prepare for such trips by reviewing publications collected in this country, doing research at the Library of Congress, et cetera. Exclusive of trips from Washington, D. C., to New York City, officials of the Soviet Military Office alone took 16 trips

- 12 -

35. *(Continued)*

to various areas of the country in 1958 and 1959. They visited 26 states in 1958 and 37 in 1959. They covered most of the strategic areas of the country and covered some areas as many as four times. During these trips they followed a definite pattern of visiting chambers of commerce, driving around the perimeter of industrial facilities and wherever possible circled military, naval and air installations in the areas visited. They collected all available literature and maps relating to industrial facilities, transportation systems, power plants, dams, chemical factories, et cetera, and wherever possible took photographs in addition to making extensive notes.

7. *PROPAGANDA AND PERSONAL APPEARANCES*

Exploitation of our freedoms has also taken the form of propaganda. Not content with the distribution of over 20,000 copies of the illustrated monthly magazine, "USSR," which is in reciprocity for distribution of a similar American magazine in the Soviet Union, the Soviet Embassy has a carefully planned program of distributing press releases. As of February, 1960, the Press Department of the Soviet Embassy was distributing press releases to almost 7,000 individuals and institutions in the United States, including newspaper editors, business leaders, radio stations, public libraries, television stations, teachers, labor leaders, scientists, and leaders in trade and commerce.

In addition, since January 1, 1959, 30 different officials attached to the Soviet Embassy have made, or were scheduled to make, 74 public appearances (not including 7 additional invitations for appearances by the Soviet Ambassador) before various groups in this country. Nineteen other Soviets attached to the Soviet Delegation to the United Nations, employed by the United Nations Secretariat or assigned to Intourist, made, or were scheduled to make, 39 public appearances during the same period.

These public appearances normally involved speeches or participation in forums on the part of the Soviet officials and were made before various types of groups, including high school, college, and university groups, parent-teacher associations, advertisement and civic clubs, fraternities, professional associations or clubs, religious and cultural groups, travel clubs and community centers. Some of these were television appearances. It is apparent that the Soviets are taking every opportunity to spread the gospel of communism by exploitation of the intense desire of Americans to learn more about the Soviet Union.

- 13 -

35. *(Continued)*

8. USE OF THE UNITED NATIONS

Attention is called to the fact that many of the incidents and cases previously cited involved Soviet employees of the United Nations. They are guests of the United States and are supposedly dedicated to the cause of international peace but they are, in fact, carefully selected envoys of the international communist conspiracy, trained in trickery and deceit and dedicated to the concept of fully exploiting the freedoms of the countries they seek to destroy. It is too much to expect that they would not prostitute the United Nations.

9. "ILLEGAL" OPERATIONS

Although Soviet-bloc intelligence services have made extensive use of their officials stationed in foreign countries for espionage purposes throughout the years, they have, in addition, operated a parallel clandestine espionage system known as the "illegal" system. As previously noted, "illegal" Soviet agents were dispatched to the United States as early as the 1920's. Such "illegal" agents have no ostensible connection with the Soviet-bloc official establishments in the United States, but operate clandestinely, usually under false identities, making full use of secret communications channels and other clandestine techniques of operation. Their dual function is to bolster the espionage activities of the Soviet-bloc officials and to be prepared to take over all espionage operations in the event of war or other emergency which would cause a break in diplomatic relations.

It is apparent that during the decade 1950-1960 the Soviets have placed increasing emphasis on "illegal" operations. One former intelligence officer of the Soviet Ministry of State Security has advised that a special directorate was created in 1947 for the purpose of handling "illegal" agents. Another former intelligence officer, Reino Hayhanen, has stated that he was told, while in Moscow in 1952, that plans were being made to change over Soviet contacts from "legal" to "illegal" operations. Another former officer of the Soviet Ministry of State Security has advised that as early as June, 1952, an order was sent to intelligence agents in all western countries to prepare "illegal" organizations which could function without interruption under any conditions.

That this policy was followed with respect to the United States is illustrated by the fact that in August, 1956, a female Soviet agent attempted to enter the United States from

- 14 -

35. *(Continued)*

Canada at Detroit using an authentic copy of a birth certificate previously issued to an American. Detected by the United States border screening process, she was refused entry. Less than a year later, Rudolf I. Abel, a colonel in the Soviet Committee of State Security, was arrested in New York City where he was posing as an American photographer under the name Emil R. Goldfus. Abel had entered the United States in 1948 using a passport issued to a naturalized American in 1947 to visit relatives behind the Iron Curtain and who never returned to this country. Abel was subsequently convicted of espionage and sentenced to 30 years imprisonment, which sentence he is now serving.

It is interesting to note that in October, 1952, the Soviets sent Reino Hayhanen to the United States to act as Abel's assistant. Hayhanen, prior to leaving Russia, had been given instructions by Mikhail N. Svirin, a Soviet intelligence officer. After his arrival in this country, Svirin, who had become First Secretary of the Soviet Delegation to the United Nations, met with Hayhanen and subsequently, during the period 1952-1953, Hayhanen operated under his supervision. It was not until 1954 that Svirin gave instructions for Hayhanen to contact Abel and to act as Abel's assistant.

The case involving Abel and Hayhanen is a striking example of Soviet use of "illegal" agents against the United States. In dispatching such agents to this country, we can be certain that the Soviet-bloc intelligence services will, as they have with their representatives who are dispatched to this country as diplomats, take full advantage of the freedoms of this country which are guaranteed by our Constitution.

<u>10. *INTERNATIONAL ASPECTS OF SOVIET ESPIONAGE*</u>

The United States has not been the only target of the Soviet-bloc intelligence organizations. Many other countries of the world have felt the barbs of the Soviet espionage attack. The disclosures of the Royal Commission in Canada which followed the 1945 defection of Igor Gouzenko, a Soviet code clerk, revealed a Soviet espionage apparatus which on a broad scale had recruited and subverted Canadian citizens while seeking to infiltrate the Canadian Government and drain off its secrets. The admissions of Klaus Fuchs in 1950 that he betrayed the free world when, as a member of the British Atomic Energy Team, he passed atomic secrets to the Russians clearly indicate the Soviet designs on information in possession of the British Government. The flight of the British scientist Dr. Bruno Pontecorvo in 1950 and the British diplomats Guy

- 15 -

35. *(Continued)*

Burgess and Donald MacLean in 1951 behind the Iron Curtain adds additional proof. The report of the Royal Commission of the Commonwealth of Australia in 1955 following the defection of Vladimir and Evdokia Petrov, Soviet espionage agents assigned to the Soviet Embassy in Australia, disclosed an extensive Soviet espionage apparatus directed against Australia. Many similar examples could be cited to illustrate that Soviet espionage is international in character and the expulsion of two Soviet officials from Switzerland during the past month clearly indicates that Soviet espionage is currently international in character.

Practically every one of the cases cited above, although based in other countries, had ramifications in the United States. For example, information furnished to the Russians by Dr. Allan Nunn May, who was uncovered by Gouzenko, had been obtained when May visited a laboratory in Chicago in 1944. Klaus Fuchs worked on atomic energy in the United States from early 1944 through September, 1945, and supplied information to the Russians while in this country. The British diplomats Burgess and MacLean had been stationed in the United States prior to their disappearance behind the Iron Curtain. In spite of the use of third countries by the Soviet Union to commit espionage against the United States, Premier Khrushchev has made strong threats of reprisal against his neighboring countries which he assumes have been used as bases for United States aerial reconnaissance of the Soviet Union.

11. AIMS OF INTERNATIONAL COMMUNISM

The world-wide espionage networks of the Soviet Union are an essential and integral part of the over-all communist plan to completely dominate the world. However, to understand the significance of the intelligence activity, it is necessary to examine the basic aims and principles of communism.

The highly authoritative "History of the Communist Party of the Soviet Union (Bolsheviks)" summarized the teachings of Marx and Engels on the question of for and violence. It stressed that Marx and Engels taught the impossibility of establishing a communist state by peaceful means, emphasizing that this could be achieved only through a proletarian revolution through which a dictatorship could be established and all resistance crushed. V. I. Lenin gave practical application to the teachings of Marx and Engels. Through the application of such principles the Bolsheviks seized power

- 16 -

35. *(Continued)*

in Russia in 1917 and under Lenin's guidance, established a dictatorship through which all resistance was systematically crushed. The success of the movement led Lenin to reiterate in later years that "The substitution of the proletarian state for the bourgeois state is impossible without a violent revolution."

Joseph Stalin followed the Marxist-Leninist principles. The Communist Party in the United States, since it was organized in September, 1919, and throughout the years of Stalin's rule in Russia, was unalterably bound to Moscow. In the earlier years, Party leaders openly, boastfully and defiantly proclaimed their allegiance to and support of Soviet objectives. The nature of the Communist Party, USA, was exposed in 1949 and its leaders convicted in a court of law where the evidence laid out before the jury constituted irrefutable proof that the Communist Party, USA, advocated the overthrow and destruction of the Government of the United States by force and violence. The policies and activities of the Communist Party, USA, have not changed to date. The current leaders of the Communist Party, like their predecessors, unwaveringly follow the lead of the Communist Party of the Soviet Union.

Time and again, Soviet Premier Khrushchev has claimed that the Soviet Union does not and will not interfere in the affairs of other nations. Yet, in practically every country in the world to date the Soviet Union has established fifth columns in the form of Communist Parties which are under the complete domination and control of the Soviets and are sworn to uphold and aid the Soviet dream for world conquest. Through the directives it furnishes to these subversive forces, the Soviet Union clearly interferes with the political, social, and economic affairs of other nations on a continuing basis in the relentless drive toward world domination.

Today, the rallying cry of world communism is "peaceful coexistence." However, on May 5, 1960, Premier Khrushchev, addressing the Supreme Soviet in Moscow, paid tribute to V. I. Lenin and stated "The Soviet people are proud to know that the cause of our great leader and teacher lives and triumphs and that Lenin's dreams are being translated into reality by hundreds and millions of people--builders of socialism and communism--and that Lenin's cause is winning all upright men on earth." Referring to the triumph of the ideas of Marx, Engels, and Lenin, Khrushchev went on to reaffirm "Marxist-Leninist ideas" as the guide to the ultimate triumph of world communism.

- 17 -

35. *(Continued)*

> Thus, the fact remains that the basic principles of Marxist-Leninist philosophy, demanding the use of force and violence, represent the guides for communism to achieve world conquest. The extensive espionage activities directed against the United States which, in the past, have utilized communists and communist sympathizers in this country as well as other individuals who could be subverted, can be better understood when regarded as essential tools in the relentless and fanatical drive of international communism to conquer the world.

PART II

SELECTED VENONA MESSAGES

Part II:
Selected Venona Messages

A Note on the Translations and List of Messages

The release of Venona translations involved careful consideration of the privacy interests of individuals mentioned, referenced, or identified in these documents. In very few cases, names have not been released because doing so would constitute an invasion of privacy.

In some of the Venona translations, the analytic footnotes indicated that the person referred to by covername had not been identified. Another—usually later—message may have footnoted that same covername with an identification. For example, in some early message translations, the covernames MER and ALBERT were footnoted as unidentified, but analysts subsequently determined (as footnoted in later translations of other messages) that the person in question was Iskhak A. Akhmerov, the KGB's chief illegal officer in the United States. Unfortunately for readers, the KGB occasionally re-used covernames; consequently, a single covername can designate two different persons. Even so, readers often can determine from context or geographic location which person is being referred to.

Finally, the Venona messages are replete with specialized Soviet intelligence terminology. The following are definitions of some of the more common terms and phrases.

The Russian word *klichka* (sobriquet or nickname) appears in the Venona translations as "covername." There are hundreds of covernames in the translations, including many seen in the messages included in this volume, such as ALBERT, LIBERAL, and ALES. Covernames designated Soviet officers, active or retired assets, valued contacts, and sometimes even prominent figures (such as CAPTAIN for President Roosevelt) and were periodically changed. Assets and contacts, however, rarely knew their covernames, which were to be used primarily in cable traffic. To complicate matters further, a Soviet intelligence officer like illegal *rezident* Iskhak Akhmerov typically had a covername (MER, and later ALBERT), aliases he used in his cover identity (William Grienke and Michael Green, among others), and "street names" he used in the company of assets and contacts ("Bill").

Fellow countrymen were members of the local Communist Party.

An **illegal** was a KGB or GRU officer, often a Soviet citizen, working abroad under alias with neither diplomatic cover nor visible connections to legal Soviet establishments. An individual illegal's cover story was his or her **legend**. Iskhak Akhmerov was the KGB's principal illegal in the United States before 1946 and thus was regarded as the illegal *rezident*. He apparently was succeeded in this role by Rudolf Abel. Several KGB and GRU illegals were shown in Venona messages to be operating in the United States, Mexico, and other countries. Although some Soviet illegals later used radios for direct clandestine communication with Moscow, illegals in the United States during World War II generally transmitted and received messages through Soviet diplomatic missions.

A **leader** (or group leader) was a KGB officer or an experienced local agent who handled and supervised a network or sub-network of assets. Such an officer might have either worked for an official Soviet entity or operated as an illegal. Venona messages showed that such agents as Jacob Golos and Sergei Kurnakov, while not themselves KGB officers, were nonetheless given significant responsibilities for certain networks. In many cases where the KGB gained control of older Comintern or GRU networks, the existing leader was left in charge for months or even years.

A **line** was a grouping of KGB officers by operational tasks. Some of these entities seen in Venona communications were the Second Line (which focused on ethnic groups of interest to Moscow, such as Ukrainians or Latvians); the Fifth Line (responsible for the security of the Soviet merchant fleet and its personnel); the White Line (concerned with White Russian emigres); and the Economic Line (a scientific and technical sub-residency, headed by Leonid Kvasnikov, in the New York consulate).

The KGB and the GRU referred to one another as the **neighbors**. In KGB parlance, Near Neighbors meant the GRU-Naval auxiliary, while the GRU proper was referred to as Far Neighbors.

Probationers was the cover term for KGB agents. The term—which apparently fell out of usage after the 1940s—was sometimes applied to KGB officers who were temporarily not attached to a diplomatic mission and hence were being run as agents.

To put on ice (sometimes rendered **in cold storage**) meant to suspend use of an agent.

The *rezident* was the KGB chief at a particular location; his station was called a **residency** *(rezidentura)*. The New York residency supported a sub-residency, under Leonid R. Kvasnikov, to collect scientific and technological secrets.

A **worker** (sometimes referred to as a cadre) was the KGB's usual term for its own officers working in a diplomatic or official Soviet establishment such as the TASS press agency or the Amtorg trading company.

Access to the Venona Translations

All the Venona translations—roughly 2,900 KGB, GRU, and GRU-Naval messages—are being released to the public. Paper copies have been sent to the National Archives and Records Administration at College Park, Maryland, and to various federal repositories (typically at large state universities). The National Cryptologic Museum, adjacent to NSA headquarters at Ft. George G. Meade, Maryland, also has a complete set of the translations. Each release of the Venona translations in 1995 and 1996 was accompanied by an original explanatory monograph authored by Robert Louis Benson, co-editor of this volume. The translations and monographs can also be found on the Internet's World Wide Web, NSA's Homepage, at http://www.nsa.gov:8080\. This conference volume can be found on the World Wide Web, CIA's Center for the Study of Intelligence Homepage, at http: //www.odci.gov/csi.

Translations included:[1]

1. Moscow [Comintern] 117, 121 to the US, 21 and 23 March 1936.
2. London [GRU] to Moscow, 10 August 1941. *Klaus Fuchs interview*
3. New York 854 to Moscow, 16 June 1942. *Recruiting proposals*
4. Moscow 424 to New York, 1 July 1942. *More recruiting proposals*

5. Washington [Naval-GRU] 2505-12 to Moscow, 31 December 1942.
6. Washington [Naval-GRU] 834, 846-8 to Moscow, 18 April 1943.
7. New York 782 to Moscow, 26 May 1943. *Duncan Lee, OSS*
8. New York 777-781 to Moscow, 26 May 1943. *MI School*

9. New York 786-7 to Moscow, 26 May 1943. *Mrs. Roosevelt*
10. New York 812 to Moscow, 29 May 1943. *Agent "19"*
11. New York 887 to Moscow, 9 June 1943. *OSS*
12. New York [GRU] 927-8 to Moscow, 16 June 1943. *GRU and Amerasia*

13. New York [GRU] 938 to Moscow, 17 June 1943. *Joseph Milton Bernstein*
14. New York 1132-3 to Moscow, 13 July 1943. *Recruiting proposals*
15. New York [GRU] 1325 to Moscow, 11 August 1943. *GRU espionage*
16. Washington [Naval-GRU] 1969 to Moscow, 13 August 1943. *S&T*

17. Washington [Naval-GRU] 1983 to Moscow, 14 August 1943. *SALLY*
18. Moscow 142 (Circular), 12 September 1943. *Comintern dissolved*
19. San Francisco 441 to Moscow, 31 October 1943. *Pobjeda codebook*
20. Moscow 232-3 to all Residents, 2 December 1943. *PETROV on security*

21. San Francisco 510 to Moscow, 7 December 1943. *Olga Khlopkova*
22. Mexico City 158 to Moscow, 23 December 1943. *Assault to free Mercader*
23. San Francisco 31 to Moscow, 17 January 1944. *Espionage against aircraft*
24. New York 195 to Moscow, 9 February 1944. *Gold meets Fuchs*

25. San Francisco 65 to Moscow, 10 February 1944. *Kuznetsova deserts*
26. Moscow [unnumbered], 25 April 1944. *Keypad indicator change*
27. New York 588 to Moscow, 29 April 1944. *Perlo group*
28. New York 598-9 to Moscow, 2 May 1944. *CPUSA political analysis*

29. New York 601 to Moscow, 2 May 1944. *Norman Jay*
30. New York 618 to Moscow, 4 May 1944. *Jack Katz's cover*
31. New York 625 to Moscow, 5 May 1944. *Jack Soble's cover*
32. New York 628 to Moscow, 5 May 1944. *Recruitment of Al Sarant*

[1] All cables are KGB messages unless otherwise noted.

33. New York 640 to Moscow, 6 May 1944. *Infiltration of an organization*
34. New York 655 to Moscow, 9 May 1944. *Report from Greg Silvermaster*
35. New York 687 to Moscow, 13 May 1944. *Perlo group, again*
36. New York 696-7 to Moscow, 16 May 1944. *Walter Lippman*

37. New York 732 to Moscow, 20 May 1944. *William Perl*
38. Moscow 334 to Mexico City, 30 May 1944. *The Fishers*
39. New York 786 to Moscow, 1 June 1944. *Try to bribe Niles in White House*
40. New York 824 to Moscow, 7 June 1944. *"The Ten"*

41. New York 847B-848 to Moscow, 15 June 1944. *Walter Lippman, again*
42. New York 850 to Moscow, 15 June 1944. *Report from Klaus Fuchs*
43. New York 1053 to Moscow, 26 July 1944. *Recruiting Max Elitcher*
44. New York 1043 to Moscow, 25 July 1944. *FBI attempt to enter Consulate*

45. New York 1065 to Moscow, 28 July 1944. *Browder, Bentley, Mary Price*
46. New York 1076 to Moscow, 29 July 1944. *KGB officers*
47. New York 1088-90 to Moscow, 30 July 1944. *Problems with seamen*
48. New York 1102-3 to Moscow, 2 August 1944. *Fisher case*

49. New York 1105-10 to Moscow, 2/3 August 1944. *Donald Maclean*
50. New York 1119-21 to Moscow, 4/5 August 1944. *Harry Dexter White*
51. New York 1203 to Moscow, 23 August 1944. *Document forgery*
52. New York 1251 to Moscow, 2 September 1944. *New covernames*

53. New York 1271-4 to Moscow, 7 September 1944. *HOMER, again*
54. New York 1313 to Moscow, 13 September 1944. *I. F. Stone*
55. New York 1314 to Moscow, 14 September 1944. *William Perl, again*
56. New York 1325-6 to Moscow, 15 September 1944. *OSS "Reds" list*

57. Moscow 954 to New York, 20 September 1944. *"Reds" list*
58. New York 1340 to Moscow, 21 September 1944. *Ruth Greenglass*
59. New York 1388-9 to Moscow, 1 October 1944. *White and Silvermaster*
60. New York 1410 to Moscow, 6 October 1944. *CPUSA work for KGB*

61. New York 1433-5 to Moscow, 10 October 1944. *I. F. Stone, again*
62. New York 1437 to Moscow, 10 October 1944. *Maurice Halperin*
63. New York 1442 to Moscow, 11 October 1944. *Disputes at KGB residency*
64. New York 1469 to Moscow, 17 October 1944. *Document photography*

65. New York 1506 to Moscow, 23 October 1944. *I. F. Stone might help*
66. Moscow 374 to San Francisco, 7 November 1944. *Order of the Red Star*
67. New York 1585 to Moscow, 12 November 1944. *Theodore Hall recruited*
68. New York 1600 to Moscow, 14 November 1944. *Greenglass, Sarant*

69. Moscow 379 to San Francisco, 16 November 1944. *Fifth Line reorganized*
70. New York 1613 to Moscow, 18 November 1944. *Laurence Duggan*
71. New York 1634 to Moscow, 20 November 1944. *Aid to Harry D. White*
72. New York 1635 to Moscow, 21 November 1944. *Reward for Silvermaster*

73. New York 1657 to Moscow, 27 November 1944. *Ethel Rosenberg*
74. New York 1699 to Moscow, 2 December 1944. *Listing atomic scientists*
75. New York 1715 to Moscow, 5 December 1944. *Rosenberg, again*
76. New York 1749-50 to Moscow, 13 December 1944. *Rosenberg ring*

77. New York 1751-3 to Moscow, 13 December 1944. *Silvermaster*
78. New York 1773 to Moscow, 16 December 1944. *Rosenberg; ENORMOZ*
79. New York 1797 to Moscow, 20 December 1944. *Michael Sidorovich*
80. New York 12-3, 15-6 to Moscow, 4 January 1945. *ALBERT reports*

81. New York 18-9 to Moscow, 4 January 1945. *Boris Morros*
82. New York 27 to Moscow, 8 January 1945. *Judith Coplon*
83. Moscow 14 to New York, 4 January 1945. *Communist Party business*
84. New York 79 to Moscow, 18 January 1945. *KGB in Treasury*

85. New York 82 to Moscow, 18 January 1945. *GRU asks KGB aid*
86. Moscow 200 to New York, 6 March 1945. *Bonus for Rosenberg*
87. Moscow 284 and 286 to New York, 28 March 1945. *Flora Wovschin*
88. Washington 1793 to Moscow, 29 March 1945. *HOMER, again*

89. Washington 1822 to Moscow, 30 March 1945. *ALES interviewed by KGB*
90. Moscow 298 to NY, 31 March 1945. *Evaluating ENORMOZ take*
91. Moscow 337 to New York, 8 April 1945. *Delivering Silvermaster take*
92. New York 776 to Moscow, 25 May 1945. *Transfer of KGB agents*

93. New York 777-9 to Moscow, 25 May 1945. *Berger and Krafsur*
94. New York 781-7 to Moscow, 25/26 May 1945. *KGB political analysis*
95. Moscow 709 to New York, 5 July 1945. *MLAD (Theodore Hall)*
96. New York 1052-3 to Moscow, 5 July 1945. *Rewards to agents*

97. Moscow 34 to London, 21 September 1945. *Gouzenko crisis*
98. San Francisco 568 to Moscow, 7 November 1945. *Kuznetsova aboard*
99. Moscow 46 to London, 17 September 1945. *Kim Philby's information*

1. Moscow [Comintern] 117, 121 to the US, 21 and 23 March 1936.

~~TOP SECRET~~ EIDER MASK
NO: 5471/U.S.A.
DATE: 24 March 1936

FROM: MOS
TO: U.S.
NO: 117
DATE: 21 March 1936

Urge you speed up departure of (1 group) students for radio school. Furthermore urge that party choose 3 comrades especially reliable and tested, with good American passports for our chief work. Furthermore urge you choose 5 young comrades well tested and especially vouched for by party knowing well photography and with good American passports. Please reply immediately.

~~TOP SECRET~~ EIDER MASK

TOP SECRET EIDER MASK
NO: 5539/U.S.A.
DATE: 30 March 1936

FROM: MOS
TO: U.S.
NO: 121
DATE: 23 March 1936

In addition to previous communication please inform us on following:-
1. What short term courses for radio operators are there in your country, and of what duration are they.
2. Are there private courses, under whose control are they, are people who finish these courses registered somewhere or take over (1 group) engagements.
3. What are conditions for admission and what fees asked for.

~~TOP SECRET~~ EIDER MASK

2. London [GRU] to Moscow, 10 August 1941.

95

~~TOP SECRET~~

(TRINE)

USSR

Reference No : 3/PPDT/131
(Previously issued as 3/NBF/T1478)

Issued : 11/10/1968

Copy No :

1. BARCh's MEETING
2. FUCHS AND PROBABLE REFERENCE TO ATOMIC ENERGY PROJECT

From: LONDON
To: MOSCOW
No: 2227

10th August 1941

To DIRECTOR

On 8th August BARCh[i] had a meeting with [C% a former acquaintance], Doctor FUCHS [FUKS] [a], who [1 group unidentified] [b] that

[10 groups unrecovered]

[in] [c] BIRMINGHAM [ii]

[34 groups unrecovered]

[B% in] three months [B% time] and then all the material [d] will be sent to CANADA for industrial production [e] [C% .] [1 group unidentified] [f] the fact that in GERMANY, in LEIPZIG [LEJPTsIG] [g]

[9 groups unrecovered]

Professor HEISENBERG [KhEJSENBERG] [iii]

[34 groups unrecovered]

1000 tons of dynamite.

(Report when opportunity occurs [DOKLAD OKAZIEJ]. [h]

No. 430

BRION [iv]

Notes [a] The following is an alternative reading:
"... had a meeting with [C% a former acquaintance] of Doctor Fuchs who ....."
On technical grounds there is nothing to choose between these two versions. Without collateral it is impossible to say which is the correct one.

[b] It appears from the two previous occurrences of this group that the general sense is "said".

/[c]

2. (Continued)

- 2 -

[c] Inserted by the translator. The case ending indicates that the preposition "in" must precede "BIRMINGHAM".

[d] It is almost certain that this means "papers", "documents", etc.

[e] This is a literal translation. The sense is probably:
"... will be sent to CANADA so that industrial methods may be used."
It is known from collateral that laboratory facilities were found to be inadequate and that the decision was taken to use industrial plant.

[f] There is some evidence that the value of this group is:
"Draws attention to"

[g] The structure of the sentence suggests that LEIPZIG should be an adjective and that the passage should read:
"... in the LEIPZIG..."
However the adjectival ending has been tried without success.

[h] This is an elliptical expression which it is exceedingly hard to interpret without the full context.
"OKAZIEJ", or more correctly "S OKAZIEJ", is equivalent to the French "a l'occasion". To send a report or letter "S OKAZIEJ" means to send it when the opportunity arises.
"DOKLAD OKAZIEJ" thus suggests that a report was to be sent when an opportunity for sending one arose. If so, the report was presumably to be sent in writing. (BRION could have signalled a report at any time and need not have waited for a suitable opportunity.)

Comments: [i] BARCh: Simon Davidovich KREMER.

[ii] FUCHS moved to BIRMINGHAM on 27th May 1941 and took up his research duties on the following day.

[iii] HEISENBERG: Professor Werner HEISENBERG who was Professor of Theoretic Physics at LEIPZIG University 1927-1941.

[iv] BRION: Lt.Col. I.A. SKLYaROV.

3. **New York 854 to Moscow, 16 June 1942.**

VENONA
~~TOP SECRET~~

USSR

Ref. No: ███████ (of 11/6/1957)
Issued: ███ /30/4/1964
Copy No: 204

2nd RE-ISSUE

PROPOSED RECRUITMENT OF SEVERAL AGENTS
INCLUDING "UCN/29" AND JANE FOSTER (1942)

From: NEW YORK
To: MOSCOW
No: 854   16 June 42

To VIKTOR.[i]

Reference No. 2359.[a]

The signing on of "UCN/29"[ii] was delayed because of his prolonged absence and the necessity for checking additional information. He arrived today and we shall report results.

[1 group unrecovered] "LIZA"[iii], we are cultivating the American Jane FOSTER[iv] with a view to signing her on. She is about 30 years old and works in WASHINGTON in the Dutch [2 groups unrecovered][B% translator] of Malay languages. FOSTER is a FELLOWCOUNTRYWOMAN[ZEMLYaChKA],[v]

[86 groups unrecoverable]

[D%.....SK] was given [1 group unrecovered].

Her vetting was carried out by us. She is a FELLOWCOUNTRYWOMAN. She is described by the FELLOWCOUNTRYMEN[ZEMLYaK] as a [1 group unrecovered], dedicated person. .....TER[vi] has also been reported on favourably by "███"[vii] who is a friend.

We intend to sign her on with a view to making use of her connections and [2 groups unrecovered] [B% her] [1 group unrecovered] SOUTH AMERICA our tasks [1 group unrecovered]. We urgently request approval.

No. 552   MAKSIM[viii]

Distribution   [Note and Comments overleaf]

~~TOP SECRET~~
VENONA

3. *(Continued)*

Note: [a] Not available.

Comments:
- [i] VIKTOR : Lt. Gen. P. M. FITIN.
- [ii] UCN/29 : Unidentified cover-name. See also NEW YORK's No. 253 of 19th February 1943 ( ) and No. 955 of 21st June 1943 ( ).
- [iii] LIZA : Unidentified cover-name. First occurrence in this lane.
- [iv] FOSTER : Later given the cover-name "SLANG". **Employed by Netherlands Study Unit: later by BEW, then by OSS.**
- [v] FELLOWCOUNTRYWOMAN: Member of the Communist Party.
- [vi] ...TER : The full name cannot be FOSTER. It will however be a fairly short name since TER is preceded by a single group probably of one or two syllables.
- [vii] FAN : Unidentified cover-name. First known occurrence.
- [viii] MAKSIM : Vasilij ZUBILIN, Soviet Vice-Consul in NEW YORK.

4. Moscow 424 to New York, 1 July 1942.

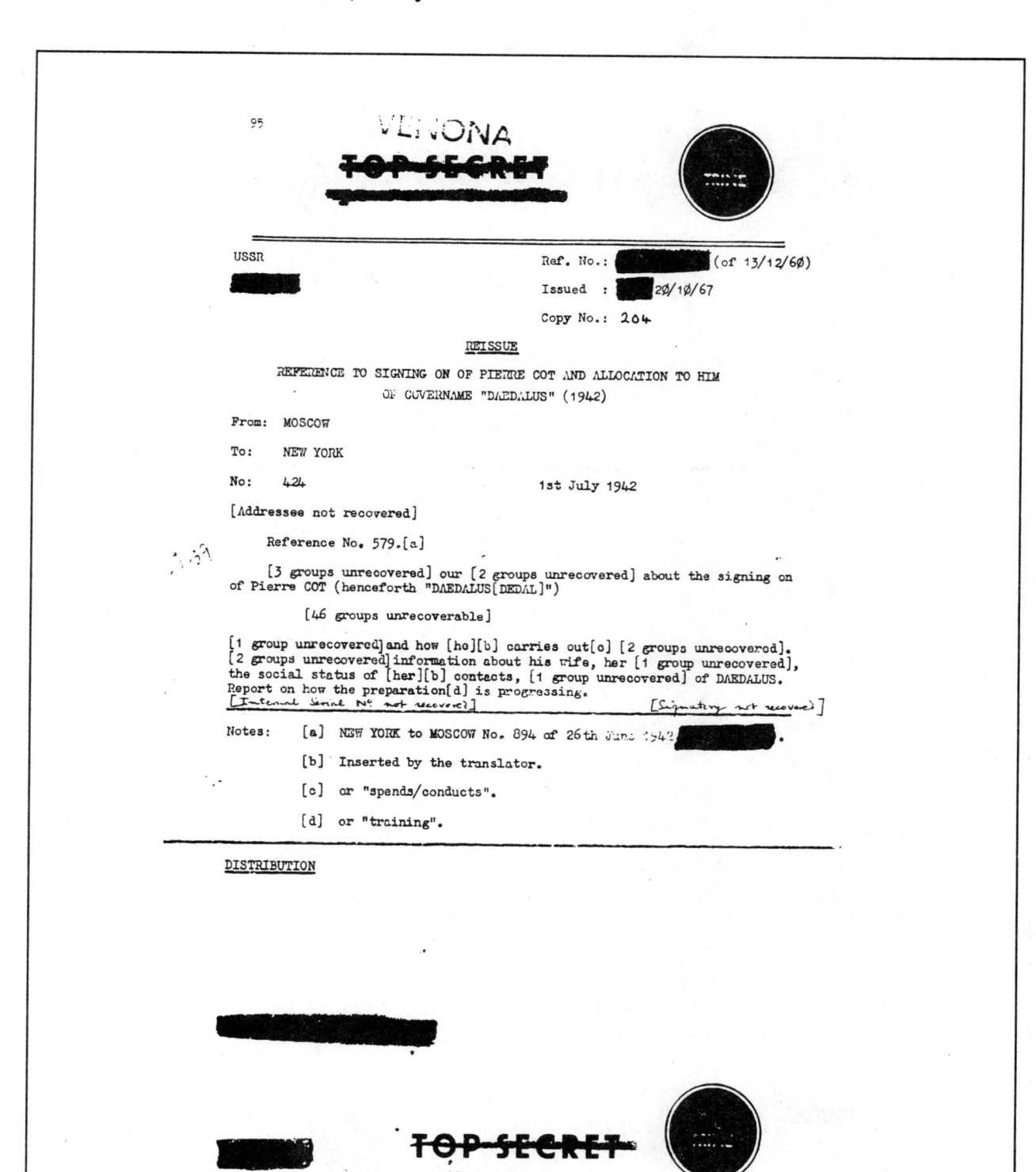

VENONA
~~TOP SECRET~~

USSR	Ref. No.: ███ (of 13/12/60)
	Issued : ███ 20/10/67
	Copy No.: 204

REISSUE

REFERENCE TO SIGNING ON OF PIERRE COT AND ALLOCATION TO HIM
OF COVERNAME "DAEDALUS" (1942)

From: MOSCOW
To: NEW YORK
No: 424   1st July 1942

[Addressee not recovered]

Reference No. 579.[a]

[3 groups unrecovered] our [2 groups unrecovered] about the signing on of Pierre COT (henceforth "DAEDALUS[DEDAL]")

[46 groups unrecoverable]

[1 group unrecovered] and how [he][b] carries out[c] [2 groups unrecovered]. [2 groups unrecovered] information about his wife, her [1 group unrecovered], the social status of [her][b] contacts, [1 group unrecovered] of DAEDALUS. Report on how the preparation[d] is progressing.

[Internal Serial No not recovered]   [Signature not recovered]

Notes: [a] NEW YORK to MOSCOW No. 894 of 26th June 1942.
      [b] Inserted by the translator.
      [c] or "spends/conducts".
      [d] or "training".

DISTRIBUTION

~~TOP SECRET~~
VENONA

5. Washington [Naval-GRU] 2505-12 to Moscow, 31 December 1942.

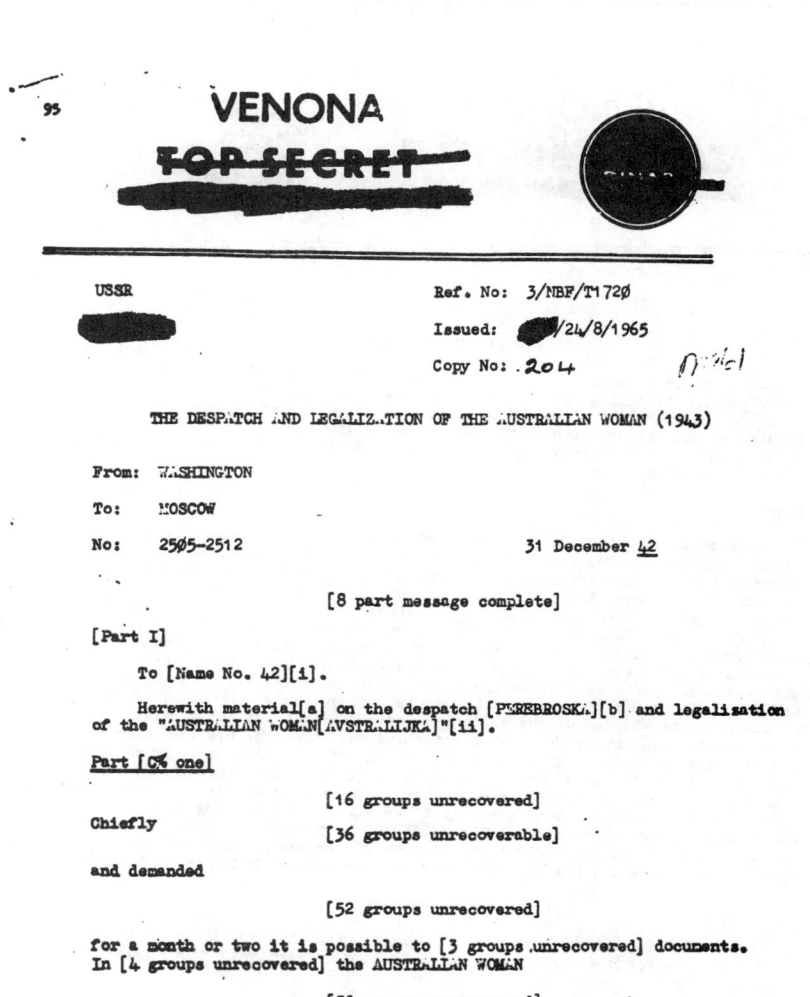

VENONA

~~TOP SECRET~~

USSR

Ref. No: 3/NBF/T1720
Issued: /24/8/1965
Copy No: 204

THE DESPATCH AND LEGALIZATION OF THE AUSTRALIAN WOMAN (1943)

From: WASHINGTON
To: MOSCOW
No: 2505-2512   31 December 42

[8 part message complete]

[Part I]

To [Name No. 42][i].

Herewith material[a] on the despatch [PEREBROSKA][b] and legalisation of the "AUSTRALIAN WOMAN [AVSTRALIJKA]"[ii].

Part [C% one]

[16 groups unrecovered]

Chiefly   [36 groups unrecoverable]

and demanded

[52 groups unrecovered]

for a month or two it is possible to [3 groups unrecovered] documents. In [4 groups unrecovered] the AUSTRALIAN WOMAN

[32 groups unrecovered]

(establishments[KhoZYaJSTVO])[c]

[104 groups unrecovered]

Distribution:

3/NBF/T1720 ~~TOP SECRET~~

VENONA

5. *(Continued)*

VENONA

- 2 -

3/NBF/T1720

[6 groups unrecoverable]

presentation of documents, three referees and the completion of a detailed questionnaire including such questions as the names and addresses of previous employers[d], places of residence, particulars of parents, relations, etc, after which all the papers go to the F.B.I. (counter-intelligence) for checking. It is impossible at present for the AUSTRALIAN WOMAN to get work in these establishments.

[Part II]

2. The basic document which gives proof of American citizenship is the birth certificate. The birth certificate does not, as a rule, serve as an everyday means of identification. The ordinary, everyday documents are the driver's licence, the draft registration card (for men) and various passes and identity papers issued by establishments, businesses, companies and firms. The NEIGBOURS[SOSED][e] are of the opinion that birth certificates were formerly issued by the churches. Now they are issued by hospitals. Archives of birth records are carefully preserved by the Americans and checking a copy of a birth certificate does not cause the F.B.I. any great difficulty. The driver's licence [2 groups unrecoverable] [B% each] adult. As the name and address of the holder are recorded on it, it also serves as an ordinary, everyday means of identification. Licences are issued by the transport department of the City Police (Traffic Department). To obtain them one has to fill up a short questionnaire giving basic biographical details and present a licence from another state or pass a written examination on the traffic regulations of the city in question and a driving test. An American needs no other papers. The NEIGBOUR who promised to draw up a birth certificate said the other day that, in view of the postponement of his appointment to CANADA, his opportunities in this respect had come to naught.

[13 groups unrecovered]

posting to CANADA for this purpose. In his opinion it is possible in the last resort to forge a birth certificate at home or simply to do without papers at first.

[Part III]

[29 groups unrecoverable]

The prospects of a new system of documentation being instituted in the USA are uncertain. The F.B.I. insists on registration and on taking[f]

[38 groups unrecoverable]

about 20 million persons have been fingerprinted. These are mainly: aliens (all aliens are fingerprinted), merchant seamen and crews of ships coming here, servicemen, employees and workers in defence plants and government establishments. The issue of fingerprint identifications to [2 groups unrecovered] is becoming popular. A number of TAYLOR's[iii] people had their fingerprints taken in order to get passes into the ports.

[Continued overleaf]

3/NBF/T1720

VENONA

5. *(Continued)*

[Part IV]

3. The landing of an illegal[g] from our ship requires careful organization. The "GREENS[ZELENYE]"[iv] keep a watchful eye on our ships and people. During the period from September to December 1942 there were two cases of attempts to inspect two ships for a second time. The following cases are known:

   (a) During the inspection of a ship, the passengers and crew were checked a second time on a trivial pretext.

   (b) There was a personal search of members of a crew going into the city "in order to discover smuggled letters[h]". [2 groups unrecovered] to search

[41 groups unrecoverable]

naval intelligence [3 groups unrecovered] with the object of recruitment. There are repeated cases of our sailors not returning to their ships. Individual members of crews are questioned as to whether there are any outsiders on board.

[Part V]

Contrary to the previous arrangements, the Americans only admit the crews of our ships into the city if they show their passes. They are permanent passes and are kept by the Captain. They are issued to each sailor arriving in the USA for the first time after his fingerprints have been taken. The information[MATERIAL][a] on the pass is checked on departure from the port and on return. The number of check points varies. Crews of ships

[45 groups unrecoverable]

in principle remains as before. All objects brought here which are being taken away[j], packages and letters are inspected.

4. In clothing and appearance, our women [B% serving] on ships are clearly distinguishable from the local women. This is because of their stockings, their berets (American women wear hats), their handbags and their untidiness. They do not take any trouble over their hair or their make-up. Suits or overcoats of medium quality differ little from the American ones.

[Part VI]

5. The possible landing ports are SAN FRANCISCO and PORTLAND. Up to 15 of our ships arrive in PORTLAND each month. 6 to 7 arrive in SAN FRANCISCO.

   <u>SAN FRANCISCO</u>

   Advantages:

   (a) A large city in which it is easy to disappear.

   [Continued overleaf]

3/NBF/T1720

5. (Continued)

- (b) Easier to get a hotel room or a [furnished][k] room if necessary.
- (c) Easier to buy a train ticket.
- (d) Less danger of the AUSTRALIAN WOMAN's meeting

[60 groups unrecoverable]

[PORTLA]ND[k]

Advantages:

- (a) DAVIS[DĒVIS][v] can be relied on. His work is such that he sees personally to the ships and is in the port practically all the time.
- (b) If necessary DAVIS can avail himself of the help of our other people there.

Disadvantages:

- (a) The city is small. It would be harder to disappear in it. It is necessary to [2 groups unrecovered] on the day of landing.
- (b) It is harder to get a hotel room and practically impossible to take a [furnished][k] room. Our people have been watched and are well known. It would be more difficult to pass the time until the departure of the train.
- (c) DAVIS is overburdened with his own work.

[Part VII]

6. Sleeper tickets on long distance trains may be bought at the ticket office two or three days in advance. Names and addresses are required when making a reservation. Two or three trains a day leave for NEW YORK. The trip takes up to five days and one must change in CHICAGO. The southern route through NEW ORLEANS should be rejected.

[55 groups unrecoverable]

The press reports that the checking of cars is in force along the west coast, especially around LOS ANGELES and to the south. To combat desertion, the military police check the papers of enlisted men in trains at PORTLAND and SAN FRANCISCO. Civilians are not liable to have their papers checked. Carriages on long distance trains consist of common sleepers and separate compartments - there are compartments for one-person (roomettes) and for two or three persons (compartments) and special class compartments (drawing-rooms). In this instance a roomette would be the most suitable. One boards the train 20 to 30 minutes in advance. One can eat in the restaurant car or order in the compartment.

[Continued overleaf]

3/NBF/T1720

5. *(Continued)*

VENONA
~~TOP SECRET~~

- 5 -   3/NBF/T1720

[Part VIII]

7. <u>Money</u>

    The F.B.I. keeps a strict check of all the numbers and series of banknotes. My expenditure is also subjected to checking through the bank. Money received in the homeland by our citizens who come here

[15 groups unrecoverable]

series.

    End of part one[l].

No. 745-752　　　　　　　　　　　　　　　[Name No. 91][vi]

Notes:
- [a] The Russian word MATERIAL is often used in the sense of "documents" or "documentary material". In this context it appears to mean "information".
- [b] PEREBROSKA generally means the transfer of troops or goods from one place to another. In conspiratorial language it means the despatch of an agent to a given country.
- [c] KhoZYaJSTVO is very difficult to translate out of context. it can mean "economy", "farm", "establishment", "household".
- [d] Literally "the designations and addresses of previous service".
- [e] Or "NEIGBOUR".
- [f] There is technical evidence that the word after "taking" is "fingerprints".
- [g] I.e. "an illegal agent".
- [h] This can either be interpreted as "contraband and letters" or "contrabandletters" i.e. "smuggled letters".
- [j] Literally "all objects being transported, being carried away...". This presumably means "all objects brought here by ship and taken out of the dock area".
- [k] Inserted by translator.
- [l] I.e. part one of the material on the despatch and legalization of the AUSTRALIAN WOMAN. There is no indication that part two will be sent later.

[Continued overleaf]

3/NBF/T1720

~~TOP SECRET~~
VENONA

5. *(Continued)*

VENONA

~~TOP SECRET~~

- 6 - 3/NBF/T1720

Comments: [1] [Name No. 42] : Possibly Capt. (1st Rank) M.A. VORONTsOV.

[ii] AUSTRALIAN WOMAN : Probably Francia Yakil'nilna MITYNEN (exact spelling not verified) who is probably identical with Edna Margaret PATTERSON.

[iii] TAYLOR : Unidentified cover-name. Also mentioned in messages passed between 14/2/1943 and 8/6/1943; the latest message was No. 997 of 8/6/1943 (3/NBF/T1201).

[iv] GREENS : Members of a non-Soviet counter-espionage agency.

[v] DAVIS[DĒVIS] : Unidentified cover-name. Also mentioned in WASHINGTON's 1040-1041 of 13/5/1943 and 1209 of 5/6/1943.

[vi] [Name No. 91] : Probably Capt. (1st Rank) I.A. EGORIChEV.

[vii] NEIGHBOUR : Soviet Intelligence Organization other than that of the Naval Attaché

3/NBF/T1720

~~TOP SECRET~~

VENONA

6. Washington [Naval-GRU] 834, 846-8 to Moscow, 18 April 1943.

Reissue (T1274)

From: WASHINGTON
To: MOSCOW
Nos: 834, 846-848

18 April 1943

[Part I] To [Name no. 42][i].

[5 groups unrecovered] the following about the NATIVES[TUZEMTsY][ii] and their methods of work with the personnel [5 groups unrecovered].

1. Commander ERDMAN[iii] -- head of a group of NATIVES,

[7 groups unrecovered].

In a drunken condition he spoke indiscreetly

[13 groups unrecoverable]

I assume during the period 1918-21.

[11 groups unrecovered],

evacuated to

[10 groups unrecovered]

(D% these languages

[37 groups unrecoverable]

ERDMAN

[9 groups unrecovered]

a) ERDMAN

[4 groups unrecovered]

Concerning this one of the interpreters who has been assigned to us (Lieutenant PLATKIPS[iv]) spoke indiscreetly [2 groups unrecovered] refused to fulfill this

[62 groups unrecoverable]

d) I switched MOL"s[v] telephone over to my switchboard for monitoring.

e) At a reception at MOL"s place in a conversation with Captain Third Rank KhMYROV[vi] he[a] stated that they wanted to get him drunk and that our people behave "like snakes in the grass".

6. *(Continued)*

VENONA

2.

[Part II] f) In a personal letter the Chief of the Shipbuilders, who is in contact with us on shipbuilding matters, said that he could not give us radar. This was discovered when FINK[vii] put some oblique questions to the Department of the Navy [MORSKOE MINISTERSTVO].

g) Under [1 group unrecovered] of ERDMAN Captain DONALD[viii], one of the acceptance officers at the plant[b] who is loyal to us, has been taken off the work.

2. [C% Informants] of the Intelligence Service [RAZVEDKA].

a) Interpreters: Lieutenant ANIKEEV[ix] who came from ODESSA in 1922, Lieutenant PLOTKINS who is the son of a SARATOV merchant, emigrated in 1926 and (2 groups unrecovered) was the only worker free

[22 groups unrecoverable]

readily[c], old sailors (over 40 years of age) no doubt dressed [B% in civilian clothes], sailors or intelligence men dressed as sailors who speak Russian, a unit of whom were specially moved to Florida, military intelligence men of the American Army particularly -- [C% Poles], clerks [1 group unrecovered] [D% at the] bases and others.

[Part III] Organization and method of work:

1. Secret surveillance by counter-espionage agents, for example at the tailor's where our people order uniforms, several cases of shadowing etc. have been noticed.

2. Special surveillance in key bases.

3. Throwing light on the functions of Deputy Commanders and their real role (Deputies for Political Matters[POMPOLIT]).

4. Discovering the attitude of the enlisted men towards the command, towards drink and women.

5. Finding out how Comrade STALIN is regarded and attempting to discredit him in the eyes of Red Fleet seamen.

6. Bringing to light dissatisfaction among Red Fleet seamen, boasting about their own standards of living, and attempting to win their confidence.

7. Attempting to get them drunk and to corrupt them by using women.

8. The suggestion made to Red Seaman BUShUEV[x]

[14 groups unrecoverable]

carbon paper

[11 groups unrecovered]

the NATIVES.

10. Finding out the geographical

VENONA

6. *(Continued)*

[Part IV]   [30 groups unrecovered].

I have given instructions to RUSSEL[ROSSEL'][xi][2 groups unrecovered] with ERDMAN and the NATIVES

[30 groups unrecovered]

with the NATIVES by well-wishers

[35 groups unrecovered]
[45 groups unrecoverable]

not to give a visa[d] for permanent work with us[xii]. When the opportunity occurs this material should be used for presenting the NATIVES with the bill. Discipline in the unit is good and many NATIVES make favorable comments [2 groups unrecovered] there was the case of the two Red Seamen LADYGIN and LADYShKIN who were sent back in a drunken condition. Details by letter. I[e] gave KENT[xiii] and JIM[DZhIM][xiv] instructions [2 groups unrecovered] a search locally and to brief RUSSEL's people.

3. A report about ERDMAN should be sent to the People's Commissariat of Foreign Affairs[NARKOMINDEL]. I advise against sending the crews of the next minesweepers until the ships [have reached a state of][f] preliminary readiness. Please [1 group unrecovered] this material to STEPANOV[xv].

Nos. 287, 294, 296   [Name no. 91][xvi]

Notes: [a] The antecedent is not clear.
[b] "plant," "factory" or "yard"[ZAVOD].
[c] readily[BOJKO]: This could possibly be the surname BOJKO, but in this context the adverb seems more likely.
[d] "visa" or "visas."
[e] "I," "we," "he," or "they."
[f] Inserted by translator.

Comments:
[i] [Name no. 42]: Possibly Capt. (1st Rank) M.A. VORONTsOV.
[ii] TUZEMTsY: the NATIVES, an unidentified cover-term. (Also see Stockholm-Moscow message nos. 698-699 of 1 March 1943.)
[iii] Commander Robert Park ERDMAN who in February 1943 was Officer in Charge of Liaison Personnel with the Soviet Government. As of 1942 he was to act as Liaison Officer for the Russian officers and crew who were to man minesweepers being built at the Tampa Shipbuilding Corporation.
[iv] Presumably an error for Lt. Maurice Frank PLOTKINS who was assigned to the staff of Cmdr. ERDMAN in ST. PETERSBURG, Florida in December 1943.
[v] MOL': Capt. (3rd Rank) Mikhail Nikolaevich MOL' of the Soviet Government Purchasing Commission.
[vi] Capt. (3rd Rank) Evgenij A. KhMYROV, a Soviet Marine Inspector who was assigned to the Tampa Shipbuilding Company, TAMPA, Florida in January 1943.
[vii] FINK: Possibly Capt. (1st Rank) Pavel A. PANTsYRNYJ.
[viii] Captain DONALD: Unidentified.
[ix] Lt. Nicholas Michael ANIKEEV, U.S. Navy interpreter, who assisted in the transfer of American ships to the Soviet Navy under the Lend-Lease program.
[x] BUShUEV: Probably the Soviet seaman Vasilij BUShUEV who deserted in the U.S. in 1943. (See WASHINGTON-MOSCOW no. 1646 of 17 July 1943).
[xi] RUSSELL: Unidentified.
[xii] See WASHINGTON's no. 762 of 17 April 1943 -- "The NATIVES are waiting for visas."

6. *(Continued)*

```
Comments (cont'd.):
   [xiii]  KENT:  Probably Capt. Nikolaj Alekseevich SKRYaGIN, As-
           sistant Naval Attache, WASHINGTON.
    [xiv]  JIM:  Lt. Georgij Stepanovich PASKO, Secretary to the
           Soviet Naval Attache, WASHINGTON.
     [v]   STEPANOV:  Vice-Adm. G.A. STEPANOV, Acting Chief of
           Naval Staff.
    [xvi]  [Name no. 91]:  Probably Capt. (1st Rank) I. A. EGO-
           RIChEV, Soviet Naval Attache in WASHINGTON.
```

1 March 1971

7. New York 782 to Moscow, 26 May 1943.

VENONA

Reissue

26 May 1943

From: NEW YORK
To: MOSCOW
No: 782

To VIKTOR[i]

"KOCH"[KOKh][ii] reports that at the "CAPTAIN"[iii]--"BOAR"[iv] conference [1 group garbled]

[16 groups unrecovered]

known, "IZBA"[v] has no

[40 groups unrecoverable]

information from ISTANBUL [8 groups unrecovered]

[D% known to the Rumanian ambassador but in the situation after]

[53 groups unrecovered]

thousand dollars in support of an underground [B% diversion and] espionage group in France.

In the middle of June KOCH is going [2 groups unrecovered] month to CHUNKING to acquaint himself there with the work of the IZBA group. With him will go an American army colonel [1 group unidentified] at CHUNGKING [3 groups unrecovered] espionage group. If it is considered necessary to establish [6 groups unrecovered] with him there, we will arrange a password.

We discussed with KOCH the question of his removing documents for photographing. KOCH said that in some cases he [B% agrees] to do this, but as a rule he considers it inexpedient. He promised to think [6 groups unrecovered]

MAKSIM[vi]

[i] VIKTOR: Lt. Gen. P. M. FITIN.
[ii] KOCH: Duncan C. LEE.
[iii] CAPTAIN: Franklin Delano ROOSEVELT.
[iv] BOAR: Winston Leonard Spencer CHURCHILL.
[v] IZBA: Office of Strategic Services.
[vi] MAKSIM: Vasilij Mikhajlovich ZUBILIN.

5 May 1978

VENONA

8. New York 777-781 to Moscow, 26 May 1943.

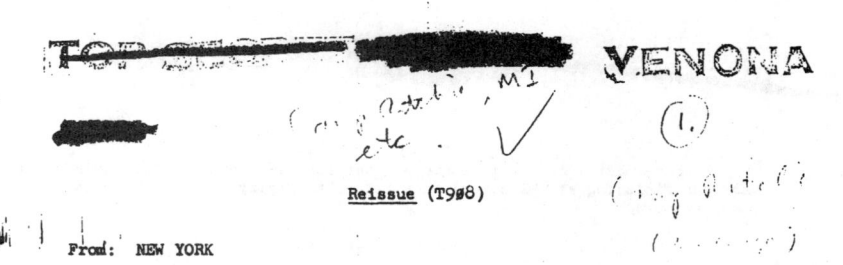

VENONA

Reissue (T908)

From: NEW YORK
To: MOSCOW
Nos: 777-781

26 May 1943

[Part I] To VIKTOR[i].
"SLAVA"[ii] reports that the "Military Intelligence Training Center" school is situated at RITCHIE, Maryland. [5 groups unrecovered] Russian section.

The school has 4 sectors:

1. Interrogation work with prisoners of war, has an Italian and German sections. [6 groups unrecovered][C% Italian] section, but it

[36 groups unrecovered]

, Far Eastern, Arabian, Turkey, USSR, England.

3. Counterintelligence, [6 groups unrecovered] [D% who have served] in enemy armies and the "[1 group unidentified]ness' of their own students.

4. Photographic sector, they study [2 groups unrecovered],

[18 groups unrecovered]

everyone in the sector goes through a general course

[86 groups unrecovered]

and one each: Italian, French, English, Arabian, Spanish, [3 groups unrecovered], Russian, Turkish, a section of officers, counterintelligence, photographic and [2 groups unrecovered] section of China and Japan. (The basic school of the "Far East" is at SAVAGE[iii]

[35 groups unrecoverable]

Military Intelligence G2) [4 groups unrecovered]. The school prepares [5 groups unrecovered].

[Part II] In the school at RITCHIE instruction is given to enlisted men and officers. They [1 group unrecovered] together and go through one and the same course.

[19 groups unrecovered]

lieutenants, captains and several majors.

VENONA

219

8. (Continued)

- 2 -

The students of the photographic section are recruited from among airmen and upon finishing at the school they return to flying units. Students of the other sectors

[22 groups unrecovered]

in divisions, corps etc. [3 groups unrecovered] groups

[36 groups unrecovered]

sergeants [11 groups unrecovered] sergeant first class

[58 groups unrecoverable]

lecturers know little about the Red Army and

[67 groups unrecovered]

[Part III]   [16 groups unrecovered]

in May 3 officers and 11 enlisted men [9 groups unrecovered] the Russian section. In the first year study was conducted only on the English language, gave

[10 groups unrecoverable]

and third classes of the air sector were [21 groups unrecovered] KISLITsIN[iv], former [C% teacher], has been living in the USA since

[18 groups unrecovered]

and was included in the regular teaching staff. In [7 groups unrecovered] sector.

In the Russian section 3 members graduated:

1. Vadim GONTsOV[v] -- age 28 years,

[19 groups unrecovered]

2. Sergej GLADILIN[vi],

[10 groups unrecovered]

3. Nikolaj KRIKARYaNETs[vii] -- GRIGOR'EV [3 groups unrecovered]. Emigrated to the USA

[45 groups unrecovered].

Before joining the school he was

[12 groups unrecovered].

He has a good command of the Russian language. He graduated with honor. [6 groups unrecovered].

[Part IV]   5. Lieutenant [2 groups unrecovered]ROV[viii], [8 groups unrecovered]

8. *(Continued)*

- 3 -

    [D%6. Lieutenant] HACKNER[ix], 30 - 32 years old, a Polish Jew. Pro-Soviet feelings.

    7. [D%Stepan] SUDAKAV[x], 21 years old. [3 groups unrecovered] emigrated from China.

    [15 groups unrecovered]

    8. [1 group unrecovered] GRADASOV[xi], 21 years old. Emigrated from China where his parents remained. [6 groups unrecovered]. Leans to the right [1 group unrecovered].

    9. [1 group unrecovered OROShKO[xii], 21 years old, emigrated from China.

    10. [15 groups unrecoverable] a Jew from WARSAW. [6 groups unrecovered]. He lived in PARIS where he was a correspondent [2 groups unrecovered] Jewish newspaper. Pro-Soviet feelings[xiii].

    11. Aleksandr ORLEY(OVChAROV)[xiv], 32 - 33 years old, a Jew. He has a [1 group unidentified] business in NEW YORK.

    12. Osya LYaPID[xv], 24 - 28 years old, a Jew from Poland. The Russian language [3 groups unrecovered] in the army at the beginning of the year. Before joining the school [5 groups unrecovered].

[Part V]   [5 groups unrecovered]:

    1. Nisen ChIPChIN[xvi] [1 group unrecovered] school. 31 - 33 years old, [4 groups unrecovered] Jew. He lives in TYRE[xvii] at the address 3871 Sedgewick Avenue Bronx

    [10 groups unrecoverable]

982[a]. He is a teacher at the school. He is drawn in exclusively during examinations. Pro-Soviet feelings

    [55 groups unrecoverable]

LEBEDEV[xviii] thus graduated in the French section.

    The director of the Russian section is Lieutenant ZANDER[xix]

    [39 groups unrecovered]

in the hospital attached to the school, complement and description of the students. SLAVA was warned about appropriate secrecy and caution. For the time being we are carrying out work with him through [4 groups unrecoverable]

No. 427   LUKA[xx]

VENONA

8. *(Continued)*

VENONA

- 4 -

Notes: [a] 982: The telephone number of Julius Epstein, brother-in-law of Nelson Chipchin and resident of the Sedgewick Ave. address was KINGSBRIDGE 3 - 1982. This telephone number would exactly fill the 10 unrecoverable groups.

Comments:
- [i] VIKTOR: Lt. Gen. P.M. FITIN.
- [ii] SLAVA: Ilya Elliott WOLSTON.
- [iii] SAVAGE: Camp Savage, Minnesota.
- [iv] KISLITsIN: Alexander J. KESLITZIN graduated from the 4th class, section 9 at Camp Ritchie.
- [v] GONTsOV: Vadim Feodor GONTZOFF, stage name Victor KENDALL, naturalized at Hagerstown, Md. 19 May 1943.
- [vi] GLADILIN: Unidentified.
- [vii] KRIKARYaNETs: Believed to be identical with Nicholas GREGORIEV (Nicolai I. KRIKORIANTZ-GRIGORIEFF) who became a naturalized U.S. citizen in February 1943.
- [viii] .....ROV: There is a possibility that this name is MAJSUROV. According to Benjamin WAID a certain Donald K. MAISSUROV was known to him at Camp Ritchie.
- [ix] HACKNER: Believed to be identical with Lt. Allan Jacob HACKNER, commissioned in February 1943.
- [x] SUDAKOV: Also known as Stephen SUDYKOFF and said to have been a member of Section 10, Class 6 at Camp Ritchie.
- [xi] GRADASOV: Evgenij Sergeevich GRADASOV, attended Russian liaison classes at Camp Ritchie with Ilya WOLSTON from March until July 1943. Was granted U.S. citizenship in 1943 at which time he changed his name to Eugene GARSON.
- [xii] OROShKO: A M/Sgt. Joseph W. OROZCO is known to have been at Camp Ritchie in September 1943.
- [xiii] This information could refer to Benjamin WAID, aka Isaac GURFINKEL, who was granted U.S. citizenship in June 1943.
- [xiv] ORLEY: Aleksandr ORLEY was a member of Section 10, Class 6 at Camp Ritchie.
- [xv] LYaPID: Identical with Jerry LAPID, member of Section 10, Class 6 at Camp Ritchie.
- [xvi] ChIPChIN: Also known as Nelson CHIPCHIN, naturalized in Hagerstown, Md. in February 1943.
- [xvii] TYRE: NEW YORK CITY.
- [xviii] LEBEDEV: There is known to have been a S/Sgt. Andrew M. LEBEDEFF at Camp Ritchie in September 1943.
- [xix] ZANDER: Lt. Randolph ZANDER is known to have been an instructor at Camp Ritchie in September 1943.
- [xx] LUKA: Pavel P. KLARIN.

7 May 1970

VENONA

9. New York 786-7 to Moscow, 26 May 1943.

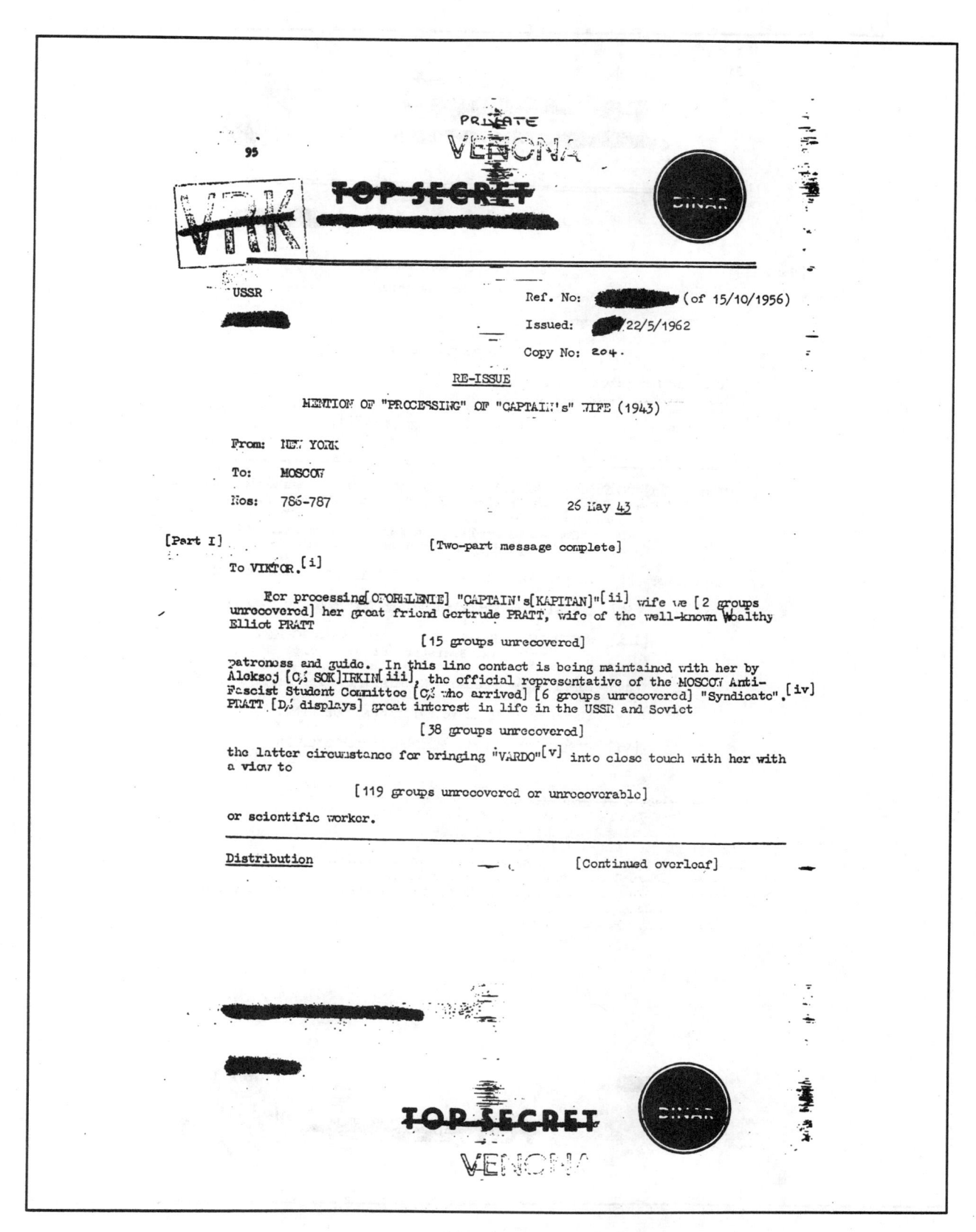

USSR

Ref. No: ▓▓▓▓ (of 15/10/1956)
Issued: ▓▓ 22/5/1962
Copy No: 204

RE-ISSUE

MENTION OF "PROCESSING" OF "CAPTAIN's" WIFE (1943)

From: NEW YORK
To: MOSCOW
Nos: 786-787   26 May 43

[Part I]   [Two-part message complete]

To VIKTOR.[i]

For processing[OFORMLENIE] "CAPTAIN's[KAPITAN][ii] wife we [2 groups unrecovered] her great friend Gertrude PRATT, wife of the well-known wealthy Elliot PRATT

[15 groups unrecovered]

patroness and guide. In this line contact is being maintained with her by Aleksej [C% SOK]IRKIN[iii], the official representative of the MOSCOW Anti-Fascist Student Committee [C% who arrived] [6 groups unrecovered] "Syndicate".[iv] PRATT [D% displays] great interest in life in the USSR and Soviet

[38 groups unrecovered]

the latter circumstance for bringing "VARDO"[v] into close touch with her with a view to

[119 groups unrecovered or unrecoverable]

or scientific worker.

Distribution   [Continued overleaf]

9. *(Continued)*

95

~~TOP SECRET~~

2

[Part II]   [87 groups unrecovered]
                         [64 groups unrecoverable]

"CAPTAIN[1 group unrecovered][a]".

                         [71 groups unrecovered]

for further processing.

No. 432   MAKSIM[vi]

Note: [a] This unidentified group is not simply an inflexion added to KAPITAN. It is possible that it is added to form an oblique case of the word KAPITANSHA – "Captain's wife" which might have been adopted to replace the form "wife of "CAPTAIN" which is used at the opening of the message.

Comments: [i] VIKTOR : Lt. Gen. P. M. FITIN.

        [ii] CAPTAIN : Franklin Delano ROOSEVELT.

        [iii] SOKIRKIN : Possibly the Aleksej P. SOKIRKIN who by 1950 was 1st Secretary at the Soviet Embassy in WASHINGTON

        [iv] SYNDICATE: People's Commissariat for Foreign Affairs.

        [v] VARDO : Elizaveta Yur'evna ZUBILINA.

        [vi] MAKSIM : Vasilij Mikhajlovich ZUBILIN, Soviet Vice-Consul in NEW YORK.

~~TOP SECRET~~

10. New York 812 to Moscow, 29 May 1943.

VENONA
~~TOP SECRET~~

USSR

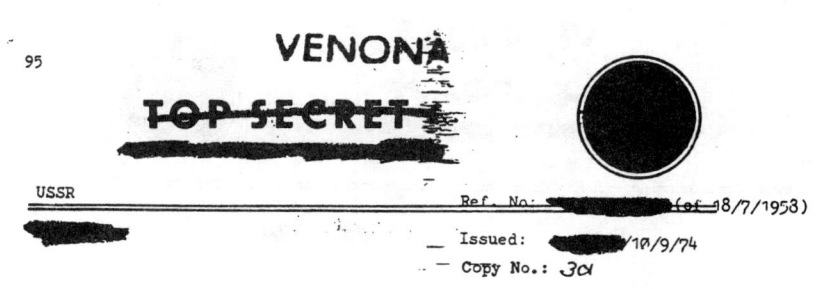

Ref. No: (of 18/7/1953)
Issued: 10/9/74
Copy No.: 301

3RD REISSUE

"19" REPORTS ON DISCUSSIONS WITH "KAPITAN", "KABAN" AND ZAMESTITEL' ON THE SECOND FRONT

(1943)

From: NEW YORK
To: MOSCOW
No: 812
29 May 1943

To VIKTOR[i].

"19"[ii] reports that "KAPITAN"[iii] and "KABAN"[iv], during conversations in the "COUNTRY [STRANA][v]", invited "19" to join them and ZAMESTITEL'[vi] openly told "KABAN"

[10 groups unrecovered]

second front against GERMANY this year. KABAN considers that, if a second front should prove to be unsuccessful, then this [3 groups unrecovered] harm to Russian interests and [6 groups unrecovered]. He considers it more advantageous and effective to weaken GERMANY by bombing and to use this time for "[4 groups unrecovered] political crisis so that there may be no doubt that a second front next year will prove successful."

ZAMESTITEL' and

[14 groups unrecovered]

". 19 thinks that "KAPITAN" is not informing ZAMESTITEL' of important military decisions and that therefore ZAMESTITEL' may not have exact knowledge of [1 group unrecovered] with the opening of a second front against GERMANY and its postponement from this year to next year. 19 says that ZAMESTITEL' personally is an ardent supporter of a second front at this time and considers postponement

[Continued overleaf]

VENONA
~~TOP SECRET~~

10. *(Continued)*

```
                    VENONA
                    TOP SECRET


                         2              (of 18/7/1958)

                 [15 groups unrecovered]

can shed blood

                 [13 groups unrecoverable]

recently shipping between the USA and

                 [40 groups unrecovered]

The "COUNTRY" hardly [9 groups unrecovered] "insufficient reason for
delaying a second front."

No. 443                                            MER[vii]


Footnotes:  [i]    VIKTOR      : Lt. Gen. P.M. FITIN.

            [ii]     19        : Unidentified cover designation.

            [iii]  KAPITAN     : i.e. "CAPTAIN"; Franklin D. ROOSEVELT.

            [iv]   KABAN       : i.e. "BOAR"; Winston CHURCHILL.

            [v]    COUNTRY     : U.S.A.

            [vi]   ZAMESTITEL' : i.e. Deputy - therefore possibly
                                 Henry Agard WALLACE, who was
                                 ROOSEVELT's Deputy (Vice-President)
                                 at this time: later he is referred to
                                 by the covername "LOTSMAN".

            [vii]  MER         : Probably Iskhak Abdulovich AKhMEROV.


                    VENONA
                    TOP SECRET
```

11. New York 887 to Moscow, 9 June 1943.

~~TOP SECRET TRINE~~ VENONA

From: NEW YORK
To: MOSCOW
No.: 887

9 June 1943

To VIKTOR[i].

1. "ZAYaTs"[ii] reports that according to information of a [C% branch] of the "IZBA"[iii]

[73 groups unrecovered]

in ITALY. Also Italian workers are returning from GERMANY.

2. "KOKh"[iv] reports that the "IZBA" has received from its [C% branch] in SIDON[v] two confidential reports on [3 groups unrecovered]. One of them from 30 April says that EDEN is inclined to side with the Poles but "KABAN"[vi] takes a more moderate position proposing to cede [D% BYELORUSSIA] and the UKRAINE to the USSR and Eastern PRUSSIA to POLAND

[13 groups unrecovered]

Poles and the chances for

[18 groups unrecovered]

"IZBA" from

[30 groups unrecoverable]

PLIT-GALATs[vii]

[13 groups unrecovered]

diplomatic relations of [a] the USSR.

No. 490　　　　　　　　　　　　　　　　　　　　　　　　　　　　LUKA[viii]

Notes:
    [a] Could alternatively be "with, by" etc. The preposition is uncertain.

Comments:
    [i] VIKTOR: Lt. Gen. P.M. FITIN.
    [ii] ZAYaTs: i.e. "HARE" or "STOWAWAY". Maurice HALPERIN, who became chief of the Latin American Section of the Research and Analysis Branch of O.S.S.
    [iii] IZBA: Office of Strategic Services.
    [iv] KOKh: i.e. KOCH. Duncan C. LEE of the Far Eastern Section of O.S.S.
    [v] SIDON: LONDON.
    [vi] KABAN: i.e. "BOAR". Winston CHURCHILL.
    [vii] PLIT-GALATs: Possibly a reference to Marcel PILET-GOLAZ, at this time a member of the Swiss Federal Council responsible for foreign affairs.
    [viii] LUKA: Pawel P. KLARIN, Soviet Vice-Consul in NEW YORK.

31 October 1968

~~TOP SECRET TRINE~~ VENONA

12. New York [GRU] 927-8 to Moscow, 16 June 1943.

~~TOP SECRET TRINE~~ VENONA

GRU

From: NEW YORK
To: MOSCOW
Nos.: 927 - 928

16 June 1943

[Part I] To the Director.

1. MARQUIS[MARKIZ][i] has established friendly relations with T.A. BISSON, (in future "ARTHUR[ARTUR]") who has recently left BEW[ii]; he is now working in the Institute of Pacific Relations and in the editorial office of MARQUIS's periodical. ARTHUR evidently is well informed and has [C% agents] in government institutions.

2. ARTHUR passed to MARQUIS, so that as his colleague in the editorial office he might get acquainted with them, copies of four documents:

   (a) his own report for BEW with his views on working out a plan for shipments of American troops to China;

   (b) a report by the Chinese embassy in WASHINGTON to its government in China about the dimensions and means of trade between the Japanese in the occupied territories and Chinese industrialists in free Chinese [B% territory][a];

   (c) a brief BEW report of April 1943 on a general evaluation of the forces of the sides on the Soviet-German front and the prospects of the German summer offensive;

   (d) a report by the American consul in VLADIVOSTOK, WARD, on the economic and political situation in the VLADIVOSTOK area.

3. The reports are in translated form. We will pass on valuable points [B% by telegraph].

4. A check on ARTHUR's personal connections will be undertaken on the spot. At the same time make use of the Centre's opportunities for checking.

[Part II] 5. Concerning JACK[DZhEK][iii][:]

   (a) No transactions were arranged. A few days ago COX[KOKS][iv] met RUDI[v]. The latter [13 groups unrecovered]

   [35 groups unrecoverable]

   [13 groups unrecovered]

. To ask RUDI [C% to replace] JACK is useless since he considers him the best of the possible candidates.

   (b) RUDI and JACK have put forward one person to set up a group of sources in NEZhIN[vi]. COX had [3 groups unrecovered] to use this person on pay by the month (180 American dollars). My instructions to him were - having received JACK's proposal, to give his views on the use and payment of the person for forwarding to the Centre. Now COX is asking the Centre to [C% agree] to the use and pay of the [C% proposed] person for three months to check his [b] possibilities. This person is a former member of one of the [B% local] committees of the KORPORATsIYa[Mil], a woman, name L. GORDON. I think payment for three months should be

- 1 -

~~TOP SECRET TRINE~~ VENONA

12. *(Continued)*

~~TOP SECRET TRINE~~ VENONA

- 2 -

allowed, at the same time insisting on her being directed personally by COX ([6 groups unrecovered]).

6. BREME[BREM][viii] has been detained by the school for several days to continue his training. He will return about the **th June[c].

7. Reference your No. 9474 [d]. The instruction to cease [C% correspondence] with the [C% city] [1 group unrecovered] ([1 group unrecovered] only on my part) has been put into effect (this was permitted by you in May 1942, telegram No. 5466 [d]). As soon as possible with [2 groups unrecovered] in their name.

8. The ship's departure is being held up until 26th June. MOK[ix] will be put on board on 22nd or 23rd June.

No. 168   MOLIÈRE[MOL'ER][x]

T.N.: [a] See New York to Moscow #989 of 24 June 1943, paragraph 1, which corrects this statement.

[b] Inserted by the translator. The "his" in the Russian is to be explained by the fact that the word used for "person" - ChELOVEK - is masculine.

[c] A date between 16th and 22nd June.

[d] Not available.

Comments:
[i] MARKIZ: Joseph Milton BERNSTEIN.

[ii] BEW: Board of Economic Warfare.

[iii] DZhEK: Unidentified.

[iv] KOKS: Unidentified.

[v] RUDI: Unidentified.

[vi] NEZhIN: Unidentified, probably a city. *(presumably NYC)*

[vii] KORPORATsIYa: the Communist Party.

[viii] BREM: Thomas BABIN.

[ix] MOK: Unidentified.

[x] MOL'ER: Pavel P. MIKhAJLOV, GRU Resident in NEW YORK.

15 April 1968

~~TOP SECRET TRINE~~ VENONA

13. New York [GRU] 938 to Moscow, 17 June 1943.

~~TOP SECRET TRINE~~ VENONA

GRU

From: NEW YORK
To: MOSCOW
No. 938

17 June 1943

To the Director.

I am transmitting the main points of a report of BEW[i] (compiled in April) reviewing the evaluation of the American and British Intelligence Services of the forces in the Soviet-German front in 1943 (the report was given by MARQUIS[MARKIZ][ii] from ARTHUR[ARTUR][iii]):

1. The main conclusion in the [C% report]

   [20 groups unrecoverable]

2. The evaluation of the British Intelligence Service:

   The ground and air forces of the USSR considerably exceed the German. The USSR's production of tanks and aircraft exceeds by far the German. The economic and possibly the military potential of the USSR have not reached their peak, but the German is on the decline. On the front by March there were 250 Soviet divisions, German (in the equivalent) 160-170, not considering Rumanian and others. Aircraft correspondingly 4,000-4,500 and 1,600.

3. [The evaluation][a] of the American [Intelligence Service][a]:

   "It is inadequately defined: all the German losses on the front will be replaced by summer; by [C% 1 June of this year] 30-40 new divisions will be formed and trained. The aim of the Germans in 1943 is as before - the destruction of the Red Army in offensive operations."

4. The BEW's own conclusions:

   a) British Intelligence grossly exaggerates the Russian forces and underestimates the German forces, but the Americans do the opposite.

   b) A full-scale offensive by the Germans is beyond the limits of their possibilities. At the same time the economy of the USSR is so strained that the armed forces cannot be, from the point of view of ability to conduct operations, at the 1942 level for more than a year.

   c) In the summer the Russians will have considerable superiority on the ground and undisputed mastery in the air.

   d) The superiority of the Germans is in transport both in the rear and along the front for regrouping.

   e) If by the summer Germany can replace all her losses and there will be no risk in weakening her garrisons in Europe, she can launch an offensive on a scale almost equal to that of 1942. The German Command probably would not consider advantageous a transition to defense on all fronts. Their main task in 1943 will [C% therefore] be the destruction of the armed strength of the USSR.

- 1 -

~~TOP SECRET TRINE~~ VENONA

13. *(Continued)*

~~TOP SECRET TRINE~~ VENONA

- 2 -

    f) The ability of the Russians to withstand for a long time the impact

[43 groups unrecoverable]

No. 169   MOLIERE[MOL'ER][iv]

Notes: [a] Inserted by translator.

Comments:
    [i]   BEW: Board of Economic Warfare.
    [ii] MARKIZ: Joseph Milton BERNSTEIN.
    [iii] ARTUR: Thomas Arthur BISSON.
    [iv] MOL'ER: Pavel P. MIKhAJLOV.

15 April 1968

~~TOP SECRET TRINE~~ VENONA

14. New York 1132-3 to Moscow, 13 July 1943.

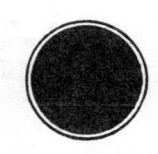

VENONA
~~TOP SECRET~~

USSR	Ref. No.: ▇▇▇ (of 27/2/1957)
	Issued: ▇▇▇ / 13 August, 1974
	Copy No.: 301

<u>3RD REISSUE</u>

DETAILS OF VLADIMIR ALEKSANDROVICH POZNER ("PLATON") AND HIS CONTACTS IN THE USA

(1943)

From: NEW YORK
To : MOSCOW
Nos : 1132, 1133   13th July 1943

[2-part message complete]

[Part I]   To VIKTOR[i]

We are planning to use Vladimir Aleksandrovich POZNER (henceforth "PLATON"[ii]) a Jew, born in LENINGRAD no earlier than 1897. Until 1925 he lived in GERMANY, from 1925 to 1941 in FRANCE. In October 1939 he was called into the French army as an officer-candidate because of [C% his [knowledge] [iii] of military aviation] and in August 1940 was demobilized. In the COUNTRY[STRANA] [iv] since May 1941. [3 groups unrecovered] petition for citizenship and received his first papers. In 1943 as a Lithuanian citizen [2 groups unrecovered] Soviet citizenship. He studied in secondary schools in LENINGRAD, BERLIN, and PARIS where he received a bachelor's degree from the PARIS University in 1926. [2 groups unrecovered] special courses in mathematics and applied [1 group unrecovered] at the SORBONNE, after which he worked until 1932

[13 groups unrecoverable]

[Continued overleaf]

VENONA
~~TOP SECRET~~

14. *(Continued)*

VENONA

~~TOP SECRET~~

(of 27/1/1957)

UNT[v], SAINT MAURICE in FRANCE[.] [iii] From 1932 to 1933 he worked as a sound recording engineer [5 groups unrecovered] to 1938

[6 groups unrecovered]

and from 1938 to 1939 was the chief engineer of the European branch of the MGM Studios in PARIS. He is a prominent specialist on the various aspects of sound recording.

[19 groups unrecovered]

studio

[12 groups unrecovered]

Studio U...

[48 groups unrecoverable]

studios in SPAIN, BELGIUM, FRANCE and SWITZERLAND. In 1939 on a business trip for MGM for three months he studied production methods and organization of films in the best film studios of the "COUNTRY". At the present time he is head of the Russian section of the film department of the "ARSENAL" [vi]. He has contacts in the COUNTRY which are of interest to us. He is also connected with "GERTsOG" [vii].

[PART II]   A secretary at "PLATON's" [2 groups unrecove ed] [C% Liza [2 groups unrecovered]evna [viii] who is being redeveloped by us for use in connection with "PLATON"

[15 groups unrecovered]

there film director

[37 groups unrecoverable]

[3 groups missed] his sister - Elena KAGEN [ix] [4 groups missed],works in the "OFFICE OF PR[x]

[50 groups unrecoverable]
[13 groups unrecovered]

). He is characterized by KALISTRAT [xi] and other

[7 groups unrecovered]

(of 27/2/1957)

VENONA

~~TOP SECRET~~

14. (Continued)

VENONA
~~TOP SECRET~~

3   (of 27/2/1957)

by GERTsOG

[33 groups unrecovered]

, but in the interests of our business was withdrawn.

Please check PLATON and sanction his use as a probationer [STAZhER] and a source of leads [NAVODChIK].

[11 groups unrecoverable]

No. 630   LUKA [xii]

Footnotes:
- [i]   VIKTOR   : Lt. Gen. P.M. FITIN.
- [ii]   PLATON   : i.e. "PLATO".
- [iii] Inserted by translator.
- [iv]   COUNTRY   : U.S.A.
- [v]   ...UNT   : The preceding gap is the right length for this to be the end of "STUDIOS PARAMOUNT".
- [vi]   ARSENAL   : U.S. War Department.
- [vii] GERTsOG   : ie "DUKE"; unidentified covername. Also occurs in NEW YORK's Nos. 865 of 8th June 1943 and 1148 of 14th July 1943, 853 of 16th June, 1944 and possibly (as G.) in 1930 of 21st November 1943.
- [viii] LIza ..Evna : Not traced
- [ix]   Elena KAGEN : Ellen POZNER, aka Helene KAGEN-POZNER, sister of Vladimir Aleksandrovich POZNER.

(of 27/2/1957) **VENONA**
~~TOP SECRET~~

14. *(Continued)*

VENONA
~~TOP SECRET~~

4.   (of 27/2/1957)

[x]   Office of Pr   :   Presumably Office of Price Administration.

[xi] KALISTRAT   :   i.e. "CALISTRATUS"; Aleksandr Semenovich FOMIN, clerk in the Soviet Consulate, NEW YORK (1941-1946).

[xii] LUKA   :   Pauel KLARIN, Soviet Vice-Consul in NEW YORK.

(of 27/2/1957)

VENONA
~~TOP SECRET~~

15. New York [GRU] 1325 to Moscow, 11 August 1943.

GRU

From: NEW YORK
To: MOSCOW
No. 1325

11 August 1943

To the Director.

[69 groups unrecoverable]

Pereulok [a], house 14 and Rozaliya ZARETsKAYa, Khoromnyj Tupik [a], house 2/6. In December 1936 went to Spain with the first [B% group] of the Lincoln Brigade. [B% There] held the post of aide-de-camp to the commander of the 15th Division, then staff officer in the Republican Army as [C% interpreter] in the line [1 group unrecovered] our [C% advisors]. Returned to the U.S.A. in [C% November] 1938. Up to 1 August 1943 worked in various explosives factories; last post assistant director of the T.N.T. factory in WILLIAMSPORT, Pennsylvania. Has now accepted an invitation to the post of [C% production] safety [b] [C% inspector] attached to the Explosives Division [UPRAVLENIE] of the War Department (the Division is in CHICAGO). PHIL[FIL][i] evidently has already had a conversation with him as he has passed on material received from him on the technology of the production of an explosive called pentolite (a mixture of TNT and penta-eritritol-tetra-nitrate) which is used for shells, bombs, and torpedoes. We await your instructions. The question of the means of liaison [B% can be] decided later. [ii]

2. MITRON[iii] just did not turn up for the first meeting.

3. MARQUIS[MARKIZ][iv] [1 group unrecovered] a two weeks' vacation.

No. 212   MO.......[c][v]

T.N.: [a] These are street names. The first word of the first name is not recoverable.

[b] BEZOPAsNOST':- This can also mean "security".

[c] The remaining letters of the signature are unrecoverable.

Comments:
[i] FIL: Not identified.

[ii] The information contained in this paragraph relates to Daniel Abraham ZARET.

[iii] MITRON: Not identified.

[iv] MARKIZ: Joseph Milton BERNSTEIN.

[v] Almost certainly MOL'ER - Pavel P. MIKhAJLOV, GRU Resident in NEW YORK.

15 April 1968

16. Washington [Naval-GRU] 1969 to Moscow, 13 August 1943.

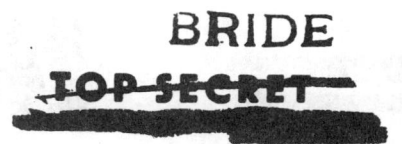

BRIDE

~~TOP SECRET~~

USSR

Ref. No: 3/NBF/T1139 (of 12/6/1959)
Issued: 13/7/1960
Copy No: 204

RE-ISSUE

LETTER FROM CARTER (1943)

From: WASHINGTON
To: MOSCOW
No: 1969   13 Aug. 43

To: [Name No. 42][i]

CARTER [KARTER][ii] has sent a letter via STELLA.[iii]

Since 26th July he has been working at the R.C.A. Laboratory, PRINCETON, NEW JERSEY. It has a staff of 20 engineers. They are developing two projects by contract with the Army Signal Corps. These are to be ready by October - November 1943. Both projects are basically for the improvement of radar and its use in radio navigation for blind bombing (that is from a high altitude and a great [2 groups unrecovered]) without visual bearings and without optical sights. It is meant to be fitted on Flying Fortresses. CARTER has been entrusted with drawing up instructions and a manual for the use of this apparatus. There is an opportunity of collaborating with other engineers. In an explanatory note CARTER mentions the advantages of the new system over the British: it is not subject to interception and has great accuracy.

CARTER mentions his contacts with four engineers who are working in important war establishments. For checking purposes we have told the NEIGHBOURS, [SOSEDI][iv] about the last three of them. All are Communists.

Philip FIELD [FILIPP FIL'D]. Aged 30. Mechanical engineer. Jew. Wife OL'GA is Russian (party member). At present working in a military establishment (we will let you have the name later).

Distribution   [Continued overleaf]

3/NBF/T1139   ~~TOP SECRET~~
                         BRIDE

16. (Continued)

~~TOP SECRET~~ ~~DAUNT~~

2   3/NBF/T1139

Sidney BOROVICh [SIDNEJ BOROVICh][a]. Aged 25. Engineer-physicist [INZhENER-FIZIK]. From a Polish-Jewish family. Works in the WESTERN ELECTRIC COMPANY on inter-aircraft radio communication.

William MILES [VIL'YaM MAJLS]. Aged 29. Rubber chemist. Friend of CARTER. Lives in NEW YORK. Works as an assistant in the BELL TELEPHONE COMPANY's laboratory. For the last eight years has been taking an active part in party work. Is not under suspicion with the company.

A radio engineer. Works in the SANDY HOOK [SENDI KhUK] Army Signal Corps laboratory. His wife is a party organizer in the NEW YORK organization and is a friend of William MILES.

An engineer-physicist, - Director of the SPERRY laboratory. Works on secret systems for electro-mechanical gun sights and ship and aircraft control.

We will let you have more precise information and the surnames later [a] when we get them [a].

From further information which has been reported to them about CARTER's biography, the NEIGHBOURS have come to the conclusion that CARTER has been in contact [BYL SVYaZAN] with ~~the~~ our military[b].

No. 626   [Name No. 91][v]

Notes: [a] Or "greater".

[a] BOROVICh : First encoded as BORVICh, repeated as BOROVICh.

[b] "Our military": This is plural: perhaps means "members of our armed forces".

Comments: [i] Name No. 42 : ~~Unidentified~~ Probably Capt. (1st Rank) M.A. VORONTSOV

[ii] CARTER : Eugene Franklin COLEMAN.

[iii] STELLA : Unidentified cover-name.

[iv] NEIGHBOURS : Members of another Soviet intelligence organization.

[v] Name No. 91 : ~~Unidentified~~ Probably Capt. (1st Rank) I.A. EGORICHEV, Soviet Naval attaché in Washington.

3/NBF/T1139   ~~TOP SECRET~~ ~~DAUNT~~

17. Washington [Naval-GRU] 1983 to Moscow, 14 August 1943.

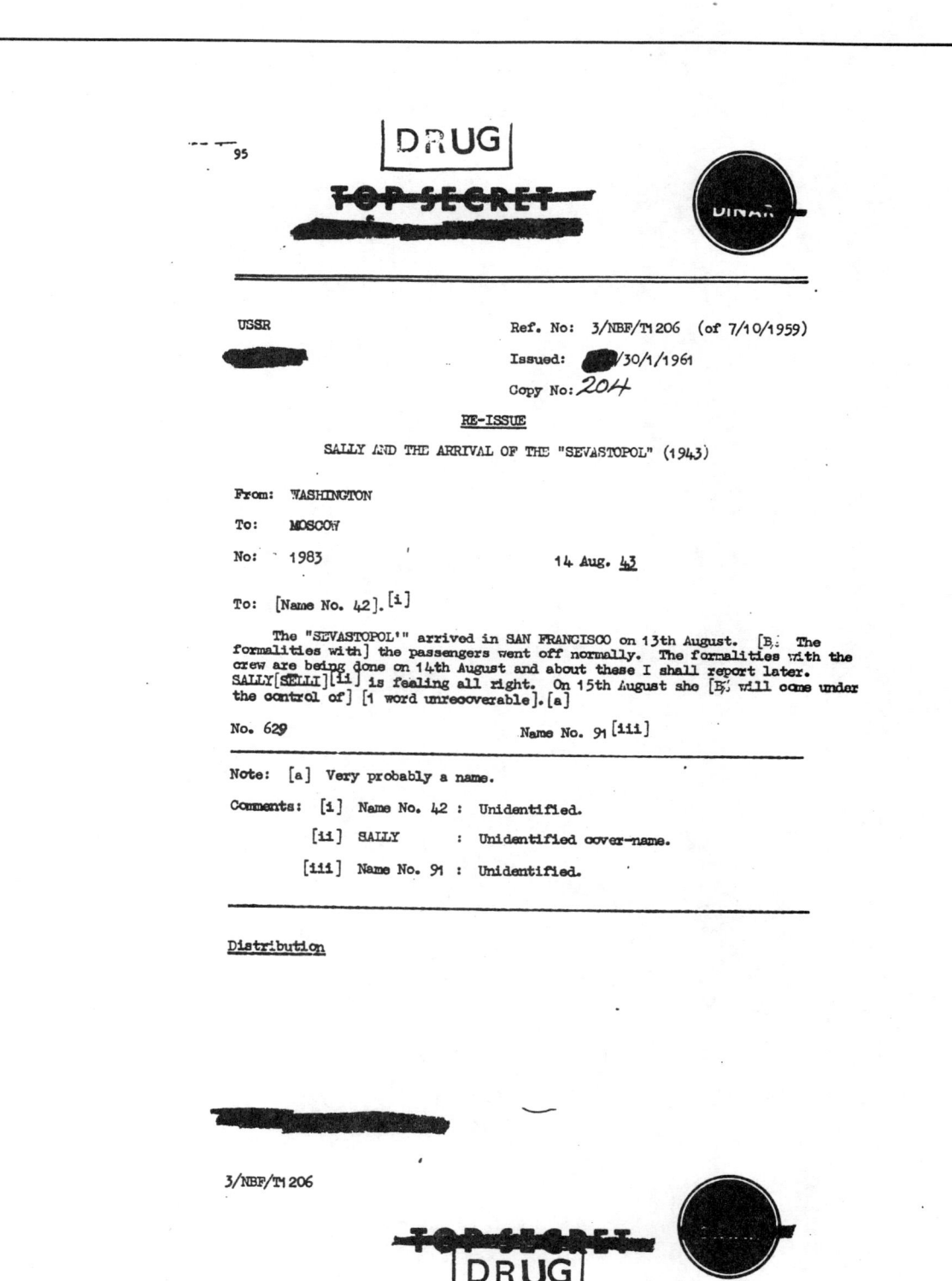

DRUG

~~TOP SECRET~~

DINAR

USSR

Ref. No: 3/NBF/T1206 (of 7/10/1959)
Issued: /30/1/1961
Copy No: 204

RE-ISSUE

SALLY AND THE ARRIVAL OF THE "SEVASTOPOL" (1943)

From: WASHINGTON
To: MOSCOW
No: 1983   14 Aug. 43

To: [Name No. 42].[i]

    The "SEVASTOPOL" arrived in SAN FRANCISCO on 13th August. [B: The formalities with] the passengers went off normally. The formalities with the crew are being done on 14th August and about these I shall report later. SALLY[SELLI][ii] is feeling all right. On 15th August she [B: will come under the control of] [1 word unrecoverable].[a]

No. 629   Name No. 91 [iii]

Note: [a] Very probably a name.

Comments: [i] Name No. 42 : Unidentified.
         [ii] SALLY : Unidentified cover-name.
         [iii] Name No. 91 : Unidentified.

Distribution

3/NBF/T1206

~~TOP SECRET~~
DRUG

18. Moscow 142 (Circular), 12 September 1943.

TOP SECRET VENONA

USSR

Reissue

From: MOSCOW
To: CANBERRA
No: 142[a]

12 September 1943

1. A change in circumstances - and in particular the dissolution of the "BIG HOUSE [BOL'ShOJ DOM]"[i] - necessitates a change in the method used by the workers of our residencies to keep in touch with the leaders of the local FELLOWCOUNTRYMAN [ZEMLYaChESKIJ][ii] organizations on intelligence matters.

2. Our workers, by continuing to meet the leaders of the FELLOWCOUNTRYMEN, are exposing themselves to danger and are giving cause [1 group unidentified][b] local authorities to suspect that the "BIG HOUSE" is still in existence.

3. We propose:

a) That personal contact with leaders of the local FELLOWCOUNTRYMAN organizations should cease and that FELLOWCOUNTRYMAN material should not be accepted for forwarding to the "BIG HOUSE."

b) That meetings of our workers may take place only with special reliable undercover [ZAKONSPIRIROVANNYJ] contacts of the FELLOWCOUNTRYMAN [D° organizations], who are not suspected by the [1 group unidentified][b] local authorities, exclusively about specific aspects of our intelligence work (acquiring [1 group unidentified] contacts, leads [NAVODKI], rechecking of those who are being cultivated, etc.). For each meeting it is necessary to obtain our consent.

[1 group unrecovered]
[1 group missing]

representative of the Soviet Union.

No. 4048   VIKTOR[iii]

Notes: [a] This message is known to have been sent also to NEW YORK, SAN FRANCISCO and OTTAWA.
        [b] The unidentified group is the same in both cases. - organ of

Comments:
        [i]   BIG HOUSE: The COMINTERN.
        [ii] FELLOWCOUNTRYMAN(-MEN): Communist(s).
        [iii] VIKTOR: Lt. Gen. P.M. FITIN.

17 August 1971

TOP SECRET VENONA

19. San Francisco 441 to Moscow, 31 October 1943.

~~TOP SECRET DINAR~~ VENONA

From: SAN FRANCISCO
To: MOSCOW
No.: 441   31 October 1943

  I confirm receipt of Code "075-B"[i] copy No.27. Code "POBEDA"[ii] will be destroyed [2 groups unidentified] after [B% such] code has been received in TYRE [TIR][iii].

242   CHARON [KhARON][iv]

Comments:
  [i] KOD "075-B": The code designated ▓▓▓▓▓ and ▓▓▓▓▓ under different system of pad-page identification. The "B" stands for BEZOPASNOST' (Security), that is, "for use by the NKGB."

  [ii] KOD "POBEDA": The code designated ▓▓▓▓▓ "POBEDA" means "Victory."

  [iii] TIR: New York.

  [iv] KhARON: Grigorij KhEJFETs

~~TOP SECRET DINAR~~ VENONA

20. Moscow 232-3 to all Residents, 2 December 1943.

~~TOP SECRET~~ VENONA

Reissue

From: MOSCOW
To: CANBERRA
No: 233, 232

2 December 1943

[Part I] Circular[a].

Once again we direct your attention to the insufficient secrecy in the work of the leaders and operational workers of the residencies. Some operational workers are being initiated into affairs of the residencies which have no relation to the work which they are carrying out. Of course this is the result of talkativeness and the inevitable responses of brotherly relations which are maintained among our workers. It is necessary to all [6 groups unrecovered] but each individual operational worker should know on the general work of the residency only what is necessary in order to carry out the work on his own assignment. In the premises of the embassy, legation, consulate (in the studies and work rooms of the residents) and in the private apartments, probably fitted with special [1 group unidentified], discussions are being conducted on operational questions. There have even been cases of setting up in the work room a conference of all the workers of the residency for a collective discussion of instructions of the [C% center]. It is categorically forbidden during instruction and generally in discussion, particularly within the premises, to use the real surnames of workers and probationers [STAZhERY], names of cities and countries, officials and other objectives. All this should be encoded.

[Part II] [1 group unrecovered] considering the cases cited above it is recommended instead of conversations aloud to exchange notes, which immediately after such a "secret conversation" [1 group unidentified] are destroyed. Our workers must not at work and in private life [4 groups unrecovered] from other [1 group unidentified] apparatus and [1 group unrecovered] that it will inevitably lead to disclosure. [1 group unrecovered] other [1 group unrecovered] discussions in Russian about [5 groups unrecovered].

[5 groups unrecoverable]

violation of rules of secrecy we will take strict measures. [1 group unidentified] providing the necessary secrecy in our work to a considerable extent depends upon the leaders of the residencies themselves. The residents should not share with their subordinates communications which they are not supposed to know for the work.

No. 677   PETROV[i]

Notes: [a] This message is known to have been sent also to HAVANA, MEXICO CITY, OTTAWA, SAN FRANCISCO and NEW YORK.
Comments:
    [i] PETROV: Unidentified MOSCOW signature.

~~TOP SECRET~~   16 August 1971

VENONA

21. San Francisco 510 to Moscow, 7 December 1943.

BRIDE
~~TOP SECRET~~
EIDER

USSR

Ref. No: 3/NBF/T1045 (of 19/9/1958)
Issued: 27/1/1959
Copy No: 204

RE-ISSUE

REFERENCE TO "JULIA", "IVERI", AND "ZARĒ" (1943)

From: SAN FRANCISCO
To: MOSCOW
No: 510   7 Dec. 43

Personal to PETROV.[i]

"JULIA"[ii] has insisted that I should inform you [C% by telegraph] that "IVERI's"[iii] relationships may become a subject for discussion since IVERI's suspicions about his wife's connections with Ben GOLDSTEIN[iv] are being confirmed by "ZARĒ".[v] ZARĒ [C% in the course] [3 groups unrecovered] IVERI's wife's intimate relations with Ben and the subsequent [1 group unrecovered] IVERI [6 groups unrecovered] scandal that IVERI in his reports to you makes his wishes out to be facts [1 group unrecovered] and [3 groups unrecovered] you. By post we are sending a detailed letter of ZARĒ's on this case.

No. 286   KhARON[vi]

Comments: [i]   PETROV   : Unidentified MOSCOW addressee.
          [ii] JULIA   : Olga Valentinovna KhLOPKOVA.
          [iii] IVERI   : Probably Mikhail Konstantinovich KALATOZOV.
          [iv] GOLDSTEIN : Not known.
          [v]   ZARĒ   : Elena Konstantinovna GORBUNOVA.
          [vi] KhARON   : Grigorij Markovich KhEJFETs, Soviet Vice-Consul in SAN FRANCISCO.

Distribution

3/NBF/T1045

~~TOP SECRET~~
BRIDE
EIDER

22. Mexico City 158 to Moscow, 23 December 1943.

VENONA

USSR	Ref. No.: 3/NBF/T2242
	Issued: 10/5/77
	Copy No.: 301

LUKA'S CONTACTS, PLANS FOR SURGICAL OPERATION, $20,000 REQUIRED (1943)

From: MEXICO CITY
To: MOSCOW
No.: 158   23 December 1943

To PETROV[i].

Contact has been established by LUKA[ii]. The SURGICAL OPERATION[iii] is planned by the DOCTORS[iii] to take place in four days' time. At this stage [1 group unrecovered] by other means[iv] is impossible. Without delay transfer 20,000 in "KAPITAN's" money[v] for urgent requirements. Telegraph your [1 group unrecovered]. [2 groups unrecovered].

No. 38   YuRIJ[vi]

[Continued overleaf]

3/NBF/T2242
[2 pages]
AJV

22. *(Continued)*

VENONA

3/NBF/T2242

Footnotes:	[i] PETROV:	Lavrentij Pavlovich BERIYa.
	[ii] LUKA:	Pavel Panteleevich KLARIN: 2nd Secretary, Soviet Embassy, MEXICO CITY, from 23 November 1943 to 24 May 1944; served previously and subsequently in the USA.
	[iii] SURGICAL OPERATION, DOCTORS:	Coverwords associated with the coverword "HOSPITAL", ie "prison". They appear to denote a release from prison and those effecting it: relating here to the attempt to secure the release of TROTsKIJ's assassin (cf. MEXICO CITY's Nos. 55 of 15 January 1944 (unpublished) and 193, 194 of 14 March 1944 (3/NBF/T770)).
	[iv]	Or "with other funds [SREDSTVA]".
	[v] KAPITAN's money:	Presumably U.S. dollars: "KAPITAN", ie "CAPTAIN", is President Franklin Delano ROOSEVELT's covername on the NEW YORK lane - first occurrence on this lane.
	[vi] YuRIJ:	Lev Aleksandrovich TARASOV.

VENONA

23. San Francisco 31 to Moscow, 17 January 1944.

USSR

Ref. No: 3/NBF/T1327
Issued: 18/11/1960
Copy No: 204

1. "BUTCHER's" CONTACTS AND THE IDENTIFICATION OF "AL'MA"
2. DIRECT CIPHER LINK WITH "JULIA" (1944)

From: SAN FRANCISCO
To: MOSCOW
No: 31   17 Jan. 44

"BUTCHER[MYaSNIK]"[i] expresses [1 group unrecovered] that the chemist Leo LEVANES[ii] (in future "AL'MA") will start giving us help. AL'MA

[30 groups unrecovered]

BUTCHER in [3 groups unrecovered] through BUTCHER - AL'MA.

Among BUTCHER's contacts there are also some interesting targets in the aviation plants [1 group unrecovered] LOS ANGELES.

No. 14   CHARON[KhARON][iii]

Since a direct cipher link has been set up with "JULIA"[iv] she wants [1 group unrecovered] there the amount expended on telegraphic communication. I gave JULIA [3 groups unrecovered] the sum of 155 dollars.

No. 15

Comments:
[i]   BUTCHER :
[ii] LEVANES : An engineer with the Shell Oil Company at DOMINIQUEZ, CALIFORNIA.
[iii] CHARON : Grigorij KhEJFETs, Soviet Vice-Consul in SAN FRANCISCO.
[iv] JULIA   : Olga KhLOPKOVA.

Distribution

3/NBF/T1327

24. New York 195 to Moscow, 9 February 1944.

VENONA

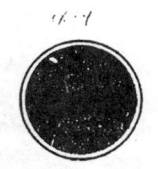

~~TOP SECRET~~

95

USSR

Ref. No.:
Issued : /25/6/1973
Copy No.: 301

MEETING BETWEEN "GUS'" AND "REST"; WORK ON ENORMOUS
(1944)

From: NEW YORK
To: MOSCOW
No.: 195   9th February 1944

Personal to VIKTOR[i].

    In reply to No. 302[ii].

    On 5th February a meeting took place between "GUS'"[iii] and "REST"[iv]. Beforehand GUS' was given a detailed briefing by us. REST greeted him pleasantly but was rather cautious at first, [1 group unrecovered] the discussion GUS' satisfied himself that REST was aware of whom he was working with. R.[iv] arrived in the COUNTRY[STRANA][v] in September as a member of the ISLAND[OSTROV][vi] mission on ENORMOUS[ENORMOZ][vii]. According to him the work on ENORMOUS in the COUNTRY is being carried out under the direct control of the COUNTRY's army represented by General SOMERVELL[SOMMERVILL][viii] and STIMSON[ix]: at the head of the group of ISLANDERS[OSTROVITYaNE][vi] is a Labour Member of Parliament, Ben SMITH[x].

[Continued overleaf]

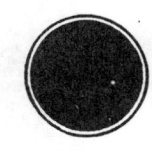

VENONA
~~TOP SECRET~~

24. (Continued)

VENONA
~~TOP SECRET~~

- 2 -

The whole operation amounts to the working out of the process for the separation of isotopes of ENORMOUS. The work is proceeding in two directions: the electron method developed by LAWRENCE[LAURENS][xi]

[71 groups unrecoverable]

separation of isotopes by the combined method, using the diffusion method for preliminary and the electron method for final separation. The work

[46 groups unrecovered]

18th February, we shall report the results.

No. 92   ANTON[xii]

Footnotes: [i] VIKTOR: Lt. Gen. P.M. FITIN.
           [ii] Not available.
          [iii] GUS':   i.e. "GOOSE"; Harry GOLD.
           [iv] REST/R.:   Dr. Emil Julius Klaus FUCHS.
            [v] COUNTRY: U.S.A.
           [vi] ISLAND, ISLANDERS: GREAT BRITAIN, British.
          [vii] ENORMOUS: a) U.S. Atomic Energy Project.
                                    b) Uranium.
         [viii] General SOMERVELL: Lt. General Brehan Burke SOMERVELL, Commanding General Army Service Forces, War Department.
           [ix] STIMSON: Henry Lewis STIMSON, Secretary of War.
            [x] Ben SMITH: Rt. Hon. Ben SMITH, Minister Resident in WASHINGTON for Supply from 1943.
           [xi] LAWRENCE: Professor Ernest Orlando LAWRENCE.
          [xii] ANTON: Leonid Romanovich KVASNIKOV.

VENONA
~~TOP SECRET~~

25. San Francisco 65 to Moscow, 10 February 1944.

VENONA

Reissue (T742)

From: SAN FRANCISCO
To: MOSCOW
No: 65

10 February 1944

To VIKTOR[i].

On the 9th of February of this year in PORTLAND second mate Elizaveta Mitrofanovna KUZNETsOVA, born 1910, deserted from S.S. "PSKOV." KUZNETsOVA without receiving permission from the immigration authorities to remain in the U.S.A. went into hiding. On this matter we are sending "MAZhOR"[a][ii] to PORTLAND.

No. 45
KhARON[iii]

T.N. [a] I.e. in the musical sense. The service rank is MAJOR in Russian.
Comments:
    [i] VIKTOR: Lt. Gen. P.M. FITIN.
    [ii] MAZhOR: i.e. "MAJOR KEY," Vyachislav Aleksandrovich MISLUK.
    [iii] KhARON: Grigorij KhEJFETs, Soviet Vice-Consul in SAN FRANCISCO at that time.

11 July 1969

VENONA

26. Moscow [unnumbered], 25 April 1944.

~~TOP SECRET~~ ACORN

Moscow (Circular)[a]
1944
[separate numeration] (25 April)

To all residents [REZIDENT"Y][a].

From 1 May[,] instead of the method of setting up the indicator group [POKAZATEL'NAYA GRUPPA] in effect at the present time, for the determination [or: definition; that is: identification] of the reciphering table [PERESHIFROVAL'NAYA TABLITSA][b] enter [or: write (down)] in clear [OTKR"ITO] at the beginning of the cipher text the first group of the table (the first indicator group[c]) with which the leaf of the pad [LIST BLOKNOTA] on the occasion[d] begins. The recipherment itself begins with the second group of the table. At the end of the cipher text enter, likewise in clear, the group following upon the last used group of the gamma [GAMMA][e] (the second indicator group). If the recipherment ends with the last group of a table, enter the first group of the following table.

[88 groups on a depth of 1, 51 groups unmatched]

[a] Sent to Habana, México, New York, Ottawa, San Francisco (no others found).

[a] Chiefs of NKGB agent systems abroad.

[b] Table of additive key [GAMMA], each such table being on one leaf [LIST] of a pad [BLOKNOT], whence table [TABLITSA] and leaf [LIST] (often referred to in AFSA as "page", since each leaf is printed on only one side) are up to a certain point interchangeable. (The table is what is written or printed on the leaf.) It is called "reciphering" because it is used in a second encrypting process (the first here being encodement with the code book).

[c] That is: now this will be the first indicator group.

[d] That is: the leaf about to be used on the respective occasion (?).

[e] Additive key.

~~TOP SECRET~~ ACORN

27. New York 588 to Moscow, 29 April 1944.

USSR

Ref. No.: 3/NBF/T110 (of 1/1/1960)
Issued: 18/10/1968
Copy No.: 204

5TH REISSUE

1. UMNITsA, ZVUK, RULEVOJ, PEL, PROBATIONERS, MAKSIM, AMT AND MER
2. KRAMER, PERLO, FLATO, GLASSER, FITZGERALD ETC: GROUP OF FELLOW COUNTRYMEN IN CARTHAGE [WASHINGTON D.C.]
(1944)

From: NEW YORK
To: MOSCOW
No: 588   29th April 1944

On 27th April UMNITsA[i] reported as follows:

"After ZVUK's[ii] death, RULEVOJ[iii]

[15 groups unrecovered]

on RULEVOJ's instructions. ZVUK

[41 groups unrecovered].

PEL[iv] used to meet R.[v] before meeting me. In future if R. permits my meeting with PEL [4 groups unrecovered] R..[vi] Even ZVUK used not to meet P.[vii] more often than once in six months."

Possibly she is making this up and exaggerating. At least [3 groups unrecovered] exclusive control of[a] the PROBATIONERS[STAZhERY] and expressed[b] an unreasoning[ZhIVOTNYJ] fear [D% that] we will contact them direct. It is essential that either MAKSIM[viii] or I should see R. and come to an agreement: that the whole group and UMNITsA

[15 groups unrecovered]

I recommended [C% asking]

[45 groups unrecovered]

[Continued overleaf]

DISTRIBUTION:

3/NBF/T110

27. *(Continued)*

95

~~TOP SECRET~~

- 2 -   3/NBF/T110

AMT[ix].

[7 groups unrecovered]

group:-

KRAMER[KREJMER][x], PERLO[PRLO][xi], FLATO[FLĒTO][xii], GLASSER[GLAZER][xiii], Edward FITZGERALD[EDUARD FITsDZhERALD][xiv] and others in a group of 7 or 8 FELLOW COUNTRYMEN[ZEMLYaKI][xv][c].

UMNITsA talked with AMT and PERLO. They told her that this group was neglected and that nobody was interested in them. KRAMER is the leader of the group. All occupy responsible posts in CARTHAGE[KARFAGEN][xvi].

[20 groups unrecovered]

AMT and PERLO

[29 groups unrecoverable]

NEIGHBOURS[SOSEDI][xvii]. For more than a year MAKSIM and I tried to get in touch with PERLO and FLATO. For some reason or other RULEVOJ did not come to the meeting and has just decided to put U.[xviii] in touch with the whole group. If we work with this group it will be necessary to remove her and [2 groups unrecovered].

Recently I met PERLO by chance in ARENA's[xix] flat.

For your information: I have never met RULEVOJ

[7 groups unrecovered]

No. 312   MĒR[xx]

Notes: [a] Literally "full monopoly over".

[b] Or "express". The group represents either 3rd person singular or 3rd plural.

[c] If it is assumed that a conjunction or punctuation has been omitted after "others", the passage could be interpreted as: "... in the group there are 7 or 8 FELLOW COUNTRYMEN".

Comments: [i] UMNITsA: i.e. "CLEVER GIRL"; Elizabeth BENTLEY.

[ii] ZVUK: i.e. "SOUND"; Jacob GOLOS, who died in November 1943.

[iii] RULEVO   i.e. "HELMSMAN"; Earl BROWDER.

[iv] PĒL: Cyrillic transliteration of English word "PAL"; Nathan Gregory SILVERMASTER.

3/NBF/T110

~~TOP SECRET~~

27. *(Continued)*

- 3 - 3/NBF/T110

Comments: [Cont'd]	[v] R.:	RULEVOJ. See comment [iii] above.
	[vi] R..:	Represents the abbreviation R. followed by the fullstop at the end of the sentence.
	[vii] P.:	PĒL. See comment [iv] above.
	[viii] MAKSIM:	Vasilij Mikhajlovich ZUBILIN.
	[ix] AMT:	John J. ABT. (Also occurs as AMT in No. 687 of 13th May 1944 (3/NBF/T910). It seems unlikely that this is a covername. Presumably it is a persistent misspelling.)
	[x] KRAMER:	Charles KRAMER.
	[xi] PERLO:	Victor PERLO. (Spelt as PRLO throughout the message; presumably a spelling mistake.)
	[xii] FLATO:	Charles FLATO.
	[xiii] GLASSER:	Harold GLASSER.
	[xiv] Edward FITZGERALD:	Edward Joseph FITZGERALD.
	[xv] FELLOW COUNTRYMEN:	Members of the Communist Party.
	[xvi] CARTHAGE:	WASHINGTON D.C.
	[xvii] NEIGHBOURS:	Members of another Soviet intelligence organisation.
	[xviii] U.	UMNITsA. See comment [i] above.
	[xix] ARENA:	Probably Mary Wolfe PRICE.
	[xx] MĒR:	i.e. "MAYOR"; probably Iskhak Abdulovich AKhMEROV.

3/NBF/T110

28. New York 598-9 to Moscow, 2 May 1944.

Reissue(T1∅2)

From: NEW YORK
To: MOSCOW
No: 598-599

2 May 1944

[Part I]   We are transmitting information written down by RULEVOJ[i] after a conversation with ERhO[ii].

1. As regards the re-election of ROOSEVELT financial and business groups are on the whole non-committal[a]. They openly support DEWEY much more than any other candidate but in support of ROOSEVELT they say very [D% little]. On the whole these circles leave the question open refraining from judgment. Such sharp propaganda of hate toward ROOSEVELT, as came out earlier from these circles, is no longer being carried on;

[36 groups unrecoverable]

ROOSEVELT (the end of April) the labor movement and the party machine of the Democratic party are for the most part carrying on. In the political circles of the Catholic Church those who had come out earlier against ROOSEVELT now are beginning [3 groups unrecovered]; FARLEY who is [3 groups unrecovered] church circles has gone over from the opposition to a neutral position. TOBIN who is a strong influence in the Church is at present leading a movement for ROOSEVELT in the circles of the AFL[AFT][iii]. The new Catholic group which is being led by Supreme Court Justice MURPHY is developing lively activity, striving for the public support of ROOSEVELT and preparing open statements of him it widely attracting prominent Catholics. Among the Republicans who were former WILKIE supporters there is a growing tendency toward going over to the side of ROOSEVELT.

3. The strategy of the Republicans still has not clearly been defined. The basic tendency apparently lies in the temptation of all

[19 groups unrecovered]

on internal questions

[62 groups unrecovered]
[29 groups unrecoverable]

[Part II] 4. Opposition to ROOSEVELT in congress is sabotaging all ROOSEVELT's undertakings, with the exception of direct military appropriations. However the Democrats who stand in opposition to ROOSEVELT consider it impossible to remain in an anti-ROOSEVELT coalition during

[22 groups unrecovered]

against ROOSEVELT, but without any success. In [5 groups unrecovered]

28. (Continued)

elections 80% of the Polish vote was [C% given] to the Democratic party, in comparison to the general figure of 65%. The British undoubtedly will support ROOSEVELT,

[37 groups unrecoverable]

will not budge. The Italian Social-Democrats together with former Fascists in every way possible are trying to turn the Italian-Americans against ROOSEVELT. An overwhelming majority of the Yugoslavs are for ROOSEVELT, even members of the mass organizations which are officially being led by supporters of MIKhAJLOVICh. The majority will come out for ROOSEVELT. Various reactionary emigré groups [3 groups unrecovered] ROOSEVELT, but they cannot attract to their side even all of those who follow them in [2 groups unrecovered].

6. If the elections were to take place at the present time ROOSEVELT would probably receive an insignificant majority of the popular vote, but he would lose the election since the votes in his favor are strongly concentrated in the South, where the huge majority of votes on his behalf in the final total count no more than 51%. For the last two months ROOSEVELT has been slowly gaining strength, but not with such speed as

[7 groups unrecoverable]

only a favorable course of the war and some bold efforts of ROOSEVELT toward a more clear-cut definition of his policy before the masses could secure his re-election.

7. According to our speculations a second front will be launched during the next few weeks. A further delay would actually assure the accession to power of the Republicans.

8. As far as we have been able to learn, the financial and business circles completely share hopes for a quick [C% agreement]. The sharp fluctuations of the "New York Times" undoubtedly reflect the sentiments of some of the groups of these circles, but in our opinion not of the most decisive groups.

No. 319   MAJ[iv]

Notes: [a] "non-committal" given in Latin spell.
Comments:
 [i] RULEVOJ: i.e. "HELMSMAN," Earl BROWDER.
 [ii] EKhO: i.e. "ECHO," Bernard SCHUSTER.
 [iii] AFT: i.e. AMERIKANSKAYa FEDERATsIYa TRUDA, American Federation of Labor.
 [iv] MAJ: i.e. "MAY," Stepan APRESYaN.

16 March 1970

29. New York 601 to Moscow, 2 May 1944.

~~TOP SECRET~~ VENONA

Reissue (T154)

From: NEW YORK
To: MOSCOW
No: 601

2 May 1944

1. The commentator of station WMCA[i] Norman JAY, henceforth "BOJKIJ"[ii], has twice sent DEDUShKA[iii] the text of his talks, which are consistently in a tone extremely friendly to us. We consider it advisable to profit by this circumstance and to invite BOJKIJ [C% to a restaurant] and get acquainted in the line of cover [LINIYa PRIKRYTIYa][a]. Telegraph what you think about BOJKIJ.

2. LEONID[iv] and ALEKSEJ[v] can hand over the "NEIGHBOR's [SOSED]"[vi] affairs to STEPAN[vii]. Advise when LEONID is to leave for home and what he can occupy himself with in our line before his departure. LEONID [3 groups unrecovered]. Are we to turn that case over to STEPAN?

3. At a meeting in the PLANT [ZAVOD][viii] GRIN[ix] [C% handed] KALISTRAT[x] a letter in which[,] in the name of the editor of "NEW MASSES", Joe NORTH[NORS], he asks for financial assistance to be given to the magazine, which is in a bad way. For the present [D% I] [1 group unrecoverable] the reason for so strange a step on GRIN's part or his appealing to KALISTRAT in particular[.] Telegraph your opinion and instructions.

No. 320 MAJ[xi]

Note: [a] LINIYa PRIKRYTIYa: That is to say that the meeting would be arranged with a member of the State Security organization in his official capacity as a member of the Consulate-General.

Comments:
- [i] Station WMCA is a NEW YORK, N.Y., broadcasting station.
- [ii] BOJKIJ: i.e. PERKY, Norman JAY.
- [iii] DEDUShKA: i.e. GRANDPAPA, Evgenij Dmitrievich KISELEV, Soviet Consul-General at NEW YORK.
- [iv] LEONID: Aleksej Nikolaevich PROKhOROV.
- [v] ALEKSEJ: Anatolij Antonovich YaKOVLEV.
- [vi] SOSED: Member of another Soviet intelligence organization
- [vii] STEPAN: Possibly Pavel Ivanovich FEDOSIMOV.
- [viii] ZAVOD: The Soviet Consulate-General at NEW YORK, N.Y.
- [ix] GRIN: If not a cover-name this may possibly refer to Abner GREEN, of the American Committee for the Protection of Foreign Born.
- [x] KALISTRAT: i.e. CALISTRATUS, Aleksandr Semenovich FOMIN.
- [xi] MAJ: i.e. MAY, Pavel Ivanovich FEDOSIMOV.

16 March 1973

~~TOP SECRET~~ VENONA

30. New York 618 to Moscow, 4 May 1944.

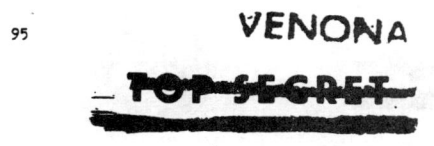

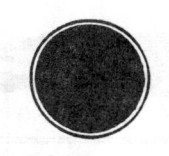

VENONA

~~TOP SECRET~~

USSR

Ref. No.: 3/NBF/T463 of 11/2/54
Issued: 18/6/75
Copy No.: 301

REISSUE

ASSESSMENT OF STUKACh'S BUSINESS DEALINGS, ASSOCIATES JOSEPH WOLFSON AND BEN, FUTURE DEVELOPMENTS (1944)

From: NEW YORK
To: MOSCOW
No.: 618   4 May 1944

Your No. 1669[i].

1. The money which STUKACh[ii] will receive will not be put into circulation by him personally. For the 5,000 he will get a loan from Joseph WOLFSON[iii], proprietor of the "MERIDEN Dental Laboratory"[iii], whose business provided STUKACh with cover for six years. About two years ago the cover fell through because S.[ii] does not work in the firm and the LEAGUE [LIGA][iv] required by law the registration of all stockholders, with an indication of their position in the firm. S. has very good personal relations with WOLFSON and the latter will undoubtedly give him a cheque for the required sum. S. will deposit the cheque received for the necessary sum in his account in the bank and then after this will [B% use] the money from the bank. If it is unsufficient, S. may be given some aid by a relative of his wife's who has a watch business.

[Continued overleaf]

VENONA

~~TOP SECRET~~

30. *(Continued)*

2. S. is organising a firm[v] of his own and with the money available he is buying manufactured goods in the shape of watches and crocodile-skin articles: BEN[vi] is assisting him in this. Thus the money will be in goods. During the last two months S. has been making a detailed study of the market for watches and crocodile-skin articles and has ascertained that these things are much in vogue and in great demand. Therefore he is sure that in the next three months [3 groups unrecoverable] will be able to sell them; thus he will not only get back the money invested but will also make a profit of three to four thousand. He will repay his debt to BEN out of the money he makes and will carry on the business without anybody's aid. We repeat, the whole business has been worked out so that S. should be the full owner of the firm and he is not inviting any partners into this [C% work]. In these conditions we can always organise any kind of business or transfer the firm to other hands. The business in its present form is safe and there should be no delay in organising it since the watches will be arriving in the COUNTRY [STRANA][vii] in the near future and must be bought up at once.

We await a reply as soon as possible.

No. 331 MAJ[viii]

4 May

Footnotes:
- [i] Not available.
- [ii] STUKACh/S.: i.e. "INFORMER"; Joseph KATZ.
- [iii] Joseph WOLFSON: Joseph WOLFSON, as working partner, and Joseph KATZ (Footnote [ii]), as owner and financier, operated the MERIDEN Dental Laboratories, MERIDEN, CONNECTICUT, from 1939 to 1943/4. In 1944 WOLFSON was the sole proprietor.
- [iv] The LEAGUE: The U.S. Government.
- [v] Firm: The "TEMPUS Import Company", NEW YORK CITY, was formed by Joseph KATZ (Footnote [ii]) in 1944 to import leather goods from South AMERICA. From 2 June 1944 KATZ employed his brother-in-law, Martin YOUNG, previously a sales agent for watches. From May 1945 YOUNG and other Communists owned and ran the firm.

30. *(Continued)*

VENONA

3/NBF/T463

Footnotes
Continued: [vi] BEN: Unidentified covername. Also occurs in NEW YORK's Nos. 1050 of 26 July 1944 (3/NBF/T22.2) and 1351 of 23 September 1944 (unpublished).

[vii] COUNTRY: The U.S.A.

[viii] MAJ: i.e. "MAY"; Stepan Zakharovich APRESYaN.

31. New York 625 to Moscow, 5 May 1944.

-95

VENONA

~~TOP SECRET~~

USSR

Ref. No.: 3/NBF/T916 (of 17/5/1957)
Issued: 23/7/69
Copy No.: 204

REISSUE

CAFETERIA AS COVER FOR ABRAM: HIS PARTNER APPEL
(1944)

From: NEW YORK
To: MOSCOW
No.: 625   5th May 1944

[Addressee unrecovered]

In mail[POChTA] No. 2 we informed you that cover had been fixed up for ABRAM[i]. He [2 groups unrecovered] directly to set up the cafeteria. For this we gave him the authorised advance of 2,000. ABRAM's partner in the cafeteria, a certain APPEL[APFEL'][ii], had several relatives in[a] the business and ABRAM came to suspect that APPEL was stealing a [C% valuable] business from him. [C% To improve control] and to expand the business, he decided to run the cafeteria himself.

-[42 groups unrecovered]

APPEL

[79 groups unrecovered]

DISTRIBUTION: [Continued overleaf]

3/NBF/T916 (of 17/5/1957)

~~TOP SECRET~~

VENONA

31. *(Continued)*

95

VENONA

~~TOP SECRET~~

- 2 -   3/NBF/T916 (of 17/5/1957)

dollars.

[9 groups unrecoverable]

[Internal Serial No. unrecovered]   [Signature unrecovered]

Note: [a]   It is assumed that "in" is understood and it has, therefore, been inserted by the translator. Without the insertion of "in", the literal translation would be ".. had the business of several relatives".

Comments: [i]   ABRAM: Jack SOBLE.

[ii]   APPEL: Available information indicates that a Sam APPEL was in some way connected with the S and V cafeteria which was set up by Jack SOBLE and his brother-in-law, Arnold WOLSTON.

3/NBF/T916 (of 17/5/1957)   - 2 -

~~TOP SECRET~~

VENONA

32. New York 628 to Moscow, 5 May 1944.

VENONA

~~TOP SECRET~~

USSR

Ref. No.:
Issued: 15/6/76
Copy No.: 301

ALFRED SARANT, A LEAD OF ANTENNA'S: PROPOSED RECRUITMENT, DETAILS (1944)

From: NEW YORK
To: MOSCOW
No.: 628   5 May 1944

Please carry out a check and sanction the recruitment of Alfred SARANT[i], a lead of ANTENNA's[ii]. He is 25 years old, a Greek, an American citizen and lives in TYRE [TIR][iii]. He completed the engineering course at Cooper Union in 1940. He worked for two years in the Signal Corps Laboratory at Fort MONMOUTH [MAMOT]. He was discharged for past union activity. He has been working for two years at Western Electric

[45 groups unrecoverable]

entry into the FELLOWCOUNTRYMAN [ZEMLYaChESKAYa][iv] [Party][v]. SARANT lives apart from his family. Answer without delay.

No. 344   MAJ[vi]

5 May

Footnotes:
[i] Alfred SARANT: Alfred Epaminondas SARANT. Later probably either covername "SKAUT"/"METR" (ie "SCOUT"/ "METRE") or covername "Kh'YuS" (ie "HUGHES").
[ii] ANTENNA: Julius ROSENBERG.
[iii] TYRE: NEW YORK CITY.
[iv] FELLOWCOUNTRYMAN: Communist.
[v] Inserted by translator.
[vi] MAJ: ie "MAY"; Stepan Zakharovich APRESYaN.

VENONA

~~TOP SECRET~~

33. New York 640 to Moscow, 6 May 1944.

~~TOP SECRET DINAR~~ VENONA

Reissue

EXPANSION OF AIDA's WORK WITH JEWS

From: NEW YORK

To: MOSCOW

No: 640   6 May 1944

HUDDSON [GUDDZON][a] proposes to place AIDA [AIDA][i] as administrative secretary to the Committee of Jewish Writers and Artists[b], where she will be able to expand her opportunities for using[c] Jewish organizations and prominent figures. Working as she does now with the United Palestine Appeal, AIDA sheds light only on the RATS [KRYSY][ii]. Sanction AIDA's shift to the new work.

350   MAY [MAJ][iii]
6 May

Translator's notes:
- [a] "GUDDZON" is presumably meant for the same name as the HUDSON [GUDZON] changed to JOHN [DZhON] in No.1403 of 5 October 1944.

- [b] The Russian ARTIST, meaning an "artiste" in the performing arts or an actor, has been used mechanically because of the etymological identity, instead of the more correct KhUDOZhNIK

- [c] The word translated "using" is OFORMLENIE. This sometimes means "clearance" (investigation into reliability etc.). But it apparently also means "inducing to help us unconsciously", "using".

Comments:
- [i] Esther Trebach RAND.
- [ii] Probably a cover word for ZIONISTS.
- [iii] Stepan Zakharovich APRESYaN, Soviet Vice-Consul in New York.

34. New York 655 to Moscow, 9 May 1944.

BRIDE
~~TOP SECRET~~

USSR

Ref No: S/NBF/T508
Issued: 7/4/1954
Copy No: 205

INFORMATION FROM "PAL".

From: NEW YORK
To: MOSCOW
No.: 655

9 May 1944

To the 3th Department.

PAL [PEL][i] advises:

According to the information of F.E.A. on 22nd April the ISLANDERS [OSTROVITYaNE][ii] gave up the plan of invading the Balkans, preferring to await the total [C% defeat] [1 group unrecovered], and after that rapidly occupy Greece and Yugoslavia.

2. The BANK [BANK][iii] is inclined to approve the USSR's intention to remove industrial equipment from Germany to replace what was destroyed. The BANK considers possible to exact reparations from Germany for 10 years. Only after this does it think it possible to allow Germany to begin the reconstruction of her own industry.

3. PROCOPE (PROKOPE)[iv] in conversations with various highly placed representatives of the LEAGUE[v] is indicating that Finland is unable to pay [1 group unrecovered] the USSR 120 million dollars in reparations.

4. The master of the COUNTRY HOUSE [DAChA][vi] in a telegram to the BANK on 15th April advised that the Soviet Government does not want [2 groups unrecovered] persistently in the talks about a loan. He considers

[Continued overleaf]

Distribution

S/NBF/T508
[2 Pages]

~~TOP SECRET~~
BRIDE

34. *(Continued)*

- 2 -　　　　　　　S/NBF/T508

~~that~~ it ~~would be~~ more in the interest of the COUNTRY [STRANA][viii] to conclude an agreement about a loan now than to wait for the end of the war.

5. NABOB [NABOB][ix] has decided to present to CAPTAIN [KAPITAN][x] a plan for a post-war trade agreement with us.

[51 groups unrecoverable]

Comments:
- [i] PEL: possibly Nathan Gregory SILVERMASTER.
- [ii] OSTROVITYaNE: the British.
- [iii] BANK: the U.S. State Department.
- [iv] Hjalmar PROCOPÉ, Finnish Minister in WASHINGTON.
- [v] LIGA: the U.S. Government.
- [vi] DACha: the U.S. Embassy in MOSCOW.
- [vii] ~~DEKRET: Lend-Lease.~~
- [viii] STRANA: the U.S.A.
- [ix] NABOB: Henry MORGENTHAU, Jr.
- [x] KAPITAN: Franklin D. ROOSEVELT.

35. New York 687 to Moscow, 13 May 1944.

~~TOP SECRET TRINE~~ VENONA

Reissue (T910)

From: NEW YORK
To: MOSCOW
No: 687

13 May 1944

On HELMSMAN's[RULEVOJ][i] instructions GOOD GIRL[UMNITsA][ii] contacted through AMT[iii] a new group [C% in CARTHAGE][C% KARFAGEN][iv]:

[53 groups unrecoverable]

MAGDOFF - "KANT"[v]. GOOD GIRL's impressions: They are reliable FELLOW-COUNTRYMEN[ZEMLYaKI][vi], politically highly mature; they want to help with information. They said that they had been neglected and no one had taken any interest in their potentialities

[29 groups unrecoverable]

"STORM[ShTORM]"[vii]. RAIDER[REJDER][viii], PLUMB[LOT][ix], TED[x] and KANT will go to TYRE[TIR][xi] once every two weeks in turn.

PLUMB and TED know PAL[PEL][xii]. We shall let you have identifying particulars later.

No. 373   MAYOR[MER][xiii]

Comments:
- [i] HELMSMAN: Earl BROWDER.
- [ii] GOOD GIRL: Elizabeth BENTLEY.
- [iii] AMT: Presumably a mistake for John ABT. See also NEW YORK to MOSCOW No. 588 of 29 April 1944. (S/NBF/T110).
- [iv] CARTHAGE: WASHINGTON, D.C.
- [v] KANT: Henry Samuel MAGDOFF.
- [vi] FELLOW COUNTRYMEN: Members of a Communist Party.
- [vii] STORM: Unidentified.
- [viii] RAIDER: Victor PERLO.
- [ix] PLUMB: Possibly Charles KRAMER.
- [x] TED: Probably Edward Joseph FITZGERALD.
- [xi] TYRE: NEW YORK CITY.
- [xii] PAL: Nathan Gregory SILVERMASTER.
- [xiii] MAYOR: Probably Iskhak Abdulovich AKhMEROV.

25 July, 1968

~~TOP SECRET TRINE~~ VENONA

36. New York 696-7 to Moscow, 16 May 1944.

Reissue (T142)

From: NEW YORK
To: MOSCOW
Nos: 696-697

16 May 1944

[Part I] To the 8th Department.

In a conversation with SERGEJ[i] IMPERIALIST[ii] said:

1. The General Staff of the COUNTRY[STRANA][iii] has no doubt of the success of the invasion of Europe. Last week CARTHAGE[KARFAGEN][iv] assured EISENHOWER that there were sufficient trained reserves in the COUNTRY to ensure the reinforcement of the units taking part in the invasion. The ISLANDERS[OSTROVITYaNE][v] have stopped objecting to the invasion. LUN''s[vi] deputy (henceforth "KAPRAL"[vii]) told IMPERIALIST that KABAN[viii] had agreed with the invasion plan proposed by the TOWNSMEN[GOROZhANE][ix]. In KAPRAL's words KABAN told him: "For a long time I could not agree to an operation of this kind. However, now despite [3 groups unrecovered]

[42 groups unrecoverable]

is sure that a break will ensue very soon. Concerning Rumania, Bulgaria and Hungary the BANK[x] supposes that they will break with Germany only after the development of decisive operations on the Western and Eastern Fronts.

Only in passing did IMPERIALIST touch upon European questions, saying that it was desirable to have a solution of the Soviet-Polish problem before the invasion: "In return for a change in the Polish Cabinet, MOSCOW ought to renounce L'VOV."

I. [xi] continues to consider the question of the participation of the USSR in the war against Japan a stumbling block in Soviet-American relations. The master of the DACHA[xii] told him that discussion of this question by the press was contrary to the interests of the COUNTRY. I. agrees with him but does not conceal that our future intentions in this matter are considered in responsible circles in the COUNTRY to be a deciding factor in the policy of the COUNTRY.

[Part II] According to IMPERIALIST's report the Americans, by the end of 1944, hope to seize the Philippines, Formosa, Singapore and

[180 groups unrecovered]
[10 groups unrecoverable]

No. 376
16 May

MAJ[xiii]

36. (Continued)

```
Comments:
   [i]    SERGEJ: Vladimir Sergeevich PRAVDIN.
   [ii]   IMPERIALIST: Walter LIPPMANN.
   [iii]  STRANA: The U.S.A.
   [iv]   KARFAGEN: WASHINGTON, D.C.
   [v]    OSTROVITYaNE: The British
   [vi]   LUN': i.e. HEN HARRIER, Cordell HULL.
   [vii]  KAPRAL: i.e. CORPORAL, Edward R. STETTINIUS, Jr.
   [viii] KABAN: i.e. BOAR, Winston CHURCHILL.
   [ix]   GOROZhANE: The Americans.
   [x]    BANK: The U. S. State Department
   [xi]   I.: i.e. IMPERIALIST.
   [xii]  DAChA: i.e. The COUNTRY HOUSE, the U. S. Embassy in
          MOSCOW.
   [xiii] MAJ: i.e. MAY, Stepan APRESYaN.
```

16 April 1974

37. New York 732 to Moscow, 20 May 1944.

~~TOP SECRET DINAR~~ DRUG

From: NEW YORK
To: MOSCOW
No: 732

20 May 1944

Data from "GNOME"[i] about the "JET [VOZDUKh]" assembly 19 A of the WESTINGHOUSE firm. The assembly

[9 groups unrecovered]

increase in speed. It consists of a compressor-internal combustion chamber-turbine. The exhaust nozzle with the cross-section regulated by a central cone. Data of the assembly:

    Weight dry - 850 pounds.
    Full length - 100 inches.
    Diameter of the installation - 19 inches.
    Diameter of the compressor - 16 inches.
    Compression ratio of the compressor - 2.75/1, number of
        stages of the compressor - 6.
    Single-stage turbine.
    Temperature of the gas in the turbine
            [3 groups unrecovered]
                            00 Fahrenheit, maximum

[67 groups unrecoverable]

nozzle
        [11 groups unrecovered]

works only when starting. The normal power of the thrust which is created by the assembly ~~is equal~~ at sea level
        [3 groups unrecovered]

[40 groups unrecoverable]

Comment: [i] GNOME: William Perl.

~~TOP SECRET DINAR~~ DRUG

38. Moscow 334 to Mexico City, 30 May 1944.

BRIDE

~~TOP SECRET~~ EIDER

USSR

Ref. No: 3/NBF/T935
Issued: 21/8/1957
Copy No: 205

M273.

PAYMENT OF A DEPOSIT FOR "THE PAIR" (1944)

From: MOSCOW
To: MEXICO CITY
No: 334   30 May 44

To YuRIJ.[i]

Payment of the deposit in the "PAIR"[ii] business we sanction on principle

[29 groups unrecovered]

from the bank of banknotes is registered by the appropriate departments [ORGANY], it is desirable in order to avoid compromise that "OKh"[iii] should pay the deposit from his own [C% money] which we will repay.

[10 groups unrecovered]

sent on from here. The Americans will not give a transit visa in MOSCOW if it is not secured in TYRE[iv] or [if][a] for this the Mexican Embassy in MOSCOW does not [1 group unrecovered] the passport on instructions from the COUNTRYSIDE[v]. We shall communicate with you after a reply about the above possibilities has been received from MAKSIM[vi].

No. 2334   VIKTOR[vii]

[Notes and Comments overleaf]

Distribution

3/NBF/T935
(2 Pages)

~~TOP SECRET~~
BRIDE EIDER

38. *(Continued)*

- 2 -　　　　3/NBF/T935

Notes: [a] Supplied by translator.

Comments:
- [i] YuRIJ : Lev A. TARASOV, 1st Secretary at Soviet Embassy in MEXICO CITY.
- [ii] The PAIR : Nicholas and Maria FISHER.
- [iii] OKh : Adolfo ORIVE de ALBA.
- [iv] TYRE : NEW YORK CITY.
- [v] COUNTRYSIDE: MEXICO.
- [vi] MAKSIM : Vasilij ZUBILIN, 2nd Secretary at the Soviet Embassy in WASHINGTON, April 1943-August 1944.
- [vii] VIKTOR : Lt. Gen. P.M. FITIN.

3/NBF/T935

39. New York 786 to Moscow, 1 June 1944.

BRIDE

~~TOP SECRET~~ SUEDE

TO BE KEPT UNDER LOCK AND KEY :
NEVER TO BE REMOVED FROM THE OFFICE.

USSR

Ref No: S/NBF/T139
Issued: 13/12/1951
Copy No:

ARRANGEMENTS FOR THE PROVISION
OF VISAS FOR "THE COUPLE".

From: NEW YORK
To: MOSCOW
No: 786   1 June 1944

To VICTOR.

Reference your telegram No. 2066.

There are three possible ways of obtaining a transit visa for THE COUPLE [CHETA][i]:

1. The normal way - "TENOR"[ii] will do everything himself. Will take several months, but the result will be favourable.

2. Through the lawyer [ADVOKAT] John KEATING [KITING] - somewhat quicker [,] will cost 300-400 dollars. Both methods are lengthy as they will involve investigation [PROVERKA][a].

3. Through CAPTAIN's [KAPITAN][iii] adviser, David NILES [NAJLS] - will take 3 - 4 days [,] will cost 500 dollars. Round NILES there is a group of his friends who will arrange anything for a bribe. Through them TENOR obtains priorities and has already paid them as much as 6000 dollars. Whether NILES takes a bribe himself is not known for certain. T.[iv] has talked to them about the [D: payment]
[12 groups unrecovered]
in the COUNTRYSIDE [DEREVNYa][v]
[9 groups unrecovered]

[Continued overleaf]

Distribution

S/NBF/T139
[2 Pages]

~~TOP SECRET~~ SUEDE
BRIDE

39. (Continued)

S/NBF/T139

COUNTRYSIDE [DEREVENSKIJ][vi] visa and a ticket as far as the COUNTRYSIDE [DEREVNYa][v].
T.[iv] declares that the latter way is one hundred percent successful and there will not be any investigation [PROVERKA][a]. I recommend the third method. Before we begin to act, THE COUPLE must obtain a COUNTRYSIDE visa and report immediately for ..'s information the amount of the surety deposited in the COUNTRYSIDE. Immediately on receipt of the COUNTRYSIDE visa and sanction to put through the manoeuvre [KOMBINATsIYa] T. will purchase a through ticket from
[13 groups unrecovered]
COUNTRYSIDE visa. T. THE COUPLE [4 groups unrecovered]
COUNTRYSIDE visa. T. [1 group unrecovered] to meet the COUPLE in [2 groups unrecovered] but later in the COUNTRYSIDE
[21 groups unrecovered]

T.N.: [a] I.e., investigation by the U.S. authorities of the genuineness of the application and the credentials of the applicants.

Comments: [i] ChETA: Nicolas and Marie (BOYKO) FISHER. Their cover-name appears to have been changed to THE REEFS [RIFI] by late 1944.

[ii] TENOR: possibly the same as BASS [BAS] – Michael W. BURD (originally WEISBURD).

[iii] KAPITAN: Franklin Delano ROOSEVELT.

[iv] T.: i.e. TENOR.

[v] DEREVNYa: MEXICO.

[vi] DEREVENSKIJ: Mexican.

W.S. No. XY-47.2

S/NBF/T139

40. New York 824 to Moscow, 7 June 1944.

~~TOP SECRET COPSE~~ M45

New York–Moscow
1944
No. 824 (7 June)

To Victor [VIKTOR].

Your no. 2310:

1. I conversed with Chemist [KhIMIK] about the DESIATKA[a]; according to] his account the DESIATKA is conscientious with the exception of Ruby [RUBIN]. Relative to the drinking bout we are sending a résumé by Chemist. There have been no other cases [or: incidents]. I shall get together before long [with] R. and IRA [separately?].....[from them?] details. I shall telegraph the results.

According to Chemist's account right now Artemius [ARTEM] and Gregory [GRIGORIJ] are living together with girl students they made the acquaintance of on the steamer. Chemist begs me to raise the question again of his wife's coming inasmuch as the DESIATKA is supposed to [stay?] here at least a year more. For the time being the DESIATKA is asking permission to send telegrams and parcels to [their] families by [designated?][b] addressees, in order that your people may intercept them and deliver them to the addressees. Telegraph.

2. By post I am sending a memorandum [or: report] [in] which I shall adopt the following conventions[c]:

    B. the Plant [ZAVOD][d].
    ZH. decipherment [RASSHIFROVKA][[,]
    YU. editorial staff [or: office] [REDAKTSIYA].
    D. the Factory [FABRIKA][e].
    CH. the Neighbor [SOSED][f].
    SH. cover [PRIKRYTIE].

~~TOP SECRET COPSE~~

40. *(Continued)*

~~TOP SECRET CORSE~~

    T. sound-recording apparatus [ZVUKOZAPIS'IVAYUSHCHAYA APPARATURA],

    S. eavesdropping [PODSLUSHIVANIYE],

    N. ?personnel? of the Office [SOSTAV? KONTOR(Y)S,

    P. the Syndicate [SINDIKAT][h],

    H. courier guard [? courier-guard or courier's guard?; KURIER(AY) OKHRANA],

    M. surveillance [NABLYUDENIYE],

    F. the Office [KONTORA][i],

    K. conspiracy [or: conspirativeness; KONSPIRATSIYA],

    L. cipher clerk [SHIFROVAL'SHCHIK],

    C. worker [RABOTNIK][j].

459

                           May [MAY]

7 June

[a]Previously rendered: the Ten. This translation, while justifiable (see below), is misleading, for it tends to suggest that the DESIATKA was necessarily composed of just ten people. Actually, its quantitative reference may be no stronger than that of, say, "the Four of Clubs" or "Eight Ball". A translation of the definition of DESIATKA in the Tolkovyy Slovar' follows; English words for the various meanings are added in brackets:

    DESIATKA, i, f. 1. The figure 10 (coll.) [a ten]. ‖ The designation of various objects numbered with this figure (coll.), e.g. billiard ball no. 10 [the ten (ball)], tramcar, autobus no. 10 [number 10]. ‖ A school mark denoted by this figure (school obs.) [a ten]. 2. A playing card having ten pips [the ten, a ten, a/the ten-spot]. 3. A ten-ruble note or coin (coll.) [like our tenner, ten-spot]. 4. A launch with ten sails (naut.).

However, speaking in favor of the quantitative interpretation is the use of TROIKA. Its meanings parallel those of DESIATKA; it can mean

~~TOP SECRET CORSE~~

40. *(Continued)*

New York-Moscow 1944 No. 304 (9 June) — 5

~~TOP SECRET CORSE~~

[a] "three horses harnessed abreast to one vehicle"; and it is famous in the history of the All-Union Communist Party (Bolshevik) for its application to various triumvirates formed by Lenin and Stalin.

[b] Possibly ANKETNYYE ADRESA = questionnaire address or interrogation-form address (meaning?).

[c] Note that the terms to be coded can all be referred to Soviet personnel and control of their actions (by surveillance, microphones, etc.). The use of the post and of a special code suggests that the contents might concern in part the cipher clerk(s) and others handling correspondence between New York and Moscow.

[d] The Soviet Consulate (in New York).

[e] The Amtorg Trading Corporation.

[f] Red Army intelligence service.

[g] Of the State Security apparatus in the Consulate.

[h] The People's Commissariat of Foreign Affairs [NARODNYY KOMISSARIAT INOSTRANNYKH DEL = NARKOMINDEL = NKID].

[i] The State Security apparatus in the Consulate.

[j] That is, operative.

~~TOP SECRET CORSE~~

41. New York 847B-848 to Moscow, 15 June 1944.

VENONA

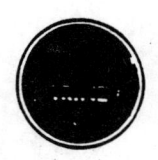

~~TOP SECRET~~

USSR

Ref. No.: 3/NBF/T24 (of 21/5/51)
Issued: 31/3/1967
Copy No.: 204

REISSUE

SERGEJ REPORTS ON U.S. POLICY TOWARDS EUROPE (1944)

From: NEW YORK
To: MOSCOW
No: 847B-848   15th June 1944

Part I

To VIKTOR[i]

SERGEJ[ii] reports the following:

1. According to statements by informed journalists who have close contacts with government circles, the question of FRANCE's future is very disturbing. These circles, which [2 groups unrecovered], [1 group unrecovered] policy of non-recognition of RAS[iii] and are afraid that it may lead FRANCE into the sphere of influence of the USSR. From conversations with IMPERIALIST[iv] and CHIEF[ShEF][v] and the correspondents LINDLEY[LINDLEJ][vi], HARSCH[HARSh][vii] and VISSON[viii], the following emerges: the policy of the USA with regard to FRANCE has been inspired, since 1940, by CALIPH[KALIF][ix], LEAHY[LEGI][x] and MURPHY[MERFI][xi]

[35 groups unrecoverable]

ZOUAVE[ZUAV][xii] with the help of COT[KOT][xiii]. CAPTAIN[KAPITAN][xiv] hoped [B% at the same time] to secure for the COUNTRY[STRANA][xv] the permanent use of DAKAR and CASABLANCA[KASABLANKA] and possibly a base in INDO-CHINA and also to oppose the attempts by the ISLANDERS[OSTROVITYaNE][xvi] to take FRANCE completely under their influence before the advantage was gained.

[27 groups unrecovered]

DISTRIBUTION: [Continued overleaf]

3/NBF/T24

~~TOP SECRET~~
VENONA

41. (Continued)

not to recognise any such agreement. According to IMPERIALIST's account HEN HARRIER[LUN'][xvii] [and][a] his deputy[xviii] are not in agreement with CAPTAIN and consider that by their policy both the COUNTRY and the ISLAND [OSTROV][xix] have already practically lost the confidence of the French while conversely our prestige there is growing. I.[xx] affirms that the BEAR CUBS [MEDVEZhATA][xxi], as well as military circles and the Navy, are in favour of recognizing R.[xxii]. Naval chiefs[RUKOVODSTVO] are not demanding the annexation of DAKAR or other bases but want a military alliance which will offer the COUNTRY their use. They also have in mind bases in the Pacific.

2. According to I., the LEAGUE[LIGA][xxiii] - contrary to its previous intentions - is not at present supporting the dismemberment of GERMANY although it still regards the award of EAST PRUSSIA to POLAND as essential. The question of the use of German manpower in the USSR and

[42 groups unrecoverable]

would have paid and fed them.

3. As regards the [B% Polish] question, [D% some circles] in the LEAGUE think, according to I., that the USSR should yield on the LWOW question in return for a change in the composition of the Polish Cabinet. I. reinforced this argument with the following observation: "The LWOW question ought not to be a matter of importance for the USSR since it considers that in any case the MIKOLAJCZYK government would not stay in power and that this would therefore only be a temporary concession which might be rectified in the future["][a].

4. I. says that Wall Street considers the forthcoming monetary conference to be pointless. It is stated in financial circles that the currency of European occupied countries cannot be stabilized at present as the prospects for their economy in the future are not known: consequently stabilization should be limited to the dollar-sterling bloc and the USSR should not be included in the conference as the rouble is stable.

5. Considering European questions to be of secondary importance, I. constantly emphasized, as in previous discussions, that it was essential for the USSR to participate in the future in the destruction of JAPAN in order to secure firm friendly relations with the COUNTRY. As regards FINLAND, I. hinted that the breaking off of diplomatic relations would depend on the breaking off by the USSR of relations with BULGARIA. However in a conversation with IDE[YaZ][xxiv], HARSCH affirmed that CAPTAIN had finally rejected the proposal by HEN HARRIER and MARSHALL[MARShAL][xxv] to break with FINLAND on the grounds that this would be inexpedient before the elections.

6. I. is well acquainted with DULLES[DALLES][xxvi], one of FISTs[KULAK][xxvii] [C% group of] political advisers. D.[xxviii] consulted [I.][a] as to how the BEAR CUBS' position on the question of postwar GERMANY should be set out and included I.'s statement of the position in a speech of FIST's in May.

No. 453 MAY[MAJ][xxix]

3/NBF/T24

41. *(Continued)*

VENONA
~~TOP SECRET~~

- 3 -   3/NBF/T24

Notes: [a] Inserted by the translator.

Comments:
- [i] VIKTOR: Lt. Gen. P.M. FITIN.
- [ii] SERGEJ: Vladimir Sergeevich PRAVDIN, TASS representative in U.S.A.
- [iii] RAS: General Charles de GAULLE.
- [iv] IMPERIALIST: Walter LIPPMANN.
- [v] CHIEF: Unidentified covername.
- [vi] LINDLEY: Ernest Kidder LINDLEY.
- [vii] HARSCH: Joseph C. HARSCH.
- [viii] VISSON: Andre VISSON.
- [ix] CALIPH: William Christian BULLITT.
- [x] LEAHY: Admiral William D. LEAHY.
- [xi] MURPHY: Robert Daniel MURPHY.
- [xii] ZOUAVE: Unidentified.
- [xiii] COT: Possibly Pierre COT.
- [xiv] CAPTAIN: Franklin D. ROOSEVELT.
- [xv] COUNTRY: U.S.A.
- [xvi] ISLANDERS: The British.
- [xvii] HEN HARRIER: Cordell HULL
- [xviii] Cordell HULL's: Edward R. STETTINIUS, Jr.
- [xix] ISLAND: Great Britain.
- [xx] I.: i.e. IMPERIALIST, Walter LIPPMANN.
- [xxi] BEAR CUBS: U.S. Republican Party.
- [xxii] R.: i.e. RAS/General Charles de GAULLE
- [xxiii] The LEAGUE: U.S. Government.
- [xxiv] IDE: Simon Samuel KRAFSUR, of the TASS News Agency.
- [xxv] MARSHALL: General George Catlett MARSHALL.

3/NBF/T24

~~TOP SECRET~~
VENONA

41. *(Continued)*

~~TOP SECRET~~

- 4 -   3/NBF/T24

Comments: [xxvi] DULLES: John Foster DULLES.
(Cont'd)
      [xxvii] FIST: Thomas Edmund DEWEY.
      [xxviii] D.: i.e. DULLES.
      [xxix] MAY: Stepan Zakharovich APRESYaN.

3/NBF/T24

~~TOP SECRET~~

42. New York 850 to Moscow, 15 June 1944.

BRIDE
~~TOP SECRET~~
FROTH

USSR

Ref No:
Issued: 16/6/1954
Copy No: 105

REFERENCE TO THE PROBABLE DEPARTURE OF "REST".

From: NEW YORK
To: MOSCOW
No.: 850

15 June 1944

To VIKTOR[i].

[1 group unrecovered][a] received from REST[ii] the third part of report MSN - 12 Efferent Fluctuation in a Stream [STRUYa]

[37 groups unrecoverable]

Diffusion[b] Method - work on his speciality. R.[iii] expressed doubt about the possibility of remaining in the COUNTRY [STRANA][iv] without arousing suspicion. According to what R. says, the ISLANDERS [OSTROVITYaNE][v] and TOWNSMEN [GOROZhANE][vi] have finally fallen out as a result of the delay in research work on diffusion. The TOWNSMEN have told the representative of the ISLAND[vii] that construction of a plant in the ISLAND "would be in direct contradiction to the spirit of the agreement on ENORMOUS [ENORMOZ][viii] signed together with the Atlantic Charter." At present the ISLAND's director [RUKOVODITEL'] in CARTHAGE [KARFAGEN][ix] is ascertaining the details of the transfer of work to the ISLAND. R. assumes that he will have to leave in a month or six weeks.

No. 458
15th June

MAY [MAJ][x]

[T.N. and Comments overleaf]

Distribution

[2 Pages]

~~TOP SECRET~~ FROTH
BRIDE

42. (Continued)

- 2 -

T.N.: [a] This is a garbled group possibly representing a cover-name, or alternatively an adverb (one possibility being "finally") with "we" or "I" being understood immediately following.

      [b] Only the latter part of the word has been recovered, but "diffusion" is probable from the context.

Comments: [i] VIKTOR: probably Lt.-General P.M. FITIN.

      [ii] REST: Emil Klaus Julius FUCHS.

      [iii] R.: i.e. REST.

      [iv] STRANA: the U.S.A.

      [v] OSTROVITYaNE: the British.

      [vi] GOROZHANE: the Americans.

      [vii] OSTROV: Great Britain.

      [viii] ĒNORMOZ: the Manhattan Engineering District.

      [ix] KARFAGEN: WASHINGTON, D.C.

      [x] MAJ: MGB resident in NEW YORK.

W.S. No.: PH-60 (Revision)

43. New York 1053 to Moscow, 26 July 1944.

Reissue(T282)

From: NEW YORK
To: MOSCOW
No: 1053

26 July 1944

To VIKTOR[i].

In July ANTENNA[ii] was sent by the firm for ten days to work in CARTHAGE [KARFAGEN][iii]. There he visited his school friend Max ELITCHER[a], who works in the Bureau of Standards as head of the fire control section for warships [which mount guns][b] of over five-inch calibre. He has access to extremely valuable materials on guns.

Five years ago Max ELITCHER [MAKS E.] graduated from the Electro-Technical Department of the City College of NEW YORK, He has a Master of Science degree. Since finishing college he has been working at the Bureau of Standards. He is a FELLOW COUNTRYMAN [ZEMLYaK][iv]. He entered the FELLOW COUNTRYMEN's organization [ZEMLYaChESTVO] after finishing his studies.

By ANTENNA he is characterized as a loyal, reliable, level-headed and able man. Married, his wife is a FELLOW COUNTRYWOMAN [ZEMLYaChKA]. She is a psychologist by profession, she works at the War Department.

Max ELITCHER is an excellent amateur photographer and has all the necessary equipment for taking photographs.

Please check ELITCHER and communicate your consent to his clearance [OFORMLENIE].

No. 594
26 July   MAJ[v]

Notes: [a] Given in Roman alphabet.
       [b] Inserted by translator.
Comments:
  [i]   VIKTOR: Lt. Gen. P. M. FITIN.
  [ii] ANTENNA: Julius ROSENBERG.
  [iii] KARFAGEN: WASHINGTON, D. C.
  [iv] ZEMLYaK: Member of the Communist Party.
  [v]   MAJ: i.e. MAY, Stepan APRESYaN.

28 April 1975

44. New York 1043 to Moscow, 25 July 1944.

BRIDE
~~TOP SECRET~~

USSR	Ref.No: S/NBF/T46
	Issued: 14/3/1955
	Copy No: 205

Item 2

REISSUE

REPORT OF VISIT TO "THE PLANT" BY
REPRESENTATIVES OF THE CITY HOUSING DEPARTMENT

From: NEW YORK
To: MOSCOW
No: 1043   25 July 1944

To VIKTOR[i].

[D% Yesterday] two fellows came to see SHAH[ShAKh][ii] at the PLANT [ZAVOD][iii] and said that in the capacity of representatives of the City Housing Department they were to inspect the PLANT building and the neighbouring house. In reply to SHAH's question about [B% the purpose][of the inspection][a] the fellows said that they ~~did not have to make a report~~. SHAH managed to show them out but they hinted roughly that they might come back with people who would ensure them access. GRANDPAPA[DEDUShKA][iv] [3 groups unrecovered] ~~[O% in case of need] [1 group unrecovered]~~ [8 groups unrecoverable] plausible excuse the necessity of checking the lift mechanism (it is very [C% bad]). GRANDPAPA came to an agreement that he would send our architect to the Housing Department and he would inform [them][a] about the lifts. With this the incident was closed, but it is difficult to doubt that the fellows

[Continued overleaf]

Distribution

S/NBF/T46
[2 Pages]

~~TOP SECRET~~

BRIDE

44. *(Continued)*

- 2 -   S/NBF/T46

represented the KhATA[v].

BORIS[vi] has no special instructions on the circumstances in which he is to destroy the ciphers without reference to anyone and when it is permissible to use weapons. Please give some guidance.

No. 581.

In view of his having enciphered and sent off a telegram in the last 10 minutes before he left the point he was at and to his [B% having destroyed] the originals GRIMM[vii] requests that its receipt be confirmed. The telegram was in three parts.

No. 583.

We have received letter number 4 addressed to SON[SYN][viii]. Please explain [3 groups unrecovered] and whether to send it at the first opportunity or should we obtain from GRANDPAPA the immediate despatch of a courier.

MAY[MAJ][ix]

No. 588

T.N: [a] Inserted by the translator.

Comments:
- [i] VIKTOR: Lt.-General P.M. FITIN.
- [ii] ShAKh: Konstantin Alekseevich ChABANOV, clerk at the Soviet Consulate-General, NEW YORK.
- [iii] ZAVOD: the Soviet Consulate-General in NEW YORK.
- [iv] DEDUShKA: Evgenij Dmitrievich KISELEV, Soviet Consul-General in NEW YORK.
- [v] KhATA: the F.B.I.
- [vi] BORIS: the MGB cipher clerk in NEW YORK. possibly Aleksandr Pavlovich SAPRYGIN.
- [vii] GRIMM: probably Nikolaj Alekseevich GOLOVIN.
- [viii] SYN: not identified.
- [ix] MAJ: probably Stepan Zakharovich APRESYaN.

W.S. No.: XY-20.14 (Revision)

S/NBF/T46

45. New York 1065 to Moscow, 28 July 1944.

BRIDE
~~TOP SECRET~~

FROTH

USSR	Ref No: S/NBF/T92
	Issued: 5/5/1954
	Copy No: 205

REFERENCES TO THE WORK OF "MAYOR"

Item 2

REISSUE

From: NEW YORK
To: MOSCOW
No.: 1065   28 July 1944

To VIKTOR[i]

[Your no.][a] 3028. Some weeks ago GOOD GIRL [UMNITsA][ii] told MAYOR [MER][iii] that HELMSMAN [RULEVOJ][iv] as a result of a conversation with DIR[v] had apparently decided that DIR must be withdrawn completely from our work in order to employ her fully on FELLOW-COUNTRYMANLY [ZEMLYaChESKIJ][vi] work. In HELMSMAN's opinion DIR's nerves have been badly shaken and her health is poor, which renders her unsuitable for our work. In MAYOR's opinion it is possible to get H. [R.][vii] to change his opinion about the advisability of this decision which MAYOR suspects was made under pressure from GOOD GIRL, who for some reason dislikes DIR. MAYOR has informed G.G. [U.][viii] that if DIR is really ill she will need rather to be withdrawn for a rest, but afterwards be used on liaison [with][a] a conspirative apartment etc. She has been working for a long time and has acquired considerable experience. MAYOR proposes that she should not be employed on active FELLOW-COUNTRYMANLY[vi] work. Telegraph your opinion.

No. 596

[Continued overleaf]

Distribution

S/NBF/T92
[2 Pages]

~~TOP SECRET~~
BRIDE

FROTH

45. *(Continued)*

　　　　　　　　　　　　　　　　- 2 -　　　　　　　S/NBF/T92

　　　　Please advise whether information on the COUNTRY's [STRANA][ix] war production and war effort should be brought to the notice of the head Neighbour [SOSED][x] (of course without indicating the source). Your are aware of the danger of people possibly being sent to check our sources. Moreover, the lack of exchange of information with the Neighbour here does not contribute, in my view, to our friendly relations; nevertheless, I have not as yet established relations with him.

No. 597　　　　　　　　　　　　　　　　MAY [MAJ][xi]

T.N.: [a] Inserted by translator.

Comments: [i] VIKTOR: probably Lt.-General P.M. FITIN.
　　　　　[ii] UMNITsA: Elizabeth BENTLEY.
　　　　　[iii] MER: unidentified.
　　　　　[iv] RULEVOJ: Earl BROWDER.
　　　　　[v] DIR· possibly Mary Wolfe PRICE.
　　　　　[vi] ZEMLYaChESKIJ: i.e. Communist Party.
　　　　　[vii] R.: i.e. RULEVOJ.
　　　　　[viii] U.: i.e. UMNITsA.
　　　　　[ix] STRANA: the U.S.A.
　　　　　[x] SOSED: a member of the Soviet military intelligence organisation.
　　　　　[xi] MAJ: Pavel Ivanovich FEDOSIMOV.

S/NBF/T92

46. New York 1076 to Moscow, 29 July 1944.

VENONA
~~TOP SECRET~~

USSR

Ref. No.: 3/NBF/T492 (of 5/4/54)
Issued: 20/1/76
Copy No.: 301

REISSUE

ASSESSMENTS OF ARTEK AND LEONID, MENTION OF SERGEJ, MAKSIM, ZVUK, SECOND LINE, "A" TECHNIQUE (1944)

From: NEW YORK
To: MOSCOW
No.: 1076   29 July 1944

To VIKTOR[i].

Herewith the personal reports:

1. ARTEK[ii] controlled several probationers [STAZhERY] of the Second Nine[iii]. He ran these probationers on his own only after SERGEJ[iv] had left for home. He did not display any particular initiative.

[20 groups unrecovered].

He has a poor knowledge of the language, he barely [1 group unrecovered] the minimum. His miserable cover (messenger-guard) actually stopped him, in the conditions obtaining here, from doubling for [DUBLIROVANIE] the inspectors. With a different cover he could have acted with greater initiative and more effectively. Perhaps he is experiencing a feeling of dissatisfaction since, according to what he says, he has not been able to show his worth for many years because of his cover and [8 groups unrecovered] he stops opening doors on an equal footing with two others who are capable of nothing else.

[Continued overleaf]

VENONA
~~TOP SECRET~~

46. (Continued)

VENONA
~~TOP SECRET~~

3/NBF/T492

2. LEONID[v], before MAKSIM[vi] was given cover, was in touch with ZVUK[vii] and a number of probationers of the Second Line. Not having operational experience, he was not able to run probationers in accordance with the requirements. He is qualified in the "A" technique[viii] and successfully carried out a number of special tasks connected with documents on receiving and dispatching people. He has carried out missions consisting of checking and observing workers. He was used for tailing immediately upon MAKSIM's arrival. He acquired experience in external surveillance [NARUZhNOE NABLYuDENIE]. He has virtually no knowledge of the language and has not studied it.

[17 groups unrecovered]

". Latterly he [2 groups unrecovered] did not try to improve himself, was off-hand and even rude, conducted [1 group unrecovered] "independently". He was needlessly frank with his wife about matters concerning our work, which

[33 groups unrecoverable]

Footnotes:
[i] VIKTOR: Lt General Pavel Mikhajlovich FITIN.

[ii] ARTEK: Leonid Dmitrievich ABRAMOV, in the USA from May 1940 to 31 July 1944.

[iii] Second Line: Probably concerned with Ukrainians and other minority ethnic groups of the USSR.

[iv] SERGEJ: Vladimir Sergeevich PRAVDIN, in the USA from 19 October 1941 to Autumn 1943 and from January 1944 to 11 March 1946: cf NEW YORK's No. 1207 of 22 July 1943 (3/NBF/T903) on the transfer of "SERGEJ's" probationers.

[v] LEONID: Aleksej Nikolaevich PROKhOROV, in the USA from 1940 to 31 July 1944.

[vi] MAKSIM: Vasilij Mikhajlovich ZUBILIN, in the USA from 25 December 1941 to 26 August 1944.

[vii] ZVUK: ie "SOUND"; Jacob GOLOS.

[viii] "A" technique: Apparently the manufacture and provision of false papers. Cf references to the "A" Group and the "A" Line in NEW YORK's Nos. 626 of 5 May 1944 (3/NBF/T86), 1203 of 23 August 1944 (3/NBF/T235), 1457 and 1465 of 14 October 1944 (3/NBF/T491, 789).

VENONA ~~TOP SECRET~~

47. New York 1088-90 to Moscow, 30 July 1944.

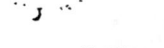

~~TOP SECRET DINAR~~ VENONA

Reissue (T529)

From: NEW YORK
To: MOSCOW
No: 1088-1090   30 July 1944

[Part I]   To SEMEN[i].

[C% As a result] [2 groups unrecovered] West Coast and [2 groups unrecovered] VITALIJ[ii] it has been established:

1. The organization

[58 groups unrecoverable]

VOVChEK's[iii] reports have been received [4 groups unrecovered] VITALIJ's concern, displayed in the opinion

[14 groups unrecovered]

seven months. During his stay and work on the ship RODINA in July of this year V.[iv] [B% received] from the captain of the ship an illegal payment [3 groups unrecovered] wages for the duration of his stay [C% with friends in Canada] [4 groups unrecovered] on shore. Unconcealed affairs with women have created around V. an atmosphere of gossip and have undermined his authority in the local apparatus and the agent network [AGENTURA] connected with it. On his side this has caused irritability, rudeness and strained relations with those around him. All this has led to exceptional slackness in operational work:

a) Contact with the ship agent network [SUDOAGENTURA] was not established on all vessels. The guarding of the ships and investigating of obvious cases of sabotage were not carried out. V. did not know how many ships and which were in port or were expected in PORTLAND or SEATTLE. The reports for
[Part II] the agent network for the most part came in haphazardly.

b) V. did not control the work of the group leaders [8 groups unrecovered] time liaison was not established with the ship agent network.

c) He did not take steps to investigate the sabotage on the ship KOMILES.

d) [7 groups unrecovered] did not take steps to ascertain the circumstances of sabotage on the ship ODESSA.

e) The serious fact of the loss of the ship IL'ICh he did not relate [C% although this affair came to the knowledge of the Center].

f) Contact with

[15 groups unrecovered]

port of VANCOUVER [2 groups unrecovered] the ship P. VINOGRADOV.

~~TOP SECRET DINAR~~ VENONA

47. *(Continued)*

~~TOP SECRET DINAR~~ VENONA

The resulting position of V. is not serious; according to all information his absentmindedness regarding cover and his desire to leave PORTLAND for Home or [3 groups unrecoverable] to recall from PORTLAND, although first having sent [B% instructions] to replace [him] which could be [3 groups unrecovered] work on the West Coast. In our opinion a suitable candidate is Viktor Vasil'evich S. Since V.'s conduct is a result of both of the prolonged absence of his family and the [D% lack]

[16 groups unrecovered]

Russian agent network on shore and on Soviet ships. For the time being I have taken the following steps:

[Part III]1. At numerous meetings with V. the way to fulfill the tasks set by you has been sketched out. At the same time steps have been taken to release V. as much as possible from work connected with his cover by using as a roof [KRYShA] VOVChEK who is his superior. The latter considers essential the control or reorganization of the method of work along the whole coast in our interests and the inclusion of himself in our work with V.

2. [11 groups unrecovered]

IGOR'[v], VLADISLAV[vi], VOVChEK, ALEKSANDR[vii] and the probationers [STAZhERY] ChEKhOV[viii] and ANCHOR [YaKOR'][ix].

3. A preliminary investigation into the circumstances of the sinking of the ship IL'ICh has been completed.

In LOS ANGELES I met PETR[x] whom I instructed on the reorganization of the work in BABYLON [VAVILON][xi] where he is finally going to the post of deputy ship repair engineer on the West Coast. On the day of the meeting PETR had no agent network in his charge. [3 groups unrecovered]

No. 606   MAY[MAJ][xii], AKIM[xiii]

Indicate the shortcomings in my telegram.

BORIS[xiv]

Comments: [i] SEMEN: Unidentified cover-name.

[ii] VITALIJ: Pavel Kuzmich REVIZOROV.

[iii] VOVChEK: Probably Aleksandr Pavlovich BOChEK.

[iv] V.: i.e. VITALIJ.

[v] IGOR': Unidentified cover-name.

[vi] VLADISLAV: Nikolaj Grigor'evich REDIN.

[vii] ALEKSANDR: Unidentified cover-name.

[viii] ChEKhOV: Unidentified cover-name.

[ix] ANCHOR: Unidentified cover-name.

[x] PETR: Aleksandr Petrovich GRAChEV.

~~TOP SECRET DINAR~~ VENONA

47. *(Continued)*

~~TOP SECRET DINAR~~

[xi] BABYLON: San Francisco.
[xii] MAY: Stepan APRESYaN.
[xiii] AKIM: Serej Grigor'evich LUK'YaNOV.
[xiv] BORIS: Aleksandr Pavlovich SAPRYKIN, MGB cipher clerk in New York.

48. New York 1102-3 to Moscow, 2 August 1944.

BRIDE

~~TOP SECRET~~   EIDER

USSR

Ref. No: S/NBF/T47 (of 27/3/1951)
Issued: /31/12/1957
Copy No: 205

RE-ISSUE

A QUESTION OF VISAS FOR "THE PAIR" (1944)

From: NEW YORK
To: MOSCOW
No: 1102, 1103.   2 Aug. 44

[Two-part message complete]

[Part I] To VIKTOR.[i]

MAKSIM[ii] has asked (us)[a] to pass on the following:

"The PAIR[ChETA][iii]

1. BASS[BAS][iv] is sending simultaneously a telegram addressed to "Railway Worker[ZhELEZNODOROZhNIK][v] WEST[VEST] that the COUNTRYSIDE[DEREVENSKIJ][vi]
[1 group unrecovered]

[46 groups unrecoverable]

filled in what was known to him, indicating that in general this was not important because when the PAIR applied to the Embassy in SMIRNA[SMIRNA][vii], they would bring all the necessary information. We consider inadmissible [3 groups unrecovered] and, most important of all, we also consider that inquiries about visas for the COUNTRYSIDE[DEREVNYa][viii] and transit visas should be made by the PAIR from "KAZAN'" because it is known here that we do not allow foreigners into SMIRNA on such business. It is necessary on the basis of BASS's telegram to "mail" the PAIR's passports to the Embassy of the COUNTRYSIDE for receipt of a visa with the request that they be sent to the Embassy of the COUNTRY[STRANA][ix] in SMIRNA

Distribution   [Continued overleaf]

S/NBF/T47 (Re-Issue)

~~TOP SECRET~~
BRIDE   EIDER

48. *(Continued)*

~~TOP SECRET~~ EIDER

— 2 —   S/NBF/T47

(merely to gain the desired time) to obtain transit visas. Simultaneously from "KAZAN" send a telegram to the Embassy of the COUNTRY with a request to issue transit visas for the passports they will receive from the Embassy of the COUNTRYSIDE. The PAIR [2 groups unrecovered] their return address and are sending a reply paid telegram saying that they have been notified by their relation BASS that they have got visas for the COUNTRYSIDE and that they have to apply for a transit visa to the Embassy of the COUNTRY.

[Part II] The latter will obviously ask the PAIR either to say why they need to come to SMYRNA or to give all necessary particulars[D%].

[51 groups unrecoverable]

Embassy of the COUNTRY in SMYRNA immediately to telegraph verbatim [1 group unrecovered].

Should complications arise the PAIR are to telegraph BASS and you me so that measures can be taken and fresh pressure brought to bear. According to BASS's information there should be no complications.

4. For your information we advise how the business of getting a visa for the COUNTRY was [0% managed]. To begin with NILES[NAJLS][x] refused to intervene in the case, explaining that he had only recently interceded for one refugee and recommended approaching Congressman KLEINS[KLaJNS]. The latter did not [6 groups unrecovered] and it was only then that NILES intervened. The affair was held up because of the Party Convention and was actually settled in the last six days. All documents, telegrams [and][a] vouchers for the money orders, the parcel and the deposit were received by BASS today in an envelope of the TEMPLE[KhRAM][xi] [8 groups unrecovered] from the BANK[xii]. The business [1 group unrecovered] extremely sound and there is every chance [of success][a]. The BANK then [0% asked the Ministry of Foreign Affairs[MID] of the COUNTRYSIDE about [9 groups unrecovered]."

No. 611   MAY[MAJ][xiii]

Note: [a] Inserted by the translator.

Comments:
[i] VIKTOR : Lt. Gen. P.M. FITIN.
[ii] MAKSIM : Vassilij Mikhajlovich ZUBILIN, 2nd Secretary at the Soviet Embassy in WASHINGTON.
[iii] THE PAIR: Nicholas and Maria FISHER.
[iv] BASS : Michael BURD.
[v] RAILWAY WORKER: It is not clear whether this is a cover-name or a reference to his occupation.
[vi] COUNTRYSIDE: Mexican. The adjectival form is used here.
[vii] SMYRNA : MOSCOW.
[viii] COUNTRYSIDE: MEXICO.
[ix] COUNTRY: U.S.A.
[x] NILES : David K NILES was Administrative Assistant to the President.
[xi] TEMPLE: Presumably the White House. Compare NEW YORK's No. 1840 of 29 December 1944 (S/NBF/T478)
[xii] BANK : U.S. Department of State.
[xiii] MAY : Stepan Zakharovich APRESYaN, Soviet Vice Consul in NEW YORK.

S/NBF/T47

~~TOP SECRET~~ EIDER

49. New York 1105-10 to Moscow, 2/3 August 1944.

VENONA

~~TOP SECRET~~

USSR

Ref. No: 3/NBF/T3 (of 21/8/50)
Issued: 30/11/1965
Copy No: 204

FOURTH REISSUE

INTELLIGENCE FROM SOURCE "H."
REFERENCE TO [C% STEPAN]
H.'S WORK FOR A COMMITTEE
(1944)

From: NEW YORK
To: MOSCOW
No: 1105-1110   2/3 August 44

[Six-part message complete]

[149 groups unrecoverable]

[Part I] [C% the army [PO ARMII]]

[37 groups unrecovered]

[Part II] [D% General EISENHOWER] CAMPBELL [KEMPBEL] [1 group unrecovered]. The Committee is [2 groups unrecovered] on [D% political] and economic questions for drawing up instructions to EISENHOWER and WILSON ~~of a political [C% nature]~~. [2 groups unrecovered] treaties[a] on civilian questions of the type already signed with Holland and Belgium and the treaty[a] with [4 groups unrecovered] [3% on [PO]] [4 groups unrecovered] Army [B% of Liberation] [ARMIya OSVOBO......]

[20 groups unrecoverable]

[B% the Allies] [1 group unrecovered] the European Advisory Commission [EVROPEJSKIJ KONSUL'TATIVNYJ SOVET][b] in SIDON[i] will

[8 groups unrecovered]

in CARTHAGE[KARFAGEN][ii] is/are taking part in the work of the Committee. Almost all the work is done by H.[G.][iii] who is present at all the sessions. In connexion with this work H.[G.] obtains secret documents [6 groups unrecovered]. The ISLANDERS[OSTROVITYaNE][iv]

[13 groups unrecovered]

The TRUST[TREST][v] in CARTHAGE

DISTRIBUTION

~~TOP SECRET~~

VENONA

3/NBF/T3

315

49. *(Continued)*

~~TOP SECRET~~

- 2 - 3/NBF/T3

[12 groups unrecoverable]

work including the personal telegraphic correspondence of BOAR[KABAN][vi] with CAPTAIN[KAPITAN][vii]

[64 groups unrecoverable]

[Part III] 2. The LEAGUE[LIGA][viii] decided to force the ISLANDERS to alter the allocation of occupation zones in Germany in accordance with the existing plan of the European Advisory Commission[b]. 6 weeks ago CAPTAIN informed BOAR that the COUNTRY[STRANA][ix] wishes to detach minimal occupation forces

[34 groups unrecoverable]

would [2 groups unrecovered] involved in the complex political problems of European countries. BOAR replied that the ISLAND's[OSTROV][x] vital interests lie in the North Sea Belgium and Holland and therefore he was not in agreement with the stationing of occupation forces a long way from these areas. CAPTAIN did not agree with this argument. At this stage the ISLANDERS continue to insist on their plan.

3. In April Richard LAW passed to the ISLAND's Government a memorandum written by the War Office and the Foreign Office setting out the ISLAND's policy with respect to the use of the Army in south-west[c] Europe. The document divides the aims to be pursued into "inescapable" and "desirable". The inescapable [aims][d] include occupation by the ISLAND of the Dodecanese to prevent a struggle for the possession of these islands among Turkey, Greece and Italy. The use in Greece of a large enough force of troops to organise relief, the despatch to Greece of military units to support [Part IV] the Greek Government, the basing in TRIESTE of adequate troops to control the Italo-Yugoslav frontier and maintain order there,

[51 groups unrecoverable]

.....ed Bulgaria[e], the despatch of adequate troops to Hungary to take part in the occupation, the despatch of troops to Albania to restore its independence which the British guarantee/d

[15 groups unrecovered]

[C% leading role]

[37 groups unrecoverable]

week(s)[f] ago H.[G.] was entrusted with the decypherment of a confidential telegram from BOAR to CAPTAIN which said that WILSON and the other generals of the ISLAND were insisting strongly on a change in the plan to invade the South of France, suggesting instead an invasion through the Adriatic Sea, TRIESTE and then north-eastwards. BOAR supported this plan. From the contents of the telegram it is clear that BOAR did not succeed in overcoming the strong objection of CAPTAIN and the COUNTRY's generals.

[Continued overleaf]

3/NBF/T3

~~TOP SECRET~~

49. *(Continued)*

VENONA
~~TOP SECRET~~

- 3 -   3/NBF/T3

[Part V]   Yesterday H.[G.] learnt of a change in the plans [4 groups unrecovered] and ANVIL[xi] will be put into effect possibly in the middle of August. Commenting on this argument

[15 groups unrecovered]

the aims that are being pursued by each: the ISLAND - the strengthening of her influence in the Balkans; the COUNTRY - the desire for the minimum involvement in European politics.

[7 groups unrecoverable]

it is clear that the COUNTRY

[72 groups unrecovered]

[4 groups unrecovered] about him and [B% STEPAN][xii] refused to pass the documents to him in view of

[22 groups unrecovered]

. When [he/she] had convinced [himself/herself]

[39 groups unrecoverable]

[Part VI]   In two weeks' time [B% on/the agreement]

[98 groups unrecovered]

[41 groups unrecoverable]

insufficient indication was given

[31 groups unrecovered]

No. 610   MAY[MAJ][xiii]

Notes: [a] Or agreement.

[b] EVROPEJSKIJ KONSUL'TATIVNYJ SOVET: This is obviously the European Advisory Commission, but the literal translation is 'European Advisory/Consultative Council'.

[c] As sent. The group for "South-East" is, however, only one digit different.

[d] Added by translator.

[e] Or: by Bulgaria.

[f] Only the last digit of the groups preceding "week(s)" has been recovered and on the basis of this digit three interpretations of this phrase are possible: (1) "3 weeks"
(2) "4 weeks"
(3) "less than a week"

[Continued overleaf]

3/NBF/T3   ~~TOP SECRET~~

VENONA

49. *(Continued)*

- 4 -   3/NBF/T3

Comments:
- [i]　　SIDON　　　: LONDON.
- [ii]　　CARTHAGE　: WASHINGTON D.C.
- [iii]　H.[G.]　　: Abbreviation for HOMER [GOMER] the covername of Donald Duart MACLEAN.
- [iv]　 ISLANDERS : The British.
- [v]　　TRUST　　　: Soviet Embassy.
- [vi]　 BOAR　　　: Winston S. CHURCHILL.
- [vii]　CAPTAIN　 : Franklin D. ROOSEVELT.
- [viii] LEAGUE　　: The U.S. Government.
- [ix]　 COUNTRY　 : U.S.A.
- [x]　　ISLAND　　: Great Britain.
- [xi]　 ANVIL　　 : Allied Codename for allied landings in the South of France.
- [xii]　STEPAN　　: Unidentified. May or may not be a covername. If a covername it is evidently not the STEPAN last reported in NEW YORK's No. 852 of 16th June, 1944 (3/NBF/T416).
- [xiii] MAJ　　　 : Stepan Zakharovich APRESYAN, Soviet Vice-Consul in NEW YORK.

3/NBF/T3

50. New York 1119-21 to Moscow, 4/5 August 1944.

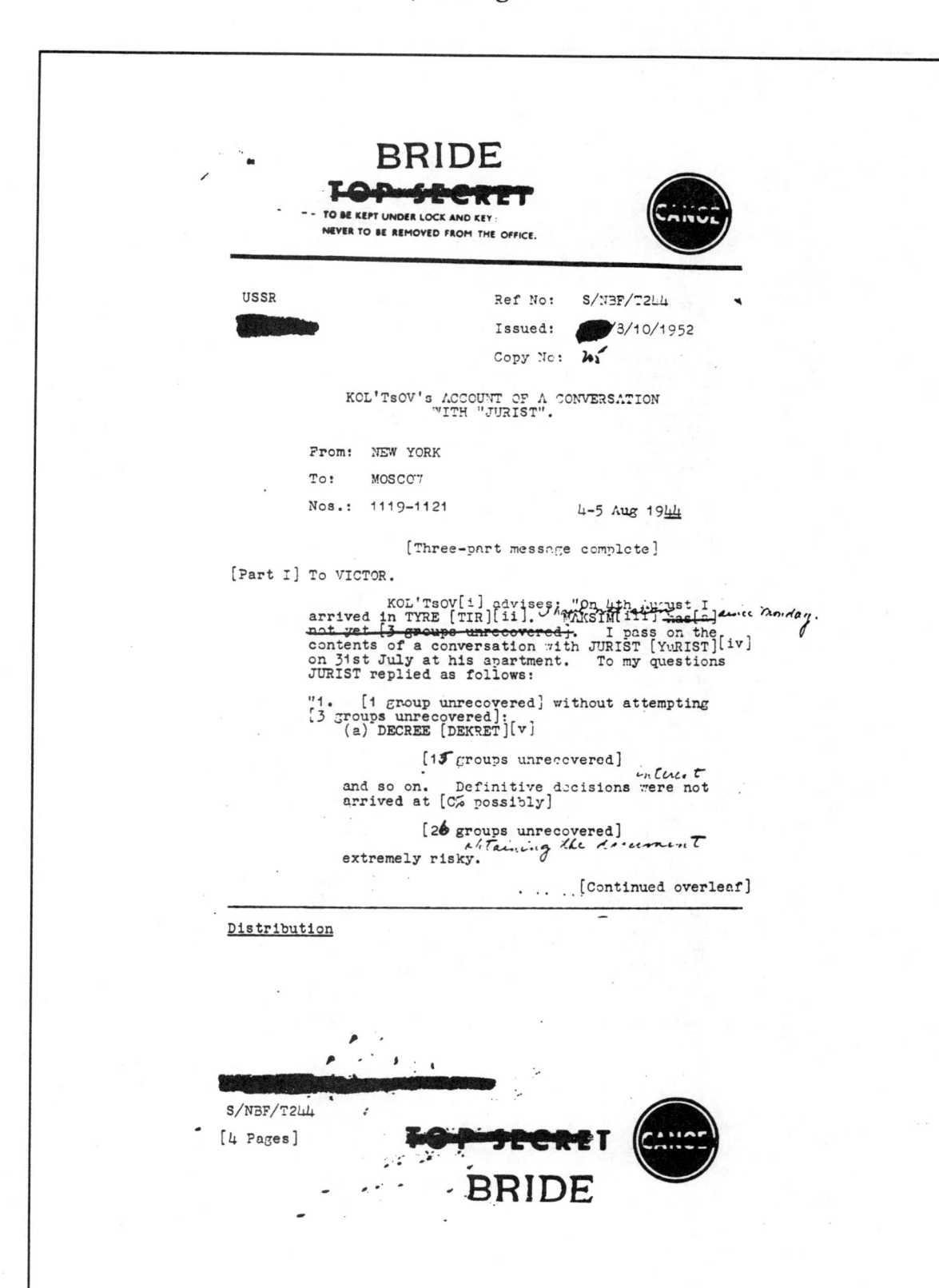

BRIDE
~~TOP SECRET~~
-- TO BE KEPT UNDER LOCK AND KEY --
NEVER TO BE REMOVED FROM THE OFFICE.

USSR

Ref No: S/NBF/T244
Issued: /3/10/1952
Copy No:

KOL'TsOV's ACCOUNT OF A CONVERSATION
WITH "JURIST".

From: NEW YORK
To: MOSCOW
Nos.: 1119-1121   4-5 Aug 1944

[Three-part message complete]

[Part I] To VICTOR.

KOL'TsOV[i] advises: "On 4th August I arrived in TYRE [TIR][ii]. [handwritten: Shapiro?] MAKSIM[iii] ~~has[a]~~ [handwritten: since Monday] ~~not yet [3 groups unrecovered]~~. I pass on the contents of a conversation with JURIST [YuRIST][iv] on 31st July at his apartment. To my questions JURIST replied as follows:

"1. [1 group unrecovered] without attempting [3 groups unrecovered]:
   (a) DECREE [DEKRET][v]

       [15 groups unrecovered]

and so on. Definitive decisions [handwritten: interest] were not arrived at [C% possibly]

       [26 groups unrecovered]
[handwritten: obtaining the document]
extremely risky.

. . . . [Continued overleaf]

Distribution

S/NBF/T244
[4 Pages]

~~TOP SECRET~~
BRIDE

50. (Continued)

- 2 - S/NBF/T244

(b) [10 groups unrecovered]

5 to 10 years

[28 groups unrecoverable]

family of nations". On the technique of control over Germany while reparations are being paid there is for the time being no definite opinion. JURIST thinks that a definite amount of reparations should be set in marks and this amount should be subsequently reviewed and reduced if Germany fulfils her obligations; if [she does][b] not, Germany should be reoccupied.

[12 groups unrecovered]

JURIST's opinion the latter

[13 groups unrecovered]

with NABOB [NABOB][vi] or CAPTAIN [KAPITAN][vii].

[Part II] (c) The trade policy of the COUNTRY [STRANA][viii] [1 group unrecovered] which will be put into effect by means of bilateral agreements with individual states covering 2-3 years. There will be no one set of conditions or removal of tariff barriers.

(d) Loans. In this sphere the only concrete thing that is being done is the preparation of a credit for us of 10 milliards

[13 groups unrecoverable]

.... The credit will be repaid by the export of our raw material to the COUNTRY [2 groups unrecovered] be caused by NABOB's not being able to get conversations on this business with CAPTAIN.

2. NABOB and JURIST's trip to SMYRNA [SMIRNA][ix] is being delayed for an indefinite period [and][b] may take place after the elections. On 5th August both are leaving for NORMANDY and SIDON[x] where [7 groups unrecovered] suppose that the ISLAND [OSTROV][xi] will [1 group unrecovered] with them about DECREE[v] payments. The fact is that the ISLAND's dollar balances have

[continued overleaf]

S/NBF/T244

50. *(Continued)*

BRIDE
TO BE KEPT UNDER LOCK AND KEY.
NEVER TO BE REMOVED FROM THE OFFICE.

— 3 —   S/NBF/T244

risen as a result of the transport work and the expenditure made by the army of the COUNTRY in Europe [;] therefore the COUNTRY is demanding partial repayment of the DECREE loan

[54 groups unrecoverable]

[D% use] of amphibians.

4. The programme of the oil conference

[5 groups unrecovered, 53 groups unrecoverable]

[Part III] 5. The role

[16 groups unrecovered]

there will be achieved a compromise agreement to exclude from the Polish Government the most hostile elements [3 groups unrecovered] Committee of Liberation [in][b] the COUNTRY

[31 groups unrecoverable]

[D% MIKOLAJ]CZYK.

7. Finland has lost the sympathy of the public in the COUNTRY, therefore the restoration of the 1940 frontier will not arouse objections from the COUNTRY.

8. As regards the Baltic Countries [PRIBALTIKA] the COUNTRY thinks that we seized them, but the restoration of the pre-war situation will not arouse any protest in the COUNTRY.

9. JURIST is convinced that CAPTAIN will win the elections if [1 group unrecovered] not [3 groups unrecovered] severe military disaster. TRUMAN's nomination is calculated to ensure the votes of the conservative wing of the party.

As regards the technique of further work with us [C% JURIST] [2 groups unrecovered] ready for any self-sacrifice[;] he himself does not think about his personal security, but a compromise [PROVAL] would lead to a political scandal and [1 group unrecovered] of all supporters of the new course[c], therefore he should be very cautious. He asked whether he should [5 groups unrecovered] his work with us. I [C% replied] that he should refrain. JURIST has no suitable apartment

be amendment

[continued overleaf]

S/NBF/T244

BRIDE

50. *(Continued)*

```
                          - 4 -            S/NBF/T244

        for a permanent meeting place[;] all his
        friends are family people.  Meetings could be
        held at their houses [0% if arranged so] that
        one meeting devolved on each every 4-5 months.
        He proposes occasional conversations lasting up
        to half an hour while driving in his automobile.

             JURIST has fixed the next meeting for
        17th-19th August and arranged appropriate
        conditions for it.  He returns to CARTHAGE
        [KARFAGEN][xii] about the 17th of August.

             I leave for CARTHAGE on the 8th of August
        and from there for SMYRNA[ix] on the 12th of
        August."

             Telegraph the date of receipt of this
        telegram.
             No. 621              MAY [MAJ][xiii]
```

T.N.: [a]   Or "had".

[b]   Inserted by translator.

[c]   NOVYJ KURS in the Russian. If correct it might be a way of translating "New Deal".

Comments: [i]   See S/NBF/T96 for another reference to KOL'TsOV.

[ii]   TIR: NEW YORK, N.Y.

[iii] MAKSIM: Vasilij Mikhajlovich ZUBILIN.

[iv]   YuRIST: Harry Dexter WHITE.

[v]   DEKRET: usually a cover-name for Lend-Lease in this traffic.

[vi]   NABOB: Henry MORGENTHAU, Jr.

[vii] KAPITAN: Franklin Delano ROOSEVELT.

[viii] STRANA: the United States of America.

[ix]   SMIRNA: MOSCOW.

[x]   SIDON: LONDON.

[xi]   OSTROV: Great Britain.

[xii] KARFAGEN: WASHINGTON, D.C.

[xiii] MAJ: Pavel Ivanovich FEDOSIMOV.

W.S. No.: XY-63.2

S/NBF/T244

50. *(Continued)*

BRIDE

~~TOP SECRET~~

USSR

Ref. No: S/NBF/T244 (of 8/10/1952)
Issued: 25/11/1958
Copy No: 204

KDL'TsOV's ACCOUNT OF A CONVERSATION WITH "JURIST".

From: NEW YORK
To: MOSCOW
Nos.: 1119-1121   4-5 Aug. 44

AMENDMENT

Amend first page to read:

[Three-part message complete]

[Part I] To VIKTOR.

KDL'TsOV[i] advises: "On 4th August I arrived in TIRE[TIR][ii]. I have not seen MAKSIM[iii] since Monday. Here is the substance of a conversation with JURIST[YuRIST][iv] on 31st July at his apartment. To my questions JURIST replied as follows:

"1. [1 group unrecovered] without attempting [3 groups unrecovered]:

   (a) DECREE[DEKRET][v]

       [15 groups unrecovered]

   interest and so on. Definitive decisions were not arrived at [or possibly]

       [26 groups unrecovered]

   obtaining the document extremely risky.

Distribution   [Continued overleaf]

S/NBF/T244 (amendment)

~~TOP SECRET~~
BRIDE

50. *(Continued)*

~~TOP SECRET~~

USSR Amendment to 3/NBF/T244 (of 8/10/1952)

Issued : 23/3/1961

Copy No: 204

KOL'TsOV's ACCOUNT OF A CONVERSATION WITH "JURIST" (1944)

From: NEW YORK
To: MOSCOW
Nos. 1119-1121 4-5 Aug. 44

AMENDMENT

On Page 3 amend the second sub-paragraph of paragraph 9 to read:

"As regards the technique of further work with us JURIST said that his wife was [B% ready] for any self-sacrifice[;] he himself did not think about his personal security, but a compromise[PROVAL] would lead to a political scandal and [B% the discredit] of all supporters of the new course[c], therefore he would have to be very cautious. He asked whether he should [5 groups unrecovered] his work with us. I [C% replied] that he should refrain. JURIST has no suitable apartment for a permanent meeting place[;] all his friends are family people. Meetings could be held at their houses in such a way that one meeting devolved on each every 4-5 months. He proposes infrequent conversations lasting up to half an hour while driving in his automobile."

Distribution

3/NBF/T244 (Amendment)

~~TOP SECRET~~

51. New York 1203 to Moscow, 23 August 1944.

BRIDE

~~TOP SECRET~~

TO BE KEPT UNDER LOCK AND KEY.
NEVER TO BE REMOVED FROM THE OFFICE.

USSR

Ref No: S/NBF/T245
Issued: ▓/8/10/1952
Copy No: 205

SETTING-UP OF TECHNICAL ENTERPRISES UNDER
"ODESSITE" AND "SECOND-HAND BOOKSELLER"

From: NEW YORK
To: MOSCOW
No.: 1203   23 Aug 1944

To VICTOR.

To organise technical point "A" in TYRE [TIR][i] we have been compelled to set up 2 independent enterprises, as ODESSITE [ODESSIT][a] covers only the second part of the technical process of the manufacture of dies [ShTAMPY]. The basic part [1 group unrecovered] can be carried out by SECOND-HAND BOOKSELLER [BUKINIST]. According to our data SECOND-HAND BOOKSELLER is a devoted and reliable person. Please authorise the use of S.-H. B. [B.] in the "A" line. We consider it essential to expand ODESSITE's enterprise by organising a stamp [ShTEMPEL'NYJ] workshop and transferring it to another part of the city. Suitable premises for this purpose have been selected. For the organisation of the two enterprises and for technical equipment 2500 dollars comprising 1000 for O.[iii] and 1500 for S.-H. B. are required. Telegraph permission.

No. 673.

[Continued overleaf]

Distribution

S/NBF/T245
[2 Pages]

BRIDE
~~TOP SECRET~~

51. *(Continued)*

- 2 -   S/NBF/T245

I am awaiting an answer to No. 650[b].

MAY [MAJ][ii]

T.N.: [a] ODESSIT: an inhabitant of ODESSA.

[b] This is the second of two messages transmitted under external serial number 1163 of 15 Aug 1944 in which MAJ asked for more information to assist in finding out about the group KREJMER [S/NBF/T239].

Comments: [i] TIR: NEW YORK, N.Y.

[ii] MAJ: Pavel Ivanovich FEDOSIMOV.

[iii] I.e. ODESSITE.

W.S. No.: XY-63.3

S/NBF/T245

52. New York 1251 to Moscow, 2 September 1944.

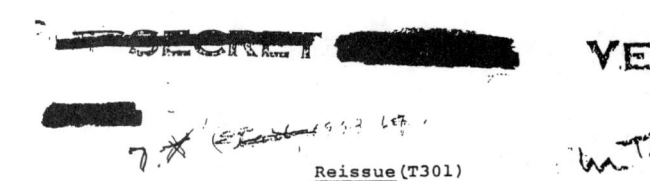

VENONA

Reissue(T301)

From: NEW YORK
To: MOSCOW
No: 1251

2 September 1944

To VIKTOR[i].

In accordance with our telegram no. 403[a] we are advising you of the new cover-names: KAVALERIST - BEK[ii], DROZD - AKhMED[iii], KLEMENS - LI[iv], ABRAM - ChEKh[v], TYuL'PAN - KANT[vi], AIDA - KLO[vii], RYBOLOV - [C% BLOK][viii], RELE - SERB[ix], ANTENNA - LIBERAL[x], GNOM - YaKOV[xi], SKAUT - METR[xii], TU.... - NIL[xiii], FOGEL' - PERS[xiv], ODESSIT - ROST[xv]. All these cover-names were selected [C% by you] with a view to economy of means. Among the new cover-names introduced by you there are disadvantageous ones which we propose to replace as follows: STELLA - ĒMILIYa[xvi], DONAL'D - PILOT[xvii], LOJER - RIChARD[xviii], DUGLAS - IKS[xix], ShERVUD - KNYaZ'[xx], [1 group unrecovered]T - ZONA[xxi], MIRANDA - ART[xxii], SEN'OR - BERG[xxiii]. All these cover-names are economical from the point of view of encoding. Please confirm. Continuation will follow later[b].

No. 700   MAJ[xxiv]
  2 September

Notes: [a] NEW YORK's no. 744 of 25 May 1944. However, no. 744 has nothing to do with the subject of this message so must be an incorrect reference.
       [b] See NEW YORK's no 1403 of 5 October 1944

Comments:
  [i]   VIKTOR: Lt. Gen. P.M. FITIN.
  [ii]   KAVALERIST - BEK: i.e. CAVALRYMAN - BECK, Sergej Nikolaevich KURNAKOV.
  [iii] DROZD - AKhMED: i.e. THRUSH - AKhMED, unidentified.
  [iv]   KLEMENS - LI: i.e. CLEMENCE - LEE, unidentified.
  [v]   ABRAM - ChEKh: i.e. ABRAM - CZECH, Jack SOBLE.
  [vi]   TYuL'PAN - KANT: i.e. TULIP - KANT, Mark ZBOROWSKI.
  [vii] AIDA - KLO: Esther Trebach RAND.
  [viii] RYBOLOV - BLOK: i.e. OSPREY - BLOCK, unidentified. BLOI is repeated as GE. There is no other occurrence of eithe
  [ix]   RELE - SERB: i.e. RELAY - SERB. RELE has been tentatively identified as Morton SOBELL. However, the only other reference to SERB is in NEW YORK's no. 50 of 11 January 1945 and would not appear to refer to SOBELL.
  [x]   ANTENNA - LIBERAL: Julius ROSENBERG.
  [xi]   GNOM - YaKOV: i.e. GNOME - YaKOV, William PERL (originally MUTTERPERL).

VENONA

52. *(Continued)*

```
Comments (cont'd.)
    [xii]   SKAUT - METR:  i.e. SCOUT - METRE, probably either Joel
                           BARR or Alfred SARANT.
    [xiii]  TU.... - NIL:  Unidentified.
    [xiv]   FOGEL' - PERS: i.e. VOGEL - PERSIAN, unidentified.
    [xv]    ODESSIT - ROST: i.e. ODESSITE - GROWTH, unidentified.
    [xvi]   STELLA - EMILIYa: Unidentified.
    [xvii]  DONAL'D - PILOT: i.e. DONALD - PILOT, William Ludwig
                             ULLMAN.
    [xviii] LOJER - RIChARD: i.e. LAWYER - RICHARD, Harry Dexter
                             WHITE.
    [xix]   DUGLAS - IKS: i.e. DOUGLAS - X, Joseph KATZ.
    [xx]    ShERVUD - KNYaZ': i.e. SHERWOOD - PRINCE, Laurence
                              DUGGAN.
    [xxi]   ....T - ZONA; i.e. ....T - ZONE, unidentified.
    [xxii]  MIRANDA - ART:  Probably ▓▓▓▓▓▓▓
    [xxiii] SEN'OR - BERG: i.e. SENOR - BERG, unidentified.
    [xxiv]  MAJ: i.e. MAY, Stepan APRESYaN.
```

20 May 1975

53. New York 1271-4 to Moscow, 7 September 1944.

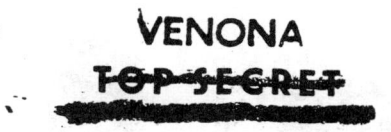

VENONA
~~TOP SECRET~~

USSR

Ref. No: 3/NBF/T81 (of 9/4/1951)
Issued: 30/11/1965
Copy No: 204

RE-ISSUE

REPORT ON INFORMATION GIVEN BY "HOMER" (1944)

From: NEW YORK
To: MOSCOW
No: 1271-1274
7 Sept. 44

[Part I] To: VIKTOR[i].

[3 groups unrecovered] HOMER's[GOMER][ii] report of 2nd September (the verbatim quotations from the report are in inverted commas):

1. In connection with the Anglo-American economic talks HOMER points out that "in the opinion of the majority of the members of the British Government the fate of ENGLAND depends almost entirely on AMERICA. They consider that ENGLAND can remain a strong and prosperous power if she maintains the volume of her imports which she can do in two ways:

   1. By getting supplies from AMERICA gratis by DECREE[DEKRET][iii] or otherwise.

   2. By restoring her exports to the required volume.

The immediate aim of the British Government consists in
[12 groups unrecovered]
will be delayed until the end of the war with JAPAN and also receiving permission

[Continued overleaf]

DISTRIBUTION

3/NBF/T81

~~TOP SECRET~~

VENONA

53. *(Continued)*

- 2 - 3/NBF/T81

[17 groups unrecovered]

NABOB[iv] to admit HEN-HARRIER[LUN'][v] and others who concentrate on internal political difficulties. In negotiations with the LEAGUE[LIGA][vi] the British will advance the following arguments:

[16 groups unrecovered]

ENGLAND and eliminate her as an economic factor but this

[39 groups unrecoverable]

ENGLAND,

[70 groups unrecovered]".

[Part II] 2. "The question as to whether the north-western and southern zones of GERMANY will be occupied respectively by the British or the Americans has not yet been decided and will be discussed by CAPTAIN[KAPITAN][vii] and BOAR[KABAN][viii] at their meeting which, as far as I know, will take place at QUEBEC about 9th September. Besides this no decision has been taken on two fundamental questions:

1. Is it desirable to attempt to maintain GERMANY on a moderately high level of economic stability and well-being or should the armies of occupation let her starve and go to pieces?

2. Is it desirable to help GERMANY to remain a single administrative [2 groups unrecovered] or should the armies of occupation do all they can to split up GERMANY into separate states?"

Citing the STRANG[ix] documents which you know of, H.[G.][x] emphasises that the plans of the British, in large measure, are based on the opinion of the British Foreign Office. A sub-committee on post-hostilities planning of the British Chiefs of Staff issued a paper on 19th August, the authors of which [1 group unrecovered] "[B% the consideration from a military point of view of all the facts for and against the division of GERMANY into separate German states and for the division of GERMANY into at least three states corresponding to the boundaries of the three zones of occupation and [C% it is recommended] that the Anglo-American armies of occupation should, as a first priority,

[52 groups unrecoverable]

divided GERMANY [25 groups unrecovered]

[C% un]divided GERMANY would more probably get into

[43 groups unrecovered]

and ENGLAND [25 groups unrecoverable]

[Part III] The Americans have created a special commission with the powers of a government department to examine policy relating to GERMANY. Among the questions which it is to discuss are:

[Continued overleaf]

3/NBF/T81

53. *(Continued)*

VENONA

~~TOP SECRET~~

- 3 - 3/NBF/T81

"1. Should GERMANY be helped (for instance by the American occupation forces) to maintain or restore order and economic stability?

2. Should GERMANY be split up into separate states?

3. How should HITLER, HIMMLER and the rest, be dealt with, if they should be caught?

4. Should the RUHR be internationalised?"

NABOB strongly opposes the first point and proposes letting economic ruin and chaos in GERMANY develop without restriction in order to show the Germans that wars are unprofitable. The assistant to the head [KhOZYaIN] of the ARSENAL[xi], McCLOY[xii], points out that such a situation would be intolerable for the army of occupation, that the responsibility for some minimum of order [4 groups unrecovered] and so forth - NABOB obtained CAPTAIN's consent to the use of yellow-seal dollars by American troops instead of military marks as had been previously agreed with the British and the Russians. The purpose of this is to turn the American occupation forces into the economic masters of GERMANY. McCLOY, LAWYER[LOJER][xiii], high officials in NABOB's establishment as well as the British, are opposed to this. The British and McCLOY are trying to get CAPTAIN to revoke this decision. McCLOY [4 groups unrecoverable] division of GERMANY averring that this attempt is doomed to failure. His views have some significance since he has direct access to CAPTAIN.

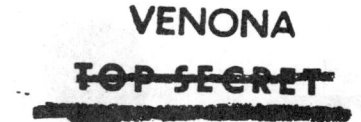

3. Under the influence of BOAR and LEEPER[LIPER][xiv], the British intend to set up and keep in power in GREECE a government well-disposed towards ENGLAND and willing to help her and hostile to communism and Russian influence. Their tactics consist in supporting the King as much as possible but also in leaning on the so-called liberal elements which might take the King's place if the opposition to him were to become too strong. For military reasons the British were forced to support EAM and ELAS to a certain extent.

[Part IV] In order to achieve their political ends the British intend to land a British division from Italy in GREECE to keep PAPANDREOU in power. As you know, this plan will be realized very soon. The LEAGUE regards the British intrigues in GREECE with some suspicion and HOMER hopes that we will take advantage of these circumstances to disrupt the plans of the British and all the more so since the IZBA[xv] still supports EAM and ELAS.

4. After Comrade STALIN had refused to allow American aircraft to land on our territory

[9 groups unrecovered]

personal message suggested to CAPTAIN that [B' he should agree to]

[30 groups unrecovered]

No. 705 MAY[MAJ][xvi]
6 September

[Comments overleaf]

3/NBF/T81

~~TOP SECRET~~

VENONA

53. *(Continued)*

~~TOP SECRET~~

-4- 3/NBF/T81

Comments:	[i] VIKTOR:	Lt. Gen. P.M. FITIN.
	[ii] HOMER:	Donald Duart MACLEAN.
	[iii] DECREE:	Lend-Lease.
	[iv] NABOB:	Henry MORGENTHAU, Jr.
	[v] HEN-HARRIER:	Cordell HULL.
	[vi] LEAGUE:	U.S. Government.
	[vii] CAPTAIN:	Franklin D. ROOSEVELT.
	[viii] BOAR:	Winston S. CHURCHILL.
	[ix] STRANG:	Sir William STRANG, U.K. Representative on European Advisory Commission.
	[x] H.	Abbreviation for HOMER, the covername of Donald Duart MACLEAN.
	[xi] ARSENAL:	War Department.
	[xii] McCLOY:	John J. McCLOY, Assistant Secretary of War.
	[xiii] LAWYER:	Harry Dexter WHITE.
	[xiv] LEEPER:	Reginald Wildig Allan LEEPER, HBM Ambassador in ATHENS.
	[xv] IZBA:	O.S.S.
	[xvi] MAY:	Stepan Zakharovich APRESYaN, Soviet Vice Consul in NEW YORK.

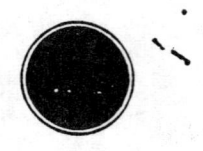

3/NBF/T81

~~TOP SECRET~~

54. New York 1313 to Moscow, 13 September 1944.

~~TOP SECRET DAUNT~~   BRIDE

T276

copy

From: NEW YORK
To: MOSCOW
No.: 1313

13 Sept 1944

To VICTOR[i].

Your number 4247[a]. SERGEJ[ii] has three times attempted to effect liaison with PANCAKE [BLIN][iii] in CARTHAGE [KARFAGEN][iv] in the line of cover[v] [C% but] each time PANCAKE declined [C% on the grounds of] being busy with trips. IDE [YaZ'] has carefully attempted to sound him, but P. [B.][vi] did not react. P. occupies a very prominent position in the journalistic world and has vast connections. To determine precisely his relations to us we will commission ECHO [EKhO][vii] to make a check.

No. 733.

Your number 4246[a]. NICK [NIK][viii] has been[b] summoned to TYRE [TIR][ix] and a meeting has been arranged

[69 groups unrecoverable]

character [KhARAKTERISTIKA] given to BOB[x] by IKS[xi]. However, BASS [BAS][xii] said that he did not intend to embark on a [C% risky][c] business as there was no need. In time he and BOB will get big commissions for the deal in CHILE. BASS said that BOB was behaving rather [C% despicably] with the companies who were intending[d] personal representation in Chile [C% and] if it had not been for BASS's insistence they would have broken off business relations with BOB. BASS says that BOB is not keen to get an appointment in Chile, preferring to remain in the COUNTRY [STRANA][xiii]. In our work with BOB allowance should be made for the difficulties which are encountered in carrying through affairs begun by others and without having received in good time exhaustive characters [KhARAKTERISTIKI] of probationers.

No. 734   MAY [MAJ][xiv]

T.N.: [a] Not available.
      [b] Or "is being".
      [c] Or [C% compromising].
      [d] A group with some such meaning as "to set up" appears to have been omitted at this point.

Comments: [i] VICTOR: possibly Lt. Gen. P.M. FITIN.

[ii] SERGEJ: Vladimir Sergeevich PRAVDIN.

[iii] BLIN: Isidor Feinstein STONE. See S/NBF/T23, Item 4, in which on 23 October 1944 MAJ reported on a meeting between SERGEJ and BLIN in WASHINGTON.

[iv] KARFAGEN: WASHINGTON, D.C.

[v] i.e. in SERGEJ's capacity as TASS representative (cf S/NBF/T23).   (OVER)

~~TOP SECRET DAUNT~~   BRIDE

54. *(Continued)*

[vi] B.: i.e. BLIN.

[vii] EKhO: possibly Bernard SCHUSTER (Communist Party name CHESTER).

[viii] NIK: Amadeo SABATINI. Compare S/NBF/T166, in which on 6 Sept 1944 MAJ said: "In DOUGLAS's opinion he should not continue to work in the West" (apparently referring to NIK). SABATINI is known to have acted as "go-between" on behalf of Grigorij KhEIFETs, Soviet Vice-Consul in SAN FRANCISCO.

[ix] TIR: NEW YORK, N.Y.

[x] BOB: Robert Owen MENAKER.

[xi] IKS: Joseph KATZ.

[xii] BAS: Michael BURD (originally WEISBURD).

[xiii] STRANA: The United States of America.

[xiv] MAJ: Pavel Ivanovich FEDOSIMOV.

55. New York 1314 to Moscow, 14 September 1944.

~~TOP SECRET~~ VENONA

Reissue (T53)

From: NEW YORK
To: MOSCOW
No: 1314

14 September 1944

To VIKTOR[i].

Until recently GNOM[ii] was paid only the expenses connected with his coming to TYRE [TIR][iii]. Judging by an appraisal of the material received and the rest [1 group garbled] sent by us GNOM deserves renumeration for material no less valuable than that given by the rest of the members of LIBERAL's[iv] group who were given a bonus by you. Please agree to paying him 500 dollars.

No. 736
14 September

MAJ[v]

Comments:
 [i] VIKTOR: Lt. Gen. P. M. FITIN.
 [ii] GNOM: i.e. GNOME, William PERL, originally MUTTERPERL.
 [iii] TIR: NEW YORK CITY.
 [iv] LIBERAL: Julius ROSENBERG.
 [v] MAJ: i.e. MAY, Stepan APRESYaN.

28 April 1975

~~TOP SECRET~~ VENONA

56. New York 1325-6 to Moscow, 15 September 1944.

~~TOP SECRET DAUNT~~ DRUG

Re-issue (T21)

From: NEW YORK
To: MOSCOW
No. 1325, 1326

15 September 1944

To VIKTOR[i].

According to ~~KOCH's~~ KOKh[ii] advice, a list of "reds" has been compiled by the Security Division of IZBA[iii]. The list contains 4 surnames of persons who are supplying information to the Russians. One of them sounds like JIMENEZ.

The list is divided into two categories: 1. Open FELLOWCOUNTRYMEN [ZEMLYaKI][iv] (among them "IZRA"[v]) and 2. Sympathizers, left-wing liberals etc. (among them "ZAYaTs"[vi]). KOKh is trying to get the list.

PILOT[vii] [2 groups unrecovered] plan dated 22 August for the transfer of the COUNTRY's[viii] air force from Europe

[11 groups unrecovered]

groups of B-24s: 10 will be sent to China-Burma-India,

[18 groups unrecovered]

groups of B-29s, [6 groups unrecovered] 33 groups of B-17s: 11 [5 groups unrecovered] 4 to the northern sector of the Pacific with a reserve of 100 percent, 6 to the southwestern part with a reserve of 100 percent

[39 groups unrecoverable]

A-26, 1 to the southwestern sector of the Pacific, 3 are remaining in Europe.

4. 3 groups of B-25s: 1 to the northern sector of the Pacific, 2 to the central.

5. 3 groups of P-[1 group unrecovered]: 2 to the COUNTRY [1 group unrecovered], 1 to the central sector of the Pacific.

6. 1 group
[8 groups unrecovered]

7. 23 groups of P-47s: the crew of 6 groups to the COUNTRY as strategic reserves, the material part is remaining in Europe as a reserve, 7 to the central sector of the Pacific, 10 are remaining in Europe.

8. 17 groups of P-51s: 4 to the COUNTRY, 2 to China India Burma with a reserve of 100 percent, 11 to the central sector of the Pacific.

9. 6 groups of P-38s: 1 to the COUNTRY, 2 to China India Burma with a reserve of 50 percent, 3 to the central Pacific.

~~TOP SECRET DAUNT~~ DRUG

56. *(Continued)*

~~TOP SECRET DAUNT~~ DRUG

10. 17 groups of military transports C-47s: 3 to the COUNTRY, 1 to China India Burma with a reserve of 25 percent, 10 1/2 to the central Pacific, 2 1/2 in Europe.

11. [5 groups unrecovered]
3 to the central Pacific, 4 in Europe.

[42 groups unrecovered]

except the A-26 and

[32 groups unrecoverable]

and 390; medium bombers 322, 323 and 386 - Yu; fighters 36, 353, 356, 358, 362, 365, 366, 373, 404 and 406; night fighters 416, 417, 427 and 415; transports 3123, 314, 53 and 78.

No. 741　　　　　　　　　　　　　　　　　　　　　MAY [MAJ][ix]

T.N. [a] The list is transmitted in New York's No. 1354 of 22 September 1944.

Comments:
   [i] VIKTOR: Lt. Gen. P.M. FITIN
  [ii] KOKh: Duncan C. LEE
 [iii] IZBA: C.O.I. - O.S.S.
  [iv] ZEMLYaKI: Members of the Communist Party.
   [v] IZRA: Donald WHEELER
  [vi] ZAYaTs: Maurice HALPERIN
 [vii] PILOT: William Ludwig ULLMANN
[viii] COUNTRY: U.S.A.
  [ix] MAJ: Stepan APRESYaN

~~TOP SECRET DAUNT~~ DRUG

57. Moscow 954 to New York, 20 September 1944.

MGB

From: MOSCOW
To: NEW YORK
No.: 954

20 September 1944

Reference no. 741[a].

Try through "KOKh"[i] to get the list of "reas." Order "MIRNA"[ii] temporarily to cease liaison with "IRA"[iii] and "AYaTs"[iv]. In future liaison may be reestablished only with our permission. Give "KOKh" the task of compiling a report on the Security Division of the "IZBA"[v].

No. 4353

[Signature unrecoverable]

Note:
  [a] No. 741 is the internal serial number of NEW YORK to MOSCOW message no. 1325 of 15 September 1944.

Comments:
  [i] KOKh: i.e. KOCH, Duncan C. LEE.
  [ii] MIRNA: i.e. MYRNA, Elizabeth BENTLEY.
  [iii] IRA: Donald WHEELER.
  [iv] AYaTs: i.e. "HARE" or "STOWAWAY," Maurice HALPERIN.
  [v] IZBA: Office of Strategic Services.

1 November 1968

58. New York 1340 to Moscow, 21 September 1944.

Reissue(T1362)

From: NEW YORK
To: MOSCOW
No: 1340

21 September 1944

To VIKTOR[i].

Lately the development of new people [D% has been in progress]. LIBERAL[ii] recommended the wife of his wife's brother, Ruth GREENGLASS, with a safe flat in view. She is 21 years old, a TOWNSWOMAN [GOROZhANKA][iii], a GYMNAST [FIZKUL'TURNITSa][iv] since 1942. She lives on STANTON [STANTAUN] Street. LIBERAL and his wife recommend her as an intelligent and clever girl.

[15 groups unrecoverable]

[C% Ruth] learned that her husband[v] was called up by the army but he was not sent to the front. He is a mechanical engineer and is now working at the ENORMOUS [ENORMOZ][vi] plant in SANTA FE, New Mexico.

[45 groups unrecoverable]

detain VOLOK[vii] who is working in a plant on ENORMOUS. He is a FELLOWCOUNTRYMAN [ZEMLYaK][viii]. Yesterday he learned that they had dismissed him from his work. His active work in progressive organizations in the past was the cause of his dismissal.

In the FELLOWCOUNTRYMAN line LIBERAL is in touch with CHESTER[ix]. They meet once a month for the payment of dues. CHESTER is interested in whether we are satisfied with the collaboration and whether there are not any misunderstandings. He does not inquire about specific items of work [KONKRETNAYa RABOTA]. In as much as CHESTER knows about the role of LIBERAL's group we beg consent to ask C. through LIBERAL about leads from among people who are working on ENORMOUS and in other technical fields.

Your no. 4256[a]. On making further enquiries and checking on LARIN[x] we received from the FELLOWCOUNTRYMEN through EKhO[xi] a character sketch which says that they do not entirely vouch for him. They base this statement on the fact that in the Federation LARIN does not carry out all the orders received from the leadership. He is stubborn and self-willed. On the strength of this we have decided to refrain from approaching LARIN and intend to find another candidate in FAECT [FAKhIT][xii].

No 751   MAJ[xiii]
   20 September

58. *(Continued)*

```
Notes:  [a]     Not available.
Comments:
         [i]    VIKTOR:  Lt. Gen. P. M. FITIN.
        [ii]    LIBERAL:  Julius ROSENBERG.
       [iii]    GOROZhANKA:  American citizen.
        [iv]    FIZKUL'TURNITsA:  Probably a Member of the Young
                Communist League.
         [v]    i.e. David GREENGLASS.
        [vi]    ĒNORMOZ:  Atomic Energy Project.
       [vii]    VOLOK:
      [viii]    ZEMLYaK:  Member of the Communist Party.
        [ix]    CHESTER:  Communist Party name of Bernard SCHUSTER.
         [x]    LARIN:  Unidentified.
        [xi]    ĒKhO:  i.e. ECHO, Bernard SCHUSTER.
       [xii]    FAKhIT:  Federation of Architects, Chemists, Engineers
                and Technicians.  See also NEW YORK's message no. 911
                of 27 June 1944.
      [xiii]    MAJ:  i.e. MAY, Stepan APRESYaN.
```

28 April 1975

59. New York 1388-9 to Moscow, 1 October 1944.

BRIDE

~~TOP SECRET~~

USSR

Ref. No:— S/NBF/T96
Issued: /26/2/1954
Copy No:

REISSUE

ACCOUNT OF A DISCUSSION WITH "ALBERT" CONCERNING "ROBERT's" GROUP.

From: NEW YORK
To: MOSCOW
Nos.: 1388 - 1389   1 Oct 1944

[Two-part message complete]

[Part I]   To VIKTOR[i].

Your telegram no. 4012[a]. ~~ALBERT~~ AL'BERT[ii] has told me that his original proposal about new cover [PRIKRYTIE] holds good and that in the near future he will send us a [C% special] note [C% on this subject]. In order to invest wisely the sum allotted by you ALBERT has to think out a number of details which will take him some time yet.

Your no. 4270[a].

[B% 1.]   On the question of the possibility of splitting ROBERT's[iv] group into smaller units ALBERT gave the following answer:

KOL'TsOV's[v] meeting with [C% RICHARD [RIChARD]][vi] and KOL'TsOV's attempt to obtain answers to a number of questions of an international

[Continued overleaf]

Distribution

S/NBF/T96
[3 Pages]

~~TOP SECRET~~

BRIDE

343

59. *(Continued)*

character produced an unfavourable impression on ROBERT. ROBERT was surprised at our decision to have recourse to the aid of a special man for raising with [C: RICHARD] questions on which ROBERT [C: himself] as leader of the group, in his own words, is working ceaselessly. "Why did we decide to ask [D: RICHARD]

[26 groups unrecoverable]

in other [C: words] this step of ours ROBERT took as a mark of insufficient confidence in his business abilities. It is true he later expressed regret at having reacted touchily [BOLEZNENNO] [6 groups unrecovered] in ALBERT's opinion shows that ROBERT is jealous about 'encroachments

[16 groups unrecovered]

not to agree to our measures calculated to "by-pass" ROBERT. ALBERT is convinced that an attempt to "remove" members of the group, however circumspectly, will be received [1 group unrecovered] unfavourably by ROBERT. I [D: said that] in that case [he][a] could in the meantime have a chat with ROBERT about the possibility of breaking the group into two or three sub-groups for greater secrecy and more effective organisation of the work, leaving however the overall direction in ROBERT's hands.

[Part II] ALBERT [C: warned me] that for the time being the question can only be put in this form and that he will discuss it with ROBERT when occasion offers. At the same time he observed that his relations with ROBERT were very good and that the latter would consent to a meeting between ALBERT himself or EL'[vii] and any member of the group. Possibly, [in][a] ROBERT's tendency not to "relinquish" anyone [, it.a. SOUND's [ZVUK][viii] education is making itself felt.

2. Your points 3, 4, 5, 6 and 7 I have passed on to ALBERT in detail.

3. ALBERT promised to write specially on your point 1. For the time being he told me the following:

ROBERT is not restricting himself to receiving material from the probationers [STAZHERY], but is giving them tasks in consultation with ALBERT. The instruction not to impersonalise [C: the group's] materials will be borne in mind (it is already being carried out). PILOT[ix] is bringing ROBERT's wife (he is not married himself) into the processing [OBRABOTKA] of materials. She is not only in the know about her husband's work, but actively helps him in the processing.

There is no information about the KHAN's[x] enquiry being finished. ROBERT is no less interested in a favourable outcome than we are and is trying to keep

[Continued overleaf]

59. (Continued)

BRIDE

~~TOP SECRET~~

- 3 -

abreast of developments. If they have not dismissed him from his present work, it means that there is no concrete information about his work for us but only suspicions connected with his FELLOW-COUNTRYMAN[xi] [D. membership]. His wife is not free from [D. suspicion]

[23 groups unrecoverable]

[D. questions] raised in your letter no. 3 and which have in the meantime remained unanswered we will remind ALBERT.

The materials on the conspiracy and the competitors[xii] of the ISLAND [OSTROV][xiii], as it turns out, have to be obtained through IZRA..[xiv] and so I am passing the task on to VADIM[xv].

No. 786 MAJ [MAJ][xvi]
1 October

T.N.: [a] not available ~~Inserted by the translator.~~

Comments: [i] VIKTOR: ~~probably~~ Lt.-General P.M. FITIN.

[ii] ~~Not available.~~

[iii] ALBERT: ~~not identified.~~ i.e. ALBERT, probably Iskhak Abdulovich AKHMEROV.

[iv] ROBERT: Nathan Gregory SILVERMASTER.

[v] KOL'TsOV: not identified.

[vi] RICHARD: ~~possibly~~ Harry Dexter WHITE.

[vii] EL': not identified.

[viii] ZVUK: Jacob GOLOS. According to Elizabeth BENTLEY, in her book "Out of Bondage", GOLOS was opposed to the Russian policy of assuming direct control of agents.

[ix] PILOT: possibly William Ludwig ULLMAN.

[x] KhAT..: the F.B.I.

[xi] ZEMLYaChESKIJ - i.e. the Communist Party. This is an adjective derived from the noun ZEMLYaK, which is used as a cover-name for a member of the Communist Party.

[xii] KONKURENTY - i.e. members of a non-Soviet intelligence organisation.

[xiii] OSTROV: Great Britain.
[xiv] IZRA..: not identified.
[xv] VADIM: Anatolij Borisovich GROMOV, M.G.B. resident in WASHINGTON, D.C.
[xvi] MAJ: Pavel Ivanovich FEDOSIMOV

~~TOP SECRET~~ (Revision)

BRIDE

59. *(Continued)*

From: NEW YORK
To: MOSCOW
No: 1389

1 October 1944

Extract[a]

Materials about the conspiracy[ZAGOVOR] and the COMPETITORS [KONKURENTY][i] of the ISLAND[OSTROV][ii], as it turns out, have to be obtained through IZRA[iii] and so I am passing the task on to VADIM[iv].

Notes: [a] This is the last paragraph of a long two-part message on an entirely different subject. The message is addressed to VIKTOR[FITIN] and signed by MAJ[APRESYaN].

Comments:
 [i] KONKURENTY: Members of a non-Soviet Intelligence Organization.
 [ii] OSTROV: Great Britain.
 [iii] IZRA: Donald Niven WHEELER.
 [iv] VADIM: Anatolij Borisovich GROMOV, MGB resident in WASHINGTON.

11 March 1978

VENONA

60. New York 1410 to Moscow, 6 October 1944.

VENONA
~~TOP SECRET~~

USSR

Ref. No. : 3/NBF/T93 (of 4/7/51)

Issued : 23.7.75

Copy No. : 391

REISSUE

1. LUKA, PAYMENT TO ATAMAN FOR PUBLICATION OF BOOK
2. PROBLEM OF UNFULFILLED ASSIGNMENTS: EKhO, IKS, RIT, RULEVOJ

(1944)

From: NEW YORK

To: MOSCOW

No.: 1410   6 October 1944

To VIKTOR[i]

In LUKA's[ii] time ATAMAN[iii] was promised 1,000 dollars to pay for the publication of a book in Polish. 500 has been paid. ATAMAN is demanding the remaining 500. Do you sanction payment?

No. 801

Recently EKhO[iv] has failed to carry out most of our tasks, pleading the unwillingness of the FELLOWCOUNTRYMEN [ZEMLYaKI][v] to co-operate. EKhO has been described to you as a worker occupying a responsible position in the FELLOWCOUNTRYMEN'S organisation. In an interview with [C% IKS][vi] quite a different picture came to light. EKhO is raising with IKS the question of our selecting another worker who occupies a more responsible

Cont'd overleaf

VENONA
~~TOP SECRET~~

60. *(Continued)*

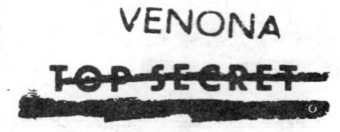

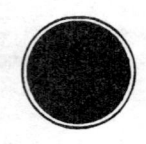

VENONA

~~TOP SECRET~~

3/NBF/195 (of 4/7/57)

position to carry out our tasks, leaving Ē.[iv] the role of go-between. He says that, because of the modest nature of his position among the FELLOWCOUNTRYMEN, he cannot

[29 groups unrecoverable]

the selection of a replacement for RIT[vii], the search for a safe house, the selection of candidates for planting in the KhATA[viii] etc remain unfulfilled for the reasons indicated above. Ē. recommends us to arrange with RULEVOJ[ix] for a responsible worker to be assigned to us, one who is capable of carrying out the necessary measures without asking permission from the authorities each time. If we do not do this, he will continue to be unable, so he says, to cope with our tasks.

No. 802
6 October
MAJ[x]

Footnotes:
- [i] VIKTOR: Lt General P.M. FITIN.
- [ii] LUKA: Pavel P. KLARIN.
- [iii] ATAMAN: Boleslaw Konstantin GEBERT.
- [iv] ĒKhO/Ē.: ie "ECHO"; Bernard SCHUSTER.
- [v] FELLOWCOUNTRYMEN: Members of the Communist Party.
- [vi] IKS: ie "X"; formerly "STUKACh", ie "INFORMER", and "DUGLAS", ie "DOUGLAS"; Joseph KATZ.
- [vii] RIT: Only occurrence; presumably an unidentified covername.
- [viii] KhATA: The Federal Bureau of Investigation.
- [ix] RULEVOJ: ie "HELMSMAN"; Earl BROWDER.
- [x] MAJ: ie "MAY"; Stepan Zakharovich APRESYaN.

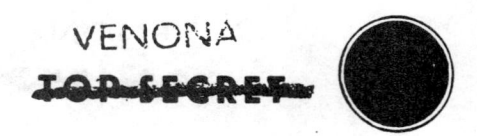

VENONA

~~TOP SECRET~~

61. New York 1433-5 to Moscow, 10 October 1944.

BRIDE
~~TOP SECRET~~

USSR

Ref No: S/NBF/T414
Issued: 9/12/1953
Copy No: 205

OPERATIONAL REPORT BY "SERGEJ" AND
"MAY's" COMMENTS ON "SERGEJ's" WORK

From: NEW YORK
To: MOSCOW
Nos.: 1433 - 1435   10 October 1944

[Three-part message complete]

[Part I]   [99 groups unrecovered]
[149 groups unrecoverable]

. SERGEJ[i] has brought in IDE [YaZ'][ii] but is not able to direct his work systematically as he sees him too rarely. Among SERGEJ's acquaintances are persons of great interest from [B-our] point of view. They are well informed and, although they do not say all they know, nevertheless they provide useful comments on the foreign policy of the COUNTRY [STRANA][iii]. Among them SERGEJ is studying Joseph BARNES and I. STONE[iv] who, however, for the time being is avoiding SERGEJ. [Among his][a] other serious targets SERGEJ has no opportunity for the [B% development] of CRITIC [KRITIK] for obtaining leads [NAVODKI] (in my opinion too CRITIC is no good for anything else ()][a].

[Part II] 2. Decisive results in the business of signing up valuable people can be obtained in only two ways, first by transferring SERGEJ to CARTHAGE [KARFAGEN][v] and secondly by making use of the FELLOW COUNTRYMEN [ZEMLYaKI][vi]

[Continued overleaf]

Distribution

~~TOP SECRET~~

S/NBF/T414
[3 Pages]

BRIDE

61. *(Continued)*

At the moment SERGEJ is trying to get the Editorial Office [REDAKTsIYa][vii] transferred to CARTHAGE. [D% Even] if

[35 groups unrecoverable]

the KhATA[viii] for the acquisition of a conspirative apartment and so on. Without the help of the FELLOW COUNTRYMEN "we are completely powerless".

MAY's [MAJ][ix] opinion:

1. In this note SERGEJ has put in a nutshell[b] his whole conception of the reasons why he has made no real advance and [his][a] approach to the next few months. His view that without CARTHAGE and HELMSMAN [RULEVOJ][x] we are doomed to vegetate is mistaken. It is not true that everything of value is in CARTHAGE and it is doubly untrue that without HELMSMAN we are "powerless". I consider that in either case we shall have to have recourse to the help of the FELLOW COUNTRYMEN, but they ought not to be the one and only base especially if you take into account the fact that in the event of KULAK's[xi] being elected this source may dry up.

2. SERGEJ will not want to be in the Office [KONTORA] itself any more than now, excepting in cases when a great deal of material requiring urgent appraisement piles up.

3. SERGEJ ought to organise the work of the Editorial Office so as to have more time for developing existing connections and starting up new ones. He should not carry the whole Editorial Office on his own shoulders; then he could go to CARTHAGE more, which is undoubtedly important.

[Part III] 4. The signing up of BARNES is obviously not only inadvisable but unrealisable; however, it is desirable to use him without signing him up.

SERGEJ helps me to decide operational questions connected with informational work[c] and to brief workers [RABOTNIKI] and probationers [STAZhERY] on current tasks. Questions on work with probationers

[27 groups unrecoverable][d]
[C% cover] the best for our [C% system]. I hope that we will not have to engage in the "theoretical" education of SERGEJ after all these years.

Telegraph your opinion and possible counsels.

No. 815
10th October   MAY

[T.N. and Comments overleaf]

S/NBF/T414

61. *(Continued)*

- 3 - S/NBF/T414

T.N.: [a] Inserted by the translator.

[b] "In a nutshell" is given in English in the original.

[c] I.e. questions for which a knowledge of the possible sources (both institutions and persons) would be helpful.

[d] The last digit of the last of those groups is the same as the last digit of the group for "his".

Comments:
[i] SERGEJ: Vladimir Sergeevich PRAVDIN, TASS News Agency correspondent.

[ii] YaZ': Simon Samuel KRAFSUR.

[iii] STRANA: the U.S.A.

[iv] Isidor Feinstein STONE.

[v] KARFAGEN: WASHINGTON.

[vi] ZEMLYaKI: members of the Communist Party, in this case of the U.S.A.

[vii] REDAKTsIYa: TASS News Agency.

[viii] KhATA: the F.B.I.

[ix] MAJ: Pavel Ivanovich FEDOSIMOV.

[x] RULEVOJ: Earl BROWDER.

[xi] KULAK: Thomas E. DEWEY.

S/NBF/T414

BRIDE

62. New York 1437 to Moscow, 10 October 1944.

MGB

~~TOP SECRET TRINE~~ VENONA

From: NEW YORK
To: MOSCOW
No.: 1437

10 October 1944

To the 6th Department.

ZaYaTs[i] reports that a telegram from BARI of 25 September has arrived in the BANK[ii], in which is discussed the introduction by TITO of strict regulations [governing](a) the movements and activities of the military missions of the COUNTRY [STRANA][iii] and the ISLAND [OSTROV][iv]. In the telegram it is stated that the ISLAND has replied by stopping supplies to the partisans and the evacuation of wounded. The telegram considers that the probable cause of the introduction of strict measures is TITO's intention to conceal from the missions the present control that he exercises over the whole country.

No. 817

[signature unrecoverable]

See below for complete message

Notes:
    [a] Inserted by translator.

Comments:
    [i] ZAYaTs: i.e. "HARE" or "STOWAWAY," Maurice HALPERIN.
    [ii] BANK: U.S. State Department.
    [iii] STRANA: U.S.A.
    [iv] OSTROV: GREAT BRITAIN.

4 November 1968

~~TOP SECRET TRINE~~ VENONA

63. New York 1442 to Moscow, 11 October 1944.

BRIDE
~~TOP SECRET~~

USSR

Ref. No: S/NBF/T1175 (of 2/4/1952)

Issued: /24/4/1958

Copy No: 205

RE-ISSUE

COMPLAINT FROM "SERGEJ" ON "MAY's" SHORTCOMINGS (1944)

From: NEW YORK
To: MOSCOW
No: 1442, 1447   11 Oct. 44

[Two-part message complete]

[1] To VIKTOR.[i]

Experience of the work of the OFFICE[KONTORA][ii] during the six months which have elapsed since MAY's[MAJ][iii] arrival has shown that he is incapable of coping with the tasks which are set him. Your instructions giving me responsibilities equal to MAY's can only partially make up for the shortcomings in the work. Conditions of enormous pressure of work in the line of cover; the necessity for security measures which do not allow frequent lengthy visits to the premises of the OFFICE; the great pressure of work on our permanent staff workers [KADROVIKI] in the line of cover - make it impossible for me to take an adequate part in the direction of all lines of work.

I am making every effort to assist MAY in all matters [.] However, assistance with advice and recommendations cannot make up for the lack of adequate organisational

[47 groups unrecoverable]

side, meetings of fellow workers with him. In answer to my inquiry about the result of the meeting MAY replied that he knew just as little about ALBERT's[iv] work before the meeting with him. There are many examples of this sort of thing. In a conversation with VADIM[v] it came to light that [7 groups unrecovered] telegrams which

---

Distribution   [Continued overleaf]

S/NBF/T175
(2 Pages)

~~TOP SECRET~~
BRIDE

63. (Continued)

~~TOP SECRET~~ EIDER

- 2 - S/NBF/T1 75

he signs. As for people, MAY is utterly without the knack of dealing with them, frequently showing himself excessively abrupt and inclined to nag and too rarely finding time to chat with them. Sometimes our operational workers who work in the same establishment with him cannot get an answer to an urgent question from him for several days at a time. Our permanent staff [KADROVYJ SOSTAV], noting MAY's inexperience and remoteness from the details of everyday work, do not consider him an authoritative leader [RUKOVODITEL'], which has an effect on working discipline.

Part II] Although since the receipt of your instructions I have formally known about [2 groups unrecovered] work of the OFFICE [2 groups unrecovered]

[55 groups unrecoverable]

in fact it turns out quite differently. [3 groups unrecovered] opportunities for rendering assistance to MAY [C% and so as a result of] inexperience and failure to understand that his appointment as leader does not signify recognition of his capability, but means that he has been given an opportunity to demonstrate his capabilities in this post, my cooperation cannot make a marked improvement in the position. The appointment as Master of the OFFICE in TYRE[TIR][vi] of a worker without experience of work abroad is an experiment apparently necessitated by the absence of a qualified candidate.

In my opinion you must decide whether to send here some other experienced leader. MAY will need to work under the supervision of such a permanent staff worker [KADROVIK]. Written instructions from you to MAY cannot make up for lack of experience and knowledge. A worker who has no experience of work abroad cannot cope on his own with the work of directing the TYRE OFFICE.

No. 820   SERGEJ[vii]
11th October

Comments: [i]   VIKTOR: Lt. Gen. P.M. FITIN.
          [ii] OFFICE: MGB Office in the Consulate-General in NEW YORK.
          [iii] MAY   : Stepan Zakharovich APRESYaN, Soviet Vice Consul in NEW YORK.
          [iv] ALBERT: Unidentified cover-name.
          [v]   VADIM : Anatolij Borisovich GROMOV, 1st Secretary at the Soviet Embassy, WASHINGTON.
          [vi] TYRE : NEW YORK.
          [vii] SERGEJ: Vladimir Sergeivich PRAVDIN, Editor of the TASS News Agency in NEW YORK.

S/NBF/T1 75   ~~TOP SECRET~~ EIDER

64. New York 1469 to Moscow, 17 October 1944.

Reissue(T1308)

From: NEW YORK
To: MOSCOW
No: 1469

17 October 1944

To VIKTOR[i].

Today we received from ROBERT[ii] 56 undeveloped films including the following materials:

1. Reviews by the Ministry of Economic Warfare on the Far East according to information of the economic COMPETITION[KONKURENTsIYa][iii].

2. A review by the Ministry of Economic Warfare on the economic situation of GERMANY.

3. A memorandum for KAPITAN[iv] on DECREE[DEKRET][v] to the French.

4. A review by the Ministry of Economic Warfare about

[22 groups unrecoverable]

negotiations of the COUNTRY[STRANA][vi] and the ISLAND[OSTROV][vii] about DECREE.

7. Reports of the Embassy of the COUNTRY in SIDON[viii] about [1 group unrecovered] GREECE.

8. Measures taken [6 groups unrecovered] in Sweden.

9. Negotiations on DECREE with FRANCE.

10. [8 groups unrecovered] about the situation in ITALY.

11. A report of the Embassy of the COUNTRY in MADRID about German assets in Spain.

12. The economic scale of defense.

13. A memorandum [3 groups unrecovered] for KAPITAN on the question of DECREE for [1 group unrecovered].

14. A telegram to the BANK[ix] from the Embassy of the COUNTRY on [2 groups unrecovered].

15. A memorandum of the executive committee on

[19 groups unrecovered]

64. (Continued)

~~TOP SECRET~~ VENONA

2.

16. [5 groups unrecovered] international cartels.

17. Instructions on the dissolution of the National Socialist Parties of GERMANY and affiliated organizations.

18. The situation on economic control of

[10 groups unrecovered]

20. A general review [4 groups unrecovered] crises of the COUNTRY.

The materials are recent.

[15 groups unrecovered]

at once the undeveloped films.

No. 835   MAJ[x]

Comments:
- [i] VIKTOR: Lt. Gen. P.M. FITIN.
- [ii] ROBERT: Nathan Gregory SILVERMASTER.
- [iii] COMPETITION: Non-Soviet Intelligence Organization.
- [iv] KAPITAN: i.e. CAPTAIN, Franklin D. ROOSEVELT.
- [v] DECREE: Lend Lease.
- [vi] COUNTRY: The United States.
- [vii] ISLAND: Great Britain.
- [viii] SIDON: LONDON.
- [ix] BANK: State Department.
- [x] MAJ: i.e. MAY, Stepan APRESYaN, Soviet Vice-Consul in NEW YORK.

7 December 1971

65. New York 1506 to Moscow, 23 October 1944.

~~TOP SECRET TRINE~~ VENONA

Reissue (T23.4)

From: New York
To: Moscow
No.: 1506

23 October 1944

To VIKTOR[i].

SERGEJ[ii] in CARTHAGE[iii] has made the acquaintance of PANCAKE[BLIN][iv]. Earlier SERGEJ had several times tried to [B% contact] him personally and also through IDE[YaD'][v] but the impression had been created that PANCAKE was avoiding a meeting. At the first conversation SERGEJ told him that he had very much desired to make his acquaintance since he greatly valued his work as a correspondent and had likewise heard flattering

[23 groups unrecoverable]

PANCAKE to give us information. P.[vi] said that he had noticed our attempts to [B% contact] him, particularly the attempts of IDE and of people of the TRUST [TREST][vii], but he had reacted negatively fearing the consequences. At the same time he implied that the attempts at rapprochement had been made with insufficient caution and by people who were insufficiently responsible. To SERGEJ's reply that naturally we did not want to subject him to unpleasant complications, PANCAKE gave him to understand that he was not refusing his aid but [B% one should] consider that he had three children and did not want to attract the attention of the KhATA[viii]. To SERGEJ's question how he considered it advisable to maintain liaison P. replied that he would be glad to meet but he rarely visited [B% TYRE[ix]] where he usually spent

[54 groups unrecoverable].

His fear is primarily explained by his unwillingness to spoil his career. Materially he is well secured[.] He earns as much as 1500 dollars a month but, it seems, he would not be averse to having a supplementary income. For the establishment of business contact with him we are insisting on [1 group unrecovered] reciprocity. For the work is needed a qualified [2 groups unrecovered] CARTHAGE. Telegraph your opinion.

No. 843
23 October

MAJ[x]

Comments: [i] VIKTOR: Lt. Gen. P.M. FITIN.
[ii] SERGEJ: Vladimir PRAVDIN, TASS representative.
[iii] CARTHAGE: Washington, D.C.
[iv] PANCAKE: Isidore F. STONE.
[v] IDE: Samuel KRAFSUR.
[vi] P.: i.e. PANCAKE.
[vii] TRUST: The Soviet Embassy in Washington.

~~TOP SECRET TRINE~~ VENONA

65. *(Continued)*

~~TOP SECRET TRINE~~ VENONA

- 2 -

Comments: [viii] KhATA: U.S. Federal Bureau of Investigation.
(Cont.)
        [ix] TYRE: New York City.

        [x]   MAJ: Stepan APRESYaN.

23 January 1968

~~TOP SECRET TRINE~~ VENONA

66. Moscow 374 to San Francisco, 7 November 1944.

BRIDE

~~TOP SECRET~~

USSR

Ref. No: 3/NBF/T960
Issued: 30/1/1958
Copy No: 205

NOTIFICATION OF AN AWARD (1944)

From: MOSCOW
To: SAN FRANCISCO
No: 374   7 Nov. 44

The Government has awarded you the Order of the Red Star. On behalf of us all and of the Presidium I warmly congratulate you on this high award and wish you the best of success in your work for the good of our country.

No. 5215   VIKTOR[i]

Comments: [i] VIKTOR: Lt. Gen. P.M. FITIN.

Distribution

3/NBF/T960

~~TOP SECRET~~
BRIDE

67. New York 1585 to Moscow, 12 November 1944.

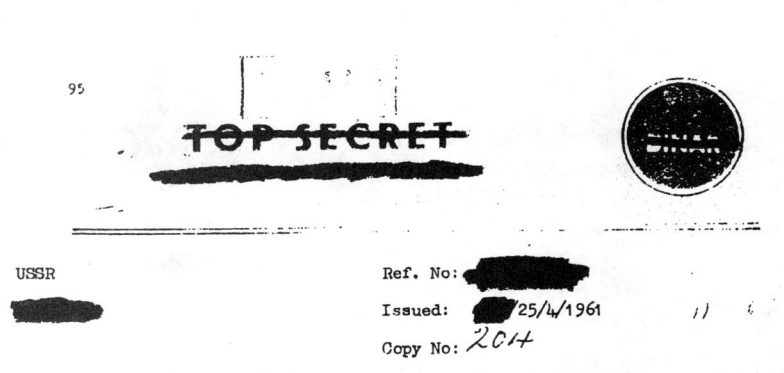

95

~~TOP SECRET~~

USSR

Ref. No:
Issued: 25/4/1961
Copy No: 204

DECISION TO MAINTAIN CONTACT WITH THEODORE HALL (1944)

From: NEW YORK
To: MOSCOW
No: 1585   12 Nov. 44

To VIKTOR.[i]

BEK[ii] visited Theodore HALL [TEODOR KhOLL],[iii] 19 years old, the son of a furrier. He is a graduate of HARVARD University. As a talented physicist he was taken on for government work. He was a GYMNAST [FIZKUL'TURNIK][iv] and conducted work in the Steel Founders' Union.[a] According to BEK's account HALL has an exceptionally keen mind and a broad outlook, and is politically developed. At the present time H. is in charge of a group at "CAMP-2"[v] (SANTA-FE). H. handed over to BEK a report about the CAMP and named the key personnel employed on ENORMOUS.[vi] He decided to do this on the advice of his colleague Saville SAX [SAVIL SAKS],[vii] a GYMNAST living in TYRE.[viii] SAX's mother is a FELLOWCOUNTRYMAN [ZEMLYaK][ix] and works for RUSSIAN WAR RELIEF. With the aim of hastening a meeting with a competent person, H. on the following day sent a copy of the report by S. to the PLANT [ZAVOD].[x] ALEKSEJ [xi] received S. H. had to leave for CAMP-2 in two days' time. He[b] was compelled to make a decision quickly. Jointly with MAY [MAJ][xii] he gave BEK consent to feel out H., to assure him that everything was in order and to arrange liaison with him. H. left his photograph and came to an understanding with BEK about a place for meeting him. BEK met S. [1 group garbled] our automobile. We consider it expedient to maintain liaison with H. [1 group unidentified] through S. and not to bring in anybody else. MAY has no objection to this. We shall send the details by post.

No. 897   [Signature missing]
11th November

Distribution   [Notes and Comments overleaf]

67. *(Continued)*

Notes: [a] I.e. Trade Union [PROFSOYuZ].
       [b] I.e. ALEKSEJ.
Comments: [i]   VIKTOR : Lt. Gen. P. M. FITIN.
          [ii] BEK   : Sergej Nikolaevich KURNAKOV.
          [iii] HALL   : Theodore Alvin HALL.
          [iv] GYMNAST : Possibly a member of the Young Communist League.
          [v]   CAMP-2 : LOS ALAMOS.
          [vi] ENORMOUS: Manhattan Engineering District - U.S. Atomic Energy Project.
          [vii] SAX
          [viii] TYRE   : NEW YORK CITY.
          [ix] FELLOWCOUNTRYMAN: Member of the Communist Party.
          [x]   PLANT   : Soviet Consulate.
          [xi] ALEKSEJ : Anatolij Antonovich YaKOVLEV, Soviet Vice-Consul in NEW YORK.
          [xii] MAY   : Stepan Zakharovich APRESYaN, Soviet Vice-Consul in NEW YORK.

68. New York 1600 to Moscow, 14 November 1944.

Reissue (T293)

From: NEW YORK
To: MOSCOW
No: 1600

14 November 1944

To VIKTOR[i].

LIBERAL[ii] has safely carried through the contracting of "Kh'YuS"[iii]. Kh'YuS is a good pal of METR's[iv]. We propose to pair them off and get them to photograph their own materials having given a camera for this purpose. Kh'YuS is a good photographer, has a large darkroom [KAMERA] and all the equipment but he does not have a Leica. LIBERAL will receive the films from METR for passing on. Direction of the probationers will be continued through LIBERAL, this will ease the load on him. Details about the contracting are in letter no. 8.

OSA[v] has agreed to cooperate with us in drawing in ShMEL'[vi] (henceforth "KALIBR" -- see your no. 5258[a]) with a view to ENORMOUS [ENORMOZ][vii]. On summons from KALIBR she is leaving on 22 November for the Camp 2 area [viii]. KALIBR will have a week's leave. Before OSA's departure LIBERAL will carry out two briefing meetings.

No. 901   ANTON[ix]

Notes: [a] Not available.
Comments:
   [i] VIKTOR: Lt. Gen. P. M. FITIN.
   [ii] LIBERAL: Julius ROSENBERG.
   [iii] Kh'YuS: i.e. HUGHES, probably Joel BARR or Alfred SARANT.
   [iv] METR: i.e. METER, probably either Joel BARR or Alfred SARANT.
   [v] OSA: Ruth GREENGLASS.
   [vi] ShMEL'/KALIBR: i.e. BUMBLEBEE/CALIBRE, David GREENGLASS.
   [vii] ENORMOZ: Atomic Energy Project.
   [viii] Camp 2: LOS ALAMOS Laboratory, New Mexico.
   [ix] ANTON: Leonid Romanovich KVASNIKOV.

1 May 1975

69. Moscow 379 to San Francisco, 16 November 1944.

DRUG

~~TOP SECRET~~

DINAR

USSR

Ref. No: 3/NBF/T798 (of 19/7/1956)
Issued: /9/10/1961
Copy No: 204

2nd RE-ISSUE

ESTABLISHMENT IN SAN FRANCISCO OF A
SUB-RESIDENCY FOR THE FIFTH LINE (1944)

From: MOSCOW
To: SAN FRANCISCO
No: 379[a]   16 Nov. 44

According to a plan approved by Comrade PETROV[i] on 26 October 1944, a special sub-residency [PODREZIDENTURA] for the Fifth Line is being established within the framework of your residency. It will not be subject to the authority

[16 groups unrecovered]

right to give independent decisions [1 group unrecovered] questions relating to the operations of the agent network and to have direct communication with the CENTRE.[ii] You [6 groups unrecovered] of the sub-residency in accordance with instructions of the TU[iii], directing the work of the sub-resident and taking the necessary steps for the successful

[63 groups unrecoverable]

, LOS ANGELES. The following changes among the permanent staff workers [KADROVIK] of the sub-residency have been approved:

1. "SMALL[MALYJ]"[iv], whom we are transferring from VANCOUVER, is appointed [C% to] help your deputy with the work in the port of SAN FRANCISCO.

2. "VITALIJ"[v] is being recalled home and "VOVChEK"[vi] is appointed senior man [STARShIJ] in PORTLAND. "YAKOV"[vii], whom we are transferring from OTTAWA, is appointed second worker in PORTLAND.

Distribution   [Continued overleaf]

3/NBF/T798

~~TOP SECRET~~
DRUG

DINAR

69. (Continued)

2   3/NBF/T798

3. "VOLKOV"[viii], who especially at the beginning will need a lot of help, remains in SEATTLE.

4. "PETR"[ix] remains in LOS ANGELES.

The permanent staff workers listed above, will for the time being work under cover of Inspectors of the Purchasing Commission. After the Merchant Fleet [MORFLOT] has succeeded in setting up in the U.S.A. a special department for vessels sailing to foreign ports [SUDA ZAGRANIChNOGO PLAVANIYa], the permanent staff workers will be transferred to the strength of that department as Personnel Inspectors. In the meantime it is essential to ensure, through the management [RUKOVODSTVO] of the Purchasing Commission, that the permanent staff workers are in a position which will give them just the right kind of influence to establish conditions favourable to [C% their] work in our line.

According to the plan approved by Comrade PETROV the sub-residency is charged with:

1. Development of counter-intelligence work among sailors of Soviet vessels to detect and suppress recruiting and anti-Soviet work by foreign intelligence services.

2. Detection of anti-Soviet and traitorous elements among the crews of vessels sailing to foreign ports.

3. Prevention of sabotage in Soviet vessels sailing to foreign ports and safe-guarding cargoes and vessels from sabotage.

Inform each permanent staff worker of these tasks, explaining them in detail and outlining practical measures. This activity will depend on the skilful co-ordination of the work of the ship and shore probationers [STAZhERY]. The work of the VLADIVOSTOK office is being reorganized to fit in with the tasks indicated, and for this purpose special instructions are also being issued by Comrade PETROV. Start carrying out the present instructions without waiting for "SERGEJ"[x] arrival. See the permanent staff workers personally and give each one a specific briefing. Proceed with the preliminary selection [2 groups unrecovered] candidates from amongst Soviet workers who have been vetted and who are connected with our vessels and port operations, with a view to employing them as contact men [SVYaZNIK] between the permanent staff workers and the ships' probationer network. The object, once the appointment of these candidates has been confirmed, is to make greater use of ships' probationers and to succeed in meeting every single one of the ships' residents.

We require:

1. that each permanent staff worker should present to you a [B% monthly] report concerning the work.

2. that a report should be sent each month, addressed to SIMEN[xi], concerning the work of the sub-residency and enclosing the reports of the permanent staff workers.

3. that the cover-names used should be reported immediately - explain

[70 groups unrecovered and unrecoverable]

3/NBF/T798   [Notes and Comments page 3]

69. *(Continued)*

DRUG

~~TOP SECRET~~

DINAR

3   3/NBF/T798

Note: [a] See MOSCOW to OTTAWA No. 568 of the same date - 3/NBF/T1275

Comments:
- [i] PETROV : Unidentified MOSCOW cover-name.
- [ii] CENTRE : MGB Headquarters in MOSCOW.
- [iii] TU : Presumably this is an abbreviation referring to some directorate [UPRAVLENIE], and T possibly stands for Transport [TRANSPORTNOE], Technical [TEKhNIChESKOE] or Territorial [TERRITORIAL'NOE].
- [iv] SMALL : Unidentified cover-name.
- [v] VITALIJ : Pavel Kuzmich REVIZOROV of the S.G.P.C.
- [vi] VOVChEK : Probably Aleksandr Pavlovich BOChEK of the S.G.P.C.
- [vii] YaKOV : Unidentified cover-name.
- [viii] VOLKOV : Andrej Romanovich ORLOV of the S.G.P.C.
- [ix] PETR : Aleksandr Petrovich GRAChEV of the S.G.P.C.
- [x] SERGEJ : Viktor Vasil'evich AFANAS'EV, described as Director of the Fifth Line in MOSCOW-NEW YORK No. 303 of 1st April 1945 (3/NBF/T1097).
- [xi] SEMEN : Unidentified MOSCOW cover-name.

3/NBF/T798

~~TOP SECRET~~
DRUG

DINAR

70. New York 1613 to Moscow, 18 November 1944.

~~TOP SECRET~~

USSR

Ref. No.: 3/NBF/T1996
Issued: /7/3/1972
Copy No.: 301

REISSUE OF ITEM I OF 3/NBF/T37
(of 7/3/1951)
DISCUSSION OF FUTURE USE OF KNYaZ': AL'BERT, CHEKh, VADIM
(1944)

From: NEW YORK
To: MOSCOW
No.: 1613   18th November 1944

To VIKTOR[i].

In mid-October AL'BERT[ii] tried to get in touch with KNYaZ'[iii]. The latter's wife stated that KNYaZ' had left for the PROVINCES[iv] and would return after Christmas. At one time KNYaZ' was compelled to resign because of the dismissal of LUN''s[v] former deputy on the grounds of organisational and political disagreement.

As a result of the election, LUN''s dismissal and the appointment of LOTsMAN[vi] in his place are not ruled out. Inasmuch as KNYaZ' is friendly with LOTsMAN [1 group unrecovered] he could count on a leading post in the BANK[vii].

[Continued overleaf]

3/NBF/T1996

~~TOP SECRET~~

70. (Continued)

- 2 - 3/NBF/T1996

About five months ago, having proposed to AL'BERT the suspension of meetings with KNYaZ', you promised to give, subsequently, instructions on how AL'BERT would explain the break to KNYaZ'. AL'BERT considers that a complicated explanation is not necessary as KNYaZ' knew of AL'BERT's chronic illness and himself recommended the latter to go away to the COUNTRYSIDE[viii] or to ARIZONA for a few months

[34 groups unrecoverable]

use:

1. If LOTsMAN gets an interesting post it goes without saying that KNYaZ' must "get in on it" by using his friendship.

2. If not, then we can try notwithstanding to use KNYaZ''s proximity to LOTsMAN to fix him up in a suitable establishment, still extracting, via him, interesting information which will [C% in any case] come LOTsMAN's way; or to send him to MI[ix] or to some other place in the PROVINCES, using the cover of representative of a firm (according to AL'BERT the PROVINCIAL[iv] experience of KNYaZ' allows him to count on any such appointment), and there to use him as the head of a private office (instead of, or with, ChEKh[x]).

If you agree I shall brief AL'BERT in this spirit.

We consider that KNYaZ' should be turned over to VADIM[xi] only after AL'BERT has ascertained his prospects.

No. 907
18th November
MAJ[xii]

Comments:
- [i] VIKTOR: Lt. Gen. P.M. FITIN.
- [ii] AL'BERT: i.e. "ALBERT"; probably Iskhak Abdulovich AKhMEROV.
- [iii] KNYaZ': i.e. "PRINCE"; possibly Laurence DUGGAN.
- [iv] PROVINCES, PROVINCIAL: Latin AMERICA(N).
- [v] LUN': i.e. "HEN-HARRIER"; Cordell HULL.
- [vi] LOTsMAN: i.e. "CHANNEL-PILOT"; Henry Agard WALLACE.
- [vii] BANK: U.S. State Department.
- [viii] COUNTRYSIDE: MEXICO.

3/NBF/T1996

70. *(Continued)*

```
                              VENONA
                           TOP SECRET

                              - 3 -           3/NBF/T1996

Comments
 [Cont'd]:  [ix] MI:        Probably CHILE.

           [x] ChEKh:       i.e. "CZECH"; Robert Owen MENAKER.

           [xi] VADIM:      Anatolij Borisovich GROMOV, First Secretary at the
                            Soviet Embassy in WASHINGTON.

           [xii] MAJ:       i.e. "MAY"; Stepan Zakharovich APRESYaN.
```

3/NBF/T1996

VENONA
TOP SECRET

71. New York 1634 to Moscow, 20 November 1944.

BRIDE
~~TOP SECRET~~   (CANOE)

USSR   Ref.No.: S/NBF/T294
                                        Issued: /22/1/1953
                                        Copy No.: 205

FINANCIAL ASSISTANCE FOR "RICHARD"

From: NEW YORK
To: MOSCOW
No.: 1634   20 Nov. 1944

To VICTOR[i].

    According to advice from ROBERT[ii] RICHARD's[iii] wife has complained recently about [D% financial]

    [65 groups unrecoverable]

in particular with business [BIZNES] since this would relieve them of heavy expenses.

    ROBERT told RICHARD's wife, who knows about her husband's participation with us, that we would willingly have helped them and that in view of all the circumstances would not allow them to leave CARTHAGE [KARFAGEN][iv]. ROBERT thinks that RICHARD would have refused a regular payment but might accept gifts as a mark of our gratitude for

    [7 groups unrecovered]

daughter's expenses which may come to up to two thousand a year.

    ALBERT said to ROBERT that in his opinion we would agree to provide for RICHARD's daughter's education and definitely advised ROBERT, PILOT[v] and the rest against attempting to offer RICHARD assistance.

    [Continued overleaf]

Distribution

S/NBF/T294
[2 pages]

~~TOP SECRET~~ (CANOE)

BRIDE

71. *(Continued)*

S/NBF/T294

— 2 —

While sharing ALBERT's opinion about the necessity for assistance we draw your attention to the fact that RICHARD has taken the offer of assistance favourably. Please do not delay your answer.

No. 912
21st November   MAY [MAJ][vi]

Comments: [i]   VICTOR: possibly Lieut.-General Pavel M. FITIN.
       [ii] ROBERT: Nathan Gregory SILVERMASTER.
      [iii] RICHARD: possibly Harry Dexter WHITE.
      [iv]   KARFAGEN: WASHINGTON, D.C.
      [v]   PILOT: William Ludwig ULLMAN.
      [vi]   MAJ: Pavel Ivanovich FEDOSIMOV.

W.S. No.: XY-70.5

S/NBF/T294

71. *(Continued)*

```
        USSR                    Ref No:   Amendment to:
                                          S/NBF/T294 (of 22/1/1953)
                                Issued:        20/1/1954
                                Copy No:   205

From:  NEW YORK
To:    MOSCOW
No.:   1634                               20 November 1944

                         AMENDMENT

        In line 3 of the last paragraph on page 1, please
amend the sentence to read "ROBERT, PILOT[v] and PA...... against
attempting to offer RICHARD assistance."




_____




Distribution






Amendment to:
S/NBF/T294
[1 Page]                          TOP SECRET  FROTH
                                     BRIDE
```

72. New York 1635 to Moscow, 21 November 1944.

BRIDE
~~TOP SECRET~~
EIDER

USSR

Ref. No: S/NBF/T177 (of 2/4/1952)
Issued: 31/5/1956
Copy No: 205

RE-ISSUE

1. REPORT FROM "ROBERT" EXPRESSING DISTRUST OF GENERAL HURLEY, AND REFERENCE TO LISTS OF GERMANS AND AUSTRIANS CONSIDERED RELIABLE BY "IZBA" AND THE "ISLANDERS" RESPECTIVELY (1944)

2. MENTION OF "ROBERT's" "PROFOUND SATISFACTION" WITH HIS REWARD, AND REFERENCES TO "ALBERT", "EL" AND "DORA" (1944)

From: NEW YORK
To: MOSCOW
No: 1635   21 Nov. 44

To VIKTOR.[i]

ROBERT[ii] reports:

1. During his visit to the Chinese 8th Army General HURLEY[a][iii] asseverated his friendship. CHOU EN-LAI should be warned that H.[Kh.] cannot be trusted. We think H. is a CHIA-HUO LU-[Q% TU].(Stooge)[a] of CHIANG KAI-SHEK. Even the BANK[iv] considers H.'s views to be in contradiction to the BANK's policy.

2. IZBA[v] has passed on to the Army a list of 20,000 "reliable Germans" with whom IZBA considers it safe to have dealings. It is impossible to obtain the list here at the moment. Perhaps it could be procured in SIDON[vi]. An analogous list of Austrians has been compiled by the ISLANDERS[OSTROVITYaNE][vii].

No. 913   [Continued overleaf]

Distribution

72. *(Continued)*

~~TOP SECRET~~ EIDER

- 2 -   S/NBF/T1 77

1. ALBERT asks for word to be passed to you that EL'[b] and he [D% profoundly]

    [20 groups unrecoverable]

2. ROBERT is sincerely overjoyed and profoundly satisfied with the reward [given him][c] [C% in accordance with your instructions]. As he says his work for us is the one good thing he has done in his life. He emphasised that he did not take this only as a [C% personal] honour, but also as an honour to his group. He wants to see the reward and the book.

3. DORA[viii] is very uneasy about the fate of her relations [and][c] again asks news of their whereabouts.

No. 914   MAY[MAJ][ix]
21st November

T.N.: [a] Given in Latin letters in the original.

[b] I.e. the Russian name for the letter "L".

[c] Inserted by translator.

Comments: [i] Lt.-Gen. P.M. FITIN.

[ii] Nathan Gregory SILVERMASTER.

[iii] Brigadier-General Patrick Jay HURLEY, appointed U.S. Ambassador to CHINA in December 1944.

[iv] U.S. Department of State.

[v] Office of Strategic Services [O.S.S.].

[vi] LONDON.

[vii] The British.

[viii] Helen (WITTE) SILVERMASTER, wife of ROBERT.

[ix] Probably Stepan Zakharovich APRESYaN, Soviet Vice-Consul in NEW YORK.

73. New York 1657 to Moscow, 27 November 1944.

VENONA

Reissue(T9.2)

From: NEW YORK
To: MOSCOW
No: 1657

27 November 1944

To VIKTOR[i].

Your no. 5356[a]. Information on LIBERAL's[ii] wife[iii]. Surname that of her husband, first name ETHEL, 29 years old. Married five years. Finished secondary school. A FELLOWCOUNTRYMAN [ZEMLYaK][iv] since 1938. Sufficiently well developed politically. Knows about her husband's work and the role of METR[v] and NIL[vi]. In view of delicate health does not work. Is characterized positively and as a devoted person.

No. 922

Advise on the possibility of using in our work the engineer MAZURIN Vladimir N. [viii]. He worked as deputy to the constructor of Plant 155. He graduated from MAI[viii] in 1936. Is now working at ARSENIJ's[ix] plant [x]. [2 groups unrecovered] [D% I request your decision on the question].

No. 923   ANTON[xi]

Notes: [a] Not available.
Comments:
  [i]   VIKTOR: Lt. Gen. P. M. FITIN.
  [ii]   LIBERAL: Julius ROSENBERG.
  [iii] Ethel ROSENBERG, nee GREENGLASS.
  [iv]   ZEMLyaK: Member of the Communist Party.
  [v]   METR: Probably Joel BARR or Alfred SARANT.
  [vi]   NIL: Unidentified.
  [vii] Vladimir Nikolaevich MAZURIN.
  [viii] MAI: i.e. MOSKOVSKIJ AVIATSIONNYJ INSTITUT, Moscow Aviation Institute.
  [ix]   ARSENIJ: Andrej Ivanovich ShEVChENKO.
  [x]   Bell Aircraft Plant, NIAGARA FALLS, N.Y.
  [xi]   ANTON: Leonid Romanovich KVASNIKOV.

1 May 1975

VENONA

74. New York 1699 to Moscow, 2 December 1944.

BRIDE

~~TOP SECRET~~   SUEDE

TO BE KEPT UNDER LOCK AND KEY:
NEVER TO BE REMOVED FROM THE OFFICE.

USSR

Ref No: S/NBF/T193
Issued: 21/5/1952
Copy No: 205

1. LIST OF SCIENTISTS ENGAGED ON THE PROBLEM OF ATOMIC ENERGY.
2. UNSUCCESSFUL EFFORTS OF AN UNIDENTIFIED PERSON (POSSIBLY "STAR") TO CONTACT NICHOLA NAPOLI AND "HELMSMAN".

From: NEW YORK
To: MOSCOW
No: 1699   2 Dec 1944

Conclusion of telegram No. 940 [sic][i].

Enumerates [the following][a] scientists who are working on the problem[ii] - Hans BETHE, Niels BOHR, Enrico FERMI, John NEWMAN, Bruno ROSSI, George KISTIAKOVSKI, Emilio SEGRE, G.I. TAYLOR, William PENNEY, Arthur COMPTON, Ernest LAWRENCE, Harold UREY, Hans STANARM, Edward TELLER, Percy BRIDGEMAN, Werner EISENBERG, STRASSENMAN
[7 groups unrecoverable]
our country addressed himself to NAPOLI[iii] and the latter, not wanting to listen to him, sent him to BECK [BEK][iv] as military commentator of the paper. On attempting to visit HELMSMAN [RULEVOJ][v] he was not admitted to him by the latter's secretary.

ANTON

[T.N. and Comments overleaf]

Distribution

S/NDF/T193
[2 Pages]

BRIDE

~~TOP SECRET~~   SUEDE

74. *(Continued)*

- 2 -   S/NBF/T493

T.N.: [a] Inserted by the translator.

Comments: [i] This internal serial number is used for the second of two messages transmitted under external serial number 1691 of 1 Dec 1944; it was signed by MAY, and dealt with an entirely different subject [see S/NBF/T37, Item 2]. The message of which the present text gives the last part probably contains material derived from MLAD [Theodore Alvin HALL]. Erroneous re-use of an internal serial number is not without precedent on this line.

[ii] To judge by the names which follow, the problem of atomic energy.

[iii] NAPOLI, Nichola, President and Manager of ARTKINO, which produces and distributes Russian motion picture films in the Western Hemisphere. Collateral suggests that the "he" of this paragraph was STAR [Saville SAX].

[iv] NEK: Sergej KURNAKOV.

[v] RULEVOJ: Earl BROWDER.

V.S. No.: XY-56.6

S/NBF/T493

75. New York 1715 to Moscow, 5 December 1944.

Reissue (T9.3)

From: NEW YORK
To: MOSCOW
No: 1715

5 December 1944

To VIKTOR[i].

Expedite consent to the joint filming of their materials by both METR[ii] and Kh'YuS[iii] (see our letter no. 8). LIBERAL[iv] has on hand eight people plus the filming of materials. The state of LIBERAL's health is nothing splendid. We are afraid of putting LIBERAL out of action with overwork.

No. 943.

Your no. 5673[a]. DIK[v] is directly in touch with FLOKS's [vi] husband and not with FLOKS herself. The intention of sending the husband to see RAMSEY [RAMZAJ][vii] is explained by [C% the possibility] of avoiding a superfluous stage for transmitting instructions.

No. 944   ANTON[viii]

Your no. 5598[a]. The sending of passengers on Liberty ships from TYRE[TIR][ix] to Soviet Northern ports has become exceptionally difficult. They can only be sent to England to await there a ship headed for the Soviet North.

No. 945   MAJ[x]
  4 December

Notes: [a] Not available.
Comments:
  [i]   VIKTOR: Lt. Gen. P. M. FITIN.
  [ii]   METR: i.e. METER, probably either Alfred SARANT or Joel BARR.
  [iii] Kh'YuS: i.e. HUGHES, probably either Joel BARR or Alfred SARANT.
  [iv]   LIBERAL: Julius ROSENBERG.
  [v]   DIK: i.e. DICK, Bernard SCHUSTER.
  [vi]   FLOKS: i.e. PHLOX, probably ▬▬▬ See NEW YORK's Nos. 619 of 4 May 1944 and 1020 of 20 July 1944.
  [vii] RAMZAJ: Possibly ▬▬▬
  [viii] ANTON: Leonid KNASNIKOV.
  [ix]   TIR: NEW YORK CITY.
  [x]   MAJ: i.e. MAY, Stepan APRESYaN.

1 May 1975

76. New York 1749-50 to Moscow, 13 December 1944.

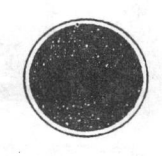

95

VENONA

~~TOP SECRET~~

USSR

Ref. No.: 3/NBF/T1290 (of 13/7/60)
Issued: 29/9/76
Copy No.: 3/1

REISSUE[i]

ORGANISATION OF WORK ON ENORMOUS AND PHOTOGRAPHY OF MATERIAL: ARNO, PERS, OSA, KALIBR, LIBERAL, "MLAD", Kh'YuS, SVET, KALISTRAT, METR (1944)

From: NEW YORK
To: MOSCOW
Nos.: 1749, 1750   13 December 1944

[2-part message complete]

[PART I] To VIKTOR[ii].

Your Nos. 5740[iii] and 5797[iii].

We consider it risky to concentrate all the contacts relating to ENORMOUS [ENORMOZ][iv] on ARNO[v] alone. This is good in that it limits the circles of [2 groups unrecovered] persons but it is dangerous to disrupt [1 group unrecovered] work on ENORMOUS

[45 groups unrecoverable]

PERS[vi]. [7 groups unrecovered] Camp-1[vii]. Our proposal

[24 groups unrecovered]

not to give [D% any more] on ENORMOUS.

2. To leave OSA[viii] and KALIBR[ix] in contact with LIBERAL[x] until [3 groups unrecovered] work.

Cont'd overleaf

MS

VENONA
~~TOP SECRET~~

387

76. (Continued)

VENONA
~~TOP SECRET~~

95

3/NBF/T1290

3. "MLAD"[xi]

[51 groups unrecoverable]

[PART II] Further [14 groups unrecovered].

Both are FELLOWCOUNTRYMEN[ZEMLYaKI][xii]. Both are helping us and both meet LIBERAL and ARNO [3 groups unrecovered]. Kh'YuS[xiii] handed over 17 authentic drawings relating to the APQ-7[xiv] (postal despatch No.9)[.] He can be trusted. The transfer of Kh'YuS alone to SVET[xv] is no way out of the situation. It will be necessary to put SVET in touch with KALISTRAT[xvi] in order to bring material for photography into the PLANT [ZAVOD][xvii]. I cannot carry material in and out of the PLANT late in the evening. I insist on bringing Kh'YuS and METR[xviii] together, putting the latter in touch with KALISTRAT or SVET and separating both from LIBERAL.

In TYRE[TIR][xix]

[14 groups unrecoverable]

round the clock. There are no major contradictions between letters 5 and 7 about LIBERAL. They complement each other. LIBERAL's shortcomings do not mean that he will be completely useless for photography. He is gradually getting used to photography.

No. 957[i] [Signature unrecoverable]

Footnotes:

[i] Part II only of this message was also published earlier, as 3/NBF/T9, Item 4.

[ii] VIKTOR: Lt General Pavel Mikhajlovich FITIN.

[iii] Not available. No. 5740 is also referred to in NEW YORK's No.1797 of 20 December 1944 (unpublished).

[iv] ENORMOUS: The U.S. Atomic Engergy Project.

[v] ARNO: Harry GOLD.

[vi] PERS: ie "PERSIAN"; formerly "FOGEL'", ie "VOGEL"; unidentified covernames. Also occur in NEW YORK's Nos. 212 of 11 February 1944, 854 of 16 June 1944 and 1251 of 2 September 1944 (3/NBF/T2053, 38, 301).

VENONA
~~TOP SECRET~~

76. *(Continued)*

~~TOP SECRET~~ VENONA

3/NBF/T1290

[vii]	Camp-1:	Not identified; probably an atomic energy site (cf references to "Camp-2" and "camps" in eg NEW YORK's No. 1585 of 12 November 1944 and 709 of 5 July 1945 (3/NBF/T1361, 223)).
[viii]	OSA:	ie "WASP"; Ruth GREENGLASS.
[ix]	KALIBR:	ie "CALIBRE"; David GREENGLASS.
[x]	LIBERAL:	Julius ROSENBERG.
[xi]	MLAD:	ie "YOUNG"; Theodore Alvin HALL.
[xii]	FELLOW-COUNTRYMEN:	Members of the Communist Party.
[xiii]	Kh'YuS:	ie "HUGHES"; Alfred Epaminondas SARANT, who was employed at the BELL Telephone Laboratories (cf. Footnote [xiv]), NEW YORK CITY, from October 1942 to September 1946.
[xiv]	APQ-7:	Or AN/APQ-7: a high-resolution airborne radar developed by the MASSACHUSETTS Institute of Technology and built by BELL Telephones (cf Footnote [xiii]) in the 1940s.
[xv]	SVET:	ie "LIGHT"; possibly Aleksandr Andreevich RAEV.
[xvi]	KALISTRAT:	ie "CALISTRATUS"; Aleksandr Semenovich FOMIN.
[xvii]	PLANT:	The Soviet Consulate.
[xviii]	METR:	ie "METRE"; Joel BARR.
[xix]	TYRE:	NEW YORK CITY.

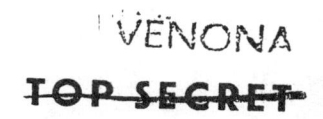

77. New York 1751-3 to Moscow, 13 December 1944.

BRIDE

~~TOP SECRET~~

SUEDE

TO BE KEPT UNDER LOCK AND KEY · NEVER TO BE REMOVED FROM THE OFFICE.

USSR

Ref No: S/NBF/T190
Issued: 21/5/1952
Copy No: 205

AMERICAN WAR DEPARTMENT AND BRITISH FOREIGN OFFICE DOCUMENTS SENT TO MOSCOW.

From: NEW YORK
To: MOSCOW
No: 1751-1753   13 Dec 1944

[Three-part message complete]

EXTRACTS

[Part I] To VICTOR.

ROBERT[i] has passed on to us a secret document "The Post-War Troop Basis of the War Department" drawn up by division [OTDEL] G-3 on the 19th of August ......[ii]

[Part III]

To the document is attached an explanation of the same date in which it is said in particular that the document replaces a provisional document drawn up on the 24th of June.

The document was sent to you by post on the 8th of December.

[5 groups unrecovered]

Telegraph whether the contents of the British Ministry of Foreign Affairs' commentary of the 3rd of July on the "Handbook on Civilian Affairs in Germany" should be telegraphed. The commentary was sent to you by the same post.[iii]

No. 953   MAY [MAJ][iv]
13th December.

[Comments overleaf]

Distribution

S/NBF/T190
[2 Pages]

BRIDE
~~TOP SECRET~~
SUEDE

77. *(Continued)*

- 2 - S/NBF/T190

Comments:
- [i] ROBERT: Nathan Gregory SILVERMASTER.
- [ii] The main body of the telegram consists of page 1 of this document containing a tabular summary of the rest of the document.
- [iii] This commentary is in the form of a letter from the Foreign Office dated 3rd July 1944 to C.B.P. PEAKE at S.H.A.E.F. commenting on the third draft of the S.H.A.E.F. Civil Affairs Handbook for Germany. An abstract of this letter was transmitted on 23 Dec 1944 in Nos. 1010-1013 (internal serial No. 937) (see PH 32).
- [iv] MAJ: Pavel Ivanovich FEDOSIMOV.

W.S. No: XY-56.8

S/NBF/T190

78. New York 1773 to Moscow, 16 December 1944.

Reissue (T1304)

From: NEW YORK
To: MOSCOW
No: 1773

16 December 1944

To VIKTOR[i].

OSA[ii] has returned from a trip to see KALIBR[iii]. KALIBR expressed his readiness to help in throwing light on the work being carried on at Camp-2[iv] and stated that he had already given thought to this question earlier. KALIBR said that the authorities of the Camp were openly taking all precautionary measures to prevent information about ENORMOUS[ENORMOZ][v] falling into Russian hands. This is causing serious discontent among the progressive [B% workers]

[17 groups unrecoverable]

the middle of January KALIBR will be in TYRE[TIR][vi]. LIBERAL[vii], referring to his ignorance of the problem, expresses the wish that our man should meet KALIBR and interrogate him personally. He asserts that KALIBR would be very glad of such a meeting. Do you consider such a meeting advisable? If not, I shall be obliged to draw up a questionnaire and pass it to LIBERAL. Report whether you have any questions of priority interest to us.

KALIBR also reports: OPPENHEIM[viii] from California and KISTIAKOWSKI[ix] (MLAD's[x] report mentioned the latter) are at present working at the Camp. The latter is doing research on the thermodynamic process. Advise whether you have information on these two professors.

No. 967
15 December

ANTON[xi]

Comments:
- [i]   VIKTOR: Lt. Gen. P. M. FITIN.
- [ii]   OSA: i.e. WASP, Ruth GREENGLASS.
- [iii] KALIBR: i.e. CALIBRE, David GREENGLASS.
- [iv]   Camp-2: Probably LOS ALAMOS.
- [v]   ENORMOZ: Manhattan Engineering Dist., U.S. Atomic Energy Project.
- [vi]   TIR: NEW YORK CITY.
- [vii] LIBERAL: Julius ROSENBERG.
- [viii] OPPENHEIM: Presumably Dr. J. Robert OPPENHEIMER, Director of the LOS ALAMOS Laboratory.
- [ix]   KISTIAKOWSKY: Dr. George Bogdan KISTIAKOWSKY, Chief of the Explosives Division at the LOS ALAMOS Laboratory.
- [x]   MLAD: i.e. YOUNG, [Theodore A. HALL]
- [xi]   ANTON: Leonid Romanovich KVASNIKOV.

20 May 1975

79. New York 1797 to Moscow, 20 December 1944.

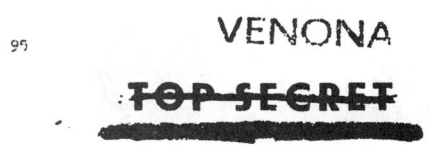

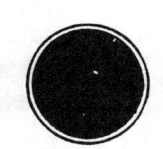

VENONA
~~TOP SECRET~~

USSR	Ref. No.: ▓▓▓▓
	Issued: ▓▓▓/16/6/76
	Copy No.: 301

1. DISCUSSION OF ARNO'S COVER AND PLAN TO SET UP LABORATORY
2. KRON
3. LINZA'S MOVE TO YaKOV'S TOWN, LIBERAL TO GO THERE AND PUT THEM IN CONTACT

(1944)

From: NEW YORK
To: MOSCOW
No.: 1797   20 December 1944

To VIKTOR[i].

Your No. 5740[ii].

We have been discussing his cover with ARNO[iii]. ARNO's note about his setting up a laboratory was sent in postal despatch No. 8 of 24 October. As the subject on which to work ARNO chose "Problems of the Practical Application Under Production Conditions of the Process of Thermal Diffusion of Gases". In his note ARNO envisages concluding agreements with firms. At first he said that our help was not needed: now he explains that not more than two thousand will be needed. For our part we consider that ARNO does not give sufficient consideration to all the difficulties of organising a laboratory and has not, as yet, adequately worked out the chances of reaching agreements with interested firms - on the conclusion of agreements with which he is counting heavily. I suggested to him that he should study the possibilities in greater detail. The picture will not become clearer before the end of January. ARNO intends to open the laboratory in his own town.

[Continued overleaf]

VENONA
~~TOP SECRET~~

[2 pages]
AJH

79. (Continued)

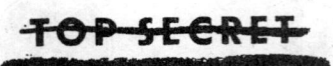

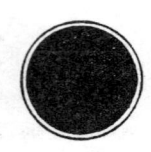

A detailed report on KRON's[iv] office was sent in postal despatch No. 9. Let us know whether we should repeat this by telegraph.

No. 978

LINZA[v] and his wife have left for YaKOV's[vi] town. At the end of December LIBERAL[vii] will go there and will put LINZA in touch with YaKOV. Before making the move, LINZA and his wife visited the town and took an apartment, the address of which we reported in letter No. 9. LINZA sold his house and spent part of the money on the move. We gave him a once for all payment of 500: I consider that

[24 groups unrecoverable]

Footnotes:
- [i] VIKTOR: Lt General Pavel Mikhajlovich FITIN.
- [ii] Not available. Also referred to in NEW YORK's No. 1749 of 13 December 1944
- [iii] ARNO: Formerly covername "GUS'", ie "GOOSE"; Harry GOLD; resident in PHILADELPHIA, PENNSYLVANNIA.
- [iv] KRON: ie "CHROME-YELLOW"; unidentified covername. Also occurs in NEW YORK's No. 19 of 4 January 1945
- [v] LINZA: ie "LENS"; Michael SIDOROVICh (wife Anne, née HANUSIAK); moved from NEW YORK State to CLEVELAND, OHIO.
- [vi] YaKOV: Formerly covername "GNOM", ie "GNOME"; William PERL (formerly MUTTERPERL).
- [vii] LIBERAL: Formerly covername "ANTENNA"; Julius ROSENBERG.

80. New York 12-3, 15-6 to Moscow, 4 January 1945.

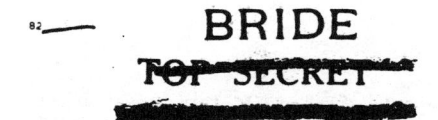

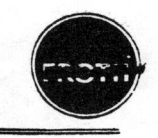

BRIDE

~~TOP SECRET~~

USSR	Ref No: S/NBF/T544
	Issued: 21/6/1954
	Copy No: 25

"ALBERT's" OBSERVATIONS ON "ROBERT".

From: NEW YORK
To: MOSCOW
Nos.: 12, 13, 15, 16   4 January 1945

[Four-part message complete]

[Part I] To VIKTOR[i].

In a special letter of 2 January, AL'BERT[ii] reports, while demonstrating to ROBERT[iii] for a long time the advisability of setting up a separate group of two or three persons whose technical work (the delivery, filming and safekeeping of materials) would not be concentrated in ROBERT's apartment.[a] AL'BERT explained that we are not proposing to deprive him of the direction of the people but we want to create the most secure possible conditions for the processing and safekeeping of materials, since, judging by well-known facts, the KhATA[iv] is probably interested in ROBERT's activities, and there is no guarantee that, as a result of some accident, materials he may have at his place when it happens will not fall into the hands of the KhATA and that our sources would not be compromised in this way since at the moment everything is concentrated in one place. After many friendly conversations on this subject ROBERT agreed in principle with our opinion.

[Continued overleaf]

Distribution

S/NBF/T544

[4 Pages]

~~TOP SECRET~~

BRIDE

80. *(Continued)*

- 2 -   S/NBF/T544

It is possible that ROBERT thought we wanted to take away some of his people counting on getting better results and concluded from this that we were not altogether satisfied with his achievements. In ALBERT's opinion he succeeded in convincing ROBERT that our sole aim was organisational security. It must be said that on the basis of our workers' information ROBERT has been inclined to be critical and dubious of our ability to deal with the probationers [STAZhERY]. Especially indicative from this point of view is the incident with KOL'TsOV[v]

[36 groups unrecoverable]

AILERON [ELERON][vi] our worker; if AL'BERT proposed this ROBERT would undoubtedly reject it. Therefore AL'BERT is trying to convince him of the necessity of setting up a small group whose technical work would be concentrated outside ROBERT's apartment, ROBERT retaining the general direction of it.

[Part II] It has been decided to train ACORN [ZhOLUD'][vii] and ZhENYa[viii] for the processing of materials in their own apartment. The couple [SUPRUGI][b] are conscientious, capable and fairly well disciplined. Notwithstanding, however, their devotion to the FELLOWCOUNTRYMEN [ZEMLYaKI][ix] and personally to ROBERT, the latter has from time to time complained of their caprices. Thus a few weeks ago DORA[x] told EL[xi] in ROBERT's and PILOT's[xii] presence that the couple were trying to get themselves free of us. ALBERT does not regard this seriously but he no longer doubts that it costs ROBERT great pains to keep the couple and the other probationers [STAZhERY] in check and to get good work out of them. Being their leader in the FELLOWCOUNTRYMANLY line ROBERT has the opportunity to give them orders.

In AL'BERT's opinion our workers would hardly manage to work with the same success under the FELLOW-COUNTRYMANLY flag. We may possibly set up direct liaison with ACORN, AILERON and the rest, but it is doubtful whether we could secure from them the same results as ROBERT, who, constantly dealing with them, has many advantages over us. The whole group [DA of ROBERT's]

[54 groups unrecoverable]

[Part III] ROBERT reacted very unfavourably saying that before AL'BERT's time somebody else tried to part him and PILOT, that he did not believe in our orthodox methods and so on. As he said, it would not be hard to separate PILOT from him, but he

[32 groups unrecoverable]

[D PILOT] will not cool off towards our work. It goes without saying that PILOT is not so deeply devoted to us as ROBERT and DORA are, for he comes from a well-to-do

[Continued overleaf]

S/NBF/T544

80. *(Continued)*

BRIDE
~~TOP SECRET~~

FROTH

- 3 -   S/NBF/T544

family of western TOWNSMEN [GOROZHANE][xiii]. In AL'BERT's opinion, for PILOT's successful work we are in large measure indebted to ROBERT and DORA, who treat PILOT very solicitously, and in the near future we shall gain nothing at the cost of separating PILOT from ROBERT. AL'BERT is trying not to permit a joint business [BIZNES] like a farm or an aerodrome and has advised ROBERT to let PILOT work out this project himself if the latter is sure of success saying that in case of need we should render PILOT some financial support. In AL'BERT's opinion the project is unrealisable and later they will drop it.

ROBERT is displeased by our interference in his personal affairs, which is what he considers the farm to be. In his words, all these years he and the others have worked at high pressure and they want to acquire a farm rather for relaxation than as a cover. For a long time PILOT and DORA have been drawing up all kinds of plans relative to the farm.

[Part IV] In PILOT's opinion the farm will be a good pretext for his absence[c] in CARTHAGE [KARFAGEN][xiv] in case of dismissal, for having been dismissed he could hardly remain in CARTHAGE even temporarily without legal[d] income. Seeing how much they were carried away by the idea AL'BERT did not consider it wise to insist

[29 groups unrecoverable]

leadership of this new group will have to be left to ROBERT.

What has been expounded does not mean that the mutual relations of AL'BERT with ROBERT are strained or that ROBERT does not want to obey us. ROBERT esteems AL'BERT highly and would not [2 groups unrecovered] any request of ours if AL'BERT insisted. AL'BERT does not doubt that ROBERT would introduce him to any of his people if AL'BERT requested, for organisationally ROBERT has become very close to us.

AL'BERT emphasises the soundness and timeliness of the award and the gift to ROBERT, who is pleased at our high evaluation [of him][e].

Note by the Office [KONTORA]. In the same letter AL'BERT adduces short biographical data on ACORN and ZhENYa which we shall send by post.

No. 6
4 January

MAY [MAJ][xv]

[T.N. and Comments overleaf]

S/NBF/T544

~~TOP SECRET~~
BRIDE
FROTH

80. *(Continued)*

- 4 - S/NBF/T544

T.N.: [a] This sentence contains a similar anacoluthon in the original. Presumably some part of the subordinate clause has been omitted.

[b] SUPRUGI means "couple" in the sense of a married couple.

[c] Presumably an error for "presence".

[d] I.e., overt.

[e] Inserted by the translator.

Comments: [i] VIKTOR: probably Lt.-General P.M. FITIN.

[ii] AL'BERT: not identified.

[iii] ROBERT: Nathan Gregory SILVERMASTER.

[iv] KHATA: the F.B.I.

[v] KOL'TsOV: not identified.

[vi] ELERON: not identified.

[vii] ZhOLUD': possibly Bella [originally Bela ?] GOLD.

[viii] ZhENYa: possibly Sonia Steinman GOLD.

[ix] ZEMLYaKI: members of the Communist Party.

[x] DORA: Helen Witte SILVERMASTER.

[xi] EL': not identified.

[xii] PILOT: possibly William Ludwig ULLMAN.

[xiii] GOROZhANE: Americans.

[xiv] KARFAGEN: WASHINGTON, D.C.

[xv] MAJ: MGB resident in NEW YORK.

W.S. No.: XY-1.06 (Revision)

S/NBF/T544

81. New York 18-9 to Moscow, 4 January 1945.

~~TOP SECRET DINAR~~

Reissue (T210.2 and 211)

From: NEW YORK
To: MOSCOW
No: 18-19

4 January 1945

[Part I] To VIKTOR[i].

Further to No.2[a]. Here is the gist of the enclosure to LOUIS's[ii] memorandum:

1. In "Memoranda on Conversations" LOUIS sets out the reactions to FROST[iii] of various persons with whom he and FROST came in contact. Opinions agree that FROST is not running the business competently, that he is making many empty promises, that he is not listening to advice and that he over-estimates his capabilities.

2. In "Summary Report" LOUIS reports about the various steps in the development of the company and FROST's mistakes which were connected with them. He considers it necessary soon to reorganize the company by setting up the following departments (in order of importance):

   1. Production.
   2. Selection of music to publish, of the artists and gramophone recordings.
   3. Promotion.
   4. Distribution.

Except for FROST LOUIS considers that none of the present personnel is adequate to deal with the tasks which confront each of these departments. In his opinion FROST should concentrate his attention on the problems of the second department; LOUIS himself, not knowing the technology of production, undertakes to head distribution. For promoting the products ability of high order is required. At present the company is failing to deal with the problem of production and this means that business is at a standstill. In this area is needed a specialist who could surround himself with experienced sound recorders, chemists and machine experts and who would know the market.

[Part II] He and 4 qualified workers could solve the personnel problem. He

[68 groups unrecoverable]

Chronological Report for 1944" LOUIS describes the activities of the company.

4 and 5. Magazine clippings and copies of postal and telegraphic correspondence on company business.

No.12   MAY[MAJ][iv]

~~TOP SECRET DINAR~~

81. *(Continued)*

~~TOP SECRET DINAR~~ VENONA

   AL'BERT[v] is urgently asking for a CONTAX camera for ACORN [ZhOLUD'][vi]. It is extremely difficult to get one here. Please telegraph YuRIJ[vii] at once.

   No.13   MAY.

   Your No.6165[b]. DDT is a disinfectant used by the army of the COUNTRY [STRANA][viii]. See our letter No.1 of 1944, the paragraph about CHROME PIGMENT [KRON][ix].

   No.14   ANTON[x]

   Your No.5351[c]. You ~~agreed~~ to the use of AKhMED[xi] in the second line. In order to decide the question of whether to use him as a group leader in this line in place of BEK[xii]. ~~Again please permit~~ NAZAR[xiii] to have a chat with AKhMED ~~for the purpose of~~ verification.

   No.15   MAY.
   4 January

Notes: [a] Not available
         [b] Not available
         [c] Not available

Comments: [i]   VIKTOR: Lt. Gen. P. M. FITIN
         [ii]   LOUIS: Alfred K. STERN.
        [iii]   FROST: Boris MORROS.
         [iv]   MAJ: Stepan Zakharovich APRESYaN.
          [v]   AL'BERT: Probably Iskhak Abdulovich AKhMEROV.
         [vi]   ZhOLUD': Bella GOLD.
        [vii]   YuRIJ: Lev A. TARASOV.
       [viii]   STRANA: U.S.A.
         [ix]   KRON: Unidentified cover-name.
          [x]   ANTON: Leonid Romanovich KVASNIKOV.
         [xi]   AKhMED: Unidentified.
        [xii]   BEK: Sergej Nikolaevich KURNAKOV.
       [xiii]   NAZAR: Stepan Nikolaevich ShUNDENKO.

82. New York 27 to Moscow, 8 January 1945.

~~TOP SECRET~~ VENONA

Reissue(T212.1)

From: NEW YORK
To: MOSCOW
No: 27

8 January 1945

TO VIKTOR[i].

SERGEJ's[ii] conversation with SIMA[iii] took place on [B% 4 January]. SIMA gives the impression of being a serious person who is politically well developed and there is no doubt of her sincere desire to help us. She had no doubts about whom she is working for and said that the nature of the materials in which we are interested pointed to the fact that it was our country which was in question. She was very satisfied that she was dealing with us and said that she deeply appreciated the confidence shown in her and understood the importance of our work.

SIMA's transfer to a new job was made at the insistence of her [D% superiors]

[64 groups unrecoverable]

generalizing materials from all departments [OTDELY]. SIMA will probably start work on 15 February.

On the basis of this preliminary information there is reason to assume that in her new job SIMA will be able to carry out very important work for us in throwing light on the activities of the KhATA[iv]. The fruitfulness of her work will to a considerable extent depend upon our ability to organize correct and constant directions. It should be remembered that SIMA from an operational point of view is quite undeveloped and she will need time to learn conspiracy and to correctly gain an understanding of the questions which interest us.

A final decision on the question of direction and liaison can be taken [B% only] after she has moved to CARTHAGE[KARFAGEN][v] when it will be ascertained [B% specifically] what her new job consists of.

No. 22 MAJ[vi]
8 January

Comments:
[i] VIKTOR: Lt. Gen. P. M. FITIN.
[ii] SERGEJ: Vladimir Sergeevich PRAVDIN.
[iii] SIMA: Judith COPLON.
[iv] KhATA: The Federal Bureau of Investigation.
[v] KARFAGEN: WASHINGTON, D. C.
[vi] MAJ: Stepan APRESYaN.

29 January 1974

~~TOP SECRET~~ VENONA

83. Moscow 14 to New York, 4 January 1945.

BRIDE
~~TOP SECRET~~
TO BE KEPT UNDER LOCK AND KEY.
NEVER TO BE REMOVED FROM THE OFFICE.

CANOE

USSR

Ref No: S/NBF/T259
Issued: 30/10/1952
Copy No: 205

1. ADDRESS FOR "FOTON's" CORRESPONDENCE WITH HIS WIFE.
2. MENTION OF LIAISON WITH MATUS.
3. FINANCES FOR "GROWTH's" ENTERPRISE.
4. INSISTENCE BY "SACHS" THAT HIS MATERIAL IS HANDED TO "THE FELLOW-COUNTRYMEN's" ORGANISATION AS WELL AS TO THE MGB.

From: NEW YORK
To: MOSCOW
No.: 14   4 Jan 1945

To VICTOR[i].

FOTON receives telegrams from his wife not from the address indicated by you in letter No. 7 but 9 Kuznetskij Most[ii][,] the RUTOVSKIJ's apartment. Advise what sort of an address FOTON ought to use.

No. 7   ANTON

[Continued overleaf]

Distribution

S/NBF/T259
[3 Pages]

BRIDE
~~TOP SECRET~~
CANOE

83. (Continued)

- 2 -   S/NBF/T259

Your number 6227[a]. The conditions for liaison with MATUS and the information [SPRAVKA] are in VADIM's[iii] possession. SERGEJ[iv] does not know anything about him. Telegraph explanation.

No. 8

For GROWTH's [ROST][v] enterprise we asked a thousand and a half. The amount assigned by you is one tenth of what is required and, it goes without saying, can produce no substantial results.

No. 9

Your number 6218[a]. I am bearing in mind your reminder about the line of conduct in respect of the leadership of the FELLOW COUNTRYMEN's organisation [ZEMLYaChESKAYa][vi]. However, as ALBERT has already firmly promised ROBERT[vii] and SACHS [SAKS] to pass on to HELMSMAN [RULEVOJ][viii] certain materials (in particular concerning the Chinese [C% FELLOW COUNTRYMEN [ZEMLYaKI]][vi]) and it is hard for him to go back on his word, please permit by way of exception the passing on of these materials to HELMSMAN through VADIM or ECHO [EKhO][ix], at the same time warning ALBERT that this is the last time. ALBERT emphasised that SACHS's attitude to this question was very jealous and he gave him to understand that he would not hand certain materials over to us without a guarantee that they would be handed over to H. [R.][x] too and, should we refuse, he might try to esatblish liaison with H. over our heads.

No. 10
4th January   MAY [MAJ][xi]

T.N.: [a] Not available.

Comments: [i] VICTOR: possibly Pavel Mikhajlovich FITIN, Lieutenant-General, head of the foreign intelligence branch of the NKGB.

[ii] 9 Kuznetskij Most, MOSCOW, is the address of several organisations, including the TORGBANK, which would presumably have correspondence with AMTORG.

[iii] VADIM: Anatolij Borisovich GROMOV, First Secretary and NKGB resident in the Soviet Embassy in WASHINGTON, D.C.

[continued overleaf]

S/NBF/T259

83. *(Continued)*

BRIDE

~~TOP SECRET~~

TO BE KEPT UNDER LOCK AND KEY
NEVER TO BE REMOVED FROM THE OFFICE.

CANOE

- 3 -   S/NBF/T259

[iv]   SERGEJ: Vladimir Sergeevich PRAVDIN.

[v]   ROST: formerly ODESSIT. See S/NBF/T245 in which on 23 Aug 1944 MAJ asked for 1000 dollars to expand "ODESSIT's enterprise" (concerned with the manufacture of dies [ShTAMPY]), and S/NBF/T248 in which on 28 Dec 1944 BORIS (MGB cipher clerk in NEW YORK) queried "the amount additionally allotted to ODESSIT's enterprise", which he had deciphered as 150. It must be assumed that MOSCOW replied that this figure was quite correct, which gave rise to the observations in the third message of the above text.

[vi]   ZEMLYaChESKAYa: the Communist Party of the country in question. Derived from the adjectival form of ZEMLYaK [FELLOW COUNTRYMAN] - a member of the Communist Party of the country in question. There is no English noun which can be used as an adequate translation.

[vii] ROBERT: Nathan Gregory SILVERMASTER.

[viii] RULEVOJ: Earl Russell BROWDER.

[ix]   EKhO: Bernard SCHUSTER (Communist Party name - CHESTER).

[x]   R.: i.e. RULEVOJ (see [viii] above).

[xi]   MAJ: Pavel Ivanovich FEDOSIMOV, secretary to the Consul-General and NKGB resident in the Soviet Consulate-General in NEW YORK.

W.S. No.: XY-66.2

S/NBF/T259

BRIDE

~~TOP SECRET~~

CANOE

84. New York 79 to Moscow, 18 January 1945.

T247 (Reissue)

From: NEW YORK
To: MOSCOW
No: 79

18 January 1945

To VIKTOR[i]

According to ROBERT's[ii] report, he may be presented with an opportunity of obtaining from RICHARD[iii] ROUBLE's[iv] appointment to RICHARD's post, as the latter will soon be appointed assistant secretary. (MAJ's[v] note: It is possible that this is a slip of the pen, for RICHARD and others are already assistants if [C% ROBERT] [1 group unrecovered] NABOB's[vi] department, where he obviously can be promoted to the post of deputy.)[vii] ROBERT has repeatedly suggested that ROUBLE be turned over to him. According to our information he could get better results from ROUBLE than our line. He suspects that ROUBLE is connected with us through other ZEMLYaChESKIJ[viii] channels. ALBERT[ix] emphasizes that ROUBLE was passive in the REJDER[x] group although he was able to give [us] valuable material. Some months ago ROBERT complained that ROUBLE was hiding important documents from ZhENYa[xi] (his secretary). If we are convinced of ROUBLE's good faith toward the ZEMLYaKI[viii], ROBERT would like to take him into his group. ROBERT has always been against appointing two of our groups to one department and [D% instead asks] that our probationers[xii] from RICHARD's department be under his direction to avoid misunderstandings. In ALBERT's opinion, if ROUBLE is reliable from our point of view he ought to be turned over to ROBERT. ROBERT does not want to promote ROUBLE to RICHARD's post unless he takes him into his group; on the other hand he is not quite sure that he will be able to get ROUBLE into this post, as it is possible that somebody else is already earmarked for it.

Wire your decision by priority telegram not later than 21 January indicating the method of establishing contact between ALBERT and ROUBLE if you agree to including ROUBLE in ROBERT's group.

No. 58   MAJ[v]
   18 January

84. *(Continued)*

Footnotes:
- [i] VIKTOR: Lt. Gen. P. M. FITIN.
- [ii] ROBERT: Nathan Gregory SILVERMASTER.
- [iii] RICHARD: Harry Dexter WHITE.
- [iv] ROUBLE: Probably Harold GLASSER.
- [v] MAJ: Pavel Ivanovich FEDOSIMOV.
- [vi] NABOB: Henry MORGENTHAU, Jr., Secretary of the Treasury.
- [vii] MAJ's confusion is due to the fact that the proposed promotion, which later took place, was from "assistant to the secretary of the treasury" to "assistant secretary of the treasury." There was probably no slip of the pen, but he sorted the positions out correctly by using the Russian words for "assistant" and "deputy" respectively.
- [viii] ZEMLYaChESKIJ (adjective) and ZEMLYaKI (noun) refer to members of the communist party of the country in question. Here, therefore, they mean "American communist party" (attributive) and "members of the American communist party" respectively.
- [ix] ALBERT: Iskhak Abdulovich AKHMEROV, alias W. GREINKE.
- [x] REJDER: i.e., RAIDER: Victor PERLO.
- [xi] ZhENYa: Sonia GOLD, nee STEINMAN, employed in the Treasury Department from 24 August 1943 to 21 August 1947. If she was in fact GLASSER's secretary at the time of this message, the statement here is a strong confirmation of the identifications of ROUBLE and ZhENYa; if she was not, it strongly suggests that one or both identifications are incorrect.
- [xii] Probationers: Agents.

29 September 1976

VENONA

85. New York 82 to Moscow, 18 January 1945.

~~TOP SECRET TRINE~~ VENONA

MGB

From: NEW YORK
To: MOSCOW
No: 82

18 January 1945

To VIKTOR[i].

Recently TSERBER[ii] asked ROBERT[iii] how he could reestablish contact with the man through whom he was connected with the "FELLOW-COUNTRYMEN[ZEMLYaKI][iv]. TSERBER works in the accounts section of PEAK's[PIK][v] department. Since you advised in no. 3937 [a] that TSERBER was a probationer of the NEIGHBORS[SOSEDI][vi] allow us to inform the head NEIGHBOR about TSERBER's request. If the NEIGHBORS have lost contact with him he [B% probably]

[13 groups unrecoverable].

ALBERT[AL'BERT][vii] also [3 groups unrecovered].

MAY[MAJ][viii]

No. 59
18 January

Notes: [a] Not available.

Comments:
[i] VIKTOR: Lt. Gen. P. M. FITIN.

[ii] TSERBER: Unidentified. Either a cover-name "CERBERUS" or a transliteration of a surname of German origin -- CERBER or ZERBER.

[iii] ROBERT: Nathan Gregory SILVERMASTER.

[iv] ZEMLYaKI: Members of the Communist Party

[v] PIK: Possibly Virginius Frank COE.

[vi] SOSEDI: Members of another Soviet Intelligence organization, here apparently the GRU.

[vii] AL'BERT: Probably Iskhak Abdulovich AKhMEROV.

[viii] MAJ: Stepan APRESYaN.

27 May 1960

~~TOP SECRET TRINE~~ VENONA

86. Moscow 200 to New York, 6 March 1945.

VENONA

~~TOP SECRET~~

USSR	Ref. No.: 3/NBF/T2208
	Issued: 17/6/76
	Copy No.: 301

BONUSES FOR SOURCES, INCLUDING LIBERAL AND NIL, GIFTS OR PAYMENTS FOR PROBATIONERS

(1945)

From: MOSCOW
To: NEW YORK
No.: 200   6 March 1945

[66 groups unrecovered]

decision was made about awarding the sources as a bonus the following sums: to LIBERAL [i] 1000 dollars[,] NIL[ii]

[58 groups unrecoverable]

either the purchase of valuable gifts for the probationers [STAZhER] or payment to them of money on the basis of well thought out cover-stories.

[28 groups unrecovered]

No. 1306   VIKTOR[iii]

Footnotes:
[i] LIBERAL: Formerly covername "ANTENNA"; Julius ROSENBERG.
[ii] NIL: ie either "(River) NILE" or a name eg "NEIL/NEALE"; formerly "TU..."; unidentified covername. "TU..."/"NIL" also occurs in NEW YORK's Nos. 863 of 16 June 1944 (3/NBF/T58), 1251 of 2 September 1944 (3/NBF/T301) and 1657 of 27 November 1944 (3/NBF/T9.2).
[iii] VIKTOR: Lt General Pavel Mikhajlovich FITIN.

VENONA

~~TOP SECRET~~

3/NBF/T2208
[1 page]
AJH

87. Moscow 284 and 286 to New York, 28 March 1945.

Reissue(T940)

From: MOSCOW
To: NEW YORK
No: 286, 284

28 March 1945

[Part I]   With Post No. 1 were received "ZORA's"[i] reports in which there are the following facts which deserve serious attention:

1. In the report of 2 February 1945 in 2 pages, she, describing the situation concerning the change of working location, names institutions of the "COUNTRY[STRANA]"[ii] by the code designations adopted by us in our telegraphic and written correspondence "CLUB[KLUB]"[iii], "BANK"[iv], "CABARET[KABARE]"[v].

2. In the reports of 1 and 3 February "ZORA" several times mentions the words "BANK", "CABARET", "HOUSE[DOM]"[vi], "CLUB". It is not a question about communications which have been [2 groups unrecovered] in the OFFICE[KONTORA][vii] in which you filled in the prearranged designations, but about [1 group unrecovered] written personally by ZORA nos. 8, 10, 111, 112.

3. In the report of [1 group unrecovered] January 1945 "ZORA" in detail sets forth the following story: "SIMA's"[viii] chief, WOOLWORTH[VUL'VORT][ix] from the Military Department of the "CLUB" entrusted "ZORA" with finding out in her

[31 groups unrecovered]

was such an informer. "ZORA" gave

[19 groups unrecovered]

John DUNNING[DANING][x] [3 groups unrecovered]. To DUNNING's question, whether [C% she] was interested in this information [1 group unrecovered] the "BANK" ZORA answered that another institution, whose name she had been forbidden to disclose, was interested in the information and that this other institution would get in touch with him. A member of the Military Department of "SIMA's" institution Aleksander SACKS[xi] [Aleksandr SAKS] in a conversation with ZORA [2 groups unrecovered] about the proposal
    [10 groups unrecovered]

by him declined. SACKS gave ZORA the task of trying to get in the "RADIO STATION[RATsIYa]"[xii] materials about Swiss-German

87. *(Continued)*

2.

financial operations [C% and]

[38 groups unrecoverable]

[Part II]   To "ZORA's" question to SACKS and WOOLWORTH, why they are not receiving material from the "RADIO STATION" through an official representative, [2 groups unrecovered] institutions of the "COUNTRY" including the "BANK", WOOLWORTH is trying to [C% seek out] [5 groups unrecovered] the CLUB. WOOLWORTH told "ZORA" that in the IZBA[xiii], BANK, RADIO STATION, FARM[KhUTOR][xiv] [4 groups unrecovered] many people who

[17 groups unrecovered]

by the next post answer:

1. Why [1 group unrecovered] ZORA.

2. Were these reports read [1 group unrecovered] by the liaison man.

3. Did "MAJ"[xv] and "SERGEJ"[xvi] see these reports.

4. Who told "ZORA" [3 groups unrecovered] and then told "[1 group unrecoverable]"

[13 groups unrecovered]

to WOOLWORTH and SACKS.

6. Why did ZORA begin to take

[33 groups unrecovered]

steps taken to curtail ZORA's dangerous activities.

   Without waiting for instructions from us after you reply to the questions which have been raised, immediately and in detail enlighten our liaison man about the serious mistakes he has committed in the work with "ZORA". As an ultimatum warn ZORA that if she does not carry out our instructions and if she undertakes steps without our consent, we shall immediately terminate all relations with her. Forbid ZORA to recruit all her acquaintances one after the other. Take all steps to see that ZORA's activities do not lead to serious political complications with the "COUNTRY". This example clearly illustrates not only the falling off in the Residency's work of controlling and educating probationers, but also the lack of understanding by our operational workers of the most elementary rules in our work.

No. 1893

[Signature unrecoverable]

87. *(Continued)*

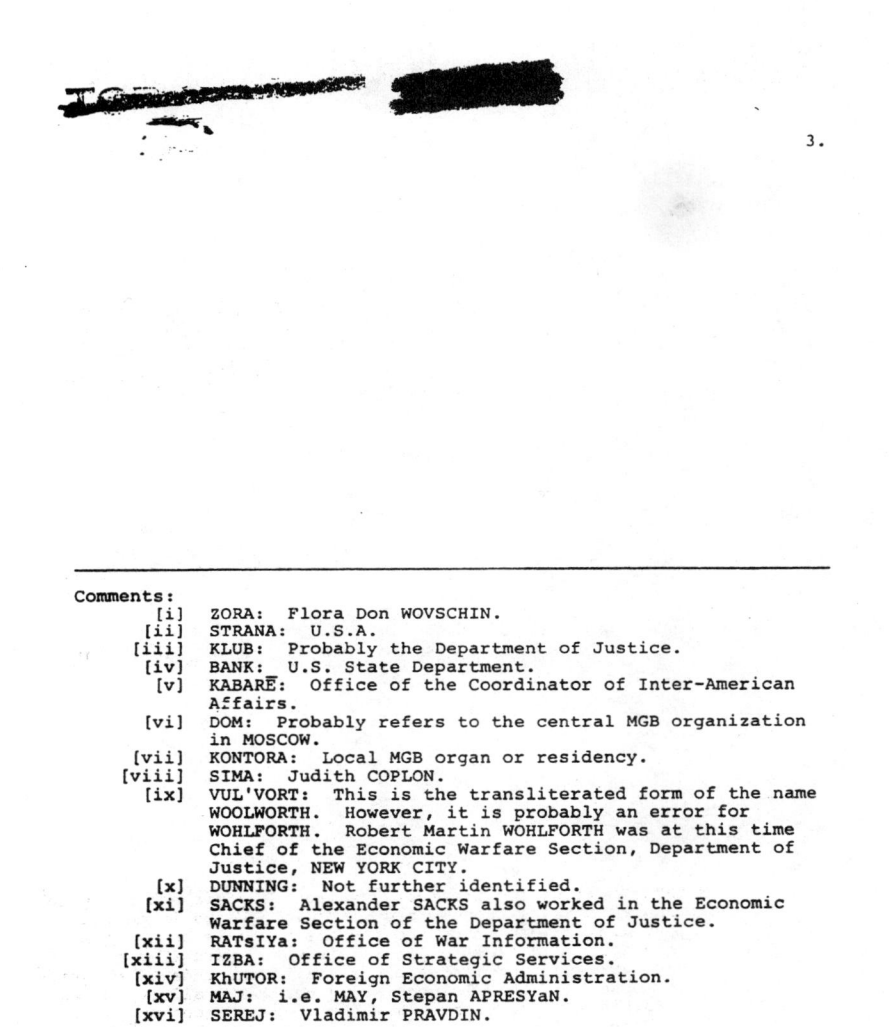

```
Comments:
    [i]    ZORA: Flora Don WOVSCHIN.
   [ii]    STRANA: U.S.A.
  [iii]    KLUB: Probably the Department of Justice.
   [iv]    BANK: U.S. State Department.
    [v]    KABARE: Office of the Coordinator of Inter-American
           Affairs.
   [vi]    DOM: Probably refers to the central MGB organization
           in MOSCOW.
  [vii]    KONTORA: Local MGB organ or residency.
 [viii]    SIMA: Judith COPLON.
   [ix]    VUL'VORT: This is the transliterated form of the name
           WOOLWORTH. However, it is probably an error for
           WOHLFORTH. Robert Martin WOHLFORTH was at this time
           Chief of the Economic Warfare Section, Department of
           Justice, NEW YORK CITY.
    [x]    DUNNING: Not further identified.
   [xi]    SACKS: Alexander SACKS also worked in the Economic
           Warfare Section of the Department of Justice.
  [xii]    RATsIYa: Office of War Information.
 [xiii]    IZBA: Office of Strategic Services.
  [xiv]    KhUTOR: Foreign Economic Administration.
   [xv]    MAJ: i.e. MAY, Stepan APRESYaN.
  [xvi]    SEREJ: Vladimir PRAVDIN.


                                                31 January 1974
```

88. Washington 1793 to Moscow, 29 March 1945.

VENONA

~~TOP SECRET~~

USSR	Ref. No: 3/NBF/T1727
	Issued: 13/10/1965
	Copy No: 204

MATERIAL FROM "H" (1945)

From: WASHINGTON
To: MOSCOW
No: 1793   29 March 45

To the 8th Department.

Material from "H[G]"[i].

I am transmitting telegram No. 2535 of 16th March, 1945 from the "NOOK[ZAKOULOK]"[ii] to the "POOL[OMUT]"[iii].

"Sent to WASHINGTON as telegram No. 2535 of 16th March and repeated to MOSCOW.

Secret

MOSCOW telegrams Nos 823 and 824.

1. [The remainder of the text (360 groups) has been largely recovered. It is a Russian translation of the telegram referred to above, which was sent by Mr. Eden (the Foreign Secretary) to Lord Halifax (British Ambassador in WASHINGTON).]

[2 groups unrecoverable][a]   [1 group unrecoverable][a]

Note: [a] The WASHINGTON MGB officer's signature and reference number are unrecoverable.

Comments: [i] "H" : Abbreviation for HOMER, the cover-name of Donald Duart MACLEAN. See comment [i] in 3/NBF/T1725 issued 13th October, 1965.

[ii] NOOK : The British Foreign Office.

[iii] POOL : British Embassy in WASHINGTON.

Distribution:

3/NBF/T1727

~~TOP SECRET~~

VENONA

88. *(Continued)*

~~TOP SECRET DINAR~~ VENONA

From: WASHINGTON
To: MOSCOW
No.: 1793   29 March 1945

To the 8th Department.

　　　　Materials of "G"[i]. I am transmitting a telegram of the "NOOK [ZAKOULOK]"[ii] No.2535 of 16 March this year to the "POOL [OMUT]"[iii].

"Sent to WASHINGTON under No.2535 of 16 March and repeated to MOSCOW.

SECRET.

Reference telegrams from MOSCOW Nos.823 and 824.

1. These telegrams arrived simultaneously with the President's message to the Prime Minister (No.718). The message shows that the President is still not inclined to support us in putting to the Russians all those questions, on which we consider it important to reach an agreement with them at this stage. From the Prime Minister's answer, transmitted in telegram No.912, you can see that he is urging the President to reconsider his position in the light of the proposals now submitted by Sir A. Clark KERR, after consultation with Mr. HARRIMAN.

2. As soon as possible please see Mr. STETTINIUS and after that, if you can, the President and show them [2 groups unrecovered] to MOLOTOV, suggested by Sir A. Clark KERR and supplemented by my telegram No.2537. You should take part in the decision of these affairs. Use all arguments at your disposal to induce them to make a concerted effort with us on the basis of this draft. We are convinced that only on such a basis will it be possible to establish a foundation for the Commission's work. We believe that if we and the Americans together take a firm position, the Russians very likely will give way on some of the points.

3. If you do not succeed in persuading the President to accept Sir A. Clark KERR's draft as it stands, in my opinion you can induce him to send Mr. HARRIMAN

　　　　　　　　　[10 groups unrecoverable]

put forth by us. (From the Prime Minister's message you will see that the point on which we cannot give way is the question of a truce). If this were done, I should be ready to instruct Sir A. Clark KERR immediately to concert with Mr. HARRIMAN in making a communication on similar lines. We fully realize the urgency of this question.

~~TOP SECRET DINAR~~ VENONA

88. *(Continued)*

~~TOP SECRET DINAR~~ VENONA

```
        4.              [10 groups unrecovered]
     specific points, which
                        [35 groups unrecoverable]
```

Comments:
   [i] G: i.e., HOMER [GOMER], Donald MacLean.
  [ii] NOOK: The British Foreign Office.
 [iii] POOL: British Embassy in Washington.

20 July 1965

~~TOP SECRET DINAR~~ VENONA

88. *(Continued)*

~~TOP SECRET TRINE~~ VENONA

From: WASHINGTON
To: MOSCOW
No: 1793

29 March 1945

Attachment

In paragraph 3 of the NSA version of the translation of this message the "10 groups unrecoverable" should contain the following:

"instructions covering at least the more important points"

Paragraph 4 should read:

"4. My immediately following telegram contains arguments on specific points which you should use with Mr. STETTINIUS and the President in addition to those contained in the Prime Minister's message no. 912."

24 May 1960

89. Washington 1822 to Moscow, 30 March 1945.

VENONA

MGB

From: WASHINGTON
To: MOSCOW
No: 1822

30 March 1945

Further to our telegram No. 283[a]. As a result of "[D% A.'s]"[1] chat with "ALES"[ii] the following has been ascertained:

1. ALES has been working with the NEIGHBORS[SOSEDI][iii] continuously since 1935.

2. For some years past he has been the leader of a small group of the NEIGHBORS' probationers[STAZhERY], for the most part consisting of his relations.

3. The group and ALES himself work on obtaining military information only. Materials on the "BANK"[iv] allegedly interest the NEIGHBORS very little and he does not produce them regularly.

4. All the last few years ALES has been working with "POL'"[v] who also meets other members of the group occasionally.

5. Recently ALES and his whole group were awarded Soviet decorations.

6. After the YaLTA Conference, when he had gone on to MOSCOW, a Soviet personage in a very responsible position (ALES gave to understand that it was Comrade VYShINSKIJ) allegedly got in touch with ALES and at the behest of the Military NEIGHBORS passed on to him their gratitude and so on.

No. 431   VADIM[vi]

Notes: [a] Not available.
Comments:
  [i]   A.: "A." seems the most likely garble here although "A." has not been confirmed elsewhere in the WASHINGTON traffic.
  [ii] ALES: Probably Alger HISS.
  [iii] SOSEDI: Members of another Soviet Intelligence organization, here probably the GRU.
  [iv] BANK: The U.S. State Department.
  [v]   POL': i.e. "PAUL," unidentified cover-name.
  [vi] VADIM: Anatolij Borisovich GROMOV, MGB resident in WASHINGTON.

8 August 1969

VENONA

90. Moscow 298 to NY, 31 March 1945.

~~TOP SECRET~~ VENONA

USSR

Ref. No: 3/NBF/T2090
Issued : A265/16/08/1979
Copy No:

REISSUE

EVALUATION OF MATERIAL ON ENORMOZ: FROM
CHARL'Z ON FUNICULAR AND FROM MLAD (1945)

From: MOSCOW

To : NEW YORK

No : 298   31 March 1945

ANTON [i]

    We are sending herewith an evaluation on ENORMOZ [ii]. Referenced are materials from "ChARL'Z" [iii] about the FUNICULAR [iv]:

    a) 5/46 [v].

[31 groups unrecovered]

gaskets [SAL'NIKI]

    b) 5/60 - [6 groups unrecovered] - contains an interesting method of calculation, which will be used during the design.

    c) 5/62 - technical data on the FUNICULAR and

[12 groups unrecovered]

    d) 7/83, paragraph 1 - about the degree of separation of the membrane [vi] - offers substantial interest.

    e) 7/84 paragraph 1 - about tests of the membrane and information about the layout of the plant - is of interest. What is needed is [7 groups unrecovered] plan of the plant.

    f) 7/83 and 84 - on the theory of the [c% stability] of the FUNICULAR - together with "ChARL'Z" materials on this question received earlier they form a full and valuable piece of information.

    2) MLAD's [vii] report about work [4 groups unrecovered]. [1 group unrecovered] great interest.

No. 1972   VIKTOR [viii]

Distribution   [continued]
Copies
  1-2   NSA (A265)
    3   FBI
    4   CIA
    5   Security Service
    6
    7   ████ (via CIA)
    8   ASIO (via NSA)
    9   Security Service/████ Representatives - WASHINGTON
  10

3/NBF/T2090

VENONA

90. *(Continued)*

~~TOP SECRET~~ VENONA

-2-   3/NBF/T2090

Footnotes:
- [i] ANTON : Leonid Romanovich KVASNIKOV
- [ii] ENORMOZ : The Manhattan Project (Development of the Atomic Bomb).
- [iii] ChARL'Z : ie CHARLES; Dr. Klaus Emil FUCHS.
- [iv] FUNICULAR: First occurence. Probably the gaseous diffusion plant K25 at CLINTON Tennessee.
- [v] A dispatch reference. The first element is probably the month or postal dispatch number and the second a running serial from the beginning of the year.
- [vi] membrane : Also referred to as "barrier" in some books.
- [vii] MLAD : Theodore M. HALL.
- [viii] VIKTOR : Lt. General Pavel Mikhajlovich FITIN

3/NBF/T2090

~~TOP SECRET~~

VENONA   CLASSIFIED BY NSA/CSSM 123-2
DECLASSIFY ON Aug. 20, 2009

91. Moscow 337 to New York, 8 April 1945.

BRIDE

~~TOP SECRET~~

USSR

Ref. No: 3/NBF/T1031 (pf 30/7/1958)
Issued: 25/11/1959
Copy No: 204

2nd RE-ISSUE

WARNING ABOUT THE COMPETITORS AND
INSTRUCTIONS FOR "ALBERT's" GROUP (1945)

From: MOSCOW
To: NEW YORK
No: 337 8 Apr. 45

According to information we have received from VADIM[i] the Competitors of the "COUNTRY"[ii] and the "ISLAND"[iii] have worked out joint measures for strengthening work

[71 groups unrecovered]

transmission of information by telegraph. Give tasks [15 groups unrecovered] ELSA[iv]

[29 groups unrecoverable]

and people devoted to us. In the work with ALBERT's[v] group it is essential to adhere to the following:

1. JULIA's[YuLIYa][vi] meeting with ART[ART][vii] or BERG[viii] should not be more than 3 times a month.
2. [15 groups unrecovered]
3. ROBERT's[ix] materials should be conveyed to TYRE[x] only on film and in small batches.
4. ELSA, BERG and ART, who are to be co-opted by ALBERT for the purpose, are to take turns in making the trip to CARTHAGE[xi] for ROBERT's materials.

Distribution [Continued overleaf]

3/NBF/T1031
(2 Pages)

~~TOP SECRET~~
BRIDE

91. *(Continued)*

                                                    2   3/NBF/T1 031

With the probationers [3 groups unrecovered] [B% ROBERT] and his wife "DORA"[xii]

5. As regards the work with the probationers in TYRE follow the same principles. Organise the work of your

                         [60 groups unrecovered]

No. 153   PETROV[xiii]

Comments: [i]   VADIM   : Anatolij Borisovich GROMOV, 1st Secretary at Soviet Embassy, Washington.
         [ii]   COUNTRY : U.S.A.
         [iii] ISLAND   : GREAT BRITAIN.
         [iv]   ELSA   : Unidentified cover-name.
         [v]   ALBERT   :   "   "
         [vi]   JULIA   : Olga Valentinovna KhLOPKOVA.
         [vii] ART   : Aleksander KORAL.
         [viii] BERG   : Unidentified cover-name.
         [ix]   ROBERT   : Nathan Gregory SILVERMASTER.
         [x]   TYRE   : NEW YORK CITY.
         [xi]   CARTHAGE : WASHINGTON, D.C.
         [xii] DORA   : Helen SILVERMASTER.
         [xiii] PETROV   : Unidentified MOSCOW signatory.

3/NBF/T1 031

92. New York 776 to Moscow, 25 May 1945.

VENONA
~~TOP SECRET~~

USSR	Ref. No: 3/NBF/T150 (of 21/1/1952)
	Issued: 9/3/1965
	Copy No: 204

REISSUE

TRANSFER OF PROBATIONERS FROM "CZECH" TO "ROMAN" AND SUBSEQUENT TRANSFER OF "CZECH" FROM "NAZAR" TO "VADIM" (1945)

From: NEW YORK
To: MOSCOW
No: 776   25 May 45

To VIKTOR[i].

Your No. 3396[a].

On 29th May "CZECH [ChEKh]"[ii] will complete the transfer to "ROMAN"[iii] of the probationers dealing with "POLECATS [KhOR'KI]"[iv] and "RATS [KRYSY]"[v]. On 1st June in accordance with the understanding with "VADIM"[vi], CZECH will be handed over by NAZAR[vii] to VADIM in TYRE[viii].

No. 483   SERGEJ[ix]
25 May 1945

Notes: [a] No. 3396 not available.
Comments: [i]   VIKTOR   : Lt. Gen. P. M. FITIN.
          [ii] CZECH   : Robert Owen MENAKER.
          [iii] ROMAN   : Robert SOBLE.
          [iv] POLECATS : Trotskyites.
          [v]   RATS   : Possibly Jews.

DISTRIBUTION   [Continued overleaf]

3/NBF/T150

~~TOP SECRET~~
VENONA

429

92. *(Continued)*

~~TOP SECRET~~

- 2 - 3/NBF/T150

Comments
[Cont'd]: [vi] VADIM : Anatolij Borisovich GROMOV, First Secretary at the Soviet Embassy in WASHINGTON.

[vii] NAZAR : Stepan Nikolaevich SHUNDENKO, an employee at the Soviet Consulate, NEW YORK.

[viii] TYRE : NEW YORK CITY.

[ix] SERGEJ: Vladimir Sergeevich PRAVDIN, TASS representative in NEW YORK.

3/NBF/T150

~~TOP SECRET~~

93. New York 777-9 to Moscow, 25 May 1945.

VENONA
~~TOP SECRET~~

USSR	Ref. No.: 3/NBF/T2 (of 19/7/1950)
	Issued : 5/9/1973
	Copy No.: 301

5TH REISSUE

JOSEPH BERGER, CONTACT OF "YaZ'": DETAILS, SUGGESTIONS FOR RECRUITMENT DURING VISIT TO MOSCOW
(1945)

From: NEW YORK
To: MOSCOW
Nos.: 777-779   25th May 1945

[3-part message complete]

[Part I]   To VIKTOR[i].

Joseph BERGER[ii], who is a lead of "YaZ'["][iii] and has already been reported on, has left for SMYRNA[iv] as a member of the COUNTRY's[STRANA][v] delegation to the Reparations Commission. BERGER - 40 years old, [1 group unrecovered], of Russian-Jewish extraction, married, has

[32 groups unrecoverable]

[Continued overleaf]

3/NBF/T2

VENONA
~~TOP SECRET~~

93. *(Continued)*

VENONA
~~TOP SECRET~~

- 2 -   3/NBF/T2

North Washington Boulevard in the city of ARLINGTON, State of VIRGINIA. Formerly he lived for a long while in the city of PROVINCETOWN in an artists' colony organised by the ROOSEVELT Administration during the depression. He took an active part in the collection of funds

[25 groups unrecoverable]

....S[vi] he wrote books for children. In 1943 he worked in the Press Section of the Department of Justice where he was given the job of writing speeches for BIDDLE[vii] and other chiefs. BERGER prepared all the materials on his own initiative, without having them approved by [1 group unrecovered]

[Part II] In 1944 he took a post in the National Democratic Committee, where, working under HANNEGAN[viii], he wrote speeches for the leaders of the party for the election campaign. HANNEGAN, who is to be appointed Postmaster General, took BERGER on as his special assistant at a salary of ten thousand dollars a year. B.[ii] will take up his duties when he returns from SMYRNA.

YaZ' has known B. [B% about] 5 years and describes him as a very progressive fellow who is well disposed towards us. He has often expressed a desire to live permanently in the U.S.S.R. During the past year [C% he has been maintaining contact] with the FELLOWCOUNTRYMEN[ZEMLYaKI][ix].

Having regard to the position he is to occupy in the future and his connections in the Democratic [B% organisation] B. could become a valuable probationer[STAZhER]. I would recommend using B.'s trip to SMYRNA for working on him and [B% possibly] signing him on. [C% By] obtaining information on the work of the delegates of the COUNTRY you could check for yourselves on the spot his potentialities.

[31 groups unrecovered]

"YaZ'" [2 groups unrecovered] in[x] CARTHAGE[KARFAGEN][xi].

[Part III] [4 groups unrecovered] YaZ' [B% and] his family, work and so on depending on how B. will [5 groups unrecovered] acquaintance in the direction necessary to us. At the meeting[xii] with YaZ' before departure B. insistently inquired [2 groups unrecovered] in SMYRNA acquaintances to whom he wanted to send greetings. If you consider such an alternative[VARIANT] acceptable, upon your request we will communicate a description of YaZ' and his wife and further facts about them, so that there should be no [2 groups unrecovered] attempt on B.'s part to check whether or not our journalists really know YaZ'.

No. 485
25 May 1945   SERGEJ[xiii]

3/NBF/T2

VENONA
~~TOP SECRET~~

93. *(Continued)*

VENONA

~~TOP SECRET~~

- 3 -   3/NBF/T2

Footnotes:	[i] VIKTOR:	Lt. Gen. P.M. FITIN.
	[ii] Joseph BERGER/B.:	Joseph Isadore BERGER; nom de plume Jeremiah DIGGES. See also details in NEW YORK's No. 705 of 17th May 1944 (3/NBF/T242).
	[iii] YaZ':	i.e. "IDE"; Simon Samuel KRAFSUR, a TASS employee.
	[iv] SMYRNA:	MOSCOW.
	[v] COUNTRY:	U.S.A.
	[vi] ....S:	Probably the last letter of BERGER's nom de plume (see Footnote [ii]).
	[vii] BIDDLE:	Francis BIDDLE, U.S. Attorney General.
	[viii] HANNEGAN:	Robert E. HANNEGAN, elected Chairman of the Democratic National Committee on 22nd January 1944.
	[ix] FELLOWCOUNTRYMEN:	Members of the Communist Party.
	[x] Or "to".	
	[xi] CARTHAGE:	WASHINGTON, D.C.
	[xii] Or "meetings".	
	[xiii] SERGEJ:	Vladimir Sergeevich PRAVDIN, Editor of the TASS News Agency in NEW YORK CITY.

3/NBF/T2

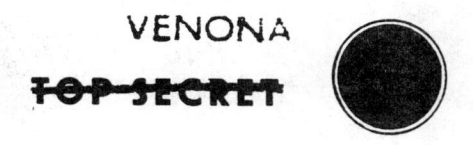

VENONA

~~TOP SECRET~~

94. New York 781-7 to Moscow, 25/26 May 1945.

VENONA
~~TOP SECRET~~

USSR

Ref. No.: 3/NBF/T27 (of 27.2.1951)
Issued: /4/8/1971
Copy No.: 301

5TH REISSUE

PRESS AND OTHER REACTIONS TO TRUMAN'S BECOMING PRESIDENT
AND FORECAST OF CHANGES IN AMERICAN FOREIGN POLICY
(1945)

From: NEW YORK
To: MOSCOW
Nos.: 781-787   25th, 26th May 1945

[7-part message complete]

[Part I]   To VIKTOR[i]. Copy to 8th Department.

As a result of MATROS's[ii] accession to power, a considerable change in the foreign policy of the COUNTRY[STRANA][iii] should be expected, first and foremost in relation to the USSR (see our No. 350[a]). [7 groups unrecovered] in economic circles which in the past were not always able to exert decisive influence in questions of principle affecting foreign policy, since this

[13 groups unrecoverable]

[Continued overleaf]

3/NBF/T27

VENONA
~~TOP SECRET~~

VENONA

~~TOP SECRET~~

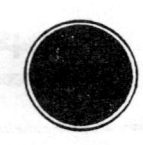

— 2 — 3/NBF/T27

[Part II] an organised campaign to "get hold of" MATROS and bring about a change in the policy of the COUNTRY towards the USSR. This campaign was reflected in the first instance in the most reactionary section of the press, which has welcomed MATROS's accession to power, emphasising particularly that henceforth the foreign policy of the COUNTRY will be decided, not independently by MATROS as it was in KAPITAN's[iv] day, but jointly with influential members of the Senate and House of Representatives (including people hostile to us). [6 groups unrecovered] MATROS is maintaining friendly relations in the Senate, not only with Democrats but also with Republicans, including such extreme reactionaries as TAFT, WHEELER[UILER], BARKLEY and others. The reactionaries are setting particular hopes on the possibility of getting direction of the COUNTRY's foreign policy wholly into their own hands, partly because MATROS is notoriously untried and ill-informed on these matters,

[26 groups unrecovered]

the press of the COUNTRY is conducting [3 groups unrecovered] of all reactionary groups, political and economic, to influence public opinion in the direction they desire

[38 groups unrecovered].

The leading protagonists of this campaign and its instigators are representatives of the BANK[v], the Army and the Navy [7 groups unrecovered] after KAPITAN's death and the end of the war in EUROPE.

[Part III] In newspaper circles in BABYLON[VAVILON][vi] and CARTHAGE [KARFAGEN][vii] it is common knowledge, as has been confirmed to me on separate [1 group unrecovered] by ShMEL'[viii], RIChARD[ix], ShEF[x], Joseph BARNES, CASSIDY, HIGHTOWER[KhAJTAUR] and many other correspondents, that the representatives of the BANK, GREW[GR'Yu], DUNN, HOLMES[GOL'MS],

[33 groups unrecoverable]

VANDENBERG, ELTON[ITON], CONALLY[KANALLI], BLOOM, Admirals KING and LEAHY[LEGI] and Generals SOMERVELL[SOMMERUEL] and MARSHALL are carrying on a systematic anti-Soviet campaign wherein many

[16 groups unrecovered]

[Part IV] The sources enumerated above said that one of the bitterest anti-Soviet propagandists is KAPITALIST[xi], who

[11 groups unrecovered].

3/NBF/T27

VENONA

~~TOP SECRET~~

94. *(Continued)*

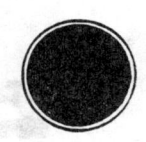

— 3 — 3/NBF/T27

In private conversations with correspondents [OF KAPITALIST] [1 group unrecovered] that the USSR is aiming at world mastery and is trying to take up a dominating position at the Conference in BABYLON. To prove his words KAPITALIST does not shrink from any chicanery. Thus for example one of his latest [1 group unrecovered] fabrications was that our delegation allegedly threatened to walk out of the Conference if our proposal about the chairmanship was not accepted.

I read the newspapers during the long journey[xii] and, in so doing, read mainly about questions of foreign policy. In all these international affairs MATROS pays great heed to the advice of the above-mentioned representatives of the BANK, the Army and the Navy. BARNES AND ShMEL' in talking with me forecast that one should expect an even greater intensification of the press campaign [9 groups unrecovered] the campaign are at present pursuing a double aim: to get MATROS firmly into their clutches and at the same time to obtain

[22 groups unrecoverable]

[Part V]   [2 groups unrecovered] has shown that the campaign of intimidation has spent itself, particularly [5 groups unrecovered] the conviction that without financial aid [1 group unrecovered] the USSR ravaged by war, is in no condition to re-establish its economy with any speed. Therefore [8 groups unrecovered] aid demanded at the present time in

[16 groups unrecovered]

economic aid [2 groups unrecovered] supplementary credit. To quote the above-mentioned sources, the foreign policy of the COUNTRY at the present time is moving in the direction of full

[59 groups unrecoverable]

the most active propaganda which, judging by its latest information, is clearly distorting the facts. In a recent conversation with me, the Director of the Institute of Pacific Affairs, CARTER, in the main confirmed RIChARD's statements about the COUNTRY's policy in CHINA (which have been reported to you [5 groups unrecoverable])

[Part VI]   ShMEL' and BARNES have expressed serious alarm at the anti-Soviet atmosphere which has arisen in the COUNTRY and were extremely indignant at what MATROS had said, [7 groups unrecovered] the ISLAND[xiii]. KAPRAL's[xiv] statement on the question of the sixteen Poles was described by ShMEL' as "disgusting servility towards EDEN". RIChARD particularly asked that our attention should be drawn to the fact that the Head of the COUNTRY's [delegation][b] to the Reparations Commission,

3/NBF/T27

94. (Continued)

VENONA

~~TOP SECRET~~

- 4 -   3/NBF/T27

PAULEY [POLE], although a private owner of oilfields, actually represents the interests of Standard Oil and in RIChARD's opinion his appointment is a "gesture of friendship" by MATROS to the oil men. There is no need to speak of the position of business circles in the campaign which has developed here, inasmuch as these circles are fully represented in the most responsible positions [C% in the BANK]

[73 groups unrecoverable]

[37 groups unrecovered]

[Part VII] Today a report was published that MATROS has sent to the USSR his personal representatives HOPKINS

[122 groups unrecoverable]

DAVIES's [xv] trip to SIDON [xvi]

[16 groups unrecovered]

No. 482   SERGEJ [xvii]

Notes: [a] Not available.
          [b] Inserted by translator.

Comments: [i]   VIKTOR: Lt.-Gen. P.M. FITIN.
          [ii] MATROS: i.e. "SAILOR"; Harry S. TRUMAN.
          [iii] COUNTRY: The U.S.A.
          [iv] KAPITAN: i.e. "CAPTAIN"; Franklin Delano ROOSEVELT.
          [v]   BANK: U.S. State Department.
          [vi] BABYLON: SAN FRANCISCO.
          [vii] CARTHAGE: WASHINGTON, D.C.
          [viii] ShMEL':   i.e. "BUMBLEBEE"; Walter LIPPMANN.
          [ix] RIChARD: i.e. "RICHARD"; Harry Dexter WHITE was known by this covername, but he seems an unlikely figure to occur in this list of newspaper correspondents.

3/NBF/T27

VENONA

~~TOP SECRET~~

94. *(Continued)*

VENONA

~~TOP SECRET~~

- 5 -   3/NBF/T27

Comments
[Cont'd]:

[x] SHEF: i.e. "CHIEF"; unidentified covername.

[xi] KAPITALIST: i.e. "CAPITALIST"; probably William Averell HARRIMAN.

[xii] Long journey: PRAVDIN, the originator of this message, returned to NEW YORK from SAN FRANCISCO on 14th May 1945.

[xiii] The ISLAND: GREAT BRITAIN.

[xiv] KAPRAL: i.e. "CORPORAL"; Edward R. STETTINIUS, Jr.

[xv] DAVIS: Joseph E. DAVIES, who was engaged on special missions to LONDON and MOSCOW as President TRUMAN's personal representative.

[xvi] SIDON: LONDON.

[xvii] SERGEJ: Vladimir Sergeevich PRAVDIN, Editor of the TASS News Agency in NEW YORK CITY. He covered the United Nations Conference at SAN FRANCISCO, which was in session from April 25th to June 26th 1945.

3/NBF/T27

VENONA

~~TOP SECRET~~

95. Moscow 709 to New York, 5 July 1945.

VENONA

Reissue (T223)

From: MOSCOW
To: NEW YORK
No: 709

5 July 1945

Your no. 613[a]. The incident involving GRAUBER[i] should be regarded as a compromise of MLAD[ii]. The cause of this is ALEKSEJ's[iii] completely unsatisfactory work with the agents [AGENTURA] on ENORMOUS[ENORMOZ][iv]. His work with [9 groups unrecovered] for this reason we consider it of the utmost importance to ensure supervision so that the C OUNTRY[b][v]

[23 groups unrecoverable]

we once more [3 groups unrecovered] attention to [2 groups unrecovered] our instructions. For the future [4 groups unrecovered] : immediately inform us by telegraph about each meeting [with the agents of ENORMOUS. In [C% the next post] [3 groups unrecovered] on this same question to send the most precise reports on meetings,

[14 groups unrecovered]

[C% every] meeting with permanent staff [KADROVYJ]

[14 groups unrecovered]

from all these areas. You

[18 groups unrecovered]

to seek safe flats in the areas of the camps[vi]. This question you must

[17 groups unrecovered]

our workers on the development

[35 groups unrecovered]

GRAUBER case meetings[c] of our operational worker with MLAD [you] must [4 groups unrecovered]

No. 4533 VIKTOR[vii]

VENONA

95. *(Continued)*

```
Notes: [a]   Not available.
       [b]   Or possibly "[in] the COUNTRY".
       [c]   Or "meeting".
Comments:
       [i]   GRAUBER:  An error for ▓▓▓▓▓▓▓▓▓▓
       [ii]  MLAD:  i.e. [YOUNG, Theodore Alvin HALL, a physicist
             employed at LOS ALAMOS.]
       [iii] ALEKSEJ:  Anatolij Antonovich YaKOVLEV, an employee
             at the Soviet Consulate in NEW YORK.
       [iv]  ENORMOUS:  Manhatten Engineering District [U.S. Atomic
             Energy Project).
       [v]   COUNTRY:  U.S.A.
       [vi]  Camps [LAGER']:  Probably a reference to atomic energy
             sites.  Camp-2 is LOS ALAMOS, New Mexico.
       [vii] VIKTOR:  Lt. Gen. P.M. FITIN.
```

25 March 1976

96. New York 1052-3 to Moscow, 5 July 1945.

~~TOP SECRET~~ VENONA

USSR
Ref. No: 3/NBF/T2277
Issued: A265/17/08/1979
Copy No: 1

NEW YORK ARGUES FOR CONTINUATION OF MONTHLY PAYMENTS TO ART AND BERG (1945)

From: NEW YORK
To: MOSCOW
No: 1052   5 July 1945

VIKTOR [i]

   Your No. 4373 [ii]. The reason for the recommendation lay in the fact that we have been paying monthly to ART [iii] and BERG [iv] 100 dollars each. I consider inappropriate the termination of their salary.

   [43 groups unrecoverable]

. With postal dispatch No.

   [28 groups unrecovered]

No. 620   SERGEJ [v]

Footnotes: [i] VIKTOR: Lt. General Pavel Mikhajlovich FITIN

[ii] Not available.

[iii] ART : Helen KORAL

[iv] BERG : formerly SEN'OR; unidentified; also occurs in NEW YORK's No. 1267 of 6 September 1944 (3/NBF/T57), 1332 of 18 September 1944 (3/NBF/T317), 1582 of 12 November 1944 (3/NBF/T305), 1636 of 21 November 1944 (3/NBF/T295), 1803 of 22 December 1944 (3/NBF/T288) and 50 of 11 January 1945 (3/NBF/T306) and MOSCOW's No. 1251 of 2 September 1944 (3/NBF/T301), 275 of 25 March 1945 (3/NBF/T867) and 337 of 8 April 1945 (3/NBF/T1031).

[v] SERGEJ: Vladimir Sergejevich PRAVDIN; TASS representative in USA.

Distribution

Copies
1-2 NSA (A265)
3   FBI
4   CIA
5   Security Service
6
7   ███ (via CIA)
8   ASIO (via NSA)
9   Security Service ███ Representatives - WASHINGTON
10

3/NBF/T2277

~~TOP SECRET~~ VENONA

CLASSIFIED BY NSA/CSSM 123-2
DECLASSIFY ON: Aug 20, 2009

96. *(Continued)*

~~TOP SECRET DINAR~~ VENONA

Reissue (T220)

From: NEW YORK
To: MOSCOW
No.: 1053   5 July 1945

To VICTOR.

Your number 4440. 1. MAShA[i]

[66 groups unrecoverable]

her attitude towards the question of placing HOOK [KhUK][ii] at our expense in a university after his discharge from the Army. We will let you know the outcome of the meeting.

URAL[iii] for liaison with SIMA[iv] is not being used but after his transfer to [4 groups unrecovered] [C% is necessary further working out].

No.629   ANTON[v]

Comments: [i] MAShA: Eufrosina DVOIChENKO-MARKOV.
         [ii] KhUK: Dmetrius DVOIChENKO-MARKOV.
        [iii] URAL: Possibly Nikolaj Prokop'evich KARPEKOV.
         [iv] SIMA: Judith COPLON.
          [v] ANTON: Leonid Romanovich KVASNIKOV.

18 May 1965

~~TOP SECRET DINAR~~ VENONA

97. Moscow 34 to London, 21 September 1945.

USSR

Ref. No.: 3/NBF/T4 (of 25/8/1950)
Issued: /21/3/1973
Copy No.: 301

9th REISSUE

REORGANISATION OF CONTACT WITH "KhIKS", "ADAM", "DZhONSON" AND
"STENLI" IN VIEW OF THE CANADIAN AFFAIR
(1945)

From: MOSCOW
To: LONDON
No.: 34   21st September 1945

To BOB[i].

In view of the "NEIGHBOURS [SOSEDI]"[ii] affair in CANADA and the circumstances which have arisen at your end as a result of this, transfer "KhIKS"[iii] at the regular meeting to "ADAM's"[iv] control. Temporarily, until further notice, cut down meetings with "KhIKS" to once a month. Urge "KhIKS" to concentrate his attention on passing us material dealing only with large fundamental issues. As "ADAM" is by nature a rather phlegmatic person, encourage him to adopt a manner at meetings with "KhIKS" which will impress the latter so that "KhIKS" senses "ADAM's" authority. On "DZhONSON's"[v] return from [2 groups unrecoverable][a] with him not oftener than once a month. The position remains the same for "STENLI"[vi] also. If, however,

[Continued overleaf]

3/NBF/T4

97. (*Continued*)

— 2 — 3/NBF/T4

you notice that, as a consequence of local circumstances, greater attention is being paid to you and to our workers by the COMPETITORS[KONKURENTY][vii], you may break off contact temporarily with the sources. For the period of the "lull" in your work with the agents[AGENTURA], try to create a pretext [2 groups unrecovered] [C% panic and cases of] carelessness. Meet them more by neutral methods of contact, go to theatres, cinemas, etc. Warn all our comrades to make a thorough check when going out to a meeting and, if surveillance is observed, not to try, under any circumstances, to evade the surveillance and meet the agent regardless. For such contingencies make use of check appointments[KONTROL'NYE YaVKI]. Come to an agreement on this with the sources. Verify once more the passwords, addresses and check appointments you have, so that, in case of loss of contact, the sources can be re-established without undue difficulty.

We agree with your proposal about handing over "DZhONSON"

[4 groups unrecoverable]

[43 groups unrecovered]

Note: [a] The word following "from" could be "colony", "colonies" or "detached duty".

Comments: [i] BOB: Probably Boris Mikhajlovich KROTOV, 3rd Secretary and Consul General in LONDON from August 1941 to March 1947.

[ii] NEIGHBOURS: Members of another Soviet intelligence organisation: in this case the GRU, from which GUZENKO defected in OTTAWA on 5th September 1945.

[iii] KhIKS: i.e. "HICKS"; probably G. F. de M. BURGESS.

[iv] ADAM: Unidentified covername.

[v] DZhONSON: i.e. "JOHNSON"; unidentified covername. Also occurs in MOSCOW's No. 47 of 18th September 1945 (3/NBF/T260).

[vi] STENLI: i.e. "STANLEY"; H. A. R. PHILBY.

[vii] COMPETITORS: Members of a non-Soviet intelligence organisation.

3/NBF/T4

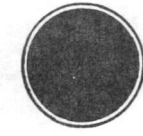

98. San Francisco 568 to Moscow, 7 November 1945.

From: SAN FRANCISCO
To: MOSCOW
No: 568

7 November 1945

To SEMEN[i].

On 4 November this year the traitor to the fatherland KUZNETsOVA[ii] was shipped to VLADIVOSTOK on the tanker "BELGOROD." Details in a supplement.

No. 295　　　　　　　　　　　　　　　　　　　　　　SERGEJ[iii]

Comments:
[i] SEMEN: Unidentified cover-name.
[ii] Elizaveta Mitrofanovna KUZNETsOVA, second mate of the ship "PSKOV" who deserted in PORTLAND on 9 February 1944.
[iii] SERGEJ: Viktor AFANAS'EV.

26 May 1978

99. Moscow 46 to London, 17 September 1945.

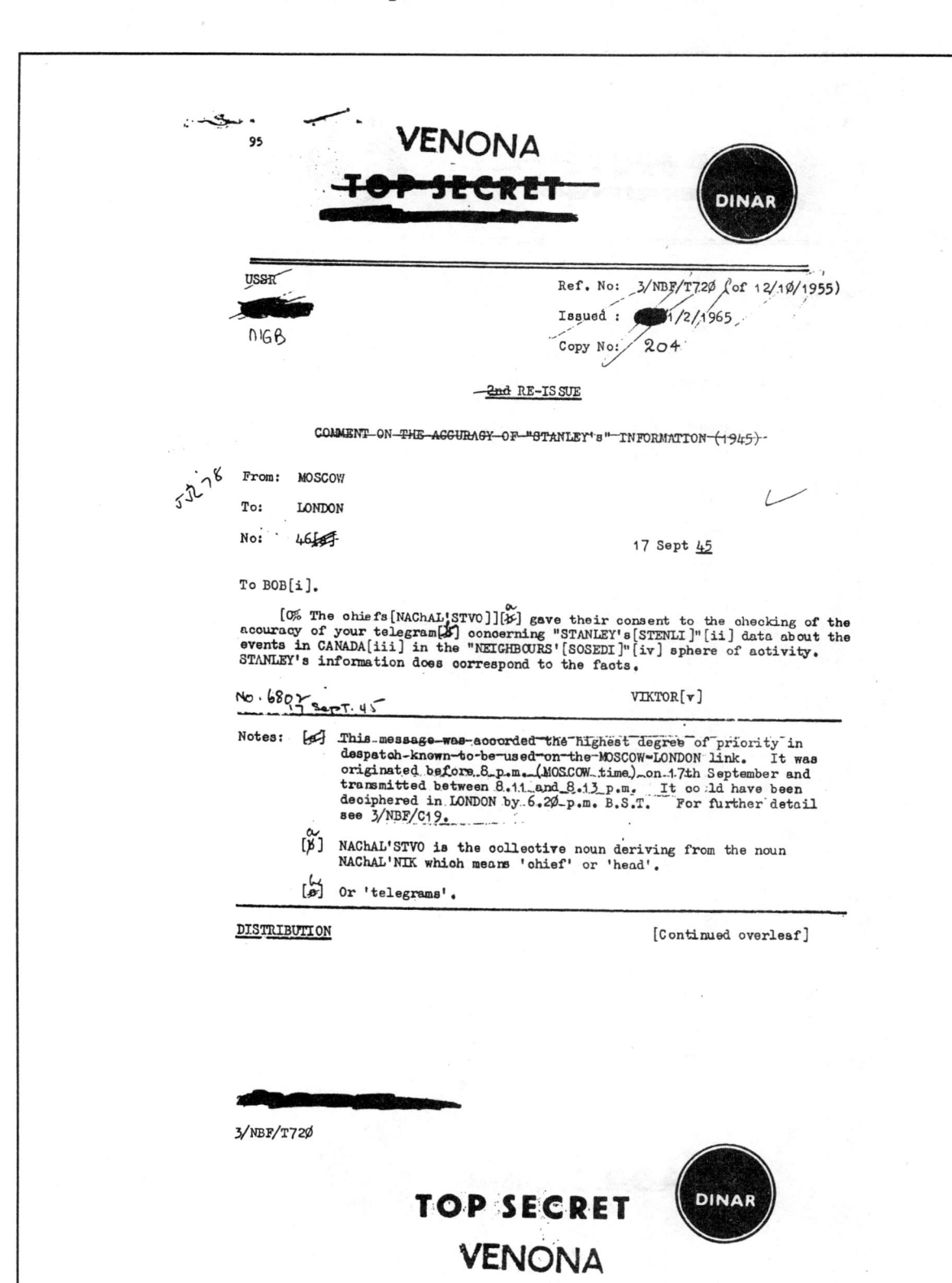

VENONA
~~TOP SECRET~~

DINAR

USSR
NGB

Ref. No: 3/NBF/T720 (of 12/10/1955)
Issued: ●●/2/1965
Copy No: 204

~~2nd~~ RE-ISSUE

~~COMMENT ON THE ACCURACY OF "STANLEY's" INFORMATION (1945)~~

From: MOSCOW
To: LONDON
No: 46

17 Sept 45

To BOB[i].

[C% The chiefs[NAChAL'STVO]][a] gave their consent to the checking of the accuracy of your telegram[b] concerning "STANLEY's[STENLI]"[ii] data about the events in CANADA[iii] in the "NEIGHBOURS'[SOSEDI]"[iv] sphere of activity. STANLEY's information does correspond to the facts.

No. 6802
17 Sept. 45

VIKTOR[v]

Notes: [a] This message was accorded the highest degree of priority in despatch known to be used on the MOSCOW-LONDON link. It was originated before 8 p.m. (MOSCOW time) on 17th September and transmitted between 8.11 and 8.13 p.m. It could have been deciphered in LONDON by 6.20 p.m. B.S.T. For further detail see 3/NBF/C19.

[a] NAChAL'STVO is the collective noun deriving from the noun NAChAL'NIK which means 'chief' or 'head'.

[b] Or 'telegrams'.

DISTRIBUTION   [Continued overleaf]

3/NBF/T720

TOP SECRET
VENONA

DINAR

449

99. *(Continued)*

~~TOP SECRET~~ DINAR

- 2 -   3/NBF/T720

Comments: [i] BOB : Unidentified LONDON Addressee.

[ii] STANLEY : Probably H.A.R. PHILBY.

[iii] GUZENKO defected in OTTAWA on 5th September 1945.

[iv] NEIGHBOURS : Members of another Soviet intelligence organization, in this instance the GRU.

[v] VIKTOR : Lt. Gen. P. M. FITIN.

3/NBF/T720

~~TOP SECRET~~ DINAR